AF306386

HERITOPIA

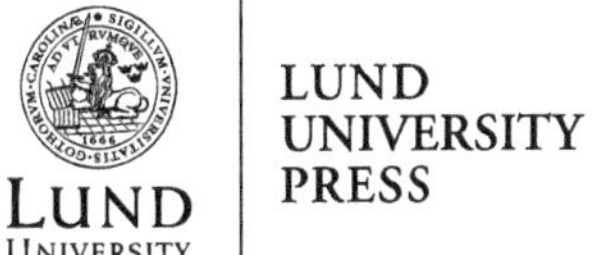

Heritopia

World Heritage and modernity

JES WIENBERG

Translated by Ian MacArthur

Lund University Press

Lund University Press
The Joint Faculties of Humanities and Theology

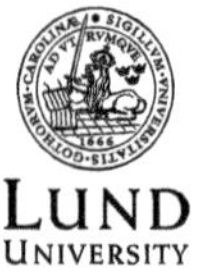

LUND
UNIVERSITY
PRESS

P.O. Box 192
SE-221 00 LUND
Sweden
http://lunduniversitypress.lu.se

Lund University Press books are published in collaboration with Manchester University Press.

British Library Cataloguing-in-Publication Data
A catalogue record for this book is available from the British Library

Lund University Press gratefully acknowledges publication assistance from the Thora Ohlsson Foundation (*Thora Ohlssons stiftelse*)

ISBN   978-91-984699-3-6   hardback

First published 2021

Typeset by
Servis Filmsetting Ltd, Stockport, Cheshire

*To write, to write, it is a forceful drive and need,
to search, and search, without knowing what I am searching for,
for if I knew what I was searching for, my search would be over.*
(The author Albert Dam in an interview with Danmarks Radio
(Danish Broadcasting Corporation), 9 February 1964)

Contents

Figures

Preface

The path to *Heritopia: World Heritage and modernity* has been a long and steep one. Not for the first time, I have written about something both because I have been thinking about it and because I want to be free to think about something else. And once again, I have tried to understand and explain so as to be able to forget and move on.

But thinking and writing take time. My interest in the meanings of the past goes back to my teens, when I read an essay called *Hvad skal vi med Historien?* ("Why do we need history?"), by the author and historian Palle Lauring (1969), whose answer was that we can learn from history. An enquiry of my own has been considered, planned, started, suspended, and resumed on numerous occasions when there was time to spare between other duties at the Department of Archaeology and Ancient History at Lund University, at home in Lund, and away in Nybro. *Heritopia* has thus been something of a Sisyphean task, in the course of which I have tried to survey and maintain order in a constantly growing number of books, articles, and press cuttings, as well as in my own ideas and those of other people. The first draft of a chapter came into being in 2006, but the work could only be completed during a more focused effort in 2015–2018. And now I can see that this investigation has been given a form that must have been shaped by my dual position as both Danish and Swedish, the distinctively Danish dimension often being defined by history and the Swedish one by modernity.

Heritopia is an attempt to stroll along the paths of curiosity without being bound by what characterises the research of today, namely strategies, deadlines, applications, budgets, running reports, and preferably answers that can be presented in advance – that is to say, without being bound by the expectations and demands of others. Instead, I have claimed for myself the mixed and time-consuming pleasure of actually reading all the literature and seeing all the films referred to, or very nearly. But I have by no means been able to visit all the World Heritage sites in the world. *Heritopia* is, in short, an attempt to conceptualise and write a book on my own terms, a book that I would like to read.

Heritopia has not been written in a state of isolation. First of all, I wish to thank my wife Bodil Petersson (Linnaeus University, Kalmar), who has followed and encouraged this work and read several versions. Next, my thanks go to Björn Magnusson Staaf (Lund University) and Asger Wienberg (Lund), who have also read the whole manuscript. All three of them have contributed both constructive and critical comments. Thanks also to two anonymous referees for Lund University Press for their helpful comments. I am grateful to the following for permission to reproduce photographs: Anders Andrén (Stockholm University) and Ingrid Berg (Uppsala University), Henrik Gerding and Lars Larsson (Lund University), Bodil Petersson (Linnaeus University, Kalmar), and Jens Vellev (Aarhus University). Thanks to Alun Richards of Manchester University Press for his help during the production stage. And finally, thanks to Marianne Thormählen of Lund University Press for providing great support through the entire process from a manuscript to a printed book.

This book is dedicated to my two children, Asger and Ingrid Wienberg.

Jes Wienberg
Lund, September 2020

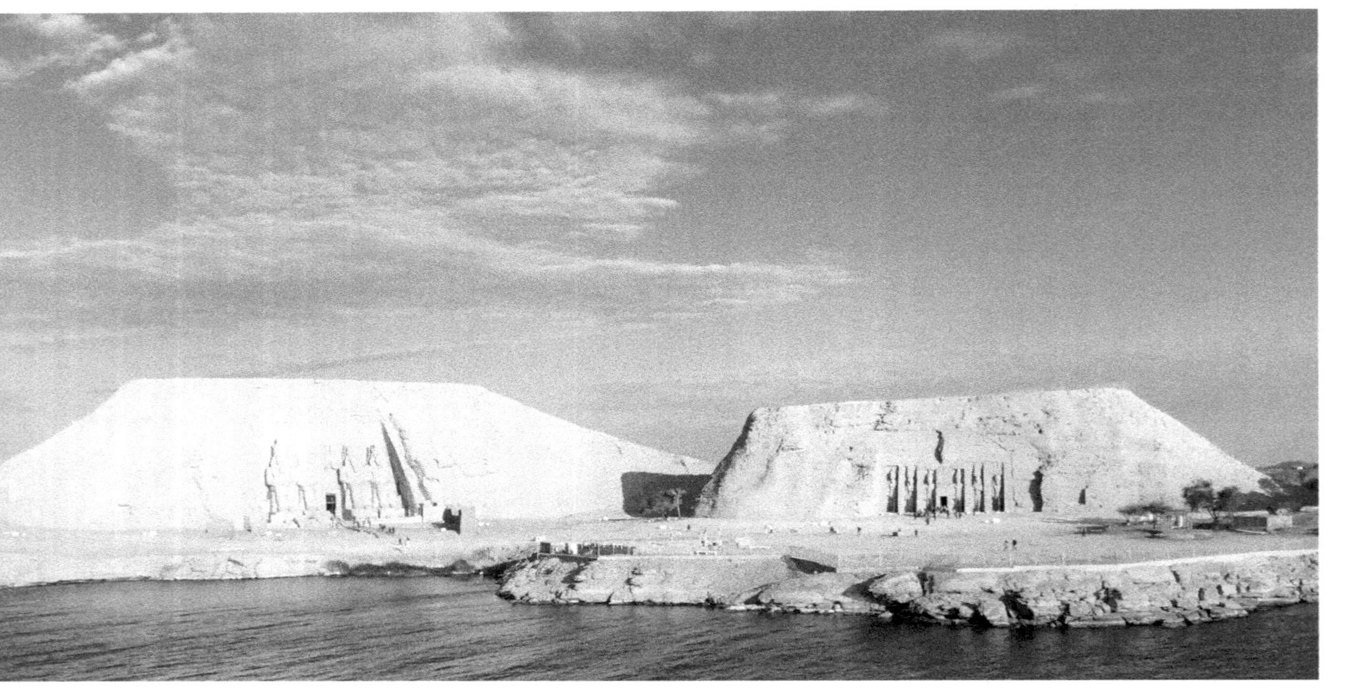

Figure 1 Abu Simbel. Photo © Ingrid Berg, 2019.

1

The past is everywhere

Drowned in the Nile

The pharaoh had been able to look at his reflection in the Nile for thousands of years. But now his face was sawn off, raised, and removed. One by one, stone blocks from the colossal statues were removed from the site. Was this because of a desire to obliterate the memory of a powerful absolute ruler? Was it an example of iconoclasm, in which the face of the god was mutilated? Were the sculptures going to be moved to a museum in the West, like so many other monuments and finds from Ancient Egypt? Or was it quite simply a case of vandalism?

The cliff temples of Abu Simbel were erected at the initiative of Pharaoh Ramses II, whose mummy is now exhibited in Cairo. The temples were carved directly out of the cliffs in the years around 1260 BCE. The great temple fronted by the four gigantic statues of Ramses II was a homage to the pharaoh himself as divine, a homage to the gods Amun-Ra, Ra-Horakhty, and Ptah, a memorial of the Battle of Kadesh, and a marker of Egyptian mastery of the Nubian border region. Twice a year, the rays of the rising sun would penetrate to the statues in the furthest depths of the temple. The nearby smaller temple was a homage to Ramses himself, his favourite wife Nefertari, and the goddess Hathor (MacQuitty 1965; Desroches Noblecourt 2007: 116ff).

But the temples of Abu Simbel were soon forgotten and covered by sand. The colossal statues were rediscovered in 1813 by the Orientalist Johann Ludwig Burckhardt, who had converted to Islam and was known in Egypt as Sheik Ibrahim ibn Abdullah; he also rediscovered Petra in Jordan. The Egyptologist Giovanni Battista Belzoni, who was hunting for antiquities along the Nile on behalf of Consul Henry Salt, heard about Abu Simbel from Burckhardt. In adventurous circumstances and in rivalry with French colleagues, Belzoni had the great temple cleared of so much sand that he was able to access its interior in 1817. After that, the temple was emptied of a few moveable items and documented. Several scientific expeditions followed during the nineteenth century (Fagan 1975: 124ff, 143ff, 172ff).

In an Egypt under British rule, a dam was erected at Aswan in 1898–1902 to regulate the Nile. The dam was subsequently raised several times. As a result of the higher water level, the temples along the river were flooded every year; but the cliff temples of Abu Simbel, with their relatively elevated location, were not. By contrast, the island of Philae, with a temple dedicated to the goddess Isis, came under water for 9 of the 12 months of the year. And in the decades following the establishment of the dam, there were several archaeological campaigns that involved investigations of threatened ancient monuments in Nubia, the gold country that is divided between Egypt and the Sudan.

The coup d'état or revolution of the Egyptian "Free Officers" in 1952 was aimed against the monarchy and the continued British influence. It was supported by the United States of America (US), the new post-war superpower. Plans were soon made to erect a new and higher Aswan dam, the Aswan High Dam, which would regulate the Nile and produce electricity, thereby contributing to the industrialisation of the country. The Aswan High Dam became a symbol of Egypt's national independence and modernisation, but its implementation was to have far-reaching consequences. After trying in vain to get the US to finance the project, President Gamal Abdel Nasser decided in 1956 to nationalise the strategically important Suez Canal so as to obtain the necessary funds. However, the subsequent Suez Crisis, in which the two old rivals and colonial powers Britain and France tried – along with Israel – to take control of the canal, clarified the new post-war world order. The US and the Soviet Union (USSR) forced the attackers to withdraw (Laron 2013).

The Aswan High Dam was not only to have political consequences. The dam would also create a lake, Lake Nasser (Lake Nubia in Sudan), which would drown the temples at Abu Simbel as well as many other traces of Ancient Nubia. The water might dissolve the sandstone of the temples. Consequently, the modernisation of Egypt threatened to drown and destroy Nubia's heritage. After millennia, the mighty pharaoh's monuments would cease to exist. Something that had been intended to be permanent would disappear. Abu Simbel risked becoming an icon of impermanence.

The modernisation involving the construction of the Aswan High Dam was carried out from 1960 to 1970. But as early as the mid-1950s, several years before the actual construction work, intensive documentation of the temples had been initiated, a project that included photogrammetry. Soon, however, the ambition was extended to salvaging as much as possible with international assistance. Both Egypt and the Sudan approached the United Nations Educational, Scientific and Cultural Organization (UNESCO) in 1959 for assistance. In 1960, the year in which work on the dam began, UNESCO made an appeal for assistance to all its member countries. In it, UNESCO's Director-General Vittorino Veronese described the monuments in a new way, as a "common heritage" that belonged not to individual countries but to the whole world, saying that "treasures of universal value are entitled to universal protection" (Veronese 1960: 7). The waters of the Nile were going to rise, but the pharaoh and his temples had to be rescued.

UNESCO organised a major international rescue campaign in which engineers, architects, archaeologists, and others cooperated over many years. Modernisation threatened the monuments; but at the same time, modern methods were applied to avert the threats and salvage the temples. The alternative to allowing the pharaoh to suffer drowning and destruction was to move the temples, just as more than 100,000 Nubians in the area were relocated.

The plan was to save the temples of Abu Simbel, even though a few argued that the temples were not sufficiently outstanding as art, and that to do so was to help to preserve the image of a megalomaniac despot (e.g. Allais 2013: 32f).

There were thorough investigations and discussions of various technical, organisational, and economic solutions. In particular, there was a protracted dispute about the technical possibilities of salvaging the temples, with several competing proposals, while the waters of the Nile were rising in a menacing manner: a French proposal to protect the temples behind their own dam; an Italian one to raise them in one piece by means of hydraulics; a British one to make them visible under the water; another French one to tow them on a raft behind a dam; and a Swedish one to cut the temples into pieces and subsequently rebuild them at a new site. The Swedish proposal made by VBB (Vattenbyggnadsbyrån; now part of Sweco), which competitors rhetorically called a "butchering", was selected, and carried out behind a temporary protective dam. In 1965, the first stone block could be lifted from Abu Simbel's ceiling, soon to be followed by the face of Ramses II.

The temples of Abu Simbel were sawn up into stone blocks that could weigh up to 30 tonnes. The blocks were lifted to a temporary storage site, whereupon they were moved and used in a reconstruction 65 metres higher up and 200 metres further inland. The great temple was divided up into 807 stone blocks and the small one into 235. The temples with their colossal statues were reconstructed under two artificial hills, both of which were supported by arched domes made of concrete. Next, the relocated temples were given lighting and ventilation.

The move of Abu Simbel was the most spectacular operation, but other temples were moved as well. So-called "cultural oases" were formed around the temples moved from Kalabsha, Wadi es-Sebua, and Amada. Some temples were transferred abroad – Debod to Madrid, Taffa to Leiden, Dendur to New York, and Ellesiya to Turin. Individual monuments, and also sculptures and reliefs, were transferred either to the Nubia Museum in Aswan or to the National Museum of Sudan in Khartoum. Frescoes from the cathedral in Faras went to Khartoum and Warsaw. The Nubian campaign culminated with the move of the temples on the island of Philae to the nearby island of Agilkia, where they could be reinaugurated in 1980. However, it was not possible to save those fortifications and churches in Nubia that had been built of sun-dried brick. At Philae, numerous clay buildings had already disappeared in the floods after the construction of the first Aswan dam.

While the Aswan High Dam was being built, extensive archaeological surveys and excavations were carried out on a selection of sites along a 500-kilometre stretch of the Nile valley which was threatened with flooding. The area was divided up into concessions that were allocated to different countries and institutions. There were agreements to the effect that museums in the assisting countries would be allowed to retain half of the finds as a reward, a model that came in for subsequent criticism. In all, 27 countries were directly involved in the investigations in the Nubia campaign and 49 countries contributed funding; they included the United Kingdom (UK) and France, which had been at war with Egypt only a few years before (Säve-Söderbergh 1987: 223ff, 232f; Hassan 2007: 80, 90ff; 2009).

The flagship of the campaign was Abu Simbel, which was and is an icon of pharaonic Egypt and a well-known tourist destination; and the campaign led to an increased flow of tourists. The temples have featured in numerous contexts since their rediscovery, for example in travel literature, novels, films, and computer games. A line runs from Napoleon's Egyptian campaign to the tourism of today. Individual trips along the Nile made by well-to-do members of society paved the way for the charter tourism of more recent times. The bestseller *A Thousand Miles up the Nile* by the author and Egyptologist Amelia B. Edwards, which depicts a long stay at Abu Simbel, was thus an inspiration for new visits (Edwards 1877: 414ff; cf. Fagan 1975: 309ff). A famous work of fiction is Agatha Christie's crime novel *Death on the Nile*, in which Abu Simbel provides exotic scenery for an attempted murder (Christie 1937). The book is said to have been written at the Old Cataract Hotel in Aswan with a view over the river, and it has been filmed several times (e.g. by Guillermin in 1978).

After many tribulations, the temples could be opened again in 1968, first for notabilities and then also for tourists, more than ever before; for the attention given to the salvage campaign had generated greater awareness of the site. The temples of Abu Simbel with the face of Pharaoh Ramses II had become world famous. Visitors now came by bus from Aswan, by cruise ship on Lake Nasser, or by way of the nearby airport in order to spend a couple of hours at the temples.

However, since the Arab Spring reached Egypt in 2011, the number of tourists has fallen drastically; the disturbances have frightened most tourists off. But it could have been worse. Because with another kind of political development in Egypt – or if Abu Simbel had been located somewhere else in the Middle East – the temples might have been deliberately blown up or bombed more or less fortuitously, as has happened to monuments in Afghanistan, Mali, Syria, Iraq, and Yemen.

The international campaign organised by UNESCO attracted a great deal of attention at the time, and this interest has continued. The campaign has thus resulted in a number of technical reports, scientific publications, popular presentations, illustrated books, guidebooks, essays, newspaper articles, and films – about the investigations, the monuments, and their rescuing (e.g. Hansen 1961; Keating 1962, 1975; MacQuitty 1965; Franck 1967 film; Desroches-Noblecourt & Gerster 1968; *The Salvage of the Abu Simbel Temples* 1976; Berg 1978; Säve-Söderbergh 1987; 1996; Kamil 1993: 98ff; Heimlich & Weidenbach 2005 film; Hassan 2007, 2009; Allais 2013; Berg 2019).

In the course of time, the campaign, and especially the salvage of the temples of Abu Simbel and the concrete structures, have been described by those involved in effusive terms such as "a complete and spectacular success" (whc.unesco.org/en/activities/172), "a miracle", "an unprecedented enterprise", "a resounding success", and "a triumph" (Desroches-Noblecourt & Gerster 1968: 7, 9, 110), "a modern cathedral or a new Temple" (*The Salvage of the Abu Simbel Temples* 1976: 162), a "triumph of civil engineering", and a "triumph for the Egyptian Government and the Egyptian authorities involved, triumph for UNESCO and its officials and for the international community" (Säve-Söderbergh 1987: 122).

And irrespective of whether it is told in the form of a travel novel or a technical report, the story of the campaign is narrated on the lines of a classic fairy tale – the threat that arises, the many obstacles and dangers that must be overcome, and the final resolution when the threat is overcome. Modernity (and humanity) threaten the heritage; but modernity (and human actions) will also bring solutions.

At the same time, these stories are infused with melancholy about Nubia, which disappears, and about the Nubian people, who are obliged to leave. And the Nubians' way of life is idealised as a contrast to the modern way of life (e.g. Hansen 1961; Keating 1975: 37ff, 208ff; Säve-Söderbergh 1987: 56ff; 1996: 193ff). Decades later, Nubians are shown recalling life at Abu Simbel, at the temples, and in the lost rural communities, while a return is being planned to a new Nubia (Heimlich & Weidenbach 2005 film). Consequently, the campaign has generated both technical innovations and existential reflections.

Abu Simbel and the campaign also play a prominent role in the story of the adoption in 1972 of the Convention Concerning the Protection of the World Cultural and Natural Heritage, or, in short, the World Heritage Convention (WHC 1972; cf. Lutyk 1987: 6ff; Säve-Söderbergh 1987: 220f; 1996: 217f; *World Heritage Information Kit*, 2008: 7f). Here, for the first time, traces of the past are recognised as a universal heritage and therefore a common responsibility across national borders. And in 1979, the monuments relocated in Nubia – from Abu Simbel in the south to Philae in the north – were inscribed in UNESCO's World Heritage List (WHL) on the strength of being a masterpiece, a testimony to a lost civilisation, and an open-air museum that represents the unfolding of a long sequence of Egyptian pharaonic history (*The World's Heritage* 2018: 56; WHL 88, 1979).

Once the Nubian campaign had ended, the Egyptologist Torgny Säve-Söderbergh was able to summarise and justify the actions taken officially on behalf of UNESCO. Säve-Söderbergh wrote that even those involved might occasionally ask whether it was morally defensible to collect funds for the campaign in a world where millions were starving, and where innumerable children were dying of hunger or did not have a hope of achieving a reasonable standard of living. But he took the view that no one would have hesitated. The ancient monuments were said to be important, especially for the historical and cultural identity of the developing countries. Their preservation was not only a moral duty, but also a matter of social and economic importance. After all, the excavations and the salvage campaigns created jobs in areas of unemployment. And once they had been saved, the monuments became tourist attractions, which provided economic benefits. Finally, the antiquities and monuments that were transferred to foreign museums were described as "new ambassadors extraordinary" of Egypt and the Sudan (Säve-Söderbergh 1987: 137ff; 1996: 114f).

But in a critical reckoning with UNESCO and its World Heritage system, the archaeologist Lynn Meskell has recently designated the prioritisation of the monuments at Abu Simbel ahead of the local population and the campaign's archaeological investigations as "another hallmark of the modern conservation industry" and the salvage of the temples as a "theatrical spectacle" (Meskell 2018: 30, 32).

The pharaoh had been reflected in the Nile for millennia before the life-giving waters of the river became a menace. Stone block by stone block, the pharaoh and his temple at Abu Simbel were moved to higher terrain, salvaged from drowning, along with other temples. The pharaoh was salvaged in an international campaign that was both praised and criticised. In a quite fundamental way, however, the campaign arouses amazement.

The paradoxes of Abu Simbel

The campaign at Abu Simbel is a source of amazement because the site and the sequence of events seem to be full of paradoxes, in this context meaning absurdity or contradictions. The paradoxes, which can be formulated as questions or statements to investigate, are like Chinese boxes, one box sitting inside the next one:

1. The impossible preservation of the past

The past is being preserved for the future; but is preservation for the future at all possible? Abu Simbel had long since been eroded by sandstorms, one of Ramses' faces had been destroyed by an earthquake already during his reign, and the external painting of the temples is gone. The temples are to be preserved for the future; but in the long run, no preservation campaign or relocation, no elevation to heritage or even World Heritage, and no consensus can prevent change, degradation, and impermanence. Even the unique and irreplaceable masterpiece will be lost.

2. *The protection, preservation, and alteration of the past*

The past is to be protected and preserved; but do these endeavours mean that the past is altered? At Abu Simbel there was a conflict not only about whether the cliff temples could be salvaged at all, but also about whether this should be done. Should the temples be preserved at their original location or might they be moved out of their context? The cliff temples of Abu Simbel were salvaged from the rising waters of the Nile; but for that to happen they had to be sawn into pieces, lifted away, and reconstructed at a new location under an arched dome made of concrete. The temples were indeed saved, but they did not remain wholly the same as before their preservation, just as their surroundings changed radically. The shape of the hills was different from that of the original cliffs, and a new built-up area emerged with a port, hotels, housing, roads, and an airport. All the attention and the elevation to a World Heritage site, with more tourist visits, can also increase the wear and tear on the temples. Preservation means change.

3. *The protection and preservation of the past as an exception*

When the past is protected and preserved in one place, does that mean that the corresponding proportion of the past disappears from other places? The spectacular temples of Abu Simbel were salvaged, but at the same time other Nubian ancient monuments, settlements, graves, churches, and fortifications had to drown in the Nile after being investigated and documented; skeletons and pottery were often left in place. An even greater number of sites and objects could never be investigated. And salvage might mean transfer to museums abroad. So for every site that is preserved, there may be several that vanish. An apparent upturn in protection and preservation may thus conceal an even greater upturn in devastation. Protection and preservation are an exception.

4. *The past and threats*

Threats may elicit history, memory, and heritage; but conversely, history, memory, and heritage may also create threats – and can the threats then themselves be transformed into history, memory, and heritage? The more Abu Simbel was threatened by drowning, the more the temples were held up as being worth telling about, remembering, and preserving. The threat was thus crucial in establishing the temples as heritage and, later, as World Heritage. Conversely, the cliff temples could have prevented the establishment of the Aswan High Dam and therefore the modernisation of Egypt. The preserved temples may also hamper a development that is not directly linked to income from tourism. In the future, then, the original threat, the dam – and perhaps also Abu Simbel's concrete arched domes – will be worthy of preservation as unique and irreplaceable testimony to the engineering skills of the 1960s. Clearly, history, memory, and heritage are interwoven with threats.

5. *The past and modernity*

Can history, memory, and heritage be a contrast to modernity while being part of modernity? The past has associations with the unchangeable, with stasis, with what has been, whereas modernity carries connotations of change, speed, and the future. Heritage was threatened by modernity; the temples of Abu Simbel were threatened by the Aswan High Dam. But heritage and World Heritage are modern phenomena. And modernity does not solely represent a threat; it can also represent a solution. The temples were salvaged by engineers and archaeologists using the most modern technology of their time, technology that may itself become history, memory, and heritage in the future. The past and modernity are also paradoxically interconnected.

6. *Modernity increases or decreases*

Can both an increase and a decrease in modernity give rise to history, memory, and heritage? That is, the more modernity, the more history, memory, and heritage; but also, the less modernity, the more history, memory, and heritage? The development of modernity leaves relics. At the same time, the decline of modernity breeds a renewed interest in the past, with more studies and an increase in preservation as well as investment in the experience economy.

Paradoxically, there thus appear to be two opposing explanations of the relationship between the past and modernity.

7. The crossing of boundaries

Ultimately, does the establishment of World Heritage sites run counter to current trends? The World Heritage area that extends from Abu Simbel to Philae is a local example of a constantly increasing category of international protection and preservation adhering to uniform principles. World Heritage represents structure, unity, a unified whole, and universalism, even though the temples of Abu Simbel were fragmented so that they could be reassembled at a new site, deconstructed so that they could be reconstructed. World Heritage thus goes against a postmodern view of the present, which is supposed to be characterised by decay, multiplicity, fragmentation, the regional, and the local. World Heritage crosses boundaries.

However, the temples of Abu Simbel are only one of innumerable heritage sites that arouse a dormant sense of wonderment. Abu Simbel is only one of innumerable places that are supposed to be threatened and need to be salvaged, places where preservation and change are in confrontation, heritage and modernity standing face to face. And Abu Simbel is only one of many World Heritage sites; that is, a place that is held to be irreplaceable for future generations.

The past is everywhere

Viewed from a satellite or on a map, the World Heritage sites appear as points and lines spread across the continents of the globe. Every year sees an increase in the number of sites included in UNESCO's World Heritage List. While the list consisted of 12 World Heritage sites in 7 countries on its inception in 1978, there are now 1121 World Heritage sites in 167 countries (WHL, July 2019; Appendix 1). But the World Heritage sites are merely the peak of a gigantic iceberg. They only represent a tiny fraction of everything considered to be worth protecting and preserving as heritage.

The past is everywhere, and the past is expansive. This is because more and more is being viewed as history that ought to be told, memory that ought to be retained, or heritage that ought to be defended and preserved. Nothing tangible or intangible, large or small, visible or hidden, old or new, near or far is neglected. Preserve not just the temples of Abu Simbel (WHL 88, 1979), but also old trees, thatched roofs, International Style housing, factories, transformer substations, bridges, windmills, station communities, battlefields, silos, bunkers, minigolf courses, neon advertising, and car mortuaries. Preserve the royal ship *Vasa* and preserve the wreck of the *Titanic*! Preserve traditions, myths and legends, books, letters, newspapers, posters, graffiti, paintings, photographs, films, sounds, Internet websites, and digital metadata! Preserve the Earth! And preserve the light from stars at night! They are all threatened by change, by lack of interest or by other priorities, by silence and amnesia, by impermanence and destruction.

Where remains of the past have burned or been bombed, have decayed or simply disappeared, a radical restoration or reconstruction can recreate the past. Many monuments have thus risen again, and several are (or have been) included in the World Heritage list – the Parthenon in Athens (WHL 404, 1987), Warsaw city centre (WHL 30bis, 1980, 2014), the Globe in London, the Stari Most bridge in Mostar (WHL 946rev, 2005), the Cathedral of Christ the Saviour in Moscow, the Church of Our Lady in Dresden (WHL 1156, 2004, delisted 2009), and mausoleums in Timbuktu (WHL 119rev, 1988). Others, such as the Berlin City Palace, are being processed; but UNESCO has given up on reconstructing the Buddha statues in Bamiyan in Afghanistan (WHL 208rev, 2003).

The current interest in the past is also seen in the constant increase in the number of museums, visitor centres, and recreated environments ranging across all periods, in places where the past is communicated and brought to life – from the copy of the Palaeolithic cave in Lascaux, France (WHL 85, 1979) via the JORVIK Viking Centre in York, England, the annual Medieval Week in Visby in Sweden (WHL 731, 1995), and the bringing to life of eighteenth-century Colonial Williamsburg in the US, to the Old Town in Aarhus in Denmark, which has a reconstructed urban neighbourhood from 1974. Here the tourist can either be an observer from a reassuring distance or participate actively in bringing another period to life. Historical role-playing games are another possibility.

A broad spectrum of literature, film, and television deals with historical themes, with a fluid dividing line between fact and fiction. This includes everything from Walter Scott's *Ivanhoe* and Umberto Eco's *The Name of the Rose* to Dan Brown's *The Da Vinci Code*, everything from *Andrei Rublev* to *Gladiator* and *Downton Abbey*. Indeed, the range of historical entertainment is enormous.

Then there is archaeology, my own discipline, which is only one of several methods of studying the past. Supported by both broad popular interest and relatively strong legislation, archaeological investigations (in Scandinavia at least) are more numerous, extensive, and ambitious than ever before. And gradually, archaeology has expanded to the point where it now covers all periods from the first humans to the present, even attempting to look far into the future.

We can investigate, preserve, and say more about the past than ever before. The methodological and technical developments have been nothing less than stupendous: aerial photography, metal detectors and georadar, pollen analyses, radiocarbon dating, dendrochronology, ice bore cores from inland ice, the use of geographic information system (GIS) mapping and drones, DNA analyses, and 3D scanning. And while we can look at the night sky with the naked eye and glimpse the Andromeda galaxy around 2.5 million light years away, we can use the Hubble telescope in an orbit around the Earth to see so far out into space, and therefore so far back in time, that we approach the birth of the expanding universe about 13.8 billion years ago.

The past is expanding, too. Almost regardless of what perspective we choose, the trend appears to be an increase, sometimes an exponential one. More history, more memory, more heritage, more World Heritage sites, more reconstructions, more museums, visitor centres, and role-playing games, more historical books and films. More archaeology, both further back in time and further ahead in time. In the wake of the upturn for heritage, there is growing heritage tourism; that is, tourism focused on traces of the past. In initiatives geared to increasing local or regional growth, the past is used as an attraction. The past is employed in order to create, strengthen, weaken, maintain, change, or discuss identities. Finally, heritage is increasing as a separate field of research and teaching.

When it comes to World Heritage, there is, in principle, global consensus. The basis for this claim is that since 1972, no less than 193 states have ratified the UNESCO Convention, while the United Nations (UN) has precisely 193 member states (whc.unesco.org/en/statesparties; www.un.org/en/member-states/index.html; September 2020; Appendix 2). Across all variations with regard to history, culture, language, religion, politics, and economics, states are hence able to agree about the meaningfulness of a universal natural and cultural heritage.

But why? Why this fascination with the past? Why so much history, memory, and heritage? Why try to retell, remember, preserve, reconstruct, bring to life, popularise, dig up, and use the past? What is the point of all this past in our present? And why the consensus?

Is the expansion an expression of a desire to attain greater knowledge about the past and therefore about ourselves, a desire accompanied by willingness to allocate more resources to such efforts? Is the expansion a symptom of a chronic nostalgia in a society in crisis, which creates an increasing need? Or is the expansion an expression of a growing moral duty to tell about, remember, or preserve remains of previous generations? Is it thus to be interpreted as an expression of progress or as a sign of decay? Are we witnessing people's increasing ability to tell about, remember, and preserve – or have people lost the ability to be silent, forget, and lose? Why not permit silence, oblivion, and impermanence? Why not simply let the past remain the past?

There is more than ever to tell about, remember, and preserve; and the desire to do these things also seems to be greater than ever, at the same time as the ability to do so is improving every day. But this endeavour can only be a postponement of the inevitable. For in the long run, no narrative, no memorial of stone or bronze, and no designation as heritage or World Heritage, no archive, library, or museum, no screen of bulletproof glass or global consensus, can resist change and therefore impermanence. This struggle is doomed to fail and therefore appears pointless. The preservation of the past is impossible, and yet efforts are constantly being made to attain this goal.

This brings to mind the myth of Sisyphus, King of Corinth, who pushes a great stone up a mountain; but then on reaching the top, the stone rolls down to the plain again. Sisyphus is the absurd hero, who toils in vain forever in the land of the dead as punishment for having once put Death in chains, that is precisely for trying to prevent impermanence. Happy or not, Sisyphus toils in sweat and dust, as he is compelled to do by Zeus the god (Camus 1942 (French): 163ff; 2005 (English): 107ff). But why then do we human beings toil with the past, if it is all in vain? Are we toiling with a stone block that is getting bigger every year? Do we have the freedom to let the stone lie, or are we forced to continue? Do we have a choice?

Multiple meanings

At first glance, protecting and preserving the past for the future may seem to be both absurd and paradoxical in that those two pursuits may be thought to be unreasonable and full of contradictions; but they are not meaningless in the sense of being without meaning. On the contrary, there is a plethora of ideas about why and how the past is actually protected and preserved – and how it can, should, or has to be protected and preserved. Indeed, the sheer quantity of perspectives, concepts, justifications, values, interpretations, explanations, and positions is overwhelming.

Numerous terms appear in the debate about the meaning of the past. They refer to perspectives, disciplines, institutions, objects, and processes: history, historicise, historicism, historicity, historical consciousness and use of history, archaeology, antiquity, artefact and ancient monument, memory, site of memory and politics of memory, monument, monumentalise and memorial, museum, musealisation and museology, heritage, heritagisation, use of heritage, politics of heritage, and heritage process.

Just as the terms are numerous, many reasons are quoted for studying, retelling, remembering, protecting, preserving, or using remains of the past. These reasons may be in the nature of arguments for a particular perspective, for the existence of an academic discipline, or for the activities of an institution: Why the disciplines of history and archaeology? Why erect monuments and memorials? Why establish archives and museums? Why categories such as heritage and World Heritage? As a source of knowledge! To be able to tell! As a moral obligation! The reasons may also be in the nature of values that are emphasised. And the choice may be between telling and staying silent, between remembering and forgetting, and between preservation and destruction.

Reasons for occupying oneself with the past are often formulated in specific situations that require a justification. A lengthy argument may then be reduced to rhetorical slogans, such as "The past for the future" and "Heritage is a resource". Differences regarding interest in the past may also be subjected to critical analyses and accounted for in the light of ideological and economic trends in society. And the importance of the past can be understood against the background of more fundamental circumstances – either humans as creatures characterised by their historical self-consciousness or society as a phenomenon dependent on its history for its ability to function. In reasons, explanations, and understanding, we recognise the three timescales of the French Annales school – the event, the conjuncture, and the long-term structure.

The field can display sharp contrasts between the rhetorical slogans for or against protection and preservation – via the critical

analyses of how the past has been or may, should, or will be used –
to categorical statements to the effect that history, memory, and
heritage are expressions of a society that is either rising or decaying.

The Past is a Foreign Country (1985), by the historian and geographer David Lowenthal, became a classic soon after its publication –
a classic that has frequently been referred to and quoted. *The Past
is a Foreign Country* thus belongs to the academic canon, has been
called the "Bible" of heritage, and was crucial to the establishment
of heritage studies as a separate field of research from the 1980s
onwards. Three decades later, Lowenthal returned with a revised
and expanded edition: *The Past is a Foreign Country – Revisited*
(Lowenthal 2015).

The Past is a Foreign Country begins by stating that "The past is
everywhere" (Lowenthal 1985: xv; 2015: 1). Lowenthal then goes
on to present, with example after example, quotation after quotation, the overwhelmingly numerous and various ways in which the
West, in particular, has viewed, related to, and used the past. The
book hence gives the impression of being a great collage, more of a
collection of examples than an analysis – a collage in which everyone can find a perspective to be inspired by, or a concrete fragment
to reuse.

The many examples and quotations blur the dividing line
between what others have written or said – and think – and whatever view Lowenthal himself may hold. And Lowenthal explicitly
says that he does not want to write a manifesto; that should be
the preserve of prelates and politicians (Lowenthal 2015: 2). But
The Past is a Foreign Country is in fact a long manifesto, held
together by a nostalgic recurring theme. Because at the same time
as Lowenthal reproaches others for making judgements about the
past, he makes judgements himself, time and again, about how the
past has been and is being put to use. Irrespective of his choice of
perspective, or of examples of how the past has been used or how
the present relates to the past, Lowenthal is consistently dissatisfied
and critical. There is too much of the past, and it is all wrong.

Here is a selection of examples and quotations to illustrate
Lowenthal's critical attitude. About anachronisms and modernisations of the past, he writes that these "ahistorical perversions are
widely accepted by the general public"; the general public "knows
less and less"; archaeological data are "elusive and slippery", and
preservation is "cramping creativity"; popularity leads to decay,
wear and tear, destruction, restrictions, and screening; tourism is
followed by the vulgarity of "constant cockneyfication"; and the

present is characterised by "historical illiteracy", while wretched history "is no longer the privileged mode of access to the past [that] it used to be" (Lowenthal 2015: 21, 394, 422ff, 590, 596). Nostalgia is characterised by such words as "epidemic", "modern malaise", and "drug" (Lowenthal 1985: 4ff; 2015: 31ff). And with the aid of a quotation from the architect Rem Koolhaas, Lowenthal compares heritage with a "metastasizing cancer" (Lowenthal 2015: 588).

Lowenthal's sweeping criticism of heritage is evident in his subsequent book, *The Heritage Crusade and the Spoils of History* (1997), which opens by stating that heritage is everywhere. Now the torrents of invective rain down on the reader. Heritage is not only good, but also "oppressive, defeatist, decadent". Heritage is "hyped", "nostalgic", "its growth [is] also alarming", it "causes chaos", and it is "rubbish" and "a sacred cow" (Lowenthal 1997: ix, 5ff, 10ff). Lowenthal writes that "[w]orship of a bloated heritage invites passive reliance on received authority, imperils rational inquiry, replaces past realities with feel-good history and saps creative innovation" (Lowenthal 1997: 12). Heritage is "corrupted by being popularized, commoditized, and politicized" (Lowenthal 1997: 87, also 88ff). History and heritage are described as mutually contradictory. "History seeks to convince by truth and succumbs to falsehood. Heritage exaggerates and omits, candidly invents and frankly forgets, and thrives on ignorance and error" (Lowenthal 1997: 121). "Heritage is immune to critical reappraisal because it is not erudition but catechism; what counts is not checkable fact but credulous allegiance" (Lowenthal 1997: 121). "To vilify heritage as biased is thus futile: bias is the main point of heritage. Prejudiced pride in the past is not a sorry consequence of heritage; it is its essential purpose" (Lowenthal 1997: 122).

After having read both the original and the later edition of *The Past is a Foreign Country* as well as *The Heritage Crusade and the Spoils of History*, and having listened to several lectures given by Lowenthal, I wonder whether the canonical status of the books is, in fact, due to the criticism, or has come about in spite of the criticism, or has perhaps evolved because many people have failed to go beyond the books' titles and lists of contents.

Lowenthal views not only the past but also his own period as if he were a tourist on a visit to a "foreign country". He takes a distanced view of the present's use of the past as something strange, without wanting to understand, without useful explanations, and without constructive proposals for improvements. There are only small and scattered attempts to understand or explain why the past is protected, preserved, used, discovered, and created, and why it changes. And yet, more than anything else, all his examples and quotations actually do show, with overwhelming empirical support, that people's relationship to the past is something essential. Without understanding or explanations, preservation becomes something absurd, something done for its own sake: "preservation has become a prime end in itself" (Lowenthal 2015: 592).

Interspersed with the criticism are small attempts at explanations. On the one hand, Lowenthal takes the view that modernisation has created anxiety and nostalgia, that the increasing tendency to tell, remember, and preserve is due to growing speed and volatility (Lowenthal 1985: 399; 2015: 417, 596). The more change, then, the greater the need for the past. On the other hand, angst and nostalgia are also said to be due to doubts about progress and modernity (Lowenthal 1985: 11ff; also 1997: 1, 10f; 2015: 36ff, 417). Consequently, Lowenthal considers that angst and nostalgia are caused by both modernism and postmodernism.

Modernism without faith is exactly what characterises postmodernism, according to the journalist and art historian Robert Hewison, who has also written critically about heritage: "Postmodernism is modernism with the optimism taken out" (Hewison 1987: 132).

The debate about the past, history, memory, and heritage thus reveals deep disagreement about most matters: the concepts that are relevant, the motives or values that are important, the interpretations or explanations that are valid, and also the attitudes that should prevail. There is also a debate about whether a newer age should be given priority ahead of an older one – for instance, whether the modern industrial heritage is more important than the Viking Age's rune-stones or the Stone Age's kitchen middens; about whether preservation is a relatively new or old phenomenon; about whether the remains of the past should be protected and preserved, can be used or even consumed; about whether or not authenticity is crucial for heritage; and about whether heritage is a reality or a construction in the present. It is thus easy to become somewhat confused when confronted by the multiplicity of concepts, justifications, values, and – not least – would-be authoritative analyses and attitudes that appear to conflict with one another.

It is tempting to regard this multiplicity as an expression of the postmodern condition. This is a concept formulated by the philosopher Jean-François Lyotard. The condition is supposed to be characterised by the dissolution of the great narratives. Religions, ideologies, and science lose their credibility. Faith in progress and the modern project has expired. What is left is the singular, subjective and individual, the multicultural and eclectic (Lyotard 1979 (French); 1984 (English)).

In the face of the postmodern condition, my investigation might come to an end. There is no reason to search any further; satisfactory answers already exist. The answers are multiple, complicated, and entangled in one another. And no answer is better than any other. So why look for more concepts, justifications, values, or theories? The world with its history, archaeology, memory, monuments, memorials, archives, museums, heritage, and World Heritage is too open and complex to be comprehensible.

Multiplicity is undoubtedly a fact; but it is debatable whether our present age is actually in a postmodern condition. First, our time is not strikingly postmodern; rather, it is hypermodern. Second, if our age is or has recently become postmodern, previous ages have certainly presented the same symptoms of multiplicity and confusion. And, third, different parts of the world may be dissimilar, so it is not possible to generalise about a prevailing global condition.

The present is not unequivocally postmodern. Consequently, the great narratives have by no means expired. It is possible that many people question faith in progress and modernity, particularly in the West, in other words in Europe and North America; but this faith is still gaining ground in other parts of the world, especially in Asia. The great global contexts are more important than ever; the economy and the climate are bringing people together around new common narratives; and religion is once more on the political agenda every day of the week. The postmodern condition is hence not dominant from a global perspective.

The concept of the postmodern condition assumes that the modern period was somehow different, an organic "golden age" of great narratives, characterised by the universal, objective, and collective, the monocultural and coherent. Here, though, the postmodern philosophers may have been seduced by the narrative of progress that they themselves criticise; or they are captives of their own rhetoric, which marks a distinction between the modern and the postmodern. For the narrative of progress gives history a direction, a direction where whatever deviates from its main line is not told, remembered, or preserved. Both the modern period and the early modern and pre-modern period possessed a multifarious abundance of small and great narratives. A canonisation of one line of development around progress closes off the alternative narratives, memories, and possibilities. All ages have been "post-modern" if the simultaneous existence of many small narratives is a crucial criterion: we have always been postmodern.

The present has always been characterised by a multiplicity of opinions, confusion, and uncertainty about the future. It is only when a distance has opened up to a period or epoch that a rounded narrative is put in place through a process of canonisation, in which something is selected as valuable ahead of something else. Something is told, remembered, and preserved while something else remains unsaid, is forgotten, and disappears. At a distance, the past can be surveyed, simplified, and fitted into a greater canonical narrative, with a given direction, about what was typical of the period. But a deeper and broader examination of earlier periods uncovers a swarm of alternative views, metaphysics, religion, superstition, speculations, and errors that are not given a place in the textbook narratives about the progress of reason and science. It is the canonised hero of reason to whom memorials are devoted, and whose intellectual legacy is protected and preserved for posterity.

A first example that may be mentioned is the view taken of the past, artefacts, and ancient monuments in Denmark and Sweden in the seventeenth century, with names such as Ole Worm and Johannes Bureus. A close study of contemporaneous sources reveals that these views about the past were intimately related to religion and magic and were much more varied and full of contradictions than previously assumed (Svestad 1995: 75ff; Jensen 2002).

A second example is the mathematician and physicist Isaac Newton, who is often presented as a pioneer of modern science but was influenced by religious motives. Newton is famous for his revolutionary theories of universal gravitation, motion, light, and colour. But at the same time, he sought to combine what should, in a modern view, be kept separate, namely the magic and the exact, the occult and the rational. Throughout his life, he studied alchemy and theology alongside mathematics and physics. Newton thus employed several methods which he regarded as equivalent in his endeavour to reach the truth and the divine (Dobbs 1991).

As a third example, the physicist Hans Christian Ørsted combined religious ideas and Romantic natural philosophy with physical experiments. When Ørsted discovered electromagnetism, he was thus inspired by Romantic ideas about the unity of natural forces. In his view, he had made an experimental demonstration of the spirit of nature, which reflected the thoughts of God (Lindborg 1998).

Multiplicity and confusion around history, memory, and heritage may also be due to the actual volume and variation of the relevant phenomenon. The past is expressed in everything from doctoral theses to novels and role-playing games, from national archives to private photo albums, and from the Abu Simbel of antiquity (WHL 88, 1979) to the modern Sydney Opera House (WHL 166rev, 2007). The field is so large, and the questions are formulated so broadly, that the path lies open to many different and mutually contradictory replies.

In addition, there is marked multiplicity in the division into disciplines and institutions, each with their own discourse or "conversation"; that is, each with its own professional language, circulation of ideas, questions, perspectives, methods, sources, practice, justifications, motives, and values. The past is illuminated by numerous subjects, each of which can be further divided into a number of sub-specialities. In the same way, there are innumerable institutions such as archives, museums, libraries, visitor centres, research centres, and administrations displaying far-reaching internal specialisation. Multiplicity may also be based on quantitative growth. There are quite simply more trained historians, psychologists, archaeologists, heritage researchers, and other specialists than ever before, and therefore also more conflicting opinions (Kristiansen 1996; Evans 1997: 171ff).

This multiplicity is a double-edged phenomenon. On the one hand, it entails an enriching pluralism, in which reality is illuminated from several vantage points. On the other hand, it easily leads to confusion and despondency. Understanding and explanation, the possibility of criticism and change disappear when numerous variations and details are allowed to dominate. Similarities and wider correlations go undetected. A unified view becomes an unachievable utopia.

However, two distinct attitudes to the traces of the past – two diametrically different cultures – run right through all this multiplicity and confusion.

Two cultures

Two cultures are separated by a gap. One is science and the other is literature (or the humanities). They do not know each other and they cannot enter into a conversation. That was the claim made by the physicist and author C. P. Snow in a lecture in Cambridge in 1959 (Snow 1959). This gap originated from a division of the scientific disciplines of the nineteenth century into analytical and explanatory natural sciences on the one side and interpretative and understanding humanities on the other. And explanation and understanding are still two complementary ways of approaching knowledge (cf. Wright 1971), so there is no concept that could unite explaining and understanding, unite causes and intentions.

Snow's idea about the two cultures had a great impact in an era in which the Cold War created a polarisation between West and East. At the same time, it is easy to see that the idea of the two cultures also sprang from Snow's personal experience as both a physicist and an author. But even if Snow's powerful pair of concepts has long been outdated, I would submit that there is a current gap between the two cultures with respect to their view of history, memory, and heritage. Despite the comprehensive affiliation to the World Heritage Convention, there is still no consensus about heritage or World Heritage.

The two cultures of heritage originate from different roles and therefore dissimilar perspectives – on the one hand antiquarian "management" and on the other hand critical studies in the academy. But the cultures share a focus on threats, in the first *to* heritage and in the second *from* heritage. In addition, the division between the two cultures often, albeit not always, coincides with the division between essentialism on the one hand and constructivism on the other. The managers thus see the past and the heritage as really existing, whereas the critics view the past and heritage as constructions for negotiation. I refer to the first culture as Canonical Heritage; the other calls itself Heritage Studies or Critical Heritage.

The first, and canonical, culture of heritage is characteristic of the heritage managers. Resting on laws and conventions, it is supported by popular engagement. It is found at international institutions such as UNESCO, national institutions such as English Heritage/Historic England, the Swedish National Heritage Board, the Directorate for Cultural Heritage in Norway, and the Danish Agency for Culture and Palaces, and at archives, libraries, museums, foundations, and associations. A characteristic of the first culture is that heritage is regarded as being under threat, and that it ought to be defended and preserved for the future. Representatives of this culture describe developments as a constant struggle against time and impermanence for better documentation, protection, preservation, and use. A boom or an upturn for history, memory, and heritage is seen as a sign of health and as progress. Heritage is already, or should be, central as a destination in a growing experience economy. And heritage is associated with words such as inheritance, memory, resource, knowledge, values, democracy, multiplicity, and sustainable development, all meant in a favourable sense.

We encounter the first culture in general works about institutions, specialist disciplines, and heritage, in which it is possible to follow developments from the very first examples of history writing, archaeological excavations, or protection up to research, management, and communication in our own age. The past, with its texts, images, objects, monuments, and landscapes, has been threatened through the ages by silence, oblivion, and destruction; but it can and should be salvaged for posterity. A consistent theme running through these narratives is threats to the heritage, and attempts to avert them. The salvage of the temples of Abu Simbel is a prime example in the first culture's own history of successful campaigns for protection and preservation. History, monuments, and heritage are presented as being worth protecting, preserving, being aware of, and visiting. In particular, all the World Heritage sites are proudly presented on signs, on websites, in adverts, in brochures, in magazines, and in abundantly illustrated works (e.g. whc.unesco.org; Lutyk 1987; Anker & Snitt 1997; Grundsten & Hanneberg 2000; Hanneberg 2012; *The World's Heritage* 2018; worldheritageswe den.se).

Heritage's second, critical, culture is found especially among a number of academics active at universities or research centres, or as independent scholars. It is present at universities, where networks are established around courses, journals, series of books, conferences, and centres with the word "critical" as their pivotal point, for example in the network called the "Association of Critical Heritage Studies" (criticalheritagestudies.org). The criticism appears across a broad scale – from criticism of the selection of heritage via criticism of how heritage is preserved and used to rejection of heritage as an idea.

One characteristic of the most radical criticism of heritage is the notion that the past is a burden and a menace to society. The unfavourable consequences of too much history, memory, or heritage are emphasised. Mass tourism to heritage destinations is a problem. An upturn for the past is thus seen as a symptom of disease and crisis. The upturn is described not as a boom, but as a mania. And history, memory, and heritage are associated with words such as myth, flight, therapy, trauma, spectacle, obsession, and inflation, madness and stress, taboo, totem and fetish, cult and crusade, industry and musealisation – all obviously intended in an unfavourable sense.

Radical critics thus describe the past as a burden, a stone of Sisyphus, and a threat to society. Stored artefacts are described as "archaeological waste" and archive documents as "archival waste" (e.g. Beckman 1998: 36f). The widespread fixation with the past is diagnosed as neurotic and repressive, an expression of a sick consciousness and fear of death (Brown 1959: 87ff). Culturalism with its notions of identity is described as an epidemic virus (Hylland Eriksen 1996). Heritage inflation is diagnosed as a narcissistic syndrome leading to either neurosis or madness (Choay 1992 (French): 187ff; 2001 (English): 164ff).

The analogy with disease is already to be found in the work of the philologist and philosopher Friedrich Nietzsche. His "untimely meditation" *Vom Nutzen und Nachteil der Historie für das Leben* (*On the Use and Abuse of History*) was originally intended to appear under the title "The Historical Disease". Nietzsche described his age's preoccupation with the past as a "consumptive historical fever" that should be countered with poison, ointments, and medicines. Nietzsche took the view that history, which ought to serve and promote life, had become a burden and a drawback. With its ideals, the art and culture of antiquity was a "yoke of the past". The present was described by Nietzsche as saturated with history, and it was to be cured by a diet of oblivion and art. For the past was hostile and dangerous. It weakened personality, fostered self-righteousness, impeded maturity, promoted epigonism, and developed both cynicism and egoism via self-irony (Nietzsche 1874 (German): Vorwort, Chapter 8, 10; 2005 (English): Preface p. 3f, Chapter VIII 47ff, Chapter X 65ff).

Another widespread analogy is with religion – also meant in an unfavourable sense. The whole sphere of history, memory, and heritage can be seen as a civil religion with relics and rituals, a religion that creates cohesion around the nation and a national identity. Museums are compared with temples or churches, the objects exhibited with relics, museum staff with priests, monuments with religious buildings, tourists with pilgrims, and mass cultural tourism with a World Church (e.g. MacCannell 1976: 42ff; Horne 1984: 1ff; Choay 1992 (French): 101ff, 128f, 158ff, 186; 2001 (English): 87ff, 111f, 139ff, 163; Beckman 1993a: 31f; 1998: 32ff; Duncan 1995: 7ff; Hylland Eriksen 1996: 85).

This criticism, in all its forms, is found in Lowenthal's work. There is criticism to the effect that UNESCO defines heritage too narrowly according to a Western way of thinking, focusing on preservation of the material; that is, the intangible, which is of greater importance in other cultures, is neglected (Lowenthal 1997: 20). Besides, the past is said to be merely preserved instead of being used creatively (Lowenthal 1985: xvii, 384; 2015: 413). There is general criticism, full of invective, of the past and heritage (Lowenthal 1985: 4ff, 64; 1997: 5ff, 10ff, 87ff, 120f, 189; 2015: 31ff, 132). The analogies to both disease and religion are in evidence here. In *The Past is a Foreign Country*, nostalgia is described as an epidemic disease (Lowenthal 1985: 4ff; 2015: 31ff). And in *The Heritage Crusade and the Spoils of History*, heritage is compared with a new folk belief, a secular religion, and a crusade, just as heritage institutions are compared with the Church (Lowenthal 1997: 1f).

But analogies with disease and religion hardly contribute to greater understanding of the importance of the past in the present. The analogies only mean that questions are given new labels, that the problem field is reformulated in new spheres which are at least as complicated or enigmatic. Then, instead, the question becomes: Why diseased? Why neurotic? Why pilgrimage? Why crusade? The purpose of the analogies appears as a rhetorical strategy, in which the choice of words is geared to demonstrating how negative or meaningless heritage is. It is about invective, not about understanding or explanation.

If there is any doubt as to which of the two cultures of heritage one is encountering, the language can be revealing. While the first, canonical, culture talks about history, memory, and heritage with respect and reverence, as something elevated, the tone in the second culture may, as an antithesis, be surprisingly disrespectful, sarcastic, derisive, or directly contemptuous of both heritage and its managers. Although the defamatory tone can be traced back to the style of Nietzsche, Lowenthal's books also seem to have set a standard here that several people with the same attitudes have striven to emulate (e.g. Beckman 1993a; 1998).

However, a critical reckoning with both traditions of heritage is long overdue (cf. Winter 2013; Aronsson 2015: 168f). The traditions have developed into conformist, self-corroborating discourses without any mutual dialogue. A continued reckoning is needed with the managing canonical tradition, whose protection and preservation are uncritically regarded as part of the Enlightenment project and progress; so is a reckoning with the critical tradition when it gets stuck in non-constructive criticism and merely repeats itself by constantly providing new examples.

On the one side are those who evidently worship the past and the cultural heritage, and on the other side are those who are discontented with them both. But if we want to understand and explain the importance of the past in the present – that is, understand and explain the importance of history, memory, and heritage – then the gap between these two cultures needs to be overcome. For an inquiry cannot focus solely on the arguments on one side – that is, either on all the good arguments for telling, remembering, and preserving, or on all the good arguments (or invective) to the contrary. My inquiry will try to bridge that gap and, if possible, fuse the canonical and the critical. In addition, greater conceptual, methodological, and empirical precision is required since, up to now, central concepts have been used in a somewhat haphazard fashion, various random examples being thrown into the debate one after another as ad-hoc arguments, and arguments often being replaced by rhetoric.

Archimedean points

The ancient mathematician Archimedes is supposed to have said, "Give me a place to stand, and I will move the earth." This wording has created the metaphor of the Archimedean Point as a name for an immoveable, secure, and certain fixed place. Now, however, the metaphor is generally used to assert that a fixed place of that kind no longer exists, insofar as it ever did. There is not supposed to be such a thing as a fixed place, a true, objective, or certain starting point. In the postmodern condition, an almost nihilistic relativism is unavoidable.

But the need for an Archimedean point becomes evident when one confronts the debate about the past. For there is great confusion here, produced by strange paradoxes, innumerable examples, multiple meanings, and conflicting explanations. So give me a fixed place where I can stand and therefore a viewpoint I can use, and then I can try to understand and explain why the past apparently turns up everywhere.

Over the years, I have considered, planned, initiated, and then rejected (at least) three different starting points for an investigation. The first was the well-known and unique, while universally valid, archaeological discovery where we stand face to face with the person of the past: the mummified body of the Tollund man at Silkeborg Museum in Denmark. I then looked at musealisation, with its shifting trends, from a long-term perspective: the founding of museums in Scandinavia as a population covering the whole spectrum from the great national museums to the Hasse & Tage Museum in Tomelilla in Sweden, called the world's smallest film museum. And finally, the spectacular blasting of a heritage – and later World Heritage – site: the destruction of the Buddha statues in Bamiyan in Afghanistan in 2001 (WHL 208rev, 2003).

Where the field of the past is great and unbounded, I choose to focus on one out of several possible perspectives, namely on heritage, an area where David Lowenthal's books, *The Past is a Foreign Country* (1985; 2015) and *The Heritage Crusade and the Spoils of History* (1997), possess canonical status. But further precision is needed.

Despite the influence of Lowenthal, studies of heritage are surprisingly often restricted to individual sites, a region, or a nation, in the same way as international perspectives are often restricted to previous colonies. Both heritage's canonical culture and heritage's critical culture generally keep to a national discussion, as if the term heritage had undergone its own independent development within the borders of a state (e.g. Anshelm 1993). This geographically restricted scope may be due to a practical dependence on the respective area of responsibility and field of interest of institutions. It may also be due to connections with questions of identity and politics, both of which are often restricted to the national stage. And the national or colonial scope may be due to linguistic limitations or convenience. But even if the nation is an important unit, it is neither natural nor unproblematic as a methodological boundary, and it needs to be explored in a global context (cf. Smith 1983; Wimmer & Glick Schiller 2002). Without a broader perspective that crosses borders and shatters the national "iron cage", it is, in my opinion, not possible to understand or explain heritage as a phenomenon, let alone to account for the global expansion of heritage.

In studies of both the past and the present, we often resort to perspectives that are characterised by dichotomies. As academic trends shift, either one or another perspective is given renewed attention: the special or particular as against the general or universal, the local as against the global, and the national as against the international. But in order to understand and explain heritage, it is necessary to unite these perspectives. Heritage as a phenomenon is both local and global – heritage is "glocal". Developments at the local level are affected by global trends – and the global has to take a position in relation to the local (Robertson 1995). But where, then, is the starting point that can shed light on heritage from a glocal perspective?

Abu Simbel in Egypt has several of the characteristics that an Archimedean point of heritage is required to possess. Thus the cliff temples of Abu Simbel hold a central position in the debate about the protection, preservation, and use of heritage. Abu Simbel is a world-famous and popular destination, even though the Arab Spring and the subsequent conflicts have reduced the number of tourists. The temples were threatened by drowning and destruction on account of the erection of the Aswan High Dam, but after several years of discussions about principles and technical solutions, the temples were salvaged in an extensive international campaign under the leadership of UNESCO. And a few years later, Abu Simbel was elevated to World Heritage status along with other Nubian monuments. But instead of remaining at Abu Simbel, the temples can be used as a vehicle for engaging in an exchange between the local and the global, from Abu Simbel to all World Heritage Sites and back again. Therefore, instead of choosing one Archimedean point I choose many; that is, the apparent stability of a growing network of many sites.

From a glocal perspective, heritage may be represented by World Heritage, which has found its way not only to Abu Simbel, but also to numerous monuments, buildings, places, and landscapes around the globe. The category of World Heritage is a growing international canon that is well defined and particularly well documented. World Heritage permits both a total overview and a focus on selected examples. World Heritage represents both the past and the present. The World Heritage sites are accompanied by various expressions defining their values, their proper use, and reasons for their status. World Heritage sites may be linked to questions related to canonisation, memory, and oblivion, crises and compensation, modernity, museums, and traditions. And World Heritage sites are relevant to current questions about economic development, politics, identity, rights, and conflicts (cf. Labadi & Long 2010). World Heritage sites, with Abu Simbel as an example, are also "good to think with" (Lévi-Strauss 1962 (French): 128 "bonnes à penser"; 1963 (English): 89).

World Heritage sites were chosen as the Archimedean points of the present investigation, partly because they can represent heritage both locally and globally and partly because they are readily accessible as empirical data, and therefore do not detract from the questions, perspectives, and debate. There is no need for time-consuming archive or storage studies or for demanding excavations, conservation, documentation, or digitalisation to make the material accessible and usable.

While new methodological conditions were created for the writing of history with the art of printing in Europe from the fifteenth century, and for archaeology and history of art with the railway and mass production of images in the nineteenth century, aspects of modernity in the form of computer technology and the Internet are creating new conditions for heritage studies in the twenty-first century. Without exertion I am able, from my location in southern Sweden, to visit World Heritage sites all over the world with the aid of Google Earth, Google Street View, and UNESCO's websites. Modernity is hence both a condition for my inquiry and part of the modernity that is to be investigated and discussed.

The World Heritage sites are complex entities. On the one hand, World Heritage is a concept, a word with a well-defined meaning which refers to a carefully defined number of sites that can, in principle, increase without end. On the other hand, every single World Heritage is an individual, unique site with its own history and own set of physical circumstances. The World Heritage sites thus represent both an abstract idea and a concrete materiality, and they must therefore be investigated from several perspectives and using several different methods. Concepts can be confronted with the material both in order to inspire and in order to meet resistance.

But do the World Heritage sites create or reflect a world? Is World Heritage something that exists and can therefore be discovered? Or is it something that is constructed, and that creates a new reality? This is the same problem as in a discussion of whether facts are discovered or constructed in a laboratory (Latour & Woolgar 1979; also Febvre 1949 (French): 239; 1973 (English): 36f), and whether a map reproduces or constructs the world (Wood 1993). Here the field of social sciences and humanities has been characterised by constructivism since the 1980s; that is, the view that we construct the world with the aid of words and images.

A World Heritage site can be discovered as a place, but it is constructed as a concept. And there is a compromise or a third standpoint between objectivism and constructivism, between discovering and constructing facts. It is not a question of knowledge either existing or being created, but of the world's being investigated with the aid of human-made instruments. But heritage and World Heritage are not only about technical instruments; they also involve the senses and language.

The world may be observed and changed from innumerable angles that complement and enrich one another. The picture of the world varies as perspectives shift. Just as colours show part of the world, and just as the Hubble telescope shows light from the cosmos in a limited section of the spectrum, a map shows the world from one of an innumerable number of possible perspectives. The map is a model of the world that connects theory with reality: it is an idealised representation of the world. And since the world is infinite and constantly changing, the map can never be more than a methodological approximation of the world (Giere 2006). So the telescope and the map are – just like the pen, the book, and the computer – tools that bridge the gap between objectivism and constructivism, between the world as it is and our view of the world. We do not experience the world as it is but as our instruments, senses, and experience permit us to perceive it (Eagleman 2016: 35).

Questions concerning the importance of history, memory, and heritage cannot be answered with a clear yes or no. Nor can they be answered with a mathematical formula or a number. There are no definitive answers. Instead, we are dealing with an interlocking of understanding and explanation where the choice of perspective is pivotal to the shaping of the answers.

Arche, archaeology, and order

The study of the past is split up among numerous subjects and institutions, each with its characteristic designation, its perspective, its methods, its source material, its period, or its preferred geographical area. And inside each subject or institution, there are discussions about objectives, boundaries, and identities, especially when the field is to be defined in relation to other fields. The universal, overarching, or common in relation to the past and the present is forced to give way to far-reaching antiquarian and academic Balkanisation. What is needed here is an amalgamation of that which has been divided, a fusion of canonical and critical perspectives.

Linguistically, the first part of archaeology as a word may have its origins in pre-Socratic philosophy. The first person to have used *archai* or *arche* as a concept is said to have been the philosopher Anaximander. *Arche* was derived from the verb *archo*, which meant "to begin" or "to reign". In philosophy, *arche* came to mean beginning, origin, first principle, ultimate cause, first material, or axiom. *Arche* was a "substrate" – an underlying layer. *Arche* was the origin of everything, boundless, eternal, immortal, and divine (OED: I, 608; Malina & Vasícek 1990: 3ff; McKirahan 1998).

In philosophy, *archaiologi'a* or archaeology then came to mean the study of a distant past, or speculation about events with regard to which there was no proof. In its earliest meaning, archaeology is hence unbounded in relation to sources, periods, and geography. But when archaeology was disciplined into a field of inquiry and then became an academic subject in the nineteenth century, it was limited to the study of material culture with the aid of the methods of typology, stratigraphy, and analogy. And archaeology then came to be associated, first and foremost, with excavation (Malina & Vasícek 1990: 3ff; Schnapp 1993 (French): 60ff, 275ff; 1996 (English): 60ff, 275ff).

Since its establishment as a subject, archaeology has itself become fragmented into a large number of subdisciplines or specialities. It was thus noted relatively recently that there are more than 100 different archaeologies with their own designations, including my own specialities "historical archaeology" and "church archaeology" (Rudebeck 2009: 18). But there is undoubtedly room for "a thousand archaeologies" in the future.

Specialisation is encouraged by an academic dynamic, in which positions and capital are sought at the "forefront of research". New perspectives are soon defined as their own specialities and, if possible, as their own subjects, which may generate a return in the form of appointments, money, and prestige. In addition, specialisation is an effective means of attaining knowledge; it may also be necessary as the quantity of methods and data increases. However, specialisation also means that we know more and more about less and less. The great questions, the overview and the syntheses, are impeded or prevented.

The concept of archaeology is still used in philosophy and in other contexts as a metaphor for a particular method. The archaeologist has become a detective looking for hidden clues. Archaeology is associated with depth, excavation, and uncovering what is hidden under the surface, as well as with stratification, the uncertain, fragments, and documentation (e.g. Lowenthal 1985: 251ff; 2015: 401ff; Ebeling & Altekamp 2004; Holtorf 2005: 16ff).

The passion that the physician Sigmund Freud had for archaeology and antiquity has attracted considerable attention, and his psychoanalysis has been compared with an archaeological excavation (Møller 1994; Thomas 2004: 149ff; Kuusamo 2011). Above Freud's famous divan in Vienna there hung a gouache, a picture of Abu Simbel from 1907 (Pollock 2006: 2 with fig. 1.1, 8f).

Another famous example is the philosopher and historian of ideas Michel Foucault, who called his own method for bringing out knowledge hidden in the archives "archaeological" (cf. Foucault 1966 (French); 1971 (English); 1969 (French); 1972 (English)).

Metaphorical archaeology is tempting with its undisciplined freedom. But my method is perhaps the opposite of archaeology. Neither non-archaeology nor pseudo-archaeology, it is a kind of anti-archaeology. Because whereas archaeology digs deep and works with materiality in a long temporal perspective, I will look up from the ground to the sky in an attempt to form an overview, working with library books and the more transient world of the computer screen.

My investigation may be an example of archaeosophy, archaeology, historical archaeology, glocal archaeology, canonical or critical heritage studies, or some seventh pursuit. But in actual fact, academic designations and divisions into subjects are uninteresting when we think and write: it must be left to others, or to the future, to bring order to a writer's identities, perspectives, and investigations (cf. Febvre 1949 (French): 231f; 1973 (English): 31; Foucault 1969: 28 (French); 1972: 17 (English)). As a didactic device, I have nonetheless chosen to assign professional labels to individuals mentioned in this text, while their national identities have been deliberately omitted.

If you follow your curiosity and conscience wherever that path may lead; formulate questions and seek answers irrespective of whether they belong to this or that discipline, culture, or tradition; freely seek enlightenment in the conviction that knowledge can bring about change; and try to cross the dividing line between knowledge, aesthetics, and ethics, as well as the dividing line between "is" and "ought" – well, then you are by necessity an engaged – and troublesome – amateur (cf. Said 1994).

The purpose of *Heritopia: World Heritage and modernity* is to try to understand and explain the importance of the past in the present by starting out from glocal examples of heritage, namely World Heritage sites. The background is my own and many others' amazement in the face of a much-debated upturn that is observable across the field of history, memory, and heritage, albeit my inquiry chooses to focus on heritage and, within that area, on World Heritage sites in particular.

In methodological terms, World Heritage sites will be included in the inquiry both as individual examples and as a statistical population. Abu Simbel will turn up regularly. But otherwise attention is generally drawn to what is different, marginal, or border-crossing, which may indirectly shed light on normality: World Heritage sites that are controversial, threatened, vandalised, or have simply been removed from the List; places that could be expected to be World Heritage sites but are nonetheless not on the List; and countries that still do not have any World Heritage, or have not even ratified the Convention.

To understand and explain the importance of the past, it is, in my view, necessary to bridge not only the gap between the two cultures of heritage, but also other trenches between different cultures, perspectives, and academic subjects that split up the field. Consequently, references will be made both to academic texts and to literary and cinematic fiction, to sciences, humanities, and social sciences – and use will be made of both qualitative interpretation and quantitative analysis. Moreover, I consider that heritage and World Heritage cannot be examined in isolation from the more general development of society. To be able to understand and explain heritage and World Heritage, we need to understand and explain present-day developments.

The main question addressed in this book may be briefly formulated as follows: What is the relationship between World Heritage and modernity? In the light of the paradoxes of heritage, a number of subsidiary questions can then be formulated: Is preservation of World Heritage for the future possible? Is World Heritage changed when efforts are made to protect and preserve it? Is the protection and preservation of World Heritage offset by more destruction at other places? Are threats of destruction a precondition for World Heritage? Is World Heritage contrary to modernity and a part of it at the same time? Is World Heritage promoted by both more and less modernity? Is World Heritage border-crossing?

The present chapter, Chapter 1, "The past is everywhere", constitutes an introduction which presents the field of problems with its paradoxes, taking Abu Simbel as its starting point. Chapter 2, "Truth, beauty, and goodness", considers reasons, motives, and values involved in preserving the past. Chapter 3, "Chronic nostalgia", discusses (mis)use of the past and crisis theories, all of which have one feature in common: they regard interest in the past as a compensation for phenomena in the present. Chapter 4, "The faces of modernity", analyses central concepts such as time, change, permanence, progress, and decay, and it presents a new perspective on modernity. Chapter 5, "Heritage in the present", examines the growth of heritage as a concept and a field, and it looks at how the concept has expanded. Chapter 6, "Destination World Heritage", examines the World Heritage Convention as a modern innovation;

the chapter discusses the list of outstanding and universal World Heritage sites as an example of canonisation and also as a reaction against an ongoing inflation of heritage. Chapter 7, "World Heritage and modernity", introduces the concept of Heritopia, and returns to Abu Simbel and other World Heritage sites in an attempt to understand and explain the seven paradoxes listed near the beginning of this introductory chapter.

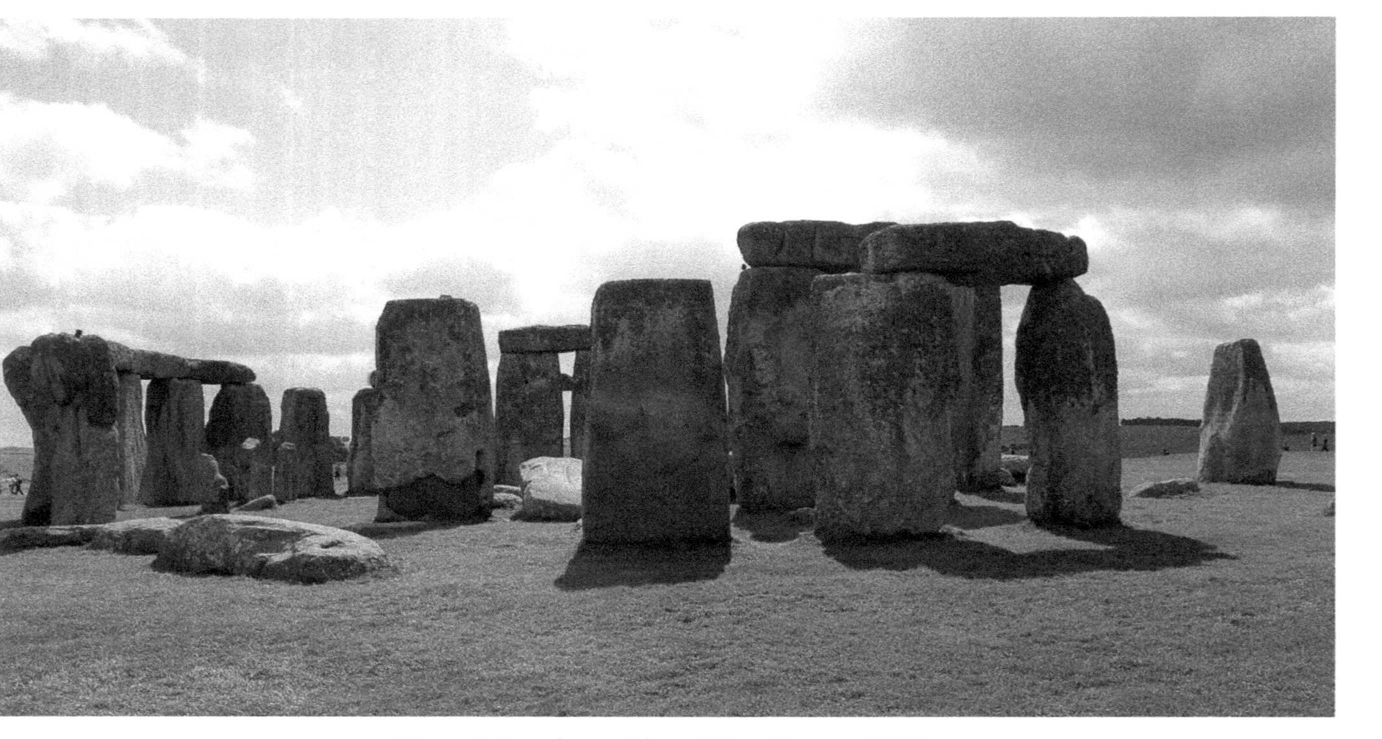

Figure 2 Stonehenge. Photo © Lars Larsson, 2008.

2

Truth, beauty, and goodness

Defence of the past

In the myth of Sisyphus, the King of Corinth pushes a great stone up a mountain, whereupon the stone rolls down to the plain again. To understand why Sisyphus apparently toils uselessly in the underworld, we can interrogate Sisyphus himself. Why are you pushing this great stone? Or we can interrogate Death, who has imposed this task, in order to secure an answer. And if Sisyphus or Death wanted, and was able, to reply, and if we could understand their answer, we could conclude our search.

Similarly, to understand the importance of history, memory, and heritage, why Ramses II's cliff temples were moved, we could interrogate the participants themselves or look for their justifications. What is the point of this enormous operation to save some old temples? Why this fascination with the past? Why tell about, remember, and preserve traces of distant ages? The intention would then be to uncover the motives through the participants' own justifications.

The justifications for the Nubian campaign were presented in 1960 by the then Director-General of UNESCO, Vittorino Veronese. An appeal described the threats from the Aswan High Dam; the difficult choice between the heritage of the past and well-being in the present and between temples and crops; and the call by the governments of Egypt and the Sudan for help from UNESCO. It stressed the possibility of new discoveries for humanity, and in return for this help the relevant countries would be opened up for archaeological excavation, with the possibility for half of all finds, as well as monuments, to go to foreign museums. The appeal described a noble cause, outlined a new era for Egyptology, and regarded the operation as a chance to demonstrate international solidarity with countries that had been at the centre of many conflicts over the centuries (Veronese 1960: 7).

Veronese described heritage in a way that pointed towards both material and intangible world heritage:

> Wondrous structures, ranking among the most magnificent on earth, are in danger of disappearing beneath the waters. … These monuments, whose loss may be tragically near, do not belong solely to the countries who hold them in trust. The whole world has the right to see them endure. They are part of a common heritage which comprises Socrates' message and the Ajanta frescoes, the walls of Uxmal and Beethoven's symphonies. Treasures of universal value are entitled to universal protection. (Veronese 1960: 7)

Today, a reader will be struck by the contrast between the elevated rhetoric and the promise later in the same text:

> In return for the help the world gives them, the governments of Cairo and Khartoum will open the whole of their countries to archaeological excavation and will allow half of whatever works of art may be unearthed by science or by hazard to go to foreign museums. They will even agree to the transport, stone by stone, of certain monuments of Nubia. (Veronese 1960: 7)

The contrast is apparent half a century later, when questions concerning the return of heritage to its original location constantly create debate and conflicts.

Justifications and motives depend on who is speaking or writing, where, and when. The justifications of a Director-General of UNESCO represent one perspective, while the motives of participating governments, institutions and funds may be different, as may the motives of the people who actually carried out the work. Behind the wording about conflicts and solidarity, it is possible to sense the Suez crisis, when the UK, France, and Israel attacked Egypt after the nationalisation of the canal in 1956, a mere four years before. Of these three countries, only France – host to the headquarters of UNESCO – contributed to the campaign, and none of them subsequently accepted temples. And before the Director-General's appeal, there were several years of contacts and initiatives between political and antiquarian actors, a minister of culture, a Deputy Director-General, an Egyptologist, and many others (Säve-Söderbergh 1987: 64ff; 1996: 59ff).

Official justifications in rhetorical phrases, which are the result of a lengthy diplomatic process and have been negotiated to create a consensus that as many countries as possible can agree on, are only part of the background. And when the campaign was over, one of the central actors – the Egyptologist Torgny Säve-Söderbergh – was able, on behalf of UNESCO, to supplement previous justifications with higher employment in the area, income from tourism, and contacts created through the transfer of antiquities and monuments to other countries (Säve-Söderbergh 1987: 137, 217f; 1996: 114).

An exploration of justifications and motives will quickly reveal that they are numerous, highly diverse, and dependent on the discourses or conversations of which they form part. Justifications and motives are to be found across the whole field of history, memory, and heritage – from general humanities to individual disciplines or investigations. Justifications and motives may be directed outwards at society as a whole, or inwards in a definition of areas of responsibility or territories; both cases involve a fight for attention and resources. Historical overviews of shifting justifications are presented; or it is possible to read the author's personal view of what are, can, or ought to be the right motives. Justifications and motives may glide from an account of why over to a methodological discussion about how; that is, about whether useful results are best achieved through freedom or control, through basic research or applied research, and through the prioritisation of one field ahead of another.

The usefulness of the humanities can be asserted in relation to economics, social science, medicine, natural science, and engineering. Motives can be discussed from a philosophy-of-history perspective, with analyses of how different periods viewed usefulness. Accounts of different motives can be presented in textbooks. Justifications that come across as rhetorical slogans for the already initiated may appear in an appeal or at the inauguration of a memorial, a new museum, or a new initiative: The past for the future! History, heritage, and memory as a resource! Democracy and dialogue! Justifications may also be given in formal decisions about archaeological investigations or the protection of buildings, and may then include references to legislation or conventions. But where the first and canonical culture of heritage is geared to expressing justifications using rhetoric, arguments, or statutory provisions, the second and critical culture of heritage wants to put in question marks as an expression of scepticism.

There is a long tradition of reflecting on what history is, can be, or should be, on the development of history, and on the history, perspectives, methods, and sources of the study of history itself. Many have argued for the usefulness of history or discussed the arguments of others. These reflections on history have been conducted by historians, but also by philosophers and others under the heading "philosophy of history".

In the course of these discussions, many participants have been inspired by the philosopher and philologist Friedrich Nietzsche and his *Vom Nutzen und Nachtheil der Historie für das Leben* (*On the Use and Abuse of History*). According to Nietzsche, the usefulness of history may be divided into three categories, the monumental, the antiquarian, and the critical. The monumental provides force for action through examples. The antiquarian admires, cultivates, and preserves the past with reverence. The critical shows the suffering person the path to emancipation (Nietzsche 1874 (German): ch. 2–3; 2005 (English): ch. II 12ff, III 17ff).

Nietzsche criticised the German society of his time, his opinion being that knowledge of past origins had come to exert an unhealthily great influence (cf. Latour 1991 (French): 93f; 1993 (English): 69). He was particularly critical of the antiquarian attitude in which all of the past was considered valuable. Nietzsche missed the balance in Ancient Greece between history and life, between knowledge and art. The three uses – the monumental, the antiquarian, and the critical – needed to be balanced.

Nietzsche's trinity has been updated and supplemented by the economic historian Svante Beckman. Employing more contemporary terms, the monumental use might, according to Beckman, contribute to social order and collective identity; the antiquarian use might contribute to knowledge and individual security; and the critical use might contribute to enlightenment and social development. Beckman then adds a fourth category, playful use, in which the past can contribute to individual experiences and entertainment. But as a typical representative of the critical culture of heritage, Beckman emphasises the unfavourable aspects: the monumental can also legitimise power and lies, assisting in repression; the antiquarian can contribute to escapism and afford false consolation; the critical can contribute to alienation and trivialisation – and the playful can contribute to lies, escape, aestheticisation, and trivialisation. The new set of four categories is based on Beckman's view that all actions can be explained with reference to norms (monumental), necessity (antiquarian), usefulness (critical), and entertainment (playful) (Beckman 1998: 39ff; 2005: 335ff; cf. 1997).

The uses of history can be identified through history itself, by exploring the justifications stated by historians themselves. Familiar and still relevant themes and motives turn up at an early stage, in Herodotus and Ibn Khaldûn, for instance: history is tremendously popular across national borders, peoples, and social groups.

History has several purposes – gathering knowledge so as to be able to describe, understand, and explain both the past and the present, narrating so as to entertain and to counter oblivion. And history searches for truth, strives after beauty in its style, and possesses both ethical and philosophical dimensions.

Herodotus, who has been called the "father of history", thus began his work *Histories* from the fifth century BCE with these words:

> What Herodotus the Halicarnassian has learnt by inquiry is here set forth: in order that so the memory of the past may not be blotted out from among men by time, and that great and marvellous deeds done by Greek and foreigners and especially the reason why they warred against each other may not lack renown. (*Herodotus* I: 1, p. 3)

The historian and politician Ibn Khaldûn supplied an insightful presentation of several purposes of history in his foreword to *The Muqaddimah: An Introduction to History* from 1377:

> HISTORY is a discipline widely cultivated among nations and races. It is eagerly sought after. The men in the street, the ordinary people, aspire to know it. Kings and leaders vie for it. Both the learned and the ignorant are able to understand it. For on the surface history is no more than information about political events, dynasties, and occurrences of the remote past, elegantly presented and spiced with proverbs. It serves to entertain large, crowded gatherings and brings to us an understanding of human affairs. [It shows] how changing conditions affected [human affairs], how certain dynasties came to occupy an ever wider space in the world, and how they settled the earth until they heard the call and their time was up. The inner meaning of history, on the other hand, involves speculation and an attempt to get at the truth, subtle explanation of the causes and origins of existing things, and deep knowledge of the how and why of events. [History,] therefore, is firmly rooted in philosophy. It deserves to be accounted a branch of [philosophy]. (Khaldûn 1958: vol. 1, Foreword, p. 6)

But history is full of varying justifications and motives. History and philosophy of history is such a broad field that there is room for a specialisation or a genre of literature that answers the question: Why history? (e.g. Southgate 1996; 2000; 2005; Evans 1997; Tosh 2008). The answers primarily reflect their time and place; but they are also an attempt to influence what direction the discipline should take in the future, and here the authors' own positions become visible.

In a surviving manuscript called *Apologie pour l'histoire ou Métier de l'historien* (*The Historian's Craft*), the Annales historian Marc Bloch began by reporting a question: "Papa, explique-moi donc à quoi sert l'histoire" ("Tell me, Daddy. What is the use of history?"). Bloch was executed by the Gestapo as a member of the Resistance, so the book that was to be the answer was never completed. Even so, the answer is clear from the subsequently published manuscript. The purpose of history is to understand the present through the past, and to understand the past through the present (Bloch 1949 (French): ix quotation, 11ff; 1992 (English): 3 quotation, 32ff).) So history is justified by a need for historical understanding, in which the past and the present are entangled.

The time and place can be almost identical and yet perspectives may differ widely, as is seen from two historians who were of the same age, were both trained in Cambridge and were both active for periods in New York, and who both wrote about Europe in the nineteenth and twentieth centuries: David Thomson and Eric Hobsbawm. While Thomson in *The Aims of History* stressed the importance of a historical attitude, of historical awareness and understanding for the intellectual enrichment of life (Thomson 1969: 11, 99ff), Hobsbawm in his article "Looking Forward: History and the Future" wanted to use history to make predictions or forecasts about the future, which he considered desirable, possible, and necessary (Hobsbawm 1981).

Archaeology focuses on excavating, documenting, analysing, interpreting, and communicating material culture, on developing new methods, and on discussing theoretical perspectives; that is, questions about what and how. On the rare occasions when the "why" of archaeology is discussed in an introduction or in a section of a chapter, this is generally done with reference both to the value of a long temporal perspective and to the specific advantages of exploring the material dimension. In both cases, the legitimation is indirectly related to the subject of history, to which a more limited perspective is ascribed, covering a relatively short period of time and wholly dependent on texts. Even in authoritative textbooks, the use of the past may be dealt with in a few lines under the heading "What use is the past?" – lines about the importance of feeling and knowing that there is a past, as well as about the importance of the past for learning more about what it means to be a human being, accompanied by a phrase such as "without our roots we are lost" (Renfrew & Bahn 2016: 583f).

One of the few exceptions to this summary treatment is to be found in an article about history of ideas by the archaeologist Carl-Axel Moberg. The article "Den nyttiga fornforskningen" ("Useful [research on] Antiquity") (Moberg 1984; written in 1947, but updated) was produced after the Second World War as an explicit reaction to the previous (ab)use of archaeology, in Germany in particular. Moberg presented varying justifications for the study of the past, drawing on examples from Sweden and Denmark since the fifteenth century. The great majority reflect how the past has been of use in legitimising the state and its ideology. Native country and nation are thus the most commonly used concepts. Other central concepts are enlightenment, education, revolution, international solidarity – and, since the 1970s, entertainment and leisure activity.

When archaeologists discuss motives, there is generally an ulterior motive somewhere. When, for instance, Michael Shanks and Christopher Tilley illustrated connections between various justifications in *Re-Constructing Archaeology*, it was in an attempt to influence both theory and practice, and to establish a critical archaeology (Shanks & Tilley 1987: 25ff, with Fig. 1.1). And when, in *From Stonehenge to Las Vegas*, Cornelius Holtorf presents different meanings of the past, his intention is to show that meaning varies over time, that it varies for different people, and that all meanings are equally important (Holtorf 2005: 78ff, 92ff). In both instances, the presentation of motives is used to promote a relativist programme.

Despite the multiple motivations and motives, it is possible to observe some expressions of concern that turn up at regular intervals in the debate – words such as threat, crisis, defence, and usefulness. The past is said to be threatened both from the outside and from the inside; consequently, the field is in crisis and needs to be defended, and this is then done with reference to its potential usefulness.

What these expressions have in common is that threat is both a concrete reality and a rhetorical figure. The texts and images of history are threatened by impermanence, but they may be preserved for posterity in archives and libraries. Memory is threatened by oblivion when new generations grow up, unless it is passed on by means of narration or documented. And heritage is threatened by decay and destruction and needs to be safeguarded. The cliff temples of Abu Simbel were threatened by flooding, but salvaged by being moved. New times mean new threats, which must be countered by new methods. Moreover, the whole field of humanities with history, memory, and heritage is seen as threatened by inner decay, which has allegedly deprived the field of its credibility and thereby rendered it useless; this is often attributed to harmful influences from modernity, Marxism, postmodernism, or postcolonialism.

Every time someone cries "crisis", however, it is necessary to ask oneself what their intention – their explicit or hidden agenda – might be. For instance, when the humanities were said to be in crisis in 1970s Sweden, this was about a new generation wanting to reshape the field so as to make it more relevant to contemporary society (e.g. Forser 1978). And now that the humanities are described as being in crisis four or five decades later, it has to do with some people's contention that the criticism and influence from Marxism have gone too far (e.g. Nordin 2008). The word crisis is used to create attention, set a new agenda, redefine a field, and then reprioritise resources.

External and internal threats demand a defence. The past needs to be defended against threatening changes through archiving, documentation, conservation, restoration, relocations, or legislation. The past needs to be defended against threats from other competing fields according to which the past is of no use. Finally, the past needs to be defended against threats within the field which undermine its credibility. The defensive position is seen directly in book titles such as *Apologie pour l'histoire …* (*The Historian's Craft*; Bloch 1949) and *In Defense of History* (Evans 1997). The fundamental point, in my view, is that the occurrence of numerous justifications and motives, as well as the febrile identification of values, actually constitutes a manifestation of the fact that history, memory, and heritage are, or are perceived as being, under attack on several flanks.

The threats are met by going on the offensive and asserting the use of the humanities and the past. We thus see titles of articles and books that could easily have ended with exclamation marks: "Den nyttiga fornforskningen" ("Useful [research on] Antiquity"), *Why History Matters*, *Why the Past Matters*, *Archaeology Matters*, and *The Value of the Humanities* (Moberg 1984; Tosh 2008; Little 2007; Sabloff 2008; Small 2013).

In a time, at a place, and in a society in which C. P. Snow's two cultures are again being marshalled against each other in the fight for limited resources, in which a distinction is made between what generates and what consumes resources, in which usefulness is associated with economics, social science, medicine, natural science, and engineering, whereas pleasure is associated with humanities, literature, and art, in which usefulness is fundamentally something defined by economic growth as both a means and an end – in such a situation, the past with its history, memory, and heritage is also obliged to assert its use and value.

The values of heritage

Heritage is priceless! Every time heritage is threatened or actually destroyed, it is pointed out that heritage is priceless. The Islamic State (IS, or Daesh) had books burned and statues smashed in Mosul and blew up the ruined city of Nimrud in the spring of 2015, while I was writing this, and these are just a few topical examples in a long historical series of related events. In this context, the word "priceless" is the strongest expression that can be used in defence of heritage, and it appears across a broad field from UNESCO to the media; priceless means of very great or infinite value. The idea behind the wording is that heritage, like that which is sacred, belongs to a sphere of its own, independent of the market and of economics. So heritage neither can nor should be valued in money, or indeed measured in relation to anything else at all.

And still, paradoxically, heritage is valued all the time – and converted into money. As a rule, heritage is preserved with reference to its values, and value is a concept drawn precisely from the economic sphere. Valuations and values are therefore crucial to the selection and management of heritage. And if heritage is put up for sale – as happens every day, legally or illegally, with antiquities and art – then supply and demand on the market will soon set a price for the priceless. The statues in Mosul would also have been given a price, higher if they were originals, lower if they were copies. The market knows no limits.

Heritage's reference to values differs from history, memory, and archaeology, where justifications are normal; but every value could, in principle, be reformulated as a justification. From the outset, the values of heritage have been adopted and developed to serve national administrations of ancient or cultural monuments, but now they are also discussed and defined globally, for example in UNESCO. Consequently, the values of heritage belong first and foremost to a bureaucratic discourse in the first, canonical, culture of heritage, even though they can be discussed more widely.

One point of reference regarding the values of heritage, and an important inspiration in heritage management, has been the treatise by the art historian Alois Riegl, *Der moderne Denkmalkultus, sein Wesen und seine Entstehung* (Riegl 1903 (German); 1929

(German); 1982 (English); "The Modern Cult of Monuments: Its Character and Origin"; cf. Arrhenius 2003: 135ff; 2012: 92ff). Riegl's treatise was written by way of preparation for new legislation to protect monuments in the dual monarchy of Austria-Hungary, a legislation that was, however, never implemented.

Riegl perceived a historical development in the choice of values, took account of both feelings and reason, and distinguished between intentional and unintentional monuments ("gewollten wie [...] ungewollten Denkmahlen"), i.e. between the manifest and the latent; everything could thus become a monument. Riegl emphasised five values, divided between the past and the present – three Commemorative Values ("Erinnerungswerte"), namely Age-Value ("Alterswert"), Historical Value ("historischer Wert") and Intentional Commemorative Value ("gewollte[r] Erinnerungswert") – and two Present-Day Values ("Gegenwartswerte"), namely Use-Value ("Gebrauchswert") and Art-Value ("Kunstwert"); the latter, Art-Value, was in its turn divided into Newness-Value ("Neuheitswert") and Relative Art-Value ("relativer Kunstwert"). These values have to do with time, source value, intention, function, and aesthetics – art as new and in the present.

Riegl's original intention was to find objective criteria for selecting what was worth preserving, but he came to the conclusion that the values were relative and might come into conflict with one another. There might be a conflict between commemorative and present-day values – between, for instance, Age-Value and Use-Value, Age-Value and Art-Value – and there could also be conflicts within one of the groups, that is to say, between Age-Value, Historical Value, and Intentional Commemorative Value. And the choice of restoration method will depend on which values are given priority.

Values are therefore not something that can be discovered but something that must be constructed. Every period and culture must formulate its own values, just as they choose their own justifications and motives. Objective justifications, motives, and values are a logical impossibility. However, there are many initiatives whose purpose is to attain national or universal consensus on values – in, for example, national legislation and international conventions such as the Universal Declaration of Human Rights (1948) and the World Heritage Convention (1972).

Ever since Riegl's innovative treatise, there has been an extensive and sustained debate about heritage values. This debate takes place within and between the two cultures of heritage. The debate is primarily driven by the need that public authorities and museums have to be able to manage a constantly growing heritage in a both flexible and credible way in relation to other stakeholders in society. On the one hand, the criteria are expected to be so precise that they can be used in order to appraise and rank; on the other, they should be so open or so numerous that they can capture a constantly expanding heritage. But the debate is also driven forward by the critical culture of heritage, which has put question marks against established values and often argues for alternative ones or other priorities.

The debate has cast light on the values of varying periods from a historical perspective and discussed them in relation to various theoretical points of departure. Historical and theoretical perspectives are frequently combined in attempts to develop heritage management and produce selection and prioritisation criteria (e.g. Hygen 1996; Carlie & Kretz 1998; Navrud & Ready 2002; Pettersson 2003; Jensen 2010; Smith *et al.* 2010; Golinelli 2015). As a consequence of management needs and heritage growth, a constantly rising number of criteria are defined in sophisticated value systems.

Heritage is often managed along with the environment, so the landscape's cultural and natural environment can either complement each other or become integrated. And the wording according to which heritage is a resource, and thus has value as a kind of energy source, is taken from an environmental perspective. Explanations of the importance of heritage may hence refer to heritage being a resource without any real arguments or specific information. Heritage as a resource functions as a silently accepted slogan to which additional positive words such as "active" or "democracy" can be added. Phrases that posit heritage as a resource appear along these lines in titles of books, reports, conferences, campaigns, and centres – and they even do so across the two cultures of heritage (e.g. Tunbridge & Ashworth 1996; Weissglas *et al.* 2002; Holtorf 2005: 130ff; Liliequist 2005).

The opposite view is also abundantly represented – that heritage is a liability, a problem and an obstacle, or, in short, that heritage is of no value. This criticism was given its most forceful expression by David Lowenthal in the 1990s, with derogatory words about heritage such as oppressive, defeatist, decadent, hyped, nostalgic, alarming, causes chaos, rubbish, sacred cow, corrupted, popularised, commoditised, politicised, ignorance, error, and biased (Lowenthal 1997: ix, 5ff, 10ff, 87ff, 121f).

Heritage can also represent events or phenomena that are so controversial, unpleasant, or marginalised that dealing with them can be problematic – there is often an association with politics, war, death, crime, or disease (cf. Tunbridge & Ashworth 1996; Meskell 2002; Jönsson & Svensson 2005; Logan & Reeves 2009; Macdonald 2009). In the case of Auschwitz-Birkenau, which became a World Heritage site in 1979, the choice that was made was to preserve and remember (WHL 31, 1979). But in other cases it may be better to choose not to tell, remember, or preserve. For example, the so-called "Führerbunker" in Berlin is not accessible; instead, it was intentionally destroyed and the site built on. And even if the bunker can be claimed to form unique (negative) evidence of a cultural tradition and human history, it is not under consideration as World Heritage.

Finally, antiquarians and archaeologists want to be able, in their everyday lives, to encounter politicians, entrepreneurs, journalists, and others who claim – from the edge of the excavation site or in the media – that ancient monuments are of no value, that excavations and archaeologists are a financial liability, and that the traces of the past are an obstacle to progress.

If calculations of the monetary value of "priceless" heritage are controversial, the value of heritage for tourism and economic development is stressed in countless contexts. Heritage should be protected, preserved, and communicated to increase tourism; indeed, this is supposed to be the very *raison d'être* of heritage. And when a monument, a building, a site, or a landscape is inscribed as a World Heritage site, there are often great expectations of an increase in tourism and development; one example is when the southern part of the island of Öland in Sweden was so designated (WHL 968, 2000). It is a fact that some of the world's most important destinations are actually World Heritage sites, but they were well known to tourists long before the establishment of World Heritage as a concept – Notre-Dame in Paris (WHL 600, 1991), the pyramids in Giza in Egypt (WHL 86, 1979), the Taj Mahal in India (WHL 252, 1983), and the Statue of Liberty in New York (WHL 307, 1984). Abu Simbel thus became a tourist destination back in the nineteenth century.

Heritage tourism is an important part of a constantly growing tourist industry that boosts land, sea, and air transport and promotes shops and hotels, museums, and visitor centres; it is therefore of importance for employment and the economy. Consequently, the literature about heritage tourism and the relationship between heritage, tourism, and the economy is extensive (e.g. Kirshenblatt-Gimblett 1998; Graham *et al.* 2000: 129ff; Timothy 2011).

Sometimes the significance of heritage is reduced to its role in tourism. But to try to understand or explain the attraction of heritage by means of tourism merely amounts to reformulating the fundamental problem. What, then, are the justifications, motives, or values of the pilgrimage, the educational tour, or tourism? People from both the host country and abroad may visit heritage sites for several reasons (cf. MacCannell 1976; Löfgren *et al.* 1990; Urry 1990; Grinder-Hansen 1992); they may, for instance, go there in order to increase their knowledge or to have a good experience, or perhaps out of a sense of duty.

What can or should be heritage, how can or should the value of heritage be determined – and how is this to be carried out? Normally the whole process is handled by academically trained antiquarian experts, who work on heritage management at the local, regional, central government, or international level, on the basis of a number of qualitative criteria formulated for this specific purpose.

Under the pressure of having to act in a society in which most values are determined in a market, and in which economic growth has high priority, attempts are made to bring out the values of heritage as clear and competitive. In this context, various tendencies are discernible. There are, for instance, attempts to systematise the actual process with well-defined (objective) value criteria that can be used in heritage management (e.g. Carlie & Kretz 1998; Unnerbäck 2002). More rarely, attempts are made to convert cultural historical values into a (subjective) market price, in which valuation by consumers is given an influence (e.g. Almevik & Fridén 1996).

In both instances, the idea is that it should be possible to measure and weigh heritage in relation to other interests, such as nature, roads, railways, bridges, tunnels, building development and industry. The question is not whether heritage is valuable, but what is the right currency and amount for heritage. However, the calculation of the value of heritage using money as the metric is controversial within the canonical culture of management; it is fine for heritage to result in income, but not for it to be seen as an expense. The idea of the independence of the field must not be undermined.

Heritage and democracy are words with several meanings. The concept of democratic heritage expresses the ambition of opening the field to the public, of engaging users, and of including those users in endeavours to set priorities regarding the traces of the past (e.g. Alzén & Aronsson 2006). The intention behind the European Convention on the Value of Cultural Heritage for Society (2005), also called the Faro Convention, was thus to involve the public. But this can also be a critical strategy for intentionally or unintentionally disarming management experts, when members of the public are themselves allowed to determine what is to be heritage and what is not. Here the dividing lines between the canonical and the critical may be blurred (e.g. Holtorf 2013b; Schofield 2014).

In this context, democracy can mean another way of letting supply and demand in the market determine heritage values. The monetary market is replaced by a market of votes, under the encouragement or guidance of critical experts. But it is hardly the supply of "pastness" that governs the process, for then heritage from the very oldest periods – extremely little of which has been preserved – would be most attractive. The experience of relevance is more likely to be the decisive factor, and this brings contemporary heritage into focus along with nostalgic traces linked to people's own childhood and youth.

Irrespective of how many, how detailed, or how sophisticated the accounts of various criteria in hierarchies and systems are, values still constitute an appraisal, however. And irrespective of all the governing documents, the criteria appear to be values that are open to interpretation and therefore, of necessity, subjective. They are values that a large number of experts have been able to agree on, based on a practice regarding the ways in which heritage has been assessed historically. But they remain values that express the view of a number of individuals at a particular time and in a particular place.

Heritage values and the associated debate can easily be identified at Abu Simbel. Thus the temples of Abu Simbel have also been called priceless, for instance by the Egyptian Minister of Culture, Sarwat Okasha, who was one of the initiators of the Nubian salvage campaign (Desroches-Noblecourt & Gerster 1968: 9). At the same time, an exact price can be put on the preservation of the temples, just as their values as World Heritage have been laid down by UNESCO. The salvage campaign for the two temples at Abu Simbel alone cost about USD 40 million (Säve-Söderbergh 1987: 104).

Riegl's systematisation of values is still relevant for an understanding of Abu Simbel as heritage: the more than 3000-year-old temples testify to the passage of time; they are sources for the reign of Ramses II in particular; they were constructed as monuments to communicate political and religious messages; they are now used as tourist attractions; and they also possess an aesthetic value, both when new and today.

When a World Heritage site was established for "Nubian Monuments from Abu Simbel to Philae" in 1979, this was done on the grounds that it fulfilled three criteria: human creative genius, testimony to cultural tradition, and heritage associated with events of universal significance (WHL 88, 1979).

The temples were already visited by travellers in ancient times, as evidenced by Greek graffiti, and after their rediscovery in the nineteenth century they again became a tourist attraction. The European adventurers in the wake of Napoleon's Egyptian campaign opened the way for the mass tourism of later times. When the Nubian campaign was to be justified, one of the arguments during the process was that more tourism would entail economic benefits; and indeed Abu Simbel became a popular tourist destination (Säve-Söderbergh 1987: 217f; 1996: 210).

The temples of Abu Simbel were constructed to be seen, admired, and used – and that is also the case today. But both the material monuments and the human subjects have changed. The temples that are seen, admired, and used have been changed in some respects, just as the visitors who continuously see, admire, and use them are new; but there is no sharp distinction between then and now, between what is lasting and what has changed. By degrees, their development has been characterised by ruptures as well as by continuity. The past is both a foreign and a well-known country.

Just as there is no lack of opinions about the past, there is thus no lack of justifications, motives or values, criteria or principles, either before or now. Far from it. The field is so diverse and so densely populated that an overview is needed, a new organising structure as an alternative to Nietzsche's three perspectives. For Nietzsche's trinity has been kept alive more by his famous name than by its current relevance. His trinity must be viewed against the background of the political left–right scale with its social and economic issues, which was on the agenda in the nineteenth and twentieth centuries but has had competition, for better and worse, in the twenty-first century from issues to do with religion, culture, and identity, issues that may require another way of viewing the past and the present. Nonetheless, I find the question of where society and I myself are going more relevant and interesting than the question of where society and I are supposed to have come from, or who society and I "are".

Instead of formulating new arguments for the use of the past or defining new values, criteria, or principles to add to the existing stock, I am going to assert the reuse of a philosophical triad as a means of surveying, understanding, and explaining the whole field of history, memory, and heritage.

Truth, beauty, and goodness

Truth, beauty, and goodness are three perspectives that may serve as the starting point of three fundamental motives for understanding the meaning of the past. This triad, with roots in Western philosophy and theology, is useful both in order to obtain an overview of the multiple justifications, motives, values, and opinions about usefulness and in order to understand current conflicts around history, memory, and heritage. The triad of truth, beauty, and goodness is thus my alternative to Nietzsche's trinity of uses – the monumental, the antiquarian, and the critical.

Traditionally, the concepts of truth, beauty, and goodness are traced back through the history of philosophy to Plato. Three fields are then linked to the concepts – the fields of epistemology, aesthetics, and ethics; that is, the theories of knowledge, art, and morality, respectively. And in popular terms, the triad of truth, beauty, and goodness has come to stand both for philosophy as a project and for classical, but never irrelevant, virtues (e.g. Gardner 2011).

Truth, beauty, and goodness belong to the group of transcendental concepts. Medieval scholasticism developed a discussion about concepts said to transcend experience, concepts referred to as "the transcendentals" (*transcendentalia*). They included being (*ens*), one (*unum*), truth (*verum*), goodness (*bonum*), beauty (*pulchrum*), something (*aliquid*) and thing (*res*) (Gracia 1992). But just as truth, beauty, and goodness were not, in fact, treated as a distinct group of concepts by Plato – even though they are often presented as if they had been – scholasticism did not discuss them as a group either. The triad was only established as a distinct group when the Renaissance created a new synthesis between ancient pagan philosophy and medieval Christian theology.

Truth, beauty, and goodness were defined as a distinct group of transcendentals by the philosopher and canon Marsilio Ficino. As a commission for Cosimo de Medici, the leading businessman and politician in Florence, Ficino translated Plato's works from Greek to Latin for the first time, making them available in the West. Ficino's translation, lectures, and printed comments were of great importance for Platonism in the Renaissance and later. It was here, in the comments on Plato's dialogue *Philebus* (probably written in 1469, but only published in 1496), that the triad was established, and it was here that it was given a clear hierarchical structure. Ficino outlined a Platonic theology with three levels, from the body via the soul up to the intelligence, to being – that is, to God. According to Ficino, intelligence understands in order to attain the true, desires in order to attain the good, and acts to attain the beautiful (Allen 1975: 1ff, 48ff, 78f).

Subsequently, the triad figured in many contexts, for instance in the work of the philosopher Immanuel Kant in his three "critique" books – critique of pure reason, critique of practical reason, and critique of judgement; that is, his inquiry into the conditions for knowledge (Kant 1781 (German); 1998 (English)), ethics (Kant 1785 (German); 1998 (English)), and aesthetics (Kant 1790 (German); 2000 (English)). In the poet and theologist Esaias Tegnér, the concepts of the triad became the true, the right, and the beautiful in a poem entitled "Det Eviga" ("The Eternal"), which was written against the background of the Napoleonic Wars (Tegnér 1828: 192f). A related triad also turns up in the work of the philosopher Søren Kierkegaard in *Stadier paa Livets Vei* (*Stages on Life's Way*): the aesthetic, the ethical, and the religious (Kierkegaard 1845 (Danish); 1940 (English)). Here the aesthetic involves enjoyment and experience and the ethical concerns duty, truth being replaced by the religious dimension.

From Kant to the present, the concepts of the triad may be followed like a theme with variations in German philosophy, sociology, and history. In *Theorie des kommunikativen Handelns* (*The Theory of Communicative Action*), a discussion of the theories of the sociologist Max Weber, the sociologist Jürgen Habermas thus asserts that the transition to modernity is characterised by the institutionalisation of three types of rationality, three spheres of knowledge or values – the cognitive, the aesthetic, and the normative. These three spheres are said to correspond, in turn, to science with its criteria for truth, art with aesthetic criticism, and politics and law with rules for ethical and legal matters. With this division, mutual tensions necessarily arose between the spheres (Habermas 1981 (German): 1, 225ff, 233ff, 456; 1984 (English): 1, 157ff, 163ff, 340).

With a direct reference to Habermas, the historian Jörn Rüsen then identifies three dimensions of historical awareness, namely cognitive, aesthetic, and political values. These three are said to correspond to science, narrative, and power: reason, feeling, and will. Rüsen also stresses the possibility of tensions, imbalances, and hierarchies, perceiving them as arising between a cognitive strategy for knowledge production, an aesthetic strategy for the rhetoric and poetics of presentation, and, finally, a political strategy for collective memory. But none of the dimensions could be reduced to any one of the others (Rüsen 1994: 219ff; 2001: 49, 64, 98).

A related triad can be found in *Föreställningar om det förflutna* "Images of the Past", an inquiry into archaeological reconstructions of Prehistory and the Middle Ages in Scandinavia. Here the archaeologist Bodil Petersson uses three perspectives, knowledge, adventure, and politics: knowledge through reconstructions, time travel as an adventure, and the political use of reconstructions (Petersson 2003: 15f).

Truth, beauty, or goodness – the useful knowledge of the Enlightenment, therapeutic narratives for times of crisis, or a moral duty to remind and remember? These three perspectives and possible uses of the past often end up opposing one another, their internal ranking changing over time. I have myself employed this triad, and the categories derived from it, to understand the contemporary debate about the role of archaeology in society in the article "Agenda arkeologi – upplysning, terapi eller moral" (Wienberg 2009; "Agenda archaeology – enlightenment, therapy, or moral"). Rhetorical phrases about renewing and democratising heritage and increasing its impact may hence, in actual fact, have to do with a desire to shift the perspective from the past to the present – and from knowledge to narrative and morality.

A polarising and totalitarian tendency can sometimes be seen to operate, with each of the perspectives wanting to dominate the debate: there is truth in the centre with a striving for knowledge, while beauty and goodness are subordinate. Or there is beauty with its narratives and entertainment in the centre; everything is narratives, and truth is not crucial. Then again, there is goodness with politics in the centre, whereas truth and beauty are subordinate. In concrete terms, the conflict between these perspectives may manifest itself as a conflict between science, which is supposed to represent striving for truth and is apt to reward original research results; media and media users, who are seeking entertaining stories irrespective of whether they are fact or fiction, moving on if the story being told is not sufficiently diverting; and, finally, politicians, parties, government agencies, and others that expect or demand usefulness to society, which is likely to be a rhetorical rephrasing of a demand that the field be subordinated to their particular agenda, whatever it might be.

The triad of truth, beauty, and goodness may, at first sight, be thought of as permanent or timeless; but it most certainly is not. The triad recurs constantly in philosophy, since the concepts are open to interpretation. In their concrete form, the concepts are transitory with a short durability; each time, and also each place, has had its own ideas about the true, the beautiful, and the good. It is precisely because of their ability to change, to adapt to new conditions, to let themselves be reused with new content, that the concepts appear to be eternal. The triad is an example of how *spolia* from the past, whether material or intangible, building blocks or concepts, can be put to use in the present, carrying new meanings. In Renaissance Italy, whose style was inspired by ancient architecture, Ficino used concepts from Plato for new philosophical needs. With a more up-to-date designation, the Renaissance rebirth of Antiquity was a matter of creative reuse.

With the philologist and religious historian Georges Dumézil one can, if so inclined, identify a functional trinity in all Indo-European societies (Dumézil 1958). The reason is that sets of three concepts that embody a fascination with the geometry of the number three occur everywhere in religion, science, and politics. We find Hinduism's trimurti or trinity with the creator (Brahma), the preserver (Vishnu), and the destroyer (Shiva); the Christian Trinity with God the Father, the Son, and the Holy Ghost; the three holy kings Balthazar, Caspar, and Melchior; Islam's three holy cities Mecca, Medina, and Jerusalem; rhetoric's credibility (ethos), reason (logos), and emotion (pathos); the division into legislative, executive, and judicial power; the three kingdoms of nature – plants, animals, and minerals; the division of time into past, present, and future; the division of knowledge into reason, memory, and fantasy, or learning, experiencing, and reflecting; the archaeological system of three periods with the Stone Age, the Bronze Age, and the Iron Age; and Nietzsche's three uses – the monumental, the antiquarian, and the critical.

It is tempting to look at the triad of truth, beauty, and goodness and read three social groups into it: the thinking intellectuals, the working and entertained masses of the people, and the politicians taking action (Fredengren 2012: 196ff). This reading is a reasonable one since Plato, in his tract *The Republic*, divided citizens into three functional groups. The philosophers, like Plato himself, would govern; the artisans would work; and the soldiers would guard. According to Plato, these groups formed a hierarchy with the philosophers at the top and the artisans at the bottom. There was a parallel in the three parts of the body and the soul – the head for wisdom, the breast for will, and the stomach for desire (Plato 1997: 971ff). Plato's ideal state is later reflected in the medieval estates of the realm or the three orders, a church ideology for a society with three social and functional groups – *oratores*, those who pray, *laboratores*, those who work, and *bellatores*, those who fight (Duby 1978 (French); 1981 (English)). The Platonic triad also forms the basis of the trinity of thinking, willing, and judging that was discussed by the philosopher Hannah Arendt (Arendt 1981). But as all the examples demonstrate, there are many ways of interpreting the triad of truth, beauty, and goodness, which may also be seen either as a hierarchy or as virtues of equal standing.

Do we need the past? In *Behövs det förflutna?* ("Is the past needed?"), the philosopher Sören Halldén found three functions that can also be derived from the triad of truth, beauty, and goodness: learning from the past about the multifariousness of life, thereby gaining insights that may be put to use in solving problems; enrichment of life, such as a tourist's travels; and extension of experience, which can be used in making assessments. Halldén ends the book with the words, "this question opens up paths in different directions. It is a little like touching on the question 'Why are you alive?'" (Halldén 1983: 14f, quotation on 135).

No, it is more than a light touch on a fundamental question. For in order to give the past meaning, it is also necessary to give meaning to the present and the future. The past, the present, and the future flow into one another in an existential reflection: is the past needed – is the present needed – is the future needed? (cf. Wienberg 1999: 192, 196).

Anyone who expects to be given a clear and unequivocal answer to the question of why the past is needed must of necessity be either disappointed or deceived, for that would be the same as expecting a clear and simple answer to the question of why the present and the future are needed. In my opinion, truth, beauty, and goodness represent perspectives that complement one another with regard to what it means to be human. *Homo sapiens*, *Homo narrans*, and *Homo ethicus* – the thinking human, the storytelling human, and the engaged human.

Truth, beauty, and goodness complement one another without any internal ranking. No perspective is superior here, none can replace any other, and none can be dispensed with. Thus there is no hierarchy between the true, the beautiful, and the good, as was otherwise asserted by Ficino, Kant, and Kierkegaard; no social order, as in Plato or in the medieval notion of the estates of the realm. The true does not need to be beautiful or good; the beautiful does not need to be true or good; and the good does not need to be true or beautiful. Moreover, we are often confronted with the opposite of the triad, namely the false, the ugly, and the evil. In addition, the triad cannot be reduced to a duality without the loss of something significant. The truth, beauty, and goodness triad forms more than one complementarity, in which two parts complement one another. The three concepts constitute a "triplementarity", in which the three parts lend greater depth to one another.

The truths of knowledge

Knowledge about the past is desirable, useful, and essential. We need knowledge about the past to be able to understand or explain the present and meet the future. The ideal is truth, enlightenment, and progress, with science as the method. New knowledge is accumulated year by year.

Knowing and ability, science and knowledge, are words with immediately favourable connotations, but they can point in all directions. Knowledge can be an advantage or a disadvantage; it can enlighten or darken. Knowledge may be liberating; it can also be used to exercise power, or in an exclusionary social game. Knowledge can be seen as something that requires education and methodical training, or as something that is immediately available to everyone. In itself, knowledge is neither good nor bad. Knowledge – like the past – can be used for everything.

Knowledge is quite fundamental, however, and it is something that characterises human beings – *Homo sapiens*, the thinking and understanding human. It is sufficient to try to imagine how quickly present-day society would break down without an enormous quantity of sophisticated knowledge about how something works, is, and was. But perhaps all knowledge is not necessary? Or is some knowledge more important or more useful than other knowledge?

As a species, *Homo sapiens* is said to be characterised precisely by its will to knowledge. *Homo sapiens* uses knowledge to understand and explain its surroundings and to search for meaning. Humans try not only to gather knowledge, but also to find and interpret patterns, even in what may be quite fortuitous; they constantly endeavour to understand and explain. And this search for meaning is said to have given the species an evolutionary advantage ahead of others: the ability, will, or compulsion to constantly look for causes

and try to foresee what may come (Gärdenfors 2006). My own
sense of wonderment about the meaning of history, memory, and
heritage may thus be a typical example of a fundamental human
character trait.

Knowledge as both an end and a means to an end has frequently
been linked to the idea of progress and the Enlightenment project
since the late seventeenth century. Rational knowledge was to
replace irrationality, superstition, and dogmas. Knowledge attained
through observation and experiment was to replace ancient and
medieval speculation. Here knowledge and science in the West form
part of a clash with the Church, acquiring a secular character in
the process. Light becomes a metaphor for what is new in the Age
of Enlightenment. Knowledge is thought to liberate humans and
create an ever better future.

The ethos of the Age of Enlightenment was clearly formulated by
the philosopher Immanuel Kant in the first lines of his contribution to
a newspaper debate, "Beanwortung der Frage: Was ist Aufklärung?"
("An Answer to the Question: What is Enlightenment?"), lines that
deserve to be quoted in full:

> *Aufklärung* ist der Ausgang des Menschen aus seiner selbst verschul-
> deten Unmündigkeit. *Unmündigkeit* ist das Unvermögen, sich seines
> Verstandes ohne Leitung eines andern zu bedienen. *Selbstverschuldet*
> ist diese Unmündigkeit, wenn die Ursache derselben nicht am Mangel
> des Verstandes, sondern der Entschließung und des Muthes liegt, sich
> seiner ohne Leitung eines andern zu bedienen. *Sapere aude!* Habe
> Muth dich deines eigenen Verstandes zu bedienen! ist also der
> Wahlspruch der Aufklärung. (Kant 1784 (German): 481)
>
> *Enlightenment* is the human being's emergence from his self-incurred
> minority. *Minority* is inability to make use of one's own understanding
> without direction from another. This minority is *self-incurred* when
> its cause lies not in lack of understanding but in lack of resolution
> and courage to use it without direction from another. *Sapere aude!*
> Have courage to make use of your own understanding! is thus the
> motto of enlightenment. (Kant 1996 (English): 17)

Science has knowledge as its goal, as is seen from the roots of the
word in the Latin word *scientia*, meaning knowledge; science is the
creation of knowledge. And even though this is not always formulated as an evident goal, it is apparent from the practice of science,
in which all disciplines are very careful about their methods; that
is, how to move in a more or less systematic way from questions to
answers, using recognised methods. Historical and archaeological
source criticism is one such method that is intended to ensure that

the description of the past is founded only on sure facts. The purpose of source criticism is to uncover the way things actually were.

In the famous words of the historian Leopold Ranke (later von Ranke) from the foreword of *Geschichte der romanischen und germanischen Völker von 1494 bis 1514* (*History of the Latin and Teutonic Nations (1494 to 1514)*), history was neither to judge the past nor to be of benefit to the future, but only to show what actually happened:

> Man hat der Historie das Amt, die Vergangenheit zu richten, die Mitwelt zum Nutzen zukünftiger Jahre zu belehren, beygemessen: so hoher Aemter underwindet sich gegenwärtiger Versuch nicht: er will bloß sagen, wie es eigentlich gewesen. (Ranke 1824: Vf)
>
> (To history has been assigned the office of judging the past, of instructing the present for the benefit of future ages. To such high offices this work does not aspire. It wants only to show what actually happened.)

But contrary to Ranke, explanations, motives, and values for history, memory, and heritage have generally been characterised by a historicist perspective since the nineteenth century. In historicism, at any rate in one of the ways in which the term is used, knowledge of the past is held to be crucial to the ability to understand and explain the present and shape the future. Historicism hence points both backwards and forwards in time. Historicism belongs together with modernity, which is said to be characterised by a historical awareness focusing on origins and development (e.g. Foucault 1966 (French); 1971 (English)).

The claim of historicism that the past can be used to shape the future has been criticised, though. In *The Poverty of Historicism*, which is a reckoning with the utopian ideologies of the 1920s and 1930s, the philosopher Karl Popper rejected the notion that there can be laws governing the development of history or of society, and that it is therefore impossible to predict or shape the future (Popper 1957). Popper's arguments resemble the chaos theory formulated long afterwards in the natural sciences and known for its "butterfly effect", in which decisive importance is ascribed to small variations and matters of chance. Both history and nature are chaotic or unstable systems sensitive to small differences, systems in which large changes do not need large explanations, and in which predictions demand an awareness of the values of all the relevant variables (Reisch 1991; Gerding & Ingemark 1997). Therefore, tomorrow will always be different from what we had imagined or planned.

The idea of progress and the Enlightenment project with its optimism have been criticised, and indeed heavily attacked, in recent years – as have knowledge and science. The Enlightenment idea of progress is reduced to just one of many ideologies. Michel Foucault and many others after him see the will to knowledge as a will to power (Foucault 1976 (French); 1990 (English)). Technological and organisational progress has a share in the responsibility for the worst genocide of the twentieth century, the Holocaust (Bauman 1989). Knowledge, facts, and truth, in particular, are called into doubt as concepts, goals, and means. Knowledge is said to be a social construction that can be negotiated in a laboratory (Latour & Woolgar 1979). Enlightenment's radical doubt has been directed against enlightenment itself, reopening the door to irrationality, superstition, and dogma. Once again, human beings enter a state of folly and *Unmündigkeit* ("not of age", "incapacity"), to borrow Kant's term. The light of the Enlightenment is threatened by the darkness of dissolution.

Creating knowledge can either be a goal in itself or a means of attaining something else. When knowledge is a goal in itself, we can talk about knowledge as part of an educational project. When knowledge is a means of attaining something else, we can talk about an instrumental goal. However, the word instrumental is often used in a derogatory way in an implicit hierarchy, in which the elite's education is superior to the majority's practical knowledge.

When general education is stressed, especially in humanities disciplines, it might be expected to involve a democratic enlightenment project: Knowledge is intended to liberate human beings from the *Unmündigkeit* imposed on them. But if anything, it seems to emerge in order to disavow what is useful, instrumental, and practical. *Bildung* is ranked above mere education. In this context, the term *Bildung* may be regarded as a relic of another time, a time when the elite was supposed to acquire a broad spectrum of knowledge and proficiencies, a cultural code, so as to be able to function in state offices and mix at a distance from the rest of the population. To quote from the film *Monty Python & The Holy Grail* (1975), when King Arthur manages to complicate a question about the air-speed velocity of an unladen swallow and is therefore free to cross the Bridge of Death: "Well, you have to know these things when you're a king, you know!" In more academic terms and with a reference to the sociologist Pierre Bourdieu, it could, instead, be said that redundant knowledge is used as symbolic capital in order to create social distance (cf. Bourdieu 1979 (French); 1984 (English)).

Knowledge about the past as both an end and a means to an end is widespread, despite all the debate, doubt, and criticism. It is often so obvious and so generally accepted that there is no need to formulate it directly. In this respect, there is no interest in knowledge as a will to power or as a social marker, nor in science as an ideology. Instead, the whole focus is on how to attain knowledge. The past is narrated, remembered, preserved, excavated, reconstructed, and brought to life as both an alluring and essential source of knowledge.

The will to knowledge runs as an explicit or implicit theme though numerous examples: Herodotus, Ibn Khaldûn, Leopold Ranke, Friedrich Nietzsche, Marc Bloch, David Thomson, Eric Hobsbawm, and even Michel Foucault – they all pursued knowledge, and they all assumed that knowledge could be attained. In the introduction to *Histoire de la sexualité* (*The History of Sexuality*), Foucault thus linked the search for truth and enlightenment to liberation (Foucault 1976: 14 (French); 1990: 7 (English)); otherwise he, if anyone, represents a power-critical perspective on science and has inspired numerous postmodern relativists.

Returning to Abu Simbel, one motive for examining and salvaging the temples by moving them would be to secure them as sources of knowledge. As monuments, the temples are sources for the reign of Pharaoh Ramses II, for the art, cosmology, and politics of that period. More specifically, the great temple with its images and texts is one of several sources for the Battle of Kadesh in 1274 BCE between Egypt under the leadership of Ramses II and the Hittite Empire under the leadership of Muwatalli II. This well-documented battle, which took place at Homs in present-day Syria and in which thousands of chariots were used, is depicted as a huge victory for the pharaoh, even though that was hardly the case. A peace treaty, the earliest one known, was then made in 1258 BCE between the equally strong parties (Desroches Noblecourt 2007: 60ff, 134ff). So the depiction in the temple represents not the truth, but a partial truth, a pharaonic perspective on the past. Finally, the temples with their architecture, sculptures, images, and texts are also potential sources in a broader sense. Through the salvage campaign they have also been secured as sources in the future, sources to which scholars can return with new questions, perspectives, and methods.

With knowledge, facts, or even truth about the past both as means and ends, the good and the beautiful, morality and narrative, should be subordinate: it is irrelevant to truth how something is told, whether it is entertaining, or whether it is morally good or evil. All that matters is what something was actually like. But when the truth of the Enlightenment is called into doubt as a legitimate motive, the beauty of the narrative and the ethical demands come into play instead. It is not apparent that an increased will to knowledge is a major reason for greater present-day interest in the past.

The beauties of narrative

Narratives about the past are desirable, useful, and essential. We need narratives about the past in order to understand and explain the present, meet the future, and create social cohesion. The ideal is the beautiful, captivating, and engaging narrative – a narrative that can enlighten, entertain, and perhaps also impose an obligation. A narrative can also be ugly, harrowing, and not attended by any obligations at all, and we still listen or read eagerly in order to inhabit another time, another country, for a while.

A sense of alienation in periods of rapid economic upturn or falling expectations about the future during economic downturns can be compensated by a dose of nostalgic narrative from the country where "things were done differently". Consequently, when the UK entered a period of deindustrialisation and unemployment in the 1970s and 1980s, factories that had closed down were transformed into museums. "Real industry" was replaced by "heritage industry" (Hewison 1987). The unemployed were given work as uniformed guides, while others moved as time tourists through environments of Iron-Age settlements, trading places from the Viking era, medieval market towns, and Early Modern urban existence, all brought to life (Petersson 2003: 276ff). And at home we can be both enlightened and entertained by historical dramas such as *Downton Abbey*, about life on an English country estate in the decades after the loss of the *Titanic*. The past can offer a temporary refuge from the dreariness or problems of everyday life, and then it acts therapeutically. In narrative form, the past may contribute to health and reduce, or deflect attention from, the problems of the present (cf. Asplund Ingemark 2013).

Narratives about the past, the present, and the future are by no means new; indeed, they are something fundamental that characterises human beings – *Homo narrans*, the narrating and listening person (Niles 1999; Mankell & Vera 2000). People use narrative as a tool to transfer experience (Gärdenfors 2006: 109ff; Boyd 2009). Mixtures of fact and fiction, of what has actually happened with what might or ought to happen, are thus found in oral narratives, in literary texts such as novels and short stories, in images such as rock carvings, paintings, photographs, and film, and in sculptures ranging from the limestone figure of Venus of Willendorf to present-day memorials. Without narratives, life would undoubtedly be much poorer, and perhaps impossible.

Back in the nineteenth century, as scientific disciplines emerged with their special genre of publications, seminars, and conferences, there was a parallel boom in historical narratives with an element of escapism. As part of the reaction of Romanticism to the Enlightenment project, the French Revolution, and the Napoleonic Wars, both science and art increased. Rational science was separated from speculative inquiry at the same time as there were constant crossings of borders.

Artists have interpreted the past, and scholars have written about it in literary modes. As examples of border-crossings between fact and fiction, between scholarship and art, and between two cultures, I select a pair of personal favourites from my bookshelf. On one side is the semioticist Umberto Eco, who was able to communicate his knowledge about semiotics, philosophy, literature, and the Middle Ages in his historical detective novel *Il nome della rosa* (Eco 1980 (Italian); 1983 (English), *The Name of the Rose*). And on the other side is the journalist and author Thorkild Hansen with *Det lykkelige Arabien* (Hansen 1962 (Danish); 1964 (English), *Arabia Felix*), who created a historical documentary novel and existential narrative about a Danish expedition to Yemen in the eighteenth century, which was at that time regarded as the happy "foreign country"; here Hansen was able to use his personal experience of the Nubian campaign. But many more names and works could obviously be mentioned.

Counterfactual history forms a popular genre of its own which crosses the border between fact and fiction. It is no longer a matter of what "actually happened" but of what could or perhaps ought to have happened, if events had taken another course. What if? Here historians and others can make creative forays beyond the confines of their disciplines and examine alternative histories. Early examples are known from the seventeenth century, but the genre has had an upturn since the 1990s. It often examines whether an alternative political or military development could have taken place after a certain point in time if something had been different. Here details, individuals, incidents, events, and the weather are given key roles. One source of inspiration is chaos theory, and the intention is to methodically examine possible explanations – and undoubtedly also to entertain (Ferguson 1997; Andersson & Zander 1999; Evans 2014).

But what if the shape of Cleopatra's nose had been different, Duke William had been defeated at Hastings in 1066, Queen Kristina had not abdicated in 1654, Napoleon had been victorious at Waterloo in 1815, Gavrilo Princip had missed in 1914, Günter Schabowski had replied differently in 1989, and Donald Trump had not won the Electoral College in 2016? Or what if Pharaoh Ramses II had been defeated at the Battle of Kadesh in 1274 BCE? Then the history of Egypt would have taken another turning, the pharaoh would have left a completely different legacy, and the temples of Abu Simbel would never have been built.

The border-crossings are numerous; but something new made its appearance with the postmodern criticism of the Enlightenment project, rational science, and "grand" narratives. There is a conscious shift from truth to beauty, from science to narrative, from fact to fiction, from grand to the small narratives, and from enlightenment to entertainment. More experiments are being made now than ever before with the form and content of history, memory, and heritage. And sometimes form is becoming more important than content.

The reckoning with the Enlightenment and rational science was accompanied by a "demasking" of the rhetorical character of research and communication. The texts of scholarship were viewed as a genre that could be subjected to textual analysis, as literary texts could. There has thus been an extensive debate about differences and similarities between fact and fiction, about what stories are told about the past, and about how the past can be (re)narrated (e.g. Solli 1996).

The historian Hayden White's *Metahistory* has attracted great attention with his inquiries into the rhetorical forms of history-writing, undertaken without White's regarding himself as a postmodernist or relativist. White claimed that history-writing was shaped by the literary templates of the nineteenth century – the romance, the comedy, the tragedy, and the satire. The romance, with metaphor as its expression, represents anarchy; the comedy, with metonymy, represents conservatism; the tragedy, with synecdoche, represents radicalism; and the satire, with irony, represents liberalism. History-writing is hence said to be steered by a fundamental poetics linked to political categories in which romance liberates while tragedy brings ruin, comedy reconciliation, and satire imprisonment (White 1973).

A focus on narrative has also gained a foothold in archaeology and heritage studies. This is most clearly manifest in the work of the archaeologist Cornelius Holtorf, who in *From Stonehenge to Las Vegas* moves the focus from the past, and archaeology as a means of gaining knowledge of the past, to the present, archaeology and archaeologists becoming means of having experiences. According to this view, the meaning of archaeology is, first and foremost, located in its popularity as a metaphor for treasure hunting, adventurous fieldwork, and detective work. Furthermore, the narratives of science are no truer than other narratives about astrology, mysticism, or sacred geometry. Here and in other texts, Holtorf pushes a relativist and Enlightenment-critical line inspired by the philosopher Paul Feyerabend and his anarchist (or neoliberal) programme (Holtorf 2000; 2005; 2010). Feyerabend argued for a consistent "political relativism"; but in contrast to Holtorf, he explicitly rejected "philosophical relativism", which is the view that all traditions, theories, and ideas are equivalent (Feyerabend 1978: 82f).

Archaeology becomes part of a borderless popular culture in which people make a virtue of necessity or a virtue of a choice of political path. It is "tittytainment", a mixture of (breast) feeding and entertainment, bread and circuses, for the great mass of the population, who will not be needed in the world economy of the future; the term is said to have been coined by the sociologist and politician Zbigniew Brzezinski in a debate about the global economy of the future in San Francisco in 1995 between politicians, economists, and business leaders (cf. Martin & Schumann 1996: 13f (German); 1997: 4f (English)).

Popular culture requires no truths; nor does it require a distinction between science and literature, between history and myth, or between fact and fiction. For experience and for entertainment, it does not matter whether Bosnia has pyramids, whether Stonehenge was built by Druids, whether King Arthur existed, whether the trelleborgs were radio stations rather than Viking-age fortresses, whether the Holy Grail is hidden on Bornholm or in Scotland or Jordan, whether the Kensington Runestone is from the fourteenth or the nineteenth century, or whether Indiana Jones was actually a living person or is a fictional character (cf. Wienberg 2004; Fagan 2006).

To go back once more to Abu Simbel, one of the motives for examining and salvaging the temples was that it would be possible to have a fantastic experience (roughly) at the site in future, too. The temples were to continue to be a tourist destination. But ever since its construction, Abu Simbel has been a starting point for narratives. Ramses II had the great temple decorated with images showing how he defeated the Hittites at the Battle of Kadesh. The truth is that the battle was a draw – or even a defeat for the Egyptians. So the first narrative is a case of "alternative facts" – a propaganda lie. The temples are also the starting point for narratives about Ramses II as a powerful king with a desire to build, and about the religious ideas of the period (e.g. MacQuitty 1965). In Agatha Christie's crime novel *Death on the Nile* (Christie 1937), Abu Simbel is a backdrop to an intricate plot at the same time as the novel depicts the cruise of affluent Western tourists on the Nile, from Cairo and the pyramids in the north to the temples in the south.

A new narrative has been added since the salvage campaign of the 1960s, a narrative that focuses on the international operation and the technological achievements in moving and rebuilding the temples (e.g. Desroches-Noblecourt & Gerster 1968). And then, every visitor, every tourist, can create their own narrative in their meeting with the temples. Even if the temples had not been salvaged, but had drowned when the Aswan High Dam was erected, the narratives would not have ceased. They would simply have been given a different and probably more nostalgic character.

But copies and films can also form starting points for narratives. The Crystal Palace in London, the main building in the first World Exhibition, housed a replica, erected in 1854, of the largest temple at Abu Simbel; the replica was destroyed in a fire in 1936 (Ossian 2007). Later, copies of varying sizes have been erected in many places – Pattaya in Thailand, Shenzhen in China, in the Luxor Hotel in Las Vegas in the US, and in Legoland at Billund in Denmark. The Italian amusement park Gardaland has an attraction called "Ramses: Il risveglio" ("Ramses: Awakening"), whose main entrance is designed as the great temple at Abu Simbel in half-scale (www.gardaland.it; cf. Melotti 2011: 81ff). In Portugal in 2011, the engineer and sculptor Hany Mustafa built a travelling exhibition called "Museo del templo Abu Simbel", which contained a glass fibre copy so that people would be able to experience the temple without needing to travel to an Egypt in turmoil. Finally, it is also possible to make a virtual visit to Abu Simbel.

The salvage campaign at the temples of Abu Simbel was also used in the film *Erinnerungen an die Zukunft* (Reinl 1970; *Chariots of the Gods*), a film based on books in which the author Erich von Däniken maintained that extraterrestrials had made visits to the earth in ancient times. In view of the enormous operation, with participants from many countries, that was necessary to move the temple in the modern period, von Däniken argued that the Egyptians could not have been capable of moving stones and doing construction work 3000 years previously. It must have been aliens from space, visits by "Gods" (cf. von Däniken 1973 (German): 60, Figs. 118–119; 1976 (English): 53f, Fig. 111a).

When beauty and fiction about the past are both means and ends, truth and goodness – knowledge and morality – must assume a subordinate position. For beauty and narrative it is generally, but not necessarily always, irrelevant whether something actually happened, existed, or is authentic, and also whether something is morally good or evil. All that matters is that the narrative is entertaining or serviceable. The truth is replaced by probabilities and possibilities. However, when the truth of the Enlightenment is doubted as a legitimate motive, and beauty and narrative are regarded as secondary, all that is left is the ethical demand.

Ethical demands

It may also be an ethical duty to protect and preserve the past from decay. We ought to preserve narratives about the past, preserve people's memories, and preserve the material and intangible traces of heritage. We are under an ethical demand to work actively so that history, memory, and heritage are not given lower priority, forgotten, or destroyed.

Ethics (or morality) is something fundamental that characterises humans – *Homo ethicus*, the engaged human, who enters into social ties with other people (e.g. Prozesky 2014). The concept of ethics comes from the Greek word *ethikos*, which is about manners or customs, whereas morality comes from the Latin word *moralis*, which is about customs or practices. Ethics and morality hence have the same core meaning, and they are often used interchangeably, even though ethics is normally defined as the theoretical or abstract starting point for the more practical or concrete sphere of morality. Irrespective of the choice of term, both concern people's endeavours to think, express, and do what is right – in other words, about people's striving towards that which is good.

But what, then, are the right and the good? The question opens up a limitless field of thoughts, recommendations, orders, statutes, and penalties. Ethics can have its starting point in religion, politics, philosophy, and culture. Ethics can be divided up into normative ethics and consequence-based ethics, or into virtues and duties. Ethics can form its own academic field of knowledge with specialists, who often come from philosophy, theology, or medicine. Among the mass of philosophers, I opt for three names and bodies of work that represent different viewpoints.

My first choice is Immanuel Kant as a representative of duty-based ethics grounded in reason. In *Grundlegung zur Metaphysik der Sitten* (*Groundwork of the Metaphysics of Morals*), Kant formulates two imperatives: first, the categorical imperative; that is, the absolutely necessary, in which an act is a good end in itself – and, second, the hypothetical imperative; that is, the possible, in which an act is a means of achieving the good (Kant 1785 (German): 51; 1998 (English): 25f). The categorical imperative says: "handle nach der Maxime, die sich selbst zugleich zum allgemeinen Gesetze machen kann"; "act only in accordance with that maxim through which you can at the same time will that it become a universal law" (Kant 1785 (German): 81; 1998 (English): 31).

The second choice is Peter Singer as a representative of consequence-based ethics. Singer's starting point is utilitarianism. He argues that acts are to be judged as good when they satisfy the greatest possible number, and that no interests may be given precedence before any others. And in line with this, he argues – in *One World Now* (2016) – that in a globalised world, where questions concerning climate, economics, legislation, and politics cross national borders, there is also a need for a global ethics.

My third choice is Martha Nussbaum as a representative of virtue ethics, and her paper "Non-Relative Virtues – An Aristotelian Approach". Nussbaum draws her inspiration from ancient literature, and her point of departure is human existence. Human beings strive after the good life, using their own feelings and internal ideas to achieve this goal. Nussbaum defines the good on the basis of some common human experiences (mortality, body, pleasure and pain, cognition, reason, the child's development, attachment, and humour) in order to go beyond the local and relative (Nussbaum 1988; 1993). Nussbaum's virtues, formulated with the assistance of Aristotle, recall various attempts to define transcendentals such as the true, the beautiful, and the good.

In response to the ethical demand, it could be argued that there is no firm foundation to stand on; there is no fixed, common starting point, no Archimedes Point or *Arche*. Where is the starting point for the right or the good in a world of religious, political, philosophical, and cultural plurality? Previously, God was perhaps an indisputable Archimedes point. But then I can ask: Which God or which gods – and in which interpretation? For Kant's reason, Singer's interests and Nussbaum's feelings and experiences also open up to plurality and need to be interpreted in practice. Which reason, which interests, which feelings, which experiences – and how? The right and the good are and remain relative and therefore problematic, as the right and the good often come with a universal ambition. Without a fixed starting point, the ethical demand risks being transformed into an individual responsibility (cf. Bauman 1993). Then the ethical is easily reduced to a non-binding slogan. Of course we ought to be ethical; but why, and how?

Inspired by Kant's imperatives, I would, however, like to try to formulate two moral rules. The first is categorical: treat the past as you want yourself and others to treat the present. Or, more specifi-cally: protect, preserve, and use the past, as you want to protect, preserve, and use the present. The rule is relevant, as the traces of the past are very much part of the present. The second is hypo-thetical: act so that the past is a means of achieving the true, the beautiful, and the good. But the "you" and "others" do not need to represent a global consensus. Different individuals and groups – social, political, cultural, religious, ethnic – may have different ideas about the true, the beautiful, and the good. So morality remains contextual and therefore relative.

The ethical demand encounters the past with history, memory, and heritage in several ways. First and foremost, ethics appears as rhetoric – the past ought to be preserved! Here ethics acts as a slogan that would implicitly make further argumentation super-fluous. It appeals to common values and to a sense of collective responsibility. Heritage is elevated to an ethical sphere, being presented as priceless.

Ethics also appears as a canonical professional ethic. In view of the unethical ways in which the past was treated before our time, professional organisations have formulated rules for what is right and proper. It is stressed that there is a professional responsibility for acting in the right way. This is seen particularly clearly in the archaeological management of heritage, and it is found at both national and international level. Still, the ethical discussion can also be more (self-)critical and reflective (e.g. Vitelli 1996; Karlsson 2004; Sandis 2014; Ireland & Schofield 2015).

One example of a canonical ethics is the International Council on Monuments and Sites (ICOMOS) whose statutes, the Charter for the Protection and Management of the Archaeological Heritage, describe the archaeological heritage as a moral duty for every human being (1990: Article 3, "The protection of the archaeological heritage should be considered as a moral obligation upon all human beings"; www.icomos.org). Here ethics becomes a professional duty formalised in statute paragraphs. But it is noteworthy that a "salvage campaign" such as that at Abu Simbel must be regarded as mistaken according to ICOMOS, since preservation ought to take place *in situ*: "Any transfer of elements of the heritage to new locations represents a violation of the principle of preserving the heritage in its original context" (1990: Article 6; www.icomos.org).

There is an extensive ethical debate, a debate about the right and the good, regarding the question of whether the past has been (ab) used, generally by "others" before us or far away in the country where "things were done differently". A constantly topical question here is who has the (property) right to the heritage concerned (cf. Gillman 2010). Should heritage in the form of archaeological finds, books, art, or monuments be returned to the places from which they once came? Should the Parthenon frieze (or the Elgin Marbles) be transferred from the British Museum in London to the new Acropolis Museum in Athens (Greenfield 1996: 42ff; Bring 2015: 69ff)? But the ethical debate becomes most intensive when it approaches human beings and the human body. Nothing can generate debate like the handling of the dead – graves, crania, skeletons, mummies, and bog bodies (cf. Nilsson Stutz 2008).

Graves have been and are of central importance as expressions of collective identity. A source as early as Herodotus recounts a conversation in around 513–512 BCE in which Idanthyrus, King of the Scythians, is supposed to have said that he wanted to fight against the Persians for "our forefathers' graves". "But if nothing will serve you but fighting straightway, we have the graves of our fathers; come, find these and essay to destroy them; then shall you know whether we will fight you for those graves or no" (Herodotus, IV: 127, pp. 328f; cf. Kristiansen 2001: 148; 2004).

An ethical argument about graves appears in Sweden in the middle of the sixteenth century. The exiled Archbishop Olaus Magnus asserted that old monuments should be preserved as they had been erected with the intention of conferring immortality, just as he condemned the disturbing of graves as outrageous and a sin. The view that the graves of the dead should not be disturbed also turns up in directives and deliberations from the 1630s and up until the nineteenth century in Sweden (Olaus Magnus 1555 (Latin): I cap. xxx, pp. 49f; xvi cap. xlv–xlvi, pp. 564ff; 1982 (Swedish): 1,

Chapter 30, p. 66ff; 16, Chapters 45–46, p. 759ff; cf. Jensen 2010: 153f). In several other religions, such as Judaism and Islam, the view is still that graves should be left in peace.

A discussion across the centuries setting out justifications, motives, and values gradually leads up to the present situation, in which most countries have legislation that protects traces of the past to varying degrees. And as a consequence of legislation and the expansion of heritage, there is now also "heritage crime" as a separate concept and a growing academic field (e.g. Grove & Thomas 2014).

The ethical perspective has been given a prominent role since the Second World War. In that context, special attention has been paid to the difficult handling of the Holocaust with Auschwitz-Birkenau as the iconic example, where genocide culminated in an industrial complex. Auschwitz-Birkenau became a World Heritage site at a relatively early stage (WHL 31, 1979). But many other places and situations characterised by evil and human beings as victims raise ethical issues. How can and should victims and executioners be remembered in texts, images, memorials, and museums? Understand or explain, tell or stay silent, remember or forget, preserve or destroy – everything is tested here, including relativism (e.g. Wyschogrod 1998; Macdonald 2009). It is also more generally observed that people in the present have a responsibility for the dead (cf. Southgate 2005: 53ff).

In *Temps et récit* (*Time and Narrative*), the philosopher Paul Ricoeur linked ethics with the narrative about the past. Here we encounter the view that every story about the past is a moral statement. The historian gives the victims of the past a voice. The victims deserve not to be forgotten, not to be trivialised or hidden by the history-writing of the victors (Ricoeur 1983–1985 (French); 1984–1988 (English)).

Ought the temples of Abu Simbel to have been salvaged from drowning, as actually happened – was it an ethical duty? In 1960, when the Director-General of UNESCO, Vittorino Veronese, was going to justify the Nubian campaign as a reaction to the flooding that would be caused by the Aswan High Dam, he did not use the concepts of ethics or morality. But Veronese did describe a difficult choice, a choice that would be "between a heritage of the past and the present well-being of a people", "between temples and crops". This was exactly why Egypt and Sudan sought international support (Veronese 1960: 7).

The same problem turned up again when the campaign was over and had to be justified once more. Then the Egyptologist Torgny

Säve-Söderbergh wrote that those involved might ask "whether it was morally acceptable to collect millions of dollars for such a purpose in a world where millions of its inhabitants starve and innumerable children die of hunger or have no expectation of even a marginally decent standard of life" (Säve-Söderbergh 1987: 217f). Now, afterwards, we can conclude that the outcome was heritage, temples, crops, and electricity, but hardly welfare; that the temples were saved, but that many people continued to have relatively low living standards.

But neither Kant's, Singer's, nor Nussbaum's ethical deliberations provide any immediate guidance as to whether the temples of Abu Simbel ought to have been saved. Can their salvage be elevated to a general rule? Does their salvage satisfy as many interests as possible? Can their salvage contribute to a good life? In all three instances, the field is open to interpretation. "Salvage" of heritage can mean many things – on-site preservation, a relocation, documentation in text and photographs, and these days also digital documentation. Were the temples salvaged at all, considering the consequences of the move for their authenticity? Which group interests should be weighed against one another, and how? Who counts in this context? People living around Abu Simbel, in the Nile valley, or in Egypt; tourists, including all potential tourists; everyone in the world, including people who will live in the future? And what is the good life, and who should be allowed to have an influence on it? Without an absolute starting point, an Archimedes Point, *Arche* or God, ethics is just a finer but volatile word for *doxa*; that is, for attitudes and positions.

By way of thanks for their assistance in the Nubian campaign, several countries received temples – Debod came to Parque del Oeste in Madrid in Spain, Taffa to Rijksmuseum van Oudheden in Leiden in the Netherlands, Dendur to the Metropolitan Museum of Art in New York in the US, and Ellesiya to Museo Egizio in Turin in Italy. Ought these temples to be returned to Egypt in a postcolonial spirit, even though their move was completely legal and Egypt was not and is not a colony? With Kant, return would be a general rule. If any heritage is to be moved back, then all heritage ought to be moved back. With Singer, interests would be weighed against one another: Where can the greatest number of persons benefit from the presence of the monuments, in Nubia or in the urban centres of the West? Well, the greater number of people undoubtedly visit Madrid, Leiden, New York, and Turin (cf. Melotti 2011: 81ff). But is the context in the West meaningful, or have the temples become "places of forgetting"? Debod's temple, for instance, stands with no justification whatsoever in a park laid out in the 1890s; it used to be a rubbish dump, and it was the site of a massacre in the civil war in 1936. Or where do the monuments contribute most to the good life? The answers are not obvious.

With the ethical perspective, knowledge is probably a precondition, but narrative is subordinate. Truth and beauty have to serve goodness. To act in the right way, knowledge is needed; but the way in which it is conveyed may not be so very important.

The ethical demand is necessary, but it is problematic at the same time, both in theory and in practice. Discussion is made more difficult by a rhetoric in which ethics itself has become a watchword which is meant to make argument superfluous.

Of the three – truth, beauty, and goodness – the last is the most difficult to pin down. Even so, considering my deliberate choice of three virtues, my sympathies are with Nussbaum. The ethical demand must be determined from example to example, from situation to situation; virtues are relative. The canonical culture of heritage needs statutes, guidelines, values, and interests that can be measured and weighed. But moral rules for handling the history, memory, and heritage of the past cannot be discovered as something essentially existing. They need to be adopted through decisions made by communities, in groups, in nations, or globally; that is the only possible route to take.

The ideas of the time

We can ask Sisyphus why he is pushing a huge stone up a hill, why he is toiling uselessly. But supposing we get a reply, is it a credible one? Perhaps Sisyphus does not know why he is rolling the stone, or he has forgotten the reason. Sisyphus may reply stating what he thinks the reason ought to be, or what he believes that we would like to hear. Sisyphus may assert one reason, but act according to another. Or he can lie, and lead us on to a false trail. So we cannot be sure of our ability to uncover an actor's motives by listening to his own account of them. But irrespective of whether the stated motives are true or mendacious, they can reveal the ideas about the past and heritage that are current at a certain point in time.

The fact that we choose to interrogate Sisyphus at all is indicative of our own doubts about the meaningfulness of rolling a stone that keeps falling down again. We already have a preconceived opinion that Sisyphus's labour is futile. A "Sisyphean task" is in fact an expression used about an effort that is strenuous, but without any hope or result.

Wondering and asking why the past is recounted, remembered, and preserved, why history, memory, and heritage are having an upturn, may be a sign of crisis. For that which is obviously legitimate does not need any justifications. So when the past in conjunction with the humanities field – that is, the second culture for C. P. Snow – constantly needs to justify itself and face expectations to be useful, this may be a sign that the field is marginalised and on the defensive. The past must be defended both against concrete threats of destruction and against other priorities in society.

But questions about usefulness are nothing new. For example, the naturalist Carl Linnaeus (later ennobled as von Linné) defended his studies against the many who believed that his science was only about curiosity and a pastime for the idle: *Hwartill duger det?* [*What use is it?*] *(Cui bono?)* (Linnaeus 1752 (Latin); 1753 (Swedish)). Linnaeus argued that God had not created anything in vain, that nothing was without a use. With numerous examples, ranging from flies to grass, he demonstrated how something could be of use as, for instance, food, medicine, or building materials, either directly or indirectly. The question, which tormented Linnaeus, contains a fundamental doubt and a demand for justification current in the period, a demand rooted in the assumption that everything must be serviceable, be of use.

There are many kinds of usefulness, and as Linnaeus demonstrated, nothing is without a use. But when usefulness is demanded of the past and of the humanities, this amounts to an insistence that the field be justified within the premises of the predominant discourse of the period. Consequently, when the concepts "usefulness" and "benefit to society" are employed in the present-day debate, they mostly function as a political mantra that provides cover for a demand for profitability from something that present-day society just does not want to give priority; it is known that the question of benefit or profit will put the field on the defensive. The fact is that the defence of the past has to be formulated at a time, at a place, and in a society in which a distinction is made between what generates and what consumes resources, in which usefulness is contrasted with amusement, and in which use is often associated with economics, social science, medicine, natural science, and engineering, while amusement is associated with the humanities and literature.

What is the past good for? One recurring theme is the topicality and relevance of the past, and therefore also its usefulness, in relation to the agenda of the present, but also in relation to future needs; something can be of use now or in the longer term. Justifications, motives, and values have constantly been updated or modernised so as to be geared to the great or burning issues of the time. To obtain legitimacy, there has been a conscious or unconscious appeal to what is well known, accepted, and relevant to the present, qualities that necessarily vary over time.

The classifications of motives and practices bear the stamp of the agenda of the present. Friedrich Nietzsche's three categories stemmed from the political tendencies of his own time – the monumental, which actively orientates itself backwards to a golden age; the antiquarian, which passively preserves; and the critical, which actively seeks the golden age in the future. In simplified terms, the categories represent a reactionary, a conservative, and a revolutionary perspective – or three social and political groups that belong to Nietzsche's time: the aristocracy, the bourgeoisie, and the workers. By contrast, Svante Beckman's division into four categories comprising norms and necessity, usefulness and entertainment, forms a mirror image of sectors in the modern welfare state, in which time is divided up between external demands and personal needs, as well as between work and leisure. And my own triple categorisation into truth, beauty, and goodness can be seen as a positioning in the present debate, bridging the two cultures of heritage – a positioning legitimised by a reuse of philosophical concepts that can point out a direction, but whose content is constantly renewed. Consequently, we are unavoidably entangled in our own time.

To obtain funds for a salvage action at Abu Simbel, it was necessary for Vittorino Veronese and UNESCO to employ rhetorically persuasive expressions which were able to engender widespread comprehension in their own period. Herodotus, Ibn Khaldûn, Leopold Ranke, Alois Riegl, Marc Bloch, Torgny Säve-Söderbergh, David Thomson, Eric Hobsbawm, Michael Shanks, Christopher Tilley, and Cornelius Holtorf – all have argued in line with or against their own period. And Carl-Axel Moberg's overview, in terms of the history of ideas, of justifications for archaeological research is very much a catalogue of varying current "uses" – from evidence of the relevant country's greatness to a mere pastime (cf. Moberg 1984).

Views of what usefulness amounts to have varied over time; but these days it is usually defined in terms of economic growth as both the means and the end, surrounded by a number of secondary themes that may be either prerequisites for or consequences of growth. The past in its wide-ranging sense, encompassing history, memory, and heritage, is thus regarded as a resource for experiences, recreation, and travel – a resource that is of growing economic importance. The designation of Abu Simbel and other sites as World Heritage sites is expected to promote the influx of tourists, thereby contributing to income and jobs, even though the development of cultural tourism is not without its problems (cf. Bourdeau *et al.* 2015).

But history, memory, and heritage are a resource comprising knowledge, narratives, and experience of broader relevance. It is thus relatively easy to find current examples in which archaeologists and others wish to activate knowledge about the past in order to contribute to solving the great issues of our time; that is, issues involving sustainable development, climate change, population growth, poverty, migration, diversity, human rights, political trust, community, and peace (e.g. Silverman & Fairchild Ruggles 2007; Sabloff 2008; Little 2009; Westman & Tunón 2010; Fredengren 2012; Högberg 2013; Aronsson 2015; *Räkna med kulturarvet* ["Count on heritage"], 2017; Schiffer 2017). The narratives, finds, and sites of the past already play a central role in a cultural tourism that is able to entertain as well as enlighten. However, heritage can be used in many other contexts as well, including issues involving identity, good health, and ethics. In short, heritage can contribute to a better world (cf. Aronsson 2009).

At the same time, it must be said that if the humanities – the study of the past, history, memory, and heritage – were to focus wholly on usefulness for the present or on the great issues, if there were no place for free basic research, curiosity, and unrestricted exploration, this would amount to losing the unexpected, which has turned out to be of crucial importance from a historical point of view. Even the study of the past needs its serendipity, the fortuitous discovery of something in the past other than the very thing that was being looked for – something unexpected and "strange".

The past has had meaning and value for thousands of years and has therefore already proved its sustainability or usefulness in varying conditions, but each period has understood or explained this in its own way. The justifications, motives, and values have varied, just as the arguments for scholarly and scientific pursuits have varied over time (cf. Sundin 1996). The crucial point is whether we are in Cairo in 1813, in Basel in 1874, in Paris in 1960, or in Lund in 2020, and what matters is whether it is the sheik, the philosopher, the director-general, or the archaeologist who is supplying the justifications and making the assessments. The question of who is to be persuaded is equally crucial: is it the president, the engineer, the tourist manager, the sceptical taxpayer – or the writer personally?

What is seen as meaningful depends on the context – on who is writing or speaking and who is expected to read or listen. The words have varied along with what someone could, ought to, or wanted to express in that period, at that place, or in that situation. Hence meaning is created within or in relation to a discourse. We say what we can, ought to, or want to when speaking to power, our colleagues, the public, and perhaps our own conscience.

What is the meaning of the past, of history, memory, and heritage? We must now conclude that the method of uncovering meaning through the actors' own justifications, through motives and values, leads to new questions, since the multifarious replies are bound up with the leading ideas and practices of the period. Does that mean that the ideas of the period are a mental prison that determines what can be said, or do the ideas of the period create new opportunities? Is the episteme restricting or liberating?

In *Les mots et les choses* (*The Order of Things*) (1966 (French); 1971 (English)) and *L'archéologie du savoir* (*The Archaeology of Knowledge*) (1969 (French); 1972 (English)), Michel Foucault used the concept of the episteme, from the Greek word meaning knowledge, about how and therefore also what it was possible to think, write, and say during a particular historical period. This would mean that the classical and the modern epochs are each characterised by their own episteme or their own discursive formation. It is, however, something of a contradiction that – also according to Foucault – there can be several epistemes at the same time. Here the episteme approaches other concepts such as mentality, paradigm, and discourse. Foucault himself thus used the concept of discourse in a way that is difficult or impossible to differentiate from the episteme.

It is tempting to reuse the concepts of episteme and discourse when trying to establish how the past acquires meaning. As a concept, the episteme can be useful in understanding how history, memory, and heritage are subordinated – at an initial, fundamental level – to a requirement of usefulness: everything must self-evidently be of use in relation to its own period. Thereafter, discourse as a concept may be employed at the next level in order to understand how expressions concerning the usefulness of the past vary with and within the demands of the period.

Here conflicts may arise between different discourses, between canonical and critical heritage, between representatives of different research traditions, and in the prioritisation of either the true, the beautiful, or the good. These conflicts are manifested in a polarised debate about the right heritage policy, a debate in which each distinct tradition attempts to define the field in its own way. In relation to that debate, political parties try to define heritage so that it fits their specific agenda – heritage as something enduring or something changeable, something delimited, national, or universal.

The episteme's requirement of use is seen in both cultures of heritage. For both the canonical and the critical culture can agree that the past ought to be of use, but they coalesce around different discourses and therefore have completely different ideas concerning what is of use. Not unexpectedly, the canonical culture is most visible in the defence of the usefulness of the past, supplying justifications, motives, and values, whereas the critical culture dominates the debate about (ab)use. The starting point of my own inquiry is also subordinated to the episteme. Because asking about the importance of the past entails looking for what is of use, even if the pursuit also includes curiosity allied to a sense of wonder.

Still, the concepts of episteme and discourse can easily become a philosophical straitjacket. There is an absence of a dynamics that allows for individuality, variation, and change, permitting movements across the constructed time limits of the episteme and the enforced roles of the discourse. Human beings are denied the ability to use their imagination to think beyond their own present and situation – think in the past and the future, in other periods, at other places, and from other perspectives. The episteme and the discourse do not allow human beings any freedom – and therefore no responsibility for their actions either, neither as individuals nor as collectives.

Justifications, motives, and values may be something different from, and more than, a mechanical and enforced reflection of the ideas and roles of a period. This is, first, because human beings do not discover the meaning of the past, but create its meaning in dialogue with their present. With new justifications, motives, and values, the past is given a meaning that it did not previously possess. Meaning is therefore in constant change, constantly fluid. And, second, because new justifications, motives, and values open the way to fresh perspectives on the past which are different from those already known. So the past is a resource that can constantly be reused in new and unexpected ways. As the time, place, and situation change, new possibilities arise of making creative use of the past – as a source of knowledge, and as a starting point for narratives or ethical deliberations. The recurring theme, the relevance of the past, is an expression not of weakness but of strength: the past possesses the very ability to be relevant and sustaining as a resource in varying circumstances.

It is meaningful to ask Sisyphus why he is pushing a great stone up a hill, even though the stone rolls down to the plain again, because justifications, motives, and values create meaning and help to shape the actions of the future. Let us now take a closer look at how Sisyphus affects the stone and the stone affects Sisyphus. What meaning does, can, or should the past have, if practices are examined? What is it that actually happens to the past?

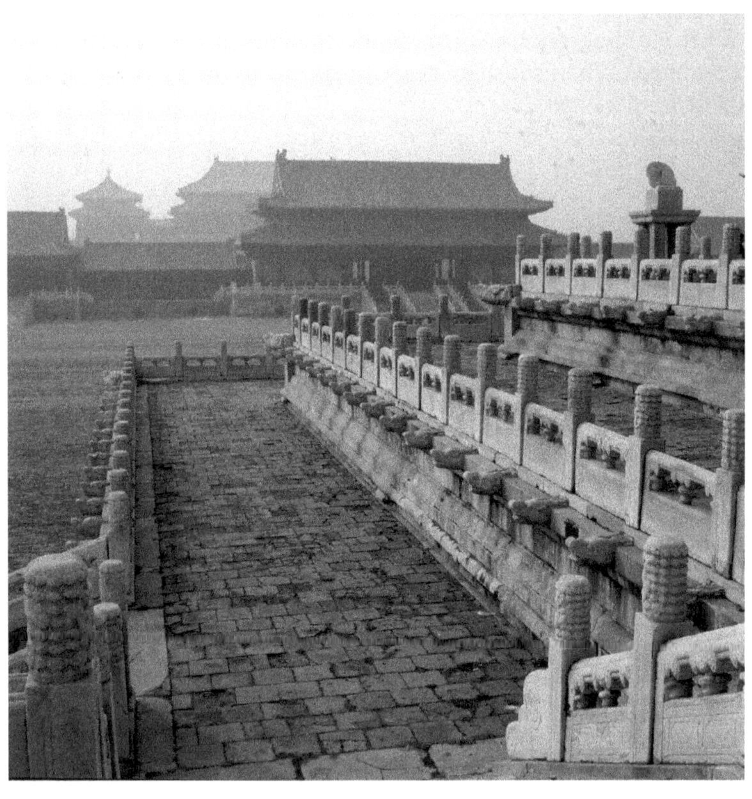

Figure 3 The Forbidden City in Beijing. Photo © Jes Wienberg, 1982.

3
Chronic nostalgia

(Ab)used histories

When focus shifts from justifications, motives, and values to practice, or from proclamations, purposes, and assessments to how history, memory, and heritage have actually been used and thereby been given meaning, the horizon darkens. Where the first, canonical culture of heritage sees resources to use, the second, critical culture of heritage sees a series of abuses. "À qui profite le crime?" ("who profits from the crime?"), as the archaeologist Alain Schnapp put it in the foreword to *La conquête du passé*, an overview of the history of archaeology (Schnapp 1993: 11). His critical title with military connotations, "The conquest of the past", was, however, transformed in the English edition into a curiosity-driven adventure, *The Discovery of the Past*, and the question about the crime disappeared (Schnapp 1996).

In the 1970s, two archaeologists initiated a wave of criticism of the use of the past and of heritage. Senake Bandaranayake published the article "Imperialism and Archaeology" (Bandaranayake 1974) under the pseudonym of "A. Gidtri". Bandaranayake wrote that in order to be able to conquer the present, colonialists also had to conquer the past. The Rosetta Stone and a statue of Ramses II, both in the British Museum in London, were stated as examples of plunder. Bandaranayake took the view that colonialists destroyed more than they preserved, and he praised the revolutionary collective of archaeologists in China that did not permit any outside interference. His article represented a postcolonial criticism that found inspiration in the China of the Cultural Revolution, even though that revolution entailed an extensive vandalising of remains from the country's past.

Bandaranayake was apparently spurred to voice this criticism on encountering the blockbuster exhibition *Treasures of Tutankhamun* at the British Museum in 1972 (Bandaranayake

1974: 431). In 1972–1981 the exhibition was on tour to the UK, the USSR, the US, Canada, and West Germany. This exhibition helped to finance the relocation of the temples on Philae to the nearby island of Agilkia (Säve-Söderbergh 1987: 168; 1996: 142f; Hassan 2007: 87).

Tutankhamun, with his well-preserved tomb and gold mask, is one of the best-known archaeological finds of the twentieth century. His tomb was discovered in 1922, in adventurous circumstances, by Howard Carter in the Valley of the Kings, Wadi el-Muluk. The expedition was financed by George Herbert, Earl of Carnarvon, the owner of Highclere Castle, the real Downton Abbey. The discovery is enveloped in popular speculation about the curse of the mummy, which is supposed to have struck the participants. I visited the tomb in the form of replicas at a travelling exhibition named *Tutankhamun – his tomb and his treasures* when it came to Malmö in Sweden in 2013.

The archaeologist Brian M. Fagan also used Egyptology as his starting point, directing harsh criticism against the colonial looting of the past in *The Rape of the Nile* (Fagan 1975). But despite his criticism, Fagan's main interest seems to have been the telling of the fascinating story of the exploration of the pharaohs' Egypt, from Napoleon's expedition in 1798 to Carter's discovery of Tutankhamun's tomb – to a great extent a race between the colonial powers France and the UK.

The temples of Abu Simbel are a well-known tourist destination in Egypt along with the Museum of Egyptian Antiquities in Cairo where Tutankhamun and his tomb have been on display, the pyramids at Giza, Luxor with Karnak, and the Valley of the Kings. Exotic trips along the Nile described by authors such as Amelia B. Edwards and Agatha Christie paved the way for the mass tourism of recent years. The tourist industry is important to the Egyptian economy, but it has been hit by several blows. The attack on tourists, guards, and a guide near Luxor in 1997 was thus both a strategic attack on the country's economy and an attack on the worship of what was seen as a non-Islamic past; there is a similarity here to the destruction by the Taliban and IS of monuments from ancient times. Then the number of tourists fell markedly with the disturbances that followed the Arab Spring in 2011.

Abu Simbel, with the colossal statues of Ramses II, is not only a tourist destination; it also serves as a set of props in Pharaonism, which constitutes a homage to pre-Islamic Egypt. Pharaonism is a national ideology which emerged in the interwar years, assigning a crucial role to Egyptology and to Tutankhamun's tomb in particular (Reid 2002; 2015). According to Pharaonism, Egypt is primarily a country with its own period of greatness and identity – and only after that period did it become an Ottoman or Arab country. After the transfer of power in 1952, however, Pharaonism was of less importance: Egypt was now presented as a leading Arab country. But a continued focus on the pharaohs, Ramses II being the most powerful, also suited the republic with its presidents, most of whom had a background in the military. The Islamic opposition notably compared the president to a pharaoh, in a derogatory sense.

Abu Simbel also touches on the debate about the removal of treasures and the demand for their return. As a reward for their efforts in the Nubian campaign and the salvage of the temples of Abu Simbel, the contributing countries were offered the possibility of retaining part of the resulting finds, as well as of receiving entire temples as "new ambassadors extraordinary". Debod went to Madrid, Taffa to Leiden, Dendur to New York, and Ellesiya to Turin, and some frescoes from the Cathedral in Faras went to Warsaw (Säve-Söderbergh 1987: 137ff; 1996: 114f). This gift policy was subsequently criticised both for plundering the heritage of Egypt and the Sudan and for entailing a division and dispersal of collections (Hassan 2007: 80, 90ff; 2009).

The criticism expressed by Bandaranayake and Fagan in the 1970s must be seen as part of a broad reckoning with the West. It is voiced against the background of decolonialisation after the Second World War, the criticism of US warfare in Vietnam and other countries, and the young people's revolt against their parents and authorities. A crucial point in this development was reached with the oil crises in 1973–1974 and again in 1978–1980, the first being triggered by the West's support of Israel in the Yom Kippur War, or October War, in 1973 between Israel, Egypt, and Syria.

Bandaranayake and Fagan were early critics. The subsequent decades saw a flood of critical debate articles and academic studies about the West's view of the "other" in time and space – a criticism formulated both outside and in the West. It includes *Orientalism* (1978) by the literary scholar Edward W. Said, a work that contains criticism of literary representations in which the "Orient" is presented as unchanging, alien, and incomprehensible – or the opposite of the West, the Occident, which is said to represent the changeable, familiar, and comprehensible.

Bandaranayake, Fagan, and Said in the 1970s were followed in the ensuing decades by numerous studies that examined, and often also criticised, the way in which the past – history and archaeology in particular – had been interpreted and used through the ages (e.g. Trigger 1984; 1989; Hedeager & Schousboe 1989; Gathercole & Lowenthal 1990; Hylland Eriksen 1996; Meskell 1998; Kane 2003; Diaz-Andreu 2007). David Lowenthal's works – *The Past is a Foreign Country* (1985; 2015) and *The Heritage Crusade and the Spoils of History* (1997) – must be included as an important part of this wave of criticism.

The criticism recapitulated above led to the establishment of both (critical) use of history and critical heritage as academic fields for research and teaching, from the 1990s onwards with their own conferences, journals, series, textbooks, networks, centres, and education programmes (e.g. *International Journal of Heritage Studies* 1994ff; cf. Aronsson 2004; Nielsen 2010; Harrison 2013). In more general terms, a great deal of attention shifted from the past in itself to the past in the present and therefore from source criticism to perspective criticism. Even so, this criticism may itself be seen as a new way of using of the past in the present.

This criticism has often focused on how the past has been used by nationalism, colonialism, imperialism, tourism, and other "isms": how selection, interpretation, and mediation have been shaped according to the needs of the present; how the past has been used to legitimise a political or military agenda – in the colonisation of Africa, in the reuse of the Roman Empire by Italian fascism, in the conduct of Nazi Germany in Eastern Europe, in Saddam Hussein's Iraq, and in the construction of a common Europe; how heritage has deliberately been destroyed to weaken identities in war zones in the Balkans, Afghanistan, Mali, and Syria; how treasures have been moved from the periphery of the colonies to central museums in the West; and how the past is used commercially and is being worn down by mass tourism. The list could be made much longer.

Motives, justifications, and values, what is spoken and written, must needs be supplemented by studies of practice in order to understand and explain the meanings of the past. And naturally, both purposes and practice must be subjected to critical assessment. It may, for instance, be useful to be reminded of how Gustaf Kossinna, Hans Reinerth, and other German archaeologists used the past as an argument in the context of German expansion – useful now that archaeology is once more brought to bear on issues of nationalism and identity (cf. Arnold 1990; 1998).

But this kind of criticism can easily come close to being banal and harmless. This happens, for instance, when the criticism condemns obvious abuse placed long ago in the poison cupboard of history. Moreover, criticism that is directed at the "other", who decided, researched, or wrote at another time and in a "foreign country", is seldom directed inwards as self-criticism. Criticism along such lines is not intended to enlighten; it functions primarily as a self-confirming social narrative. A display of criticism serves to demonstrate membership of the critical collective, confirming the existence of that community. Ethical reflection is reduced to identity-creating moralising.

Use – use and abuse – use or abuse – or only abuse? Abuse is use that someone else, later, in another place or as belonging to another tradition, regards as incorrect and therefore chooses to criticise. The use is seen as untrue, ugly, or evil. The criticism thus raises questions as to whether motives, values, use, and interpretation can be separated at all; as to whether use is unavoidable or ought to be avoided; and as to where to draw the line between use and abuse, between the true and the mendacious, the beautiful and the ugly, the good and the evil.

The word abuse carries connotations of distancing in terms of time or geography. The abuse of the past took place in the past – or somewhere else. Consequently, characterising a use as abuse often makes an unconscious assumption of either a developmental perspective or an ethnocentric attitude. We are wiser now, or we know better here. But do we have any right to judge the past, to drag the dead before an academic court without any possibility of defending themselves, to hold a day of judgement over the dead in the absence of God; that is, to pass judgement in the absence of Archimedean points for what is true, beautiful, and good? Convincing arguments are needed in each specific case. The true, the beautiful, and the good are goals to strive after; but they are not easy to achieve.

Criticism of the past is itself an example of use of the past; criticism is itself a narrative to examine, just as criticism of politics is political. Therefore, the question is what the intention is, or what is revealed in practice when others' use of the past is criticised. What is the agenda of the criticism? Its purpose may be to bring out what is untrue, ugly, or evil, so as to be able to regain the true, the beautiful, and the good. That is honourable. But criticism can also be an end in itself, serve in the creation of an identity, or be formulated in order to legitimise new perspectives or a new practice. So the criticism of the past is not only about interpreting the past, but also about the present and the future.

"Who controls the past controls the future: who controls the present controls the past" was the Party's slogan. The words from the dystopian science fiction novel *Nineteen Eighty-Four* (Orwell 1949: 37, 249 quotation) by the journalist and author Eric Arthur Blair, who wrote under the pseudonym George Orwell, are well known and perhaps hackneyed, but they are nonetheless accurate. The point of trying to control the past is to control the present and therefore also the future, even if all efforts to control the future must be in vain. The slogan is not that far from the thoughts expressed by the historian Marc Bloch at the same time: The point of history is to understand the present through the past, and to understand the past through the present (Bloch 1949 (French): 11ff; 1992 (English): 32ff). However, Bloch refrained from planning to understand, let alone control, the future.

An alternative to analysing motives, justifications, and values, or criticising practice – that is, an alternative to looking backwards – can be to work towards new goals. An archaeological activism and a reorientation, in which the public is a co-creator, emerges as a constructive counter-reaction to the intense criticism of the 1980s and 1990s. New goals are set so that the past can be of use.

Other and darker motives and values appear immediately when practice is examined. Lies and manipulation are hidden behind the ideal of truth; the ugly is to be found behind the ideal of beauty; an evil reality is revealed behind the ideal of goodness. The past has been filled with lies, looted, and raped. It has been used for treasure hunts, escapism, pastimes, and profit. The past has served all needs, nationalism, colonialism, imperialism, and tourism; it has served religion, ideology, and capital. True, beautiful, and good – or, conversely, false, ugly, and evil – and in both instances the triad's categorisation remains relevant. For there is not necessarily such a great distance between motives, justifications, and values on the one hand and the criticised practice on the other. That which is now criticised as abuse might have been perceived as useful in its time or its place. And that which is seen as useful today may be regarded as abuse in the future.

The concepts of criticism and crisis are related, their Greek roots being *kritikos*, meaning capable of judging, and *krisis*, meaning a decision or judgement. So is it the case, as many have claimed, that the use of the past increases in periods of crisis?

Crisis and the heritage industry

I believe that a civilisation which tends towards conservatism is a declining civilisation because it is afraid to go forward and ascribes

> more importance to its memories than to its future. Strong, expanding
> civilisations have no memory: they reject, they forget the past. They
> feel strong enough to be destructive because they know they can
> replace what has been destroyed. (Boulez 1976: 33)

These words were spoken by the composer and conductor Pierre
Boulez in a radio interview as a comment on the tendency, in evidence from the late nineteenth century onwards, to revive older
musical works. Boulez's statement was clear and unambiguous, but
far from unique. A broad spectrum of intellectuals have asserted,
and continue to assert, that a society that preserves is a society in
crisis. The context comprises everything from theoretical considerations to empirical examinations, from global perspectives to
selected examples. But often the crisis and the consequences of the
crisis are simply presented as facts for which no argument need be
made. For everyone seems to know that society was, or soon will
be, in a state of crisis for one reason or another, and that there
is a self-evident connection between the crisis and the expansion
of history, memory, and – especially – heritage. In times of crisis,
therapeutic consolation is sought in the past.

As the major change, modernity is supposed to be the crucial
reason why society finds itself in a state of crisis. That modernity
leads to a greater focus on the past is thus a widely held standpoint.
Modernity creates alienation, unrest, and anxiety that need to be
compensated for or balanced by narratives from the country of the
past. The reaction to modernity is said to be nostalgia as people
react to having modernity imposed on them by recalling a lost
time, the "wild strawberries" of their youth. And relics of the past
that get in the way of modernity are moved to temporal reserves, to
archives, libraries, or museums, where they are allowed to survive.

Or is it the other way round, nostalgia growing when modernity
finds itself in a state of crisis? Ever since the 1980s, there has been
a widely held view to the effect that the increased focus on the past
was caused by the decline or end of modernity. Modernity has been
succeeded by postmodernity, economic growth by decline, industrialisation by deindustrialisation, and belief in progress by belief
in a bygone golden age. The closed-down factory is transformed
into a museum, where former employees find work as guides.
Others visit reconstructed environments from the past – Iron-Age
settlements, trading places from the Viking Age, medieval market
towns, or Early Modern industries. And at home, people can be
entertained by the adventures of archaeologists on TV. The crisis

of modernity creates a yearning to escape to an apparently secure past.

In *The Past is a Foreign Country*, David Lowenthal was in no doubt that the heritage boom of the 1980s was caused by a crisis. And the numerous quotations in the book include a slight rewriting of Pierre Boulez's words: "A civilization which tends to conserve is a civilization in decline" (Lowenthal 1985: 384; 2015: 413). In a later lecture, in which Lowenthal is looking back, he refers to the background of the boom in the 1970s as a decade of unfulfilled promises, economic collapse, the closure of the Suez Canal (1967–1975), oil crises, inflation, postmodern doubt, and a revolt against modernism and the idea of progress (Lowenthal 2011 YouTube; cf. Lowenthal 2015: 36).

But in his books, Lowenthal has been unclear about the relationship between the crisis and the boom. *The Past is a Foreign Country* thus contains statements that point in several directions: he wrote that we should preserve because modernity, with its swift changes and developments, affects identity and well-being (Lowenthal 1985: xxiv). But he also wrote that nostalgia has replaced belief in progress and modernity (Lowenthal 1985: 11f; 2015: 36f). In other words, Lowenthal is inconsistent in identifying both modernity and postmodernity as being responsible for developments.

Here and there in *The Past is a Foreign Country* and its successor *The Heritage Crusade and the Spoils of History*, Lowenthal mentioned a wide range of reasons why nostalgia had crowded out belief in progress and development: increasing technological innovation, radical changes, disruptions, volatility, social decline and isolation, revolutions, immigration and industrialisation, genocide and iconoclasm, greater perishability on account of mass tourism, plus pollution, political, military, and biological disasters, longer life expectancy, and technophobia. The growth of heritage is thus regarded as reflecting traumatic losses and changes as well as fear of the future, but apparently also better living conditions, as expressed in longer life expectancy (Lowenthal 1985: 8ff, 121f, 394ff; 1997: 5ff; 2015: 36ff, 202f, 416ff).

The cultural historian Patrick Wright was clearer when he claimed in *On Living in an Old Country* that the past, tradition, and the nation would be invoked in periods of decline. The identity of the UK was said to have collapsed after the Second World War, when the Empire disintegrated and urban renewal led to anxiety and disorientation. Faced with the country's social and economic crisis in the 1970s, Margaret Thatcher's government was able to offer a rallying around national symbols. Consequently, the recovery of Henry VIII's flagship *Mary Rose* and the Falklands War, both in 1982, should be seen as two sides of the same project. Wright's view was that history should instead be geared towards the future. History can and must be created in the present and should not focus on lost fragments. A society in development ought, according to Wright's way of thinking, to be able to let an old wreck rest in peace (Wright 1985).

In his review of Wright's book, the architect Colin Ward pioneered the term "heritage industry" (Ward 1985, cf. Wright 2009: xxiii, 258, note 36). Intended to be pejorative, the term was undoubtedly inspired by the philosophers Max Horkheimer and Theodor W. Adorno, of the Frankfurt School, who formulated the concept "culture industry" in the 1940s. Horkheimer and Adorno used it about American popular culture with its films, radio, and magazines, which they viewed as solely profit-seeking; according to them, these manifestations of popular culture were standardised, commercial, conformist, and banal, and they manipulated and passivised the masses (Horkheimer & Adorno 1947 (German): 144ff; 2002 (English): 94ff; cf. Adorno 1967 (German); 1979 (English)).

A couple of years after that review, another well-written book established "heritage industry" as a general term within the framework of what was to become the critical tradition of heritage. In *The Heritage Industry*, the cultural historian Robert Hewison delivered a vigorous attack on the eponymous phenomenon. Hewison criticised the tendency to establish ever more museums, historical theme parks, and visitor centres. He claimed that heritage had become a nostalgic escape in a time of decline and uncertainty. The UK had, he said, been in crisis ever since the 1960s, beset by pessimism, devaluation, and oil crises. Modernisation had been replaced by deindustrialisation and unemployment. Industrial premises had become museums. Instead of goods, they produced superficial heritage. In Hewison's view, the heritage industry was stifling contemporary culture, and its inertia was impeding necessary renewal. What he wished to see was not more heritage and bringing to life but critical history, "real" industry, and "real" jobs (Hewison 1987).

Similarly drastic criticism was formulated by the philosopher Agnes Heller in her article "Europe – An Epilogue". From an American perspective, Heller observed a Europe in decline ever since the First World War, characterised by barbarity and totalitarianism. Worn out, Europe had turned away from progress and modernity that were, according to Heller, the essence of European culture. Instead, Europe was looking towards a nostalgic culture. Now Europe was searching for meaning in the past, as the present had nothing to offer. Its preoccupation with the past was seen as a symptom of its decline. "Old cities are rebuilt, ancient castles are refurbished, old artefacts are exhibited, old books are republished – Europeans tiptoe in their cities as museums *because they are museums*" (Heller 1988: 155; italics in the original).

This view was repeated, but now from an Eastern perspective, by Chinese state media after the vote on Brexit in 2016: "East Asia has witnessed decades of high-speed growth and prosperity. Europe stays where it was, becoming the world's center of museums and tourist destinations" (*Global Times* 25 June 2016).

Radical criticism was also presented by the historian Françoise Choay in *L'allégorie du patrimoine* (*The Invention of the Historic Monument*). Choay saw the culture industry, with its inflation of heritage and museums, as a reaction against the electronic era that had emerged since the late 1950s. In her view, a hegemonic technological network had liberated humanity from its natural and cultural restrictions, such as seasonal change. Artificial memory, greater mobility, and global communication had destabilised identity. The present was therefore characterised by repressed conflicts, anxiety, helplessness, and crisis. And Choay issued a warning about the new prosthetic human being, *homo sapiens prostheticus*, on the threshold of a new century (Choay 1992 (French): 158ff, 187ff; 2001 (English): 138ff, 164ff; italics in the original).

Similar ideas occur in *Twilight Memories* by the literary historian Andreas Huyssen. As a reaction to accelerating technological development and a crisis for modernity's faith in the future, he claimed that a "museum mania" had arisen since the 1980s. It transformed the museum from an institution for the elite into a popular mass medium. The revolution in the sphere of information had made the present chaotic, fragmentary, and liquid. Digital media spearheaded by television had blurred the difference between then and now – and between fact and fiction. The authentic materiality and contemplation offered by museums could, Huyssen suggested, compensate for the speed and superficiality of the media (Huyssen 1995: 14, 20, 25ff).

The sociologist Frank Füredi has described his own time as characterised by social anxiety. In *Mythical Past, Elusive Future*, Füredi thus claimed that the history and nostalgia of the 1980s was an expression of the decline of the West and its fear of the future. He saw the West as being characterised by economic stagnation, pessimism, and ideological emptiness after the end of the Cold War. The West had turned towards the past, with roots and tradition, to create new identities and contexts. Füredi viewed this development as a crisis of modernity, comparing his own present to the "fin de siècle" of the 1890s. He also criticised the use of the past as creating identities that are more about who people are than who they can become. Füredi wanted to see historical thinking rather than historical narrative, change rather than continuity, reason rather than roots, forward-looking progress rather than backward-looking conservatism (Füredi 1992).

In Füredi's opinion, decline and anxiety had meant a boom for the past; but at the same time, the French Revolution and the Napoleonic Wars had generated historical thinking, that is, an awareness that humans are able to shape their own future. And a romantic view of history had emerged in the nineteenth century as a conservative reaction against the Enlightenment's belief in progress and against the French Revolution (Füredi 1992: 72ff, 192ff).

The crisis and the critical jargon have also made their way to Scandinavia, even though references to the international debate may be absent. In the project "Modernisation and heritage", which resulted in the edited volume *Modernisering och Kulturarv*, the economic historian Svante Beckman wrote that the increased importance of heritage was a manifestation of the third, or perhaps the fourth, crisis of modernisation. These crises are linked to uncertainty about the future around the turns of centuries – 1800, 1900, and now 2000. Beckman also compared the fin de siècle of the 1890s to the end of the twentieth century: the same uncertainty, the same cultural shift, the same reaction to modernisation – and the same nostalgia (Beckman 1993a; 1993b).

Crisis is a common denominator of the explanations of increased interest in history, memory, and – especially – heritage. We witness a "crisis discourse" which, like a black hole, attracts and swallows all other interpretations. But crisis is an unclear concept, and it is rarely the result of an analysis. "Crisis" is used to designate a situation or change as being unfortunate or bad. But anything at all can be seen as a crisis by someone – and as unproblematic by someone else. When the word crisis crops up in a text, there is an explicit or veiled purpose. The concept is used as a rhetorical tool in shaping a narrative (cf. Magnusson Staaf 2013).

Society is in crisis; but when, how, and why? Heller saw a crisis since the First World War, Choay since the 1950s, Hewison since the 1960s, Lowenthal and Wright in the 1970s, Huyssen and Füredi in the 1980s, Beckman perhaps in the 1990s. Some write about a crisis in Europe, others in the UK, France, or – perhaps implicitly – in the West as a whole. And the crisis can be blamed on modernity, on postmodernity, or on something else again.

Another common feature is criticism directed against the increased importance of the past, against history, memory, and – especially – heritage. One example is the critique of tradition by the modernist Boulez. But it also includes criticism of heritage specifically, whereas traditional or critical history is commended. Lowenthal and Hewison thus drew a sharp distinction between history and heritage. They wanted to see more traditional or critical history, not narratives or superficial or false heritage. Lowenthal linked history to a search for truth and authenticity, but heritage to faith, fables, and construction; history could be tested, but heritage could not, a view pithily summarised in the heading "Historical fact, heritage faith" (Lowenthal 1997: 1, 119ff with heading, 250; cf. also Füredi 1992: 268). Or, as Hewison put it: "Heritage, for all its seductive delights, is bogus history" (Hewison 1987: 10, 139, 144 quotation).

This criticism is yet another example of widespread elitist contempt for the popular, perhaps spiced with a dash of envy, and it forms a repetition of the Frankfurt School's sceptical view of modernity with its commercial development; it may also be a consequence of the attitude of many text-centred historians to material remains, which are researched by archaeologists and ethnologists. Even though it is not formulated directly, it is clear that this criticism adheres to familiar hierarchical fault lines between the elite and the people, high and low culture, the academy and the general public, education and entertainment, fact and fiction. A reaction against elitist criticism was presented as early as the 1990s (e.g. Samuel 1994: 259ff; also Wright 2009: xiiff); but it is still relevant, since the views live on.

The concept of the heritage industry, which is inspired by Horkheimer and Adorno's cultural industry, is intended to be derogatory; "industry" is supposed to evoke associations to something bad. Yet paradoxically, in his criticism of the heritage industry, Hewison is actually calling for more traditional industry. So when industry expanded into the cultural sphere in the 1940s, this was a bad thing; and later on, when there was deindustrialisation in the 1970s, that was bad too.

A compensatory linkage is generally claimed between the crisis and the emergence of or increase in history, memory, and heritage. Even so, the notion that there is a causal connection here has the character of a postulate. A temporal conjunction between different trends is pointed out without any further examination. Alternatively, selected examples are put forward as arguments or "evidence". But the arbitrary nature of the choice of examples and interpretations becomes apparent when the recovery of the *Mary Rose* was used by Wright as an example of a nationalist application of the past and a nostalgic backward glance in a period of decline for the UK. A sidelong glance reveals that the Swedish warship *Vasa* from the seventeenth century was raised in 1961 (www.vasamuseet. se), while the five Viking ships from Skuldelev in Denmark were raised in 1962 (www.vikingeskibsmuseet.dk) – in both cases at a point in time when modernity, industrialisation, and the economy were making advances in Scandinavia.

However, the connections between crisis, society, and heritage can be turned around. The postulated cause and effect can be made to change places. It is the increased interest in heritage that makes the critics perceive a crisis in society. The actual "crisis" is not modernity, the decline of modernity, or deindustrialisation, but the emergence and existence of what is derogatorily described as a heritage industry. Then, depending on which concrete phenomenon is being discussed, critics arrive at somewhat dissimilar explanations and crises.

For the critics generally have a problem with heritage. They offer an unfavourable account of their own present, in which heritage is expanding. Things were better before the 1990s, 1980s, 1970s, 1960s, 1950s or the First World War, before the spread of the commercial, the popular, and the material. It is not so much the increased interest in the past that is the problem; the trouble lies in the popular expressions of this interest and the focus applied at any one time. What arouses distaste is the new role of the museums as a mass medium, the bringing to life of a reconstructed past, the shift in emphasis from education to entertainment and consumption, from the elevated to the everyday, from texts to images and materiality, from the authentic to replicas, and from older periods to modernity, the present, and the future. It can also be noted that whereas museums are perceived as a sign of crisis, archives and libraries hardly ever are, even though they also protect and preserve remains of the past.

Clearly, then, the crisis stems not from society, but from heritage. And the criticism is nostalgic. The expansion of heritage has caused a nostalgic reaction among a large number of intellectuals. Thus the fierce and sometimes sarcastic criticism is itself a reaction to crisis.

Progress and musealisation

Decline and postmodernity are not the sole explanation of the rising interest in the past or the emergence of a heritage industry. On the contrary, the debate about museums and archaeology also features a widespread view that progress and modernisation are the very reason for it. The past is thought to possess greater significance in periods of development and economic growth. History, memory, and heritage are resources that are expected to be able to compensate for the unfavourable consequences of progress.

The need to compensate for progress has been expressed most clearly in Germany, where a compensation theory has spread from philosophy to other disciplines. The theory was first formulated by the philosopher Joachim Ritter, who led the seminar called "Collegium Philosophicum" in Münster and after whom the Ritter School was named. The theory was developed further by Ritter's pupils Odo Marquard and Hermann Lübbe. It sees progress, with its technical and economic developments, as either essential or desirable. But to attain balance in society, the harmful effects of progress must be limited.

Ritter discussed the same phenomena as C. P. Snow, namely science and the humanities (or literature) (cf. Snow 1959). But while Snow lectured about the gap between the analytical and explanatory natural sciences on the one hand and the interpretative and understanding of the humanities on the other, Ritter wanted to demonstrate their dependence on each other. He asserted that the humanities were established in the nineteenth century as an existential response to the natural sciences and modernisation. Abstraction, ahistoricity, and discontinuity, which were seen as characterising modern bourgeois industrial society, were compensated for by the *Bildung*, history, language, art, literature, and philosophy of the humanities. In more concrete terms, modernisation was said to banish the "historical" to the museums (Ritter 1961).

Extending Ritter's line of thought, the philosopher Odo Marquard took the view that the modern world lacks meaning. The alienation and destructive elements inherent in modernity need to be compensated for by traditions, narratives, museums, and preservation. The ahistoricity of natural science is compensated for by humanities scholarship, which re-enchants the world with its narratives. Museums provide a refuge for what has been crowded out by progress. So modernity has two sides: both a culture of progress and a compensatory culture of memory, increasing at the same pace. The more modernity, the greater the need for humanities scholarship. And the more modernity, the greater the number of museums. He also argued that the modern idea of progress and the first museums had arisen at the same time, shortly after 1750, and that the natural sciences were established before the humanities. The concepts of compensation and "Homo compensator" kept recurring in Marquard's philosophy (Marquard 1986: 98ff; 2000: 11ff, 30ff, 50ff).

Like Marquard, the philosopher and political scientist Hermann Lübbe discussed progress and its consequences in numerous articles and books. As a general thesis, he asserted that the constantly increasing speed of progress causes the present to "shrink". The destruction and alienation inherent in progress lead to a nostalgic yearning to escape. People turn to history and museums in order to regain familiarity with their present. The main function of the museum, and of preservation, is thus to compensate for the loss of familiarity and identity resulting from the exponential dynamic of innovation in society. This is a trend that, according to Lübbe, cannot continue forever (e.g. Lübbe 1982; 1983: 9ff; 1996; also Rosa 2005 (German); 2013 (English); 2012 (German)).

In his lecture *Der Fortschritt und das Museum* ("Progress and the Museum"), Lübbe discussed the role of progress for musealisation. Using statistics and examples from the then West Germany, he demonstrated how musealisation had increased dramatically during the twentieth century. Lübbe explained this trend on the basis of the museum's core task of salvaging what had been made redundant by progress. Progress has now become so rapid that all kinds of products lose their function ever more rapidly. Hence the quantity of relics fit for museums keeps growing. According to Lübbe, musealisation increases at the same accelerating tempo as modernisation so as to be able to compensate for the destruction. Something recognisable and familiar is needed for people's identity when everything else is in a state of rapid change (Lübbe 1982; cf. also Latour 1991 (French): 93f; 1993 (English): 69).

The role of museums in the development of society was recently discussed in a European research project called EUNAMUS, or European National Museums; while there is no reference to compensation theory, the word "balance" appears frequently. The project regards national museums, in their capacity of institutions, as "agents of change" and places where society can "negotiate" about changes. Museums use, or ought to use, culture to balance continuity and change, stability and dynamism. Museums thus have a role in creating social stability, where culture can work together with politics (Aronsson 2015; www.ep.liu.se/eunamus). The role of museums for establishing a balance is fully in line with the Ritter School.

This balance, however, may either be the project's demonstration of an actual function or – as is more likely – an attempt to formulate a topical and legitimate meaning for national museums in Europe; that is, a formula for both the present and the future.

The relationship between change and preservation is clear in archaeology when ancient monuments are excavated and documented in order to "salvage" the past. When a new settlement or a new industry, motorway, railway, or gas pipeline is to be constructed, the legislation may require archaeological investigations. Remains from the past that would otherwise have been destroyed are then examined and documented. In principle, this context may entail a correlation between the extent of modernisation and the archaeological work involved. The past is threatened and is then salvaged by an archaeology that is known by several names, such as rescue archaeology, salvage archaeology, contract archaeology, and commercial archaeology. But salvaging here means investigating, documenting, and removing, as the development of society has the highest priority (Rosén 2007).

Even so, the relationship between modernisation and archaeology is complicated. The existence and design of legislation regulating archaeology will vary between countries, just as there are differences with regard to how the legislation is applied in practice. Despite strong legislation, a balance will always be struck between different needs in each instance. Nor can a simple correlation be expected between economic cycles and the scale of excavations. In boom periods, archaeology may be extensive, since many new homes and industries are built at such times. But in a recession, archaeology may be extensive too, since the government chooses to invest in infrastructure to create employment – or even initiate archaeological investigations for the same reason.

The idea of salvaging ancient monuments under threat either by giving them protection or by moving them to a museum is an idea as old as archaeological and antiquarian practice; in Sweden, for instance, it can be traced back to the middle of the seventeenth century (Jensen 2002: 266ff, 325ff; 2004). The main argument for the operation at Abu Simbel and along the Nile in Nubia was precisely to save the past – it was a salvage operation (Desroches-Noblecourt & Gerster 1968; *The Salvage of the Abu Simbel Temples*, 1971; Säve-Söderbergh 1987; 1996).

In his eulogy at the start of the Nubian campaign in 1960, the French Minister of Culture André Malraux thus described the campaign as a way of overcoming death: "Il n'est qu'un acte sur lequel ne prévalent ni l'indifférence des constellations ni le murmure éternel des fleuves: c'est l'acte par lequel l'homme arrache quelque chose à la mort" (Malraux 1960 (French/English): 11; "there is only one action over which indifferent stars and unchanging, murmurous rivers have no sway; it is the action of a man who snatches something from the death" [*sic*]).

Salvage is a flexible concept, though. In his youth, the author Malraux had seen it as a salvage operation when, as a leader of an expedition, he unlawfully removed reliefs from the abandoned temple of Banteay-Srei at Angkor in Cambodia in 1923 – an act for which he was subsequently convicted (Greenfield 1996: 6, 282ff). The removal of the Parthenon frieze, the "Elgin Marbles", has also been described as a salvage operation since the sculptures might otherwise have been vandalised or destroyed by air pollution (Greenfield 1996: 63; Bring 2015: 90, 97f).

Eric Hobsbawm turned the concepts of renewal and tradition around in a creative manner by showing that changes can create traditions. As is seen from the anthology *The Invention of Tradition*, Hobsbawm took the view that traditions can be constructions. When rapid change in society weakens or destroys social patterns, newly formed traditions become a way of showing that part of the modern world is unchanged (Hobsbawm & Ranger 1983: 1ff; also Connerton 1989: 51f, 63f, 103). Invented ritual traditions are intended to create a feeling of continuity in the midst of discontinuity, irrespective of whether changes can be described as progress or as decline.

A compensation theory was formulated for the first time by the doctor and psychologist Alfred Adler (1908 (German); 2002 (English)): neurotic behaviour and the need to compensate, or even over-compensate, were due to inferiority complexes. Marquard, however, followed his own theory back to the theodicy problem; that is, the problem of being able to combine faith in an almighty God with the existence of evil. Just as God was said to compensate for the evil in the world, the humanities were able to compensate for modernity and natural science (Marquard 2000: 15ff). Others have, by contrast, viewed compensation theory as a political project.

With its combination of belief in both progress and tradition, the Ritter or Münster School has been characterised as a conservative political philosophy. The members of the group have been classed along with other liberal-conservative or culturally conservative intellectuals from the Cold War era who accepted modern technological civilisation, but observed unfortunate consequences that needed to be compensated for (cf. Hacke 2006). Critics linked to the Frankfurt School have even described it as neoconservative (Habermas 1985 (German): 86ff; 1990 (English): 69ff).

The view that change needs to be balanced by permanence, renewal by tradition, is characteristic of a conservative policy. But when a "neo" is added in a rhetorical manner, the idea is to mark distance, and it is intended as an insult. And it can be noted that critics inspired by the Frankfurt School join the Marxist Hobsbawm in applying compensation theory in their interpretations.

David Lowenthal, Patrick Wright, and Robert Hewison are against the decline in modernity, against postmodernity, and against the way in which the decline is compensated for. Joachim Ritter, Odo Marquard, and Hermann Lübbe accept both modern development and compensation. Points they have in common are that they all perceive an increase in history, memory, and heritage, and that they see it as a compensatory reaction. However, they have completely different views of the "crisis". And whether anything at all can be viewed as a crisis depends entirely on the perspective chosen.

However, the attaching of political labels to theories or debaters cannot determine if progress or decline, renewal or tradition, modernity or postmodernity are concepts of relevance for understanding and explaining the "heritage industry" and musealisation. Other strategies are needed: there is a need both to clarify the concepts used and to conduct a concrete examination of chronological sequences and geographical connections. How are the concepts related to one another? And can correlations be observed in time and space between changes and traditions, in this case between modernity and World Heritage? Does nostalgia thus arise in periods of radical change, irrespective of whether the changes are experienced as progress or as decline?

Chronic nostalgia

In the film *Nostalghia*, the poet Andrei Gorchakov wanders around in a Tuscany full of ruins and decaying buildings. He is pathologically affected by his longing for his family and home in Russia. But after a symbolic act, when he succeeds in carrying a lit candle across a mineral pool in Bagno Vignoni, redemption becomes possible, and he dies. In the last images of the film, Gorchakov is sitting in front of his Russian home, which is placed inside the ruins of the Italian Abbey of San Galgano. Gorchakov is finally at home in both worlds, at home both there and here (Tarkovsky 1983 film).

Nostalghia, directed by Andrei Tarkovsky, is one of many artistic works, films, novels, poems, musical works, and images that express yearning for what has disappeared. Tarkovsky depicted a bleak existence abroad at a time when he was himself entering exile. Nostalgia is about being cut off from a time and a place, often from a childhood home. And the longing is so strong that it becomes unhealthy.

The concept of nostalgia appears for the first time in a medical dissertation: *Dissertatio medica de Nostalgia, Oder Heimwehe* (*Medical Dissertation on Nostalgia*), by the physician Johannes Hofer (1688 (Latin); 1934 (English)). Here, the concept "nostalgia" – from the Greek words *nostos* and *algos*, meaning "journey home" and "pain" – is used as a new term for homesickness, that is, for a melancholy and pathological longing for home. Hofer used a Swiss mercenary who lived abroad as an example. And through the eighteenth and nineteenth centuries, nostalgia was used as a medical diagnosis, especially for soldiers longing to go home (Davis 1979: 1ff; Boym 2001: 3ff; Johannisson 2001: 15ff, 51ff; Fuentenebro de Diego & Valiente Ots 2014).

Gradually, the meaning of the nostalgia concept shifted from a lost place to a lost time. It was Immanuel Kant – in a revolutionary decade and at an advanced age – who was first to link homesickness not to a place but to a lost time. According to Kant, the homesickness of the Swiss soldier was to do with the notion of a carefree and sociable childhood, a longing for the simple joys of life, which could only be disappointed on a subsequent visit when everything had changed. For, as Kant noted, youth cannot be recreated (Kant 1798 (German): 87, § 24; 2006 (English): 71f, § 32). For his own part, Kant remained faithful to his native town, Königsberg (since 1946 Kaliningrad) in East Prussia. Kant stayed at home, without needing to travel, instead having the world come to his market town, a place that he found well suited to studies (Kant 1798 (German): viii note; 2006 (English): 4, note a).

The new interpretation of the concept of nostalgia has been explained by the emergence of a new view of time in around 1800. When an older, static, cyclical or cosmological view of time was replaced by a linear and secular view of time, the past was separated from the present and the future. And the past became desirable as the time lost forever (e.g. Boym 2001: 8ff; Johannisson 2001: 22f).

However, a shift from place to time in the meaning of the nostalgia concept is debatable. First, it is a simplification to say that time changed character from being pre-modern to being modern in around 1800. Views of time are dependent on the actual situation, so there can be several different time perspectives at the same time. Second, the time and place of nostalgia are not easily separated; that is, yearning *either* for a time *or* for a place. The Swiss soldier longed to go home – or longed for the time when he would be at home again. When elderly people are nostalgic, they long for a lost childhood country such as Finnish Karelia; German East Prussia; East Germany, as in "ostalgia"; or Yugoslavia in "yugo-nostalgia": it is to do with something that has disappeared in both time and space, both a lost epoch and a partly changed landscape. Something has become different and alien, while something else remains unchanged and familiar. In other words, nostalgia is a selective feeling.

With the nineteenth-century idea of progress and modernisation, nostalgia evolved into a general social diagnosis, an irrational feeling. Nostalgia became a sign of weakness in a person unable to adapt to the modern at a time when it was possible to travel by steamship and railway. A nostalgic became a derogatory term for a person who flees from the present and the modern, someone who dreams backwards in time (Lowenthal 1985: 4ff; 2015: 31ff; Boym 2001: 16ff; Johannisson 2001: 127ff).

In the critical tradition of heritage, nostalgia is a derogatory term for people's interest in the past, and calling someone a nostalgic is insulting. Being preoccupied with the past becomes a symptom and a social diagnosis. As Lowenthal writes, "no term better expresses modern malaise" (Lowenthal 1985: xxiv, 4 quotation, 4ff; 1997: 1, 5ff, 88ff; 2015: 31ff). In line with this, I myself previously formulated the ambiguous term "chronic nostalgia" to characterise an unhealthy and painful yearning for remains of the past (Wienberg 1999: 184ff; also Boym 2001: 290).

In *The Future of Nostalgia*, the literary historian and artist Svetlana Boym expressed the view that the present is characterised by a "global epidemic of nostalgia" (Boym 2001: xiv). Boym's diagnosis was quoted two decades later by the productive sociologist Zygmunt Bauman in his final and somewhat disillusioned book *Retrotopia* (2017: 4 quotation). Bauman regretted the nostalgia of his time and its inability to construct utopias for the future.

The choice of the term nostalgia is no accident. Rhetorically, nostalgia is intended to bring trauma, disease, weakness, and sentimentality to mind; the implication being that a strong and healthy person has no need of nostalgia. Paradoxically, though, the critical tradition of heritage uses modernity's view of nostalgia as a social diagnosis at the same time as it is apt to reject modernity as an ideal.

Nostalgia improves and embellishes the past. Things were not as pleasant in the Stone Age, the Viking Age, the Middle Ages, before the First World War, or in the 1950s as people imagine. The good old times were not as good as people like to think. Probably few people would like to swap a life today for a life in an earlier epoch – or only providing they were allowed to keep their life expectancy, doctor, dentist, washing machine, and smartphone.

But nostalgia can be a force for good. Nostalgia may be a resource that is activated in order to deal with existential threats, destruction, and death. Nostalgia is important for the individual's identity and meaning when facing discontinuities; that is, in phases of radical change (Sedikides *et al.* 2004).

In *Yearning for Yesterday* (1979), the sociologist Fred Davis described his American present as an "orgy of nostalgia" with Disneyland as a "nostalgia industry". He regarded this nostalgia as a reaction to the social and political turbulence of the 1960s. However, despite his choice of term, Davis saw nostalgia as something both useful and essential. This was because, in his view, nostalgia provided relief in the transition between phases of life and in periods of change characterised by anxiety, worry, and uncertainty. Nostalgia contributes to the creation of a collective identity for generations that need to come to terms with political murders, war, depression, and natural disasters. In a modern society characterised by constant change and increasing speed, in which identities are threatened by discontinuity, nostalgia may contribute to a re-enchantment of the world. Nostalgia filters, selects, arranges, constructs, and reconstructs the past. It is the capacity of nostalgia to find an attractive past, its freedom from pain, that makes recovery possible (Davis 1979: 31ff, 97ff, 118ff).

Nostalgia may also be an expression of active opposition to developments. With the dominance of West Germany and a rapid deindustrialisation, "ostalgia" is a conscious re-selection of the old East Germany and its way of life and goods (Berdahl 1999).

Nostalgia is a way of choosing an elevating perspective on both past and present, the good and the beautiful ranking more highly than the true. The therapeutic – and thus healing – capacity of nostalgia derives precisely from its selective memory. As aptly put by the journalist Herb(ert) Caen, "Nostalgia is memory with the pain removed" (Davis 1979: 37). Consequently, nostalgia can mean returning home both with and without the concept's suffix of pain, both with and without *algos*.

Pierre Boulez took the view that a conservative, preserving civilisation is a civilisation in decline (Boulez 1976: 32f). And Lowenthal asserted in *The Past is a Foreign Country* that a society will preserve when it is incapable of making creative use of the past (Lowenthal 1985: xxiv, 384, 406; 2015: 413). But with the aid of specific examples of radical changes, it is possible to show that preservation and creativity are not mutually contradictory, and that the yearning inherent in nostalgia is not sufficient to understand and explain a greater interest in the past.

The French Revolution of 1789 and the subsequent wars up until the Battle of Waterloo in 1815 have been identified as being of crucial importance for the emergence of a modern historical awareness, with museums, monuments, memorials, historicising styles of architecture, and historical novels. For instance, the historian Peter Fritzsche asserted in *Stranded in the Present* (2004) that the nostalgia of Romanticism arose in the wake of the revolution and the wars, which created a dramatic discontinuity and mobility in both Europe and America. History offered the only possible escape from the present. Drawing on examples from literature, letters, diaries, and memoirs, Fritzsche showed how the past became associated with feelings of loss and melancholy. Ruins were transformed from manifestations of nature and impermanence to evidence of the greatness of the past in a nascent nationalism. The past was separated from the present and therefore became an object of study worth protecting and preserving.

The French Revolution itself became the archetype of radical social change. It started in 1789 with the capture and demolition of the Bastille in Paris. In that same year, a decision was made to confiscate Church property. This was followed by wave upon wave of destruction of symbols representing the old regime – quickly followed by decrees forbidding this destruction. As early as 1790, the new concept of "historic monument" (*monument historique*) was used about palaces, churches, and abbeys; and church art was gathered in a depot in the Petits-Augustins Convent, while other objects went to the Palais du Louvre, a royal residence that was converted into the Musée Central des Arts in 1793. Then, in 1794, the rhetorical word "vandalism" was used to prevent further devastation at the same time as a term was established for what was to be protected, *un héritage commun*, a common heritage. And in 1795 the depot was converted into a museum for fragments of architecture and sculpture, the Musée des Monuments Français ("Museum of French Monuments"). But when the monarchy was restored in 1815, the museum was closed and church property was returned (Choay 1992 (French): 76ff; 2001 (English): 63ff; Poulot 1995; 1997; Gamboni 1997: 31ff, 329ff; also Arrhenius 2003: 51ff, 161ff; 2012: 14ff, 138ff; Schildgen 2008: 121ff).

Another example of how radical change was followed by a new museum can be found in Copenhagen of the same period. There, the Oldnordisk Museum, the Old Nordic Museum (from 1892 the National Museum of Denmark), was founded in 1807 as a reaction to Denmark's defeat in the Napoleonic Wars, the theft of the Golden Horns, the bombardment of Copenhagen, and the loss of the fleet, developments that culminated in state bankruptcy in 1813. The idea was that the past would strengthen the absolute monarchy and national identity in a time of crisis (Kristiansen 1981: 22; 1989 (Danish): 207; 1993 (English): 23).

But the museums founded after the upheavals in Paris and Copenhagen were not nostalgic; they showed no longing for the past. On the contrary, they transformed the past into something new and useful in the present. For instance, the nationalised buildings in Paris that had not been destroyed could be given new functions, while other symbols of the monarchy and Church could be transferred to museums and be given a national and secular importance there as both sources and art. In other words, destruction and preservation can be two sides of a process in which the past is invested with new meanings (Choay 1992 (French): 76ff; 2001 (English): 63ff; Poulot 1995; 1997; Gamboni 1997: 31ff, 329ff; also Arrhenius 2003: 51ff, 161ff; 2012: 14ff, 138ff).

Historicising architecture displays the same tendency. On the face of it, the neo-Gothic style, which became popular from the 1820s, may appear to be yet another example of a nostalgic and romantic retrospective, modelled on the Middle Ages in this case (Clark 1928). But historicising style is not a Romantic invention from the nineteenth century. Both medieval Romanesque architecture and Renaissance architecture had ancient Rome as a model, while the ideal of Neoclassicism from the middle of the eighteenth century was Ancient Greece. And while neo-Gothicism, which imitated the medieval Gothic style, was indeed widespread in the nineteenth century, it had begun back in the middle of the eighteenth century (cf. Clark 1928).

Style was chosen with attention to different functions; the Italian Renaissance style was hence deemed suitable for palatial new bank offices. And historical forms were combined with the most modern technology for specific needs, Romanticism being integrated with modernity. For instance, the architect Helgo Zettervall used iron and concrete in his restorations of medieval cathedrals in Sweden, but the new materials remained hidden from view. A roof structure of iron from the 1870s lies concealed above the vaults of Lund Cathedral, invisible to visitors (Weibull 1953: 88). As a style, neo-Gothic was thus more Gothic than medieval Gothic had ever been.

In the meeting between past and present, something new is created. Developments after the French Revolution may be taken as examples: museums and monuments transformed political propaganda into sources or art; neo-Gothic combined old forms with new technology; and historical novels used the past in order to shed light on topical issues.

Nostalgia's way of reusing selected portions of the past may be reminiscent of "creative anachronism", within whose framework the European Middle Ages and Renaissance are explored and brought to life and in which the focus is on experiences and narratives, not on traditional authenticity. Past and present are deliberately mixed as a method (e.g. www.sca.org; Petersson 2017). And nostalgia can be compared with the use made by the Middle Ages of *spolia*; that is, the reuse of selected older, generally ancient, building components in medieval buildings.

Spolia from different buildings were recycled in new contexts and given new meanings, generally as part of a political or religious process of legitimation. *Spolia* evinced both breaks and continuity with the past – breaks through their fragmentation and continuity through renewed use (Fabricius Hansen 2003). One well-known example is the palace chapel of Charlemagne at Aachen (WHL 3bis, 1978, 2013), to which ideas, architectural forms, marble, columns, and sculptures were brought from both Ravenna and Rome so as to create a manifestation of the power of the emperor, pointing both backward to tradition and forward to something new (Fabricius Hansen 2003: 157ff; Tekippe 2004).

A newer example is when the balcony of the Berlin City Palace (Berliner Stadtschloss), from which Karl Liebknecht had declared the formation of the Free Socialist German Republic in 1918, was incorporated in the State Council Building (Staatsratsgebäude) in East Berlin in 1963. The City Palace, which was blown up as a Prussian symbol in 1950, has been under reconstruction since 2013 (www.historisches-stadtschloss.de). Three of four facades are being reconstructed, but the fourth is completely new, as is everything inside. That, then, is a modern example of historicising architecture that combines old and new, but without suggesting any nostalgic yearning for imperial Germany. The building will also have a new name – the Humboldt Forum (www.humboldtforum.com).

The French Revolution began a period of radical changes, but it is by no means the only revolution. In a global perspective, there are many other well-known political, economic, social, religious, technological, and scientific revolutions, just as there have been notable counter-revolutions and radical changes that have not been classed as revolutions. And revolutions and other upheavals do not necessarily generate nostalgic feelings.

Nostalgia's longing for a different time or place does not need to arise if the change or break brings liberation. If the past or the place one came from was painful, there is no point in missing it; and if the development or relocation is experienced as progress, there is no loss involved and nothing to compensate for.

Hence, nostalgia does not suffice to understand and explain the multifaceted relationship of the present to the past. Nostalgia becomes attached to the beautiful perspective with its therapeutic narratives. But historical consciousness, museums, monuments, architecture, and novels are about things other and more than beauty, and the same applies to tourism. Enlightenment knowledge and the ethical demand constitute motives, too, particularly in the emergence of museums and canonisation of monuments.

When Fritzsche wrote that history was the only possible escape in a turbulent present (Fritzsche 2004: 10), he was not convincing. First, people could physically escape to other places, that is emigrate, as many were forced to do during the French Revolution, a point that Fritzsche himself noted (Fritzsche 2004: 33ff). Second, people could move in their imagination, not only to the past but also to fictional places in the present or the future. Today, many are able – provided they have the necessary resources (passport, visa, and money) – to travel in both time and space, both in reality and in their imagination. But not all journeys are nostalgic or involve an escape. At the same time, more people than ever before are forced to flee on account of war, poverty, and oppression.

When tourists travel to Abu Simbel, this has nothing to do with nostalgia, with an unhealthy or socially determined longing for a distant age; it has to do with an enchanted place. The Egypt of the pharaohs is a foreign time in a foreign country. Here the attraction is the meeting with what is different, with the exotic. Tourism permits a temporary move to another place that may surprise, instruct, attract, and provide food for thought.

Amelia B. Edwards thus described how she felt that time stood still at Abu Simbel, how time could be traversed:

> It is a wonderful place to be alone in – a place in which the very darkness and silence are old, and in which Time himself seems to have fallen asleep. Wandering to and fro among these sculptured halls, like a shade among shadows, one seems to have left the world behind; to have done with the teachings of the present; to belong one's self to the past. (Edwards 1877: 444f)

Secularisation and immortality

The Heritage Crusade and the Spoils of History (1997) is David Lowenthal's follow-up to *The Past is a Foreign Country* (1985). In the new book, Lowenthal described heritage as a popular faith and a secular religion, just as heritage institutions were compared with the Church. Lowenthal compared the expansion of heritage with a medieval crusade, at the same time as the book itself was a crusade against the spread of heritage at the expense of history (Lowenthal 1997: 1f). Lowenthal is, however, by no means alone in comparing the handling of history, memory, and heritage to expressions of religion.

Another example is the political scientist Donald Horne, whose book *The Great Museum: The Re-Presentation of History* (1984) presents a critical, ironic, and moralising account of heritage tourism in Europe. Horne compares modern museums, exhibition objects, and tourists to medieval churches, relics, and pilgrims. Modern souvenirs and postcards are like medieval pilgrim badges. Photography has replaced participation in Mass. Graves of and monuments to national heroes are worshipped with rituals and devoutness as if they were secular saints. One example is Vladimir Lenin in the Lenin Mausoleum in Moscow, part – since 1990 – of World Heritage along with the Kremlin and the Red Square (WHL 545, 1990). Horne found the background to heritage tourism in industrialism and modernity. For him, those two phenomena had created a crisis in and nervousness about the perception of reality, a state that could be diverted in a hunt for the authentic. The pilgrimage to the past thus becomes an escape from the disturbances of industrial society (Horne 1984: 1ff, 21ff).

Many other commentators have compared museums with temples or churches, the objects exhibited with relics, museum staff with priests, monuments with sacred reliquaries, tourists with pilgrims, and mass cultural tourism with a World Church and history in general with a religion (e.g. MacCannell 1976: 42ff; Choay 1992 (French): 101ff, 128f, 159ff, 186; 2001 (English): 87ff, 111f, 139ff, 163); Beckman 1993a: 31f; 1998: 32ff; Duncan 1995: 7ff; Hylland Eriksen 1996: 85.

What is common to Lowenthal, Horne, and others who have compared heritage and museums with a religion is that the analogy is meant to be a pejorative one. As researchers and authors in a secular age, they are making comparisons with something assumed to arouse unfavourable connotations. If we step back to a time when the Church still had a central religious and ideological role in the West, we find the same analogy in use, but at that time its connotations were favourable, the analogy being employed as an argument for heritage and museums. The analogy is thus used not for analysis, understanding, or explanation, but as a rhetorical argument adapted to the expectations and values of the time.

When, in 1806, the philologist Rasmus Nyerup drew inspiration from the Museum of French Monuments in Paris to argue for the foundation of a new national museum in Denmark – a museum that was initially called the Old Nordic Museum – he was hence able to describe it both as an "asylum for the otherwise increasingly disappearing old national memorials" and as "a temple for the remains of the spirit, and the language, art, and power of the past" (Nyerup 1806: VIII).

Finally, mention may be made of the art historian Alois Riegl, whose *Der moderne Denkmalkultus, sein Wesen und seine Entstehung* ("The Modern Cult of Monuments: Its Character and Its Origin") reported the emergence in the nineteenth century of a cult, the worship of historical memorials, that had elements in common with a religious experience (Riegl 1903 (German): 18; 1929 (German): 157; 1982 (English): 29).

The analogy extends further, as is sometimes seen from the location and architecture of museums. New museums might be given a central place in the townscape, a location reminiscent of the place of the cathedral. Museums were located in or alongside the halls of power. The Old Nordic Museum in Copenhagen was located first in, and then close to, the royal palace of Christiansborg, which is now the Danish Parliament, just as the Museum Island in Berlin (WHL 896, 1999) is beside the cathedral and royal palace. Museums could also take over buildings from which power had previously been exercised, such as the Louvre in Paris (WHL 600,

1991; www.louvre.fr) and the Forbidden City in Beijing (WHL 439bis, 2004). And the architecture of a museum might assume the shape of a classical temple, such as the British Museum (www. britishmuseum.org), or of a medieval cathedral, for instance the Natural History Museum (www.nhm.ac.uk), both in London.

It can be concluded that the analogy between heritage and museums on the one hand and religion and churches on the other is, first and foremost, a rhetorical strategy, the meaning of the analogy varying with the context. Next, a subtext can be sensed in the sharp criticism of the expansion of heritage. It is a subtext about historians wanting to defend their field of research, regarding a focus on textual analysis and on critical use as a matter of greater importance than materiality and experiences. Similarly, an elitist perspective may be discerned behind the harsh criticism of mass tourism, a criticism that contains poorly concealed contempt for the popular and for mass travel. The problem is the social context and the intrusive quantity. There is certainly prestige in travelling along the trails of the peregrinations, or Grand Tours, of the past, but not in travelling like the great majority of people: nothing against a visit to Venice, but not as one of millions of tourists each year. A distance from the common folk is called for.

During the period when some critics used the analogy between heritage and religion as derogatory rhetoric, others actually wanted to see a linkage that was not fortuitous. The idea is that a gradual secularisation, or religion becoming less important, caused a greater need for heritage. The decline in faith in God owing to secularisation needs to be compensated for. An apparently constant need for community, meaning, and security means that an older religious narrative is replaced by a new one, woven around the nation and the history of the people. History, memory, and heritage are linked up with a nationalised past.

The demographer and historian Philippe Ariès, who was associated with the French Annales School, did not discuss the emergence of heritage, monuments, and museums in his *Western Attitudes toward Death*. With a broad brush, however, he outlined a connection between Romanticism's cult of the grave and worship of the nation's dead heroes. In Ariès's view, this striving for immortality emerged from the end of the eighteenth century onwards along with secularisation, industrialisation, and urbanisation (Ariès 1974: 55ff).

In *Mortality, Immortality and Other Life Strategies* (1992), Zygmunt Bauman asserted that human beings are defined by their awareness of death. Fear of death and the endeavour to achieve immortality are fundamental to human existence. In order to master their mortality, human beings try to ensure a continuation of life beyond physical death. Christianity and several other religions promise an eternal life. With modernity, human beings must instead seek a place in the memory of their survivors. Individual historical immortality was the prerogative of an elite, small in number, while the masses had to make do with immortality as a collective, as the people of the nation.

As an extension of Ariès and Bauman, the archaeologist Ola W. Jensen has shown in concrete terms how this striving after immortality for the nation's dead was manifested in a cult linked to graves, statues, monuments, and museums. Heritage became a material expression of the soul of the nation. The preservation of heritage therefore had an existential explanation (e.g. Jensen 1998; also Grundberg 2004: 13).

Death as a threat and the striving after immortality have a central role in myths, religion, psychology, and philosophy. Death, or the awareness of death, is something that needs to be overcome or compensated for. The hero tries to combat or outwit death.

King Sisyphus was punished precisely for having tried to overcome death. To obtain water for his palace in Corinth, Sisyphus had told Asopos, the river god, that Zeus had kidnapped his daughter Aegina. Zeus then sent Thanatos, the god of death, to chain Sisyphus in the underworld; but Sisyphus managed to imprison Death. Thanatos was subsequently freed by Ares, the god of war, who was annoyed that no warriors died. Sisyphus ended up with Hades in the land of the dead; but when he was allowed to visit the earth and his wife, he did not return. Sisyphus was then collected by Hermes. He would only be set free again if he succeeded in rolling a great stone up a hill, but the stone always rolled all the way back down again. His effort was in vain (cf. Camus 1942 (French): 163ff; 2005 (English): 107ff).

In philosophy, death may be identified as being essential to human beings. In *Sein und Zeit* (*Being and Time*) by the philosopher Martin Heidegger, death was thus obscurely described as an existential condition that constitutes the wholeness of life. Life was characterised both by a flight from death and by a constant decline until death. The threat of individual death with its loneliness and emptiness evokes a fundamental anxiety (Heidegger 1927 (German): §§46–53: 235ff; 1996 (English): §§46–53: 219ff).

Cognitive research also holds that human beings are unique in being aware of their own mortality. The dream of eternal life is therefore something distinctive only of human beings; and so is reflection, in a spirit of wonder, about the meaning of life (Gärdenfors 2006: 33ff).

In *Das Unbehagen in der Kultur* (*Civilization and its Discontents*), physician and psychologist Sigmund Freud held that human beings possess two fundamental drives that are both restricted by civilisation: on the one hand an erotic and creative drive and on the other the destructive death drive. However, suppression of the death drive and aggression leads to neuroses, guilt feelings, angst, and discomfort (Freud 1930 (German): 89ff; 2004 (English): 68ff).

In a reinterpretation of psychoanalysis in his *Life against Death*, the historian Norman O. Brown asserted that human beings are imprisoned by the past, just as hysterical patients cannot break free from the past. In his view, the bond of all cultures to heritage is neurotic. And the background to the human preoccupation with the past (and the future) is a fundamental fear of death, which separates human beings from animals. Civilisation and monuments are attempts to overcome death, to create immortality. Brown's purpose was to free human beings from the burden of history, the dead hand of the past (Brown 1959: 11ff, 87ff, 283ff).

Inspired by the psychoanalysis of Adler and Freud, but with a more encouraging approach, the psychologist Rollo May interpreted artistic and scientific creativity in *The Courage to Create* as a reaction to human mortality; that is, as a rebellion against death or the gods. The creative person is a rebel in his or her longing for immortality (May 1975: 25ff, 36ff).

We can only accept that death may play a central role, that death anxiety can occur, and that people can daydream about immortality, but not always and everywhere. Depicting life as a journey towards death, and creativity as a question of compensation and neuroses, is reductive. Freud asserted both a life drive and a death drive, both Eros and Thanatos. Consequently, death is not everything in life, even though death has the last word for each individual.

History, memory, and culture do, of course, have several motives, values, and potential uses. The past has multiple meanings, meanings that reach beyond a reductive and compensatory mechanics.

To be specific, gradual secularisation may be questioned as an explanation of death anxiety and the striving after immortality, or of cults based on graves, statues, monuments, museums, and heritage.

For these phenomena are not new, and they are found across cultural and religious borders. This once again brings to mind the temples of Ramses II at Abu Simbel more than 3200 years ago.

Materialised memories

The temples at Abu Simbel are striking monuments. Their dating is certain – around 1260 BCE. And their originator is well known: the Egyptian Pharaoh Ramses II, also called the Great (e.g. MacQuitty 1965; Desroches Noblecourt 2007: 116ff). But why were they erected?

Monuments are an attempt to lay down enduring memories that are readily visible and generally "monumental", that is, of an imposing size; they are intended to make an impression. But the key point about a monument is precisely the memory, as indicated by the word itself. "Monument" comes from the Latin words *monumentum/monere*, meaning to remind or exhort. But remembering may assume many forms – thinking, carrying out ritual acts, or using aids such as images and script. To create a monument is to give memories material form. And to ensure the permanence of the monument, preferably for an envisaged eternity, it is often created in durable materials such as earth, stone, or metal.

The temples at Abu Simbel are typical monuments: they are monumental and materialised in stone, carved directly out of the sandstone cliffs. And the temples mediate narratives about the past by means of hieroglyphs, painted images, and sculptures.

Dolmens, barrows, pyramids, temples, menhirs, runic stones, and churches have attracted attention by virtue of their visibility in the landscape. They also form starting points for mythical popular tales about gods, giants, and powerful individuals (cf. Burström *et al.* 1997; Gazin-Schwartz & Holtorf 1999). Then, when archaeology emerged as a method and a scholarly discipline, the monuments in the landscape became a source of knowledge for all to see. And the collective term is precisely "monument" – the monumental.

There has been a great deal of research about materialised memories since the transformation of Eastern Europe and the USSR as of 1989, which was followed by extensive iconoclasm; but the research started earlier. In theoretical terms, there has been an interest in collective memories; that is, how groups in a society or a nation create and maintain common memories (cf. Halbwachs 1992). Specifically, there has been an interest in surveying and describing national memorials from the nineteenth and twentieth centuries. The research has been carried out by ethnologists and historians and the collective term has generally been "memorial", the marking of a memory (e.g. Gillis 1994; Frykman & Ehn 2007; Adriansen 2010).

As terms, "monument" and "memorial" have essentially the same origin and meaning, and they are often used in a somewhat haphazard manner. However, the choice of term may be seen to define two distinct discourses. On the one hand, archaeologists have studied prehistoric and ancient monuments; on the other, historians and ethnologists have studied historical memorials. The history of art has taken an interest in both monuments and memorials, applying an aesthetic perspective. And with a long-term perspective, a few archaeologists have also gone beyond the chronology of the discourses (e.g. Holtorf 1997; Wienberg 2007: 241).

The anthropologist Claude Lévi-Strauss divided societies into two universal and contrasting types: "cold" primitive societies and "hot" modern ones. Cold societies were also called mechanical and were compared with clockwork, whereas hot modern societies were referred to as thermodynamic and compared with steam engines. Primitive societies remained in their original state, but they were egalitarian and in harmony with themselves and nature. Their social order was maintained with the aid of tradition. The "wisdom" of primitive societies excludes history, and they therefore seem to be ahistorical. But the primitive societies that Lévi-Strauss was thinking of were societies of hunters and gatherers that were thought to be under threat in his time, and that he clearly idealised. Warm, modern, or civilised societies came into being as a result of the introduction of agriculture; they are dynamic and therefore in imbalance. Modern societies such as the Mediterranean city states or the industrialised states of the nineteenth century extract energy from social differences. That causes disorder or entropy between people, but recreates order as culture. According to Lévi-Strauss, modern societies make slaves of people in order to create progress; and they use history as a motor in their development (Charbonnier 1961 (French): 37ff; 1969 (English): 32ff; Lévi-Strauss 1966: 121f).

Ramses II's Egypt could be characterised as a hot and civilised agricultural society to whose development social differences and history contributed. In its simple form, however, the dichotomy does not lead to greater understanding or a better explanation of the pharaoh's constructional zeal.

The notion of the "primitive society" had a fundamental position in anthropology for a long time. But the classification made by Claude Lévi-Strauss and others into primitive societies and civilisations, cold and hot societies, can be characterised as an illusion bound up with evolutionism and colonialism. The primitive cold society has never existed as an initial state; it was a consequence of colonisation. The primitive and apparently ahistorical societies made up the periphery of a world system in which only the centre was in possession of civilisation and history. The primitive society was constructed as the "other", as an antithesis or an inverted mirror image of the anthropologists' own modern Western society (Kuper 1988; Friedman 1994: 4f, 23f).

The idea that there is a linkage between power and monuments is not new. Ibn Khaldûn thus took the view that monuments – large construction works – were proportionate to the original power of a dynasty. Consequently, the monument was intended to demonstrate the strength of a dynasty (Khaldûn 1958: vol. 1, Chapter III, §16, pp. 356f).

At the same time as criticism of the (ab)use of the past appeared in the 1970s, concepts such as power, manipulation, and legitimation also became central to archaeology's interpretation of the past. The purpose of building monuments was thus to show and legitimise power – just as monuments were used to legitimise social and mental changes (Trigger 1990: 124ff). Monuments were then linked either to the establishment and consolidation of new elites and ideas or to a situation in which established elites and ideas were being challenged.

The erection of monuments has also more generally been linked to periods of crisis. A society under stress or in imbalance, threatened from within or without, would therefore be characterised by megalomaniac building. The monuments were precisely monumental, large and if possible enduring, so as to influence the landscape and memory for a long time to come; and they became connected to collective rituals. The monuments were intended to counter or conceal conflicts. From such a perspective, monuments do not testify to power and pride; rather, they should be viewed in relation to attempts at compensation when a collapse seems imminent. The monuments were intended as material communication, the use of signs increasing in periods of "social stress". The greater the monuments, the greater the desperation; or the more monuments, the closer the society is to collapse (e.g. Gren 1994). But just as the popularity of heritage may be used to postulate a crisis, the very existence of monuments can make archaeologists and others assert the existence of a crisis. Cause and effect may be turned around again.

The French project *Les Lieux de mémoire* (*Realms of Memory*), led by the historian Pierre Nora, has had a great influence on the study of memorials. In an introduction entitled "Entre mémoire et histoire" ("Between Memory and History"), Nora differentiated between memory and history, and he asserted that sites of memory are put in place when memory is threatened. The term "sites of memory" is used broadly about museums, archives, churches, anniversaries, memorials, and other entities intended to stop time and immortalise. The living and genuine memory or tradition is replaced by a constructed history – a development characterised as a secularisation. The sites of memory are thus seen as being linked to modernity, which breeds oblivion and where a break with the past is the prerequisite for nostalgia. Nora saw loss and oblivion when industrialisation brought about the disappearance of agrarian culture at the end of the nineteenth century (Nora 1984 (French); 1989 (English); 1996 (English)).

The temples of Abu Simbel were undoubtedly a manifestation of power. But when the temples were constructed, Ramses II was not actually a pharaoh who needed to legitimise his power. He had ruled for around 30 years, was the third pharaoh of the 19th Dynasty, and was himself the son of a pharaoh. Nor was he threatened by outer or inner enemies; a peace treaty had been concluded with the Hittite Empire at the time of the construction of the temples. It is hard to postulate a situation of "social stress", secularisation, or modernity, and there was no threat of collapse. The temples were constructed at the border to Nubia, so it can be claimed that there was a need to mark power and legitimacy in relation to potentially hostile neighbours. At the same time, however, Ramses II had numerous other construction works built along the Nile, far from the border. Still, the temples can certainly be described as sites of memory, since they were full of accounts of events during Ramses' reign.

With the turn in archaeology away from social and economic explanations to symbolism and cosmology, monuments have been interpreted in new ways. Monuments are nowadays related to cosmological ideas about time and space. The importance of rituals is stressed, as is the fact that monuments were constantly being reshaped according to new needs (e.g. Bradley 1993).

Cosmology is also relevant to a discussion of Abu Simbel. The great temple with its four colossal statues presents Ramses II as the ruler of both Upper and Lower Egypt and as the gods Re-en-Hekau, Heka-Taw, Mery-Amun, and Mery-Atum (Desroches-Noblecourt

& Gerster 1968: 19f). Politics and ritual were combined in the pharaoh.

Was Abu Simbel an expression of nostalgia, a yearning for a lost age? No; Ramses II was not likely to think with nostalgia of the Battle of Kadesh, which was depicted in the interior of the great temple. But a visitor will soon discover that the battle is represented as a great victory for the warrior pharaoh, which is not in fact correct. The battle ended as a kind of draw. The Egyptians had to withdraw, and a peace treaty was concluded later on (cf. MacQuitty 1965: 107ff; Desroches Noblecourt 2007: 60ff, 153ff). Abu Simbel as a monument thus had the purpose of mediating a doctored memory, "alternative facts" – or, put more clearly, a propaganda lie. The monument was intended to manipulate the visitor.

Abu Simbel is not about secularisation, and nor is it about fear of death. Even so, the centrality of death was a characteristic of Ancient Egypt. It was crucial to enter the land of the dead in the right way, to embalm the body, to provide the necessary possessions, and to take effective measures against grave plunderers. Here the word "stress" may well be used. But Abu Simbel was not a burial site. Ramses II was buried further down the Nile in the Valley of the Kings, where the burial chamber was subject to flooding, and his mummy was moved several times before it could finally be exhibited in Cairo.

A feature shared by both monuments and memorials is that, without recurrent rituals that can keep the memory alive, they soon become places of oblivion (e.g. Connerton 1989). Irrespective of whether the purpose is to remember, legitimise, or manipulate, the original message is soon forgotten. In spite of their durable materials, monuments and memorials change, are reinterpreted, or fall into decay. As the author Robert Musil puts it in the essay "Denkmale": "Es gibt nichts auf der Welt, was so unsichtbar wäre wie Denkmäler" ("There is nothing in this world as invisible as a monument") (Musil 1936 (German): 87; 2006 (English): 64). And as a closing reply to the question why memorials are then raised to commemorate great men, Musil wrote: "Es scheint eine ganz ausgesuchte Bosheit zu sein. Da man ihnen im Leben nicht mehr schaden kann, stürzt man sie gleichsam mit einem Gedenkstein um den Hals, ins Meer des Vergessens" ("This seems to be a carefully calculated insult. Since we can do them no more harm in life, we thrust them with a memorial stone hung around their neck into the sea of oblivion") (Musil 1936 (German): 92f; 2006 (English): 68).

From this, it is no great leap to assert that the real function of a monument and memorial is to allow us to forget. The monument and memorial can relieve traumatic memories. And if forgetting was not the explicit purpose, it was the unintended consequence (e.g. Rowlands 1999).

Every monument or memorial therefore comes into conflict with its own paradoxical capacity to foster forgetting. New forms for creating permanence are constantly being tested. One such example is the Holocaust monument "Denkmal für die ermordeten Juden Europas" ("Memorial to the Murdered Jews of Europe") in central Berlin, based on a drawing by the architect Peter Eisenman and inaugurated in 2005. With its 2177 concrete blocks of varying sizes and an associated underground information centre, the monument is not easy to ignore. A completely different example is the artist Gunter Demnig's *Stolpersteine* ("stumbling stones"), which are intended to be reminders of individual victims of the Holocaust in the pavement in front of their last address (www.stolpersteine.eu).

Ramses II's intention in constructing the temples of Abu Simbel was not that he and his achievements should be forgotten; quite the contrary. However, Abu Simbel was damaged in an earthquake just a few years after its inauguration. The head of one of the colossal figures at the great temple fell off. The constantly shifting sands gradually covered the front of the temples, and their stories about Ramses II and the Battle of Kadesh were forgotten. To be sure, the temples remained visible and familiar to local people, but their entrances sanded up so that their interior became inaccessible. The temples were only reopened when they were discovered by European adventurers, Johann Ludwig Burckhardt and Giovanni Battista Belzoni, early in the nineteenth century.

But here, again, Ramses II and his temples at Abu Simbel depart from expectations. For Ramses II actually did succeed in maintaining the memory of himself as a great pharaoh. His mummy is preserved in Cairo. The temples have been given a new function as a tourist destination and World Heritage site. The temples with their texts, images, and sculptures are mediated in numerous ways – through visits to the site or in reconstructions, in books and films, and on the Internet.

Sisyphus has been mentioned several times, and he will be mentioned again. The stone he is rolling may be viewed as a metaphor for the attempt to establish a memory, to place a memory stone at the top of the hill – something that constantly fails, with Ramses II as a rare exception. However, Sisyphus rolling a stone in vain may also bring to mind the many attempts made to understand and explain heritage. New perspectives, interpretations, and examples are constantly thrown into the discussion; but every single time, there is something that does not add up. The interpretative models so far have either encompassed internal contradictions, or Abu Simbel and other examples have not fitted them.

Community and meaning

It is easy to be overwhelmed, confused, or surprised in the face of the multiplicity of views, perspectives, arguments, and examples that characterise the debate about history, memory, and heritage. Conflicting positions are often uncompromising and uncomprehending about one another. But it is possible to detect (or construct) patterns in the debate that make the different positions comprehensible.

This multiplicity can be divided into two sides on the basis of the two cultures of heritage. On one side is the canonical tradition that perceives heritage as a resource to protect, preserve, document, and mediate. On the other side is the critical tradition that sees heritage as something to redefine, an obstacle, something that should be limited and, if possible, overcome. Where the canonical tradition perceives possibilities for development, the critical tradition sees symptoms of crisis and needs for compensation. The marked contrast between the positions may be an expression of different social discourses that may themselves be rooted in education and employment – "antiquarians" with the task of managing the heritage and "critics" free to comment. But that is obviously a simplification. For even if "heritage lovers" are seen among the managers and "heritage iconoclasts" among the critics, attitudes can be placed on a scale with many nuances. And individuals may move between different positions in the field, adopting dissimilar standpoints in the process.

The multiplicity can also be divided between theoretical intentions and practical realities. Here the contrast appears to run between all the justifications, motives, values, and uses on the one hand and an extensive criticism of concrete (ab)use and various crisis or compensation theories on the other. Once again, though, it is not quite that simple. For irrespective of whether it conveys praise or criticism, speaking or writing is also an act – an act whose purpose and outcome may in fact be that of creating new realities. And there are theoretical perspectives across the whole field, implicit or explicit.

Finally, the multiplicity may also be divided according to the triad of the true, the beautiful, and the good; that is, according to knowledge, aesthetics, and ethics. Different priorities that are not always explicit appear in the debate – priorities to the effect that new knowledge, entertaining narratives, or ethical duties already are, or ought to be, decisive in relation to the past. These perspectives extend across the other divisions and across discourses about intention versus practice. The triad is hence also relevant to the debate about (ab)use, since the true or false, beautiful or ugly, and good or evil can be combined in many ways.

My experience of applying the triad's perspectives to the debate about history, memory, and heritage has ended in the conclusion that nothing is obvious or indisputable. It is all a matter of making choices, of justifying priorities, where it is not possible to rely on rules that have been established once and for all. Every attempt to specifically assert one justification, one motive, one value, one use, one position, or one theory for the whole of the field, with all of its variation across time and space, must therefore be met with scepticism – including my own attempts.

In the debate, dividing lines appear between left and right that may be linked to academic environments in Frankfurt and Münster in Germany, respectively. Classic positions concerning the relationship between high and popular culture, and between theoretical education and practical experience, come to the fore as well. And the hard rhetoric, the slogans, the crisis, and the comparison with religion are comprehensible when it is understood that it is all really about politics, specifically the politics of heritage. The challenge is to be persuasive.

Nor can it come as any surprise, when faced with choices, priorities, and politics, that the present makes its mark on the debate about the past. Justifications, motives, values, uses, criticism, and theories have both senders and recipients in the present. Ideas about the past are ideas in the present. This is particularly clear in the debate about (ab)use as well as about crisis and compensation theory. Even though the subject is the past, a radical criticism of the present appears, irrespective of whether the present is regarded as modern, postmodern, or something else again. History, memory, and heritage are used as a pretext for criticism of society. The growing popularity of heritage becomes a reason to shout "crisis!". But despite criticism of nostalgia as a phenomenon, the criticism itself, paradoxically, frequently bears the unambiguous stamp of nostalgia. Everything was better before – even when it comes to the use of the past.

One after another, a whole series of critical commentators appear to have experienced a deterioration – Boulez and Wright from a focus on the future to one on the past; Lowenthal from the familiar to the foreign, from change to preservation, and from history to heritage; Horkheimer and Adorno from (high) culture to popular culture; Hewison from industry to heritage industry; Heller from progress to nostalgia; Choay from the natural to the artificial; Huyssen from fact to fiction; Füredi from thinking to narrating; Beckman from security to uncertainty; Marquard from meaning to meaninglessness; Lübbe from identity to lack of identity; Hobsbawm from continuity to discontinuity; Tarkovsky and Hofer from home to exile; Kant from childhood to adult life; Horne from harmony to nervousness; Bauman and Jensen from faith to doubt; Freud and Brown from nature to culture or civilisation; Lévi-Strauss from the primitive society to civilisation; and Nora from memory to history: a multiplicity of "falls" at different points in time, like pearls on a string.

Norman W. Brown concluded that society was neurotic and sick. The roots of its neurosis were civilisation, money, the city, and capitalism, which were repressive. He characterised his present as a "tragic crisis" in which human beings, with their death instinct and weapons of mass destruction, were threatened by ruin and disaster (Brown 1959: x, 234ff).

Both Donald Horne and Agnes Heller regarded Europe as a museum – and that was not meant as praise. As onlookers from the New World, Horne from Australia and Heller from the US, they observed a European continent sunk in its own past. Heller wrote a funeral address for Europe – the museum that she herself had left: weakened creativity, acquired idiocy and narrow-mindedness, loss of meaning and cultural masochism. She wanted to see a "new European culture", a dream of an authentic culture characterised by virtues, taste, reason, education, urbanity, joy, nobility, and dignity, as well as love of nature, poetry, music, drama, painting, piety, and erotic culture (Horne 1984: 1, 21; Heller 1988: 154, 158f).

This kind of criticism can be exposed as an example of pessimistic cultural philosophy, an activity in which intellectuals look at and criticise their present in a spirit of anxiety and nostalgia (cf. Nordin 1989). The developments leading up to the crisis-ridden present are set forth as a typical tragic narrative (cf. White 1973: 191ff).

Criticism along these lines is characterised as follows in the unfinished *Das Passagen-Werk* (*The Arcades Project*) by the philosopher and literary critic Walter Benjamin:

> Es hat keine Epoche gegeben, die sich nicht im exzentrischen Sinne
> "modern" fühlte und unmittelbar vor einem Abgrund zu stehen glaubte.
> Das verzweifelt helle Bewußtsein, inmitten einer entscheidenden Krisis
> zu stehen, ist in der Menschheit chronisch. Jede Zeit erscheint sich
> ausweglos neuzeitig. Das "Moderne" aber ist genau in dem Sinne
> verschieden wie die verschiedenen Aspekte ein und desselben Kalei-
> doskops. (Benjamin 1983 (German): II, 677)
>
> There has never been an epoch that did not feel itself to be "modern"
> in the sense of eccentric, and did not believe itself to be standing
> directly before an abyss. The desperately clear consciousness of being
> in the middle of a crisis is something chronic in humanity. Every age
> unavoidably seems to itself a new age. The "modern", however, is
> as varied in its meaning as the different aspects of one and the same
> kaleidoscope. (Benjamin 1999 (English): 545)

The kaleidoscope displays an ever-changing succession of attractive
images – social, economic, political, ideological, religious, or existential crises. Either there is too much modernity or too little. There
is always something to be worried about, always a change that can
be regarded as being for the worse. The crisis is chronic.

It is not hard to understand that crisis theory is popular, but its
explanatory capacity is an illusion. Whenever crisis theory seems to
be able to explain most things or make them comprehensible, this is
due to the complex ambiguity of the theory with its open concepts,
uncertain chronology, hand-picked or absent empirical data, and,
at times, obscure language. There may be reason to be sceptical
of theories that employ metaphors and analogies and cannot be
tested (cf. Sokal & Bricmont 1998: 8ff, 59). Nor is there a single
crisis theory; there are many, they are various, and time and again
they contradict one another. All they have in common is crisis as a
concept and, of course, criticism.

Crisis theory as a critical perspective is itself open to criticism. As
a perspective, however, it cannot in fact be falsified and is therefore
unscientific in the sense formulated by the philosopher Karl Popper
(Popper 1935 (German); 1959 (English)). And the same accusation
could be levelled at compensation theory.

But even if crisis theory is criticised and referred to as unscientific, it will not go away, as it satisfies ideological and psychological
needs for criticism of the present. Instead of a possibly vain struggle
against the paradoxical claims of the theory, alternative perspectives are called for. The criticism of the criticism must be supplemented by something constructive and concrete that opens the way
to further inquiry and debate.

So far, the debate about history, memory, and heritage has focused wholly on events and phenomena since the end of the eighteenth century. The debate has been about revolution, Romanticism, nationalism, secularisation, and modernity – and about the establishment of academic disciplines, memorials, museums, and legislation pertaining to the protection and preservation of ancient monuments. Its geographical focus is the industrialised Western world. But history, memory, and heritage are neither a relatively new nor an exclusively Western phenomenon.

When Abu Simbel is so often highlighted in this inquiry, it is because the place represents both the past and the present, both heritage and modernity, and is outside Europe. At Abu Simbel there is a time depth of thousands of years, which can supplement or correct the focus on the West in the debate. Moreover, the texts of Herodotus and Ibn Khaldûn form a simple reminder that people thought about the past long ago, too, and in other cultures.

The multiplicity of views, perspectives, arguments, and examples that characterises the debate about history, memory, and heritage can no longer come as a surprise. It is possible to explain and understand the variation that prevails in justifications, motives, values, uses, criticism, and theories. But what remains is a sense of wonder at the importance of the past in a changing present and, more specifically, puzzlement regarding the relationship between World Heritage and modernity. Is it possible to perceive a general pattern after all?

Research about human evolution can be combined with *spolia* from my inquiry; the answer will therefore be of a fundamental but also very general nature. I find three observations, in particular, useful as *spolia*: 1) presentism; that is, the view that opinions, perspectives, and arguments are generally conditioned by their present; 2) the connections between nationalism and collective memory, where the past has been used in the construction of identities; that is, who a person is seen as being by themselves or by others; 3) the similarity between heritage and museums on the one hand and religious institutions and rituals on the other, but without an implication that the analogy is somehow unfavourable. Key words are therefore currency, identity, and analogy. The inspiration comes from studies of social evolution: the past is used in order to create meaning in the present. Meaning is about who we are, have been, or are striving to become. And the similarity between heritage and museums on the one hand and religion on the other is due to the fact that they can all contribute to defining a social community.

In human evolution, culture is one of several possible aids in creating and maintaining a social community. Everything that has strengthened the community has provided an evolutionary advantage. Culture is an advantage for the survival of groups; it is one of several factors in selection and hence a precondition for the human conquest of the world (Boyd 2009; Wilson, E. O. 2012). The knowledge, narratives, and rules of heritage are means in the construction of social ties and in establishing cooperation. The true, the beautiful, and the good are all useful in evolution. History, memory, and heritage have a function in creating and maintaining communities. This is why the past has been so useful in both religion and nationalism.

Religious communities are built up around mythical narratives and texts; holy places, persons, monuments, and relics; and offices and ceremonies linked to a historical tradition. Common religious ideas play their part in strengthening social cohesion; they foster cooperation and therefore the potential for survival. Religion creates meaning and therefore motivation for both individuals and groups, and religion is an advantage in competition between groups (Wilson, D. S. 2002; Wilson, E. O. 2012: 255ff; cf. Gärdenfors 2006: 133ff). Consequently, the analogy between heritage and religion is no coincidence. But instead of employing the analogy as an element in derogatory rhetoric, it can be used to understand and explain the importance of heritage.

Similarly, ideas about the nation are built up around myths or narratives about a common past; a common country with canonical places, monuments, and events; and a common material or intangible culture mediated not least in print. Nationalism creates the nation. And nations may, to use the words of the social anthropologist Benedict Anderson, be described as "imagined communities" since not all members are able to know one another. Anderson ascribed particular significance to censuses, maps, and museums for the idea of the nation (Anderson 1991). Nationalism was and is a modern ideology for countering social disruption in industrial societies, and as such it may supplement or replace religious communities (Gellner 1983).

History, memory, and heritage are tools for creating and maintaining communities at all levels from the immediate family to humanity. But the starting points do not need to be true in a scientific sense, beautiful in an aesthetic sense, or good in an ethical sense. The common history, memory, and heritage may be magical, mythological,   mendacious,   unauthentic,   invented,   imagined, illusory, nostalgic, or creative. All that matters is its usefulness in creating meaning and cohesion.

Heritage is used creatively in order to generate meaning. Human beings are searchers for meaning, *Homo opinans*. Meaning can be found in knowledge, narratives, and rules that link up with the past. Selected parts – those that are useful – are drawn from the past; these are *spolia*. And in the encounter between past and present, between fragments of past and current needs, something new is created. The remains of the past are transformed and given new meaning. In this way, all use of the past is creative in the sense of making something that did not exist before.

With the evolutionary perspective, history, memory, and heritage become a fundamental human practice. Meanings have then been added by existentially thinking human beings. Practice goes before justifications and values. And the multiple meanings and manifold critical theories are an expression of the human search for understanding and explanation. Meanings are not discovered, but created.

Before we open the door to the laboratory where theories and concepts can be confronted with concrete specifics, it is necessary to explain the central concepts and history-of-ideas context of crisis theory. What is meant by progress, modern, modernisation, modernism, modernity, and postmodernity? Is there still progress, but without belief in the future? Is the present modern, postmodern, or hypermodern? And what is the relationship between the phases of modernity and the many expressions of nostalgia? Is nostalgia a reaction to modernity or itself part of modernity? In short, we are going to be looking at time and perceptions of time.

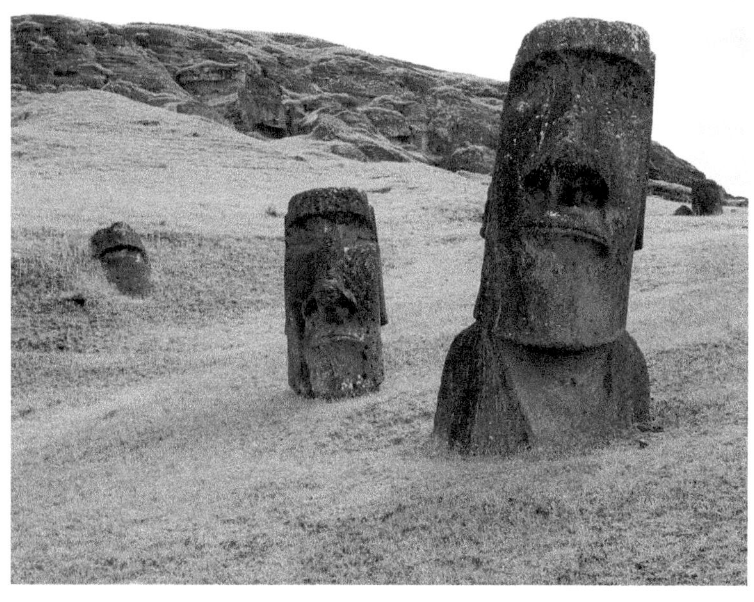

Figure 4 Easter Island statues. Photo © Lars Larsson, 2012.

4
The faces of modernity

Time, change, and permanence

Time is an enigma. Indeed, there is but one truly serious existential problem, and that is time. To determine what time means is to answer the fundamental question of existence. But in what does the enigma of time consist?

Time escapes definition; for it is difficult, perhaps impossible, to define time without including time as a category from the outset. Time can be defined as the distance between two events, that is, the distance between two changes; but what is an event without the concept of time?

Time opens up a number of questions where the meaning of the words determines the answers. Does the concept of time combine both change and permanence? If time is change, what does it mean that time changes? And if time is permanence, what does it mean that time is unchanged? Is time absolute or relative? Does time have a beginning and an end? Why does the arrow of time point specifically towards the future? Is time travel possible to the past or to the future? Is time itself changeable over time? Finally, does time exist, or is it just an illusion?

There is no consensus about the concept of time. There are varying views about what time is – whether time is to be seen as a dimension, as something that flows or as a direction away from the beginning of the universe; whether time is independent of human existence; whether time can be perceived by human beings with their senses, words, and mathematics; and whether it is at all meaningful to ask what time "is" (e.g. Bardon 2013; Rovelli 2017 (Italian); 2019 (English)).

The associations of time with change, impermanence, greater disorder (entropy), and death also give the concept a fateful ring: "Är du beredd?" ("Are you prepared?") asks Death in the film *Det sjunde inseglet* (*The Seventh Seal*) by the director Ingmar Bergman.

The knight Antonius Block tried to cheat Death while the plague was raging; by playing chess with Death, Antonius managed to gain time and save his friends Jof and Mia along with their son Mikael (Bergman 1957 film). The film with its iconic representation of Death on the beach was intended, and was apparently also able, to help Bergman come to terms with his own death anxiety.

We can play with time in fiction, too. Thus readers of the novel *Einstein's Dreams*, by the physicist and author Alan Lightman, can imagine what life would have been like in Berne in 1905 if time had behaved differently than expected; here theories about time can be applied in practice. We can dream about a time that repeats itself, stands still, and goes backwards, a time without events, a time that changes speed, varies locally, or jumps (cf. Lightman 1993). The film *Lola rennt* (English *Run Lola Run*), by the director Tom Tykwer, explores the counterfactual branches of time. Three times Lola has to run through Berlin, and each time a detail of her starting point is changed with fatal consequences. Lola has 20 minutes; but it is only during her final attempt that she manages to save both her friend's life and her own (Tykwer 1998 film).

On the one hand, there is the human experience of temporal change, the future being transformed into the present and then into the past. The tripartition of time with expectation, existence, and memory is crucial to the way in which human beings experience and understand the world. On the other hand, there is the stable spacetime of natural science, which explains the world without necessarily accepting temporal change. This contrast between human experience and the logical reality of physics, between change and permanence, has not (yet) been resolved. Instead of asking "What is time?", we are recommended to ask "What does time do?" (Bardon 2013: 79ff, 173ff). But with the question "What does time do?", every archaeologist or historian is securely back in their own field.

Time may be enigmatic, and yet time is used in a relatively unproblematic way in countless contexts as a concept, a perspective, and, especially, a unit of measurement. Without the concept of time there would be no history to tell, nothing to remember, and no heritage to examine and preserve.

Time is a prerequisite for archaeology, irrespective of whether it is associated with origins, *arche*; whether it is seen as the study of a distant past; or whether it is linked to excavation, in which different layers of time are examined stratigraphically. As an academic discipline, archaeology devotes a great deal of care to establishing times specifically in the form of datings, chronologies, and periods. For without a temporal context, it is difficult to use artefacts as sources of knowledge. And without time, there will not be any narratives about the past, nor any discoveries to reflect on.

Time is crucial for connecting events, a once-in-the-past with a now-in-the-present and a once-in-the-future, a here-in-one-place with a there-in-another-place. Time is a necessary condition of narratives, irrespective of whether they are tales of facts, counter-factuals, or fiction, and irrespective of whether they are science or literature (Wright 1971: 42ff, 103ff; Ricoeur 1984–1985 (French); 1984–1988 (English)). Time is hence a prerequisite for the ability to create meaning – at the same time as it is difficult to give time itself a meaning.

The philosopher Henri Bergson asserted that time cannot be reduced to moments that follow on from one another, to points on a line, or to successive spaces. Time is real, and it is characterised by permanence, by continuance. Experienced time is a movement, a continuing constant change. What is new in that change is dependent on the past that shaped us. And as a result of the uninterrupted growth of the new in the present, ever more past is accumulated. So the past is constantly present in a transient now, as a growing quantity of memory and matter (Bergson 1889 (French); 2001 (English)).

Paradoxically, Bergson's view of time was formulated at the point in time when film was invented. A film sequence by the photographer Louis Le Prince from Roundhay Garden in Leeds in 1888 is the first known film (*Roundhay Garden Scene*, 1888 film). Bergson's view contrasts with the idea and technology of film, in which every single moment is brought together in the form of a series of static photographs on a roll of film so as to create the illusion of movement.

With a reference to Bergson, the archaeologist Laurent Olivier has emphasised that every present is multi-temporal. The present is composed of accumulated matter from previous epochs, matter that is of differing duration. But when Olivier viewed his surroundings from his window in a farmhouse in France, he saw buildings from the seventeenth, eighteenth, and nineteenth centuries, whereas the twentieth century was only visible in details; and everything that was supposed to be typical of his own present in the 1990s was invisible. The past with its weighty matter is therefore seen as dominating the present (Olivier 1999; cf. 2008 (French); 2011 (English); also Latour 1991 (French): 101ff; 1993 (English): 74ff).

From my window in Lund in Sweden, I also look out over a mosaic of times that is, at a first glance, characterised by older periods. Archaeologicum, the building I work in, was built in 1853 and was originally the Anatomy Department of Lund University. From here I look out over Universitetsplatsen, the open space in front of the main University building, and Lundagård, with runic stones from the Viking period, busts of dead scholars, and buildings from the Middle Ages, the Renaissance, and the nineteenth and twentieth centuries in particular. Most centuries since the foundation of the city are represented. So the past is everywhere, but it is neither foreign nor distant. The past is familiar and present in my everyday life.

The architecture of Universitetsplatsen can easily be recognised in old pictures where the great changes of recent times have not yet taken place: an academic campus that wants to assert tradition and continuity in the midst of the renewal, modernity, and growth that characterise the city and the region. But the immediate experience of tradition and continuity is a double illusion.

First, the view is a piece of historical stagecraft. In several cases, the architecture is historicised and refers to the styles of previous periods. The barrow with runic stones is a memorial from 1868; the runic stones used to stand in completely different locations. The Academic Society's medieval castle is from 1850–1851; the cathedral's "Romanesque" towers were erected in 1869–1876; Kungshuset (the King's House) from the sixteenth century was greatly altered in the eighteenth and nineteenth centuries. And life both in front of and behind the facades is characterised by hurry and change. Passing through the area are pedestrians, bicycles, and the occasional car, all bearing the stamp of prevailing fashions. On the grass and benches are students with the newest smartphones and laptops connected to wireless networks. Behind their facades, the buildings are constantly being modernised in accordance with current needs and the latest technological options. All parts of this view are in constant change at different speeds.

Second, the view described above is a memory. My workplace has now been moved to LUX, a faculty campus consisting of buildings from 1917, 1961, and 2014. And the view is no longer of Universitetsplatsen and Lundagård but of the university hospital's high-rise "central block", opened in 1968, and of the accident and emergency department from 2004, where people and ambulances rush in and out.

In cosmological terms, the elements of matter originate from supernova explosions billions of years ago. And the matter of the past may be accumulated everywhere in me and in the view from my window, but a continuing past does not dominate my experience of the present; far from it. The present with its changes is extremely familiar and manifest.

Where Bergson with his "flowing" time formulated a concept of time that combined change and permanence, concepts such as heritage and modernity presuppose a separation and contrast, as do the canonical and critical traditions of heritage. Heritage refers to culture that is inherited or passed on over time; that is, to something that lasts despite changes. The concept of heritage thus emphasises continuity with the past, whereas modernity suggests discontinuity. The concept of modernity refers to the new that is created in time; that is, to something that forms a break with that which lasts. Modernity carries connotations of change, progress, and the future, while heritage has associations with the old that has survived into the present, with permanence.

Consequently, we rediscover the abstract question of the relationship between change and permanence in the relationship between modernity and heritage. Here modernity is seen as representing change and the forward-looking and accelerating time, whereas heritage is regarded as representing permanence, stasis, and the backward-looking. This dichotomy runs through the entire field of heritage, across the canonical and critical traditions of heritage and across justifications, motives, values, and crisis theories.

In the book *Zeit und Tradition* (English *Time and Tradition*), the literary scholar Aleida Assmann sets up time in the sense of change against tradition in the sense of permanence. In line with crisis theories, Assmann sees traditions as a cultural strategy for creating permanence; that is, a compensatory strategy (Assmann 1999).

But are change and permanence, modernity and heritage, necessarily opposites? Can change be a precondition for permanence and permanence a precondition for change? An examination should be made as to whether modernity and heritage might not also be inextricably entangled.

Irrespective of whether our purpose is to describe time from a psychological, mechanical, or cosmological perspective, we are obliged to employ metaphors that refer to geometrical forms, to human beings, and movement. The pictures used in the metaphors – pictures that are recognisable, but nevertheless absurd in the relevant context – are intended to establish a pattern in the enigmatic, make the incomprehensible comprehensible, and give time a meaning that we can understand (cf. Gärdenfors 2006:

105ff): Time is a point, is linear, circular, or an arrow; it is short or long, light or dark, foreign or familiar. Time stands still, walks, runs or flows, shrinks or accelerates. Time means steps forward or backward, rise or fall.

The Past is a Foreign Country by David Lowenthal had a broad impact with its anthropological look at the past. As the title suggests, and as the content of the book confirms, the idea is that the present has been alienated from the past. The past has become different, remote, and exotic – a "foreign country" (Lowenthal 1985: xvi, 406; 2015: 3f, 8ff, 358ff).

Lowenthal's title was taken from the author L. P. Hartley's novel *The Go-Between*, whose opening sentence is, "The past is a foreign country: they do things differently there" (Lowenthal 1985: xvi; 2015: 3; Hartley 1953: 9). In the novel an older Leo Colston relives, with the aid of his diary, the summer of 1900 when, as a boy, he was a guest at Brandham Hall. Colston revisits the place and the persons. But his memory and visit are paradoxically characterised by both yearning and rejection, both nostalgia and loathing. The past has become foreign to him. The foreign element in the past has to do both with the innocent and almost naive period before puberty, when the world of adults was unknown or incomprehensible, and with a British class society that met its downfall with the First World War.

The people of the past are supposed not to have been like us; they were different. They thought differently, and they lived and died differently. The past becomes an enchanted time zone, distinct from the present where the people of the past become "the others". The rise of modernity is supposed to be what has created a radical, alienating, and disenchanting break with the past. Then we can try to travel to the country of the past to attain knowledge about other forms of life, travel nostalgically in a flight from our own time, or visit the past in order to honour the dead and their memorials.

But the past cannot be described as either foreign or familiar, as either progress or decline, any more than the Middle Ages as an epoch can be described as either dark or light. What the past was, what the present is, and what the future will be depends entirely on the choice of perspective. For every change or permanence can be experienced differently. Time, change, and permanence are experienced differently depending on the perspective applied; that is, by who is looking and from where, when they are doing it, and how.

Progress and decay

There are two fundamental and mutually opposing conceptions of the changes wrought by time, one being characterised by optimism and the other by pessimism. Changes can either be viewed as progress, an improvement in relation to the past, a development – or as decline, a downturn, decay, or a fall. Irrespective of whether this division is incorrect, misleading, or irrelevant, it forms the starting point of two distinct traditions of thought about time (cf. Toulmin & Goodfield 1965: 106ff; Frängsmyr 1980).

The idea of progress is the notion that it is possible to improve human life and society. The conception of progress as both a possibility and a reality emerged gradually in Europe. It entailed a liberation from a previous, more static view of time laid down by the Church and Christianity with a predetermined development from creation, ingeniously dated at 4004 BCE, up until the expected return of Christ. The idea of progress was promoted by the Enlightenment from the seventeenth century onwards, gained new importance with the discovery of the great depths of the past in the eighteenth century, and culminated in the middle of the nineteenth century with the formulation of the theory of evolution by Charles Darwin and Alfred Russel Wallace (Toulmin & Goodfield 1965).

With the idea of progress, the past becomes something unsatisfactory, something to leave behind, "dark" Middle Ages or a "primitive" Stone Age (cf. Mommsen 1942; Kuper 1988). The present also runs a risk of rapidly becoming old and unmodern. The ideas and technology of the present must constantly be ready to be "updated" to the latest version – click here to download the new 2.0!

A number of intangible and material innovations serve as icons of progress. The intangible icons of progress are such liberal notions as reason, freedom, democracy, and equality, notions with a long history in which philosophers and politicians are agents. They gain new relevance with the Enlightenment starting in the seventeenth century, see a political breakthrough at the time of the American and French Revolutions at the end of the eighteenth century, and are, in some cases, affirmed as human rights in conventions in the twentieth century, albeit constantly disputed (e.g. Universal Declaration of Human Rights, 1948; Bring 2011).

The material icons of progress are to do with new, cross-border technologies in which inventors and engineers are agents. They are technologies that have widened the horizon and increased the range and speed of human beings. They include lenses used in spectacles, telescopes, and microscopes. They also comprise the development from the astronomer Galileo Galilei's first telescope to present-day satellite telescopes that have gradually permitted humanity to gaze into space, and therefore backwards in time. The material icons of progress include modes of transport such as the sailing ship, the steamship, the train, the car, the aircraft, and the rocket. They encompass forms of communication that join the world together, such as the telegraph, telephone, radio, TV, and the Internet. And they include technologies that permit the construction of ever-higher buildings, which are erected in a spirit of competition between states and major cities and appear to run counter to the laws of nature.

In Utopia, progress and its icons are projected into a fantastic future. The picture of an ideal society to strive towards is outlined. Utopia means "no place" and goes back to the Renaissance, when the politician and author Thomas More introduced the concept. More had to reformulate his political criticism away from the contemporaneous society to a distant and foreign place, a non-existent island called Utopia (Moro/More 1516 (Latin); 2012 (English); cf. Claeys 2011). Utopia is thus related to L. P. Hartley's and David Lowenthal's "foreign country", where they do things differently.

The most extreme expression of the idea of progress came in Futurism, which aimed to create a new future liberated from the past but was soon compromised by its link to Fascism. Futurism, with roots in anarchism, arose in a northern Italy characterised by rapid industrialisation. In 1909, the author Filippo Tommaso Marinetti formulated a manifesto that entailed a radical reckoning with the past. The Manifesto of Futurism praised the future, speed, technology, war, masculinity, the masses, and the big city, whereas the institutions of the past were to be destroyed. Futurism also observed a division into two cultures, praising forward-looking technology but rejecting backward-looking humanities:

> Nous déclarons que la splendeur du monde s'est enrichie d'une beauté nouvelle: la beauté de la vitesse. ... Nous voulons démolir les musées, les bibliothèques, combattre le moralisme, le féminisme et toutes les lâchetés opportunistes et utilitaires. ... C'est en Italie que nous lançons ce manifeste de violence culbutante et incendiaire, par lequel nous fondons aujourd'hui le *Futurisme*, parce que nous voulons délivrer l'Italie de sa gangrène de professeurs, d'archéologues, de cicérones et d'antiquaires. (Marinetti 1909 (French))
>
> We affirm that the world's magnificence has been enriched by a new beauty: the beauty of speed. ... We will destroy the museums,

libraries, academies of every kind, will fight moralism, feminism, every opportunistic or utilitarian cowardice. ... It is from Italy that we launch through the world this violently upsetting incendiary manifesto of ours. With it, today, we establish *Futurism*, because we want to free this land from its smelly gangrene of professors, archaeologists, *ciceroni*, and antiquarians. (Marinetti 1973 (English): 21f)

Progress was given metaphorical expression by Walter Benjamin. A refugee at the time, Benjamin described progress as a disastrous storm from Paradise, a storm that creates ruins. In his final essay, "Über den Begriff der Geschichte" ("Theses on the Philosophy of History"), he commented on a picture by the artist Paul Klee called "Angelus Novus":

Der Engel der Geschichte muß so aussehen. Er hat das Antlitz der Vergangenheit zugewendet. Wo eine Kette von Begebenheiten vor *uns* erscheint, da sieht *er* eine einzige Katastrophe, die unablässig Trümmer auf Trümmer häuft und sie ihm vor die Füße schleudert. Er möchte wohl verweilen, die Toten wecken und das Zerschlagene zusammenfügen. Aber ein Sturm weht vom Paradiese her, der sich in seinen Flügeln verfangen hat und so stark ist, daß der Engel sie nicht mehr schließen kann. Dieser Sturm treibt ihn unaufhaltsam in die Zukunft, der er den Rücken kehrt, während der Trümmerhaufen vor ihm zum Himmel wächst. Das, was wir den Fortschritt nennen, ist *dieser* Sturm. (Benjamin 1980 (German): 697f)
This is how one pictures the angel of history. His face is turned towards the past. Where we perceive a chain of events, he sees one single catastrophe which keeps piling wreckage upon wreckage and hurls it in front of his feet. The angel would like to stay, awaken the dead, and make whole what has been smashed. But a storm is blowing from Paradise; it has got caught in his wings with such violence that the angel can no longer close them. This storm irresistibly propels him into the future to which his back is turned, while the pile of debris before him grows skyward. This storm is what we call progress. (Benjamin 1970 (English): 259f)

Destruction was also of central importance to the economist Joseph A. Schumpeter, who developed the paradoxical concept of "creative destruction". According to Schumpeter, industrial development is both creative and destructive. Innovations mean that old modes of production are laid waste (Schumpeter 1942: 81ff). Of necessity, progress thus leaves both ideas and buildings as ruins.

While the idea of progress is about development and improvements, the idea of decay is about liquidation and deterioration. The idea of decay places its utopia in the past, as a lost paradise, an idyllic

Arcadia, a lost golden age, or a past period of greatness (Frängsmyr 1980; Lowenthal 1985: 23ff; 2015: 66ff). Previously, peace, happiness, and plenty reigned; now the rulers are war, disaster, and poverty. Once we lived in paradise, but we were expelled as in the Christian story of creation. Once, the region of Arcadia in Greece was a pristine idyll. Once, long ago, there was a golden age; but now we are seen as living in an Iron Age, as in ancient conceptions. Once the country was great and rich, but now it is diminished and poor, as in several national narratives. Once people lived in harmony with one another and with nature, but now the balance has been broken; or society and the climate are in crisis, as in the current debate.

There are several ways of applying a perspective of decay: the past can be admired with the eyes of Romanticism on ruins from Antiquity and the Middle Ages; people can use time travel to make their way back to the golden age in an escapist manner, the past serving as a nostalgic refuge, which is reconstructed and brought to life; the present can be brought back, along reactionary lines, to that magnificent state of things that was said to have existed once, before things got worse: "Make America Great Again!" There are attempts to recreate a belief, a policy, a territory, a position of power, or an organisation that has never existed in that way. The allegation of a crisis in the present and a nostalgic picture of the past pave the way for a reshaping of the present and the future.

The present can also be dismissed as decadent or in crisis, and with an added element of anxiety the future can be expected to be disastrous. The future then becomes a dystopia – an anti-utopia characterised by a breakdown of civilisation, famine, and either a nuclear winter or rising temperatures and floods. Where the Futurist wanted to pursue the speed of progress, survivalists or preppers want to prepare for the disaster by digging themselves into bunkers along with their supplies.

The relationship between progress and decay, between optimism and pessimism, has created its own genre, a genre that discusses the rise and fall of civilisations. The reason is that people who live in "civilisations" have been, and continue to be, fascinated by the development of other civilisations that have gone under. The genre covers everything from examinations of a single civilisation to global syntheses and prophetic statements about what is to be expected in the coming years. Several general theories of the development of civilisations have been formulated with phases of rise, stagnation, decline, and fall, paying attention to the importance of, for instance, religion, culture, the economy, the environment, values, and institutions (e.g. Kennedy 1987; Tainter 1988; Diamond 2005; Acemoglu & Robinson 2012).

How and why could once powerful civilisations collapse? Examples that have exerted fascination include Ancient Rome, the Maya in Central America, Angkor in Cambodia, the Norse settlements on Greenland, Easter Island, the British Empire, and the USSR. In our own time, there is a discussion about whether the US is entering a phase of decline and fall. Will China be the new superpower instead?

Ruins and wrecks are material icons of decline and decay. The sinking of the Atlantic steamer the *Titanic* in 1912 was a shock that called technological progress into question. The accident at the nuclear power station in Chernobyl in 1986 was a warning of the collapse of the USSR – after its collapse. And to the sociologist Immanuel Wallerstein, the collapse of the Twin Towers in New York after the attack in 2001 was an image of the decline of the US (Wallerstein 2003: 193ff, 198f, 202).

The genre of decay with its civilisation theories assumes that there is something that can be called civilised, in contrast to the uncivilised, savage, or barbarian. It also assumes that changes in civilisations can be described in stages of rise, stagnation, decline, and fall. Both these assumptions are dubious. Moreover, every period seems to be able to offer its own narrative as to why civilisations decayed and disappeared, its interpretation reflecting that which characterises the agenda of its own present: faith, culture, the economy, the climate, or the ability to change. Then criticism can be – and has, of course, been – levelled against the concrete interpretations (e.g. McAnany & Yoffee 2009).

Like the longing for a lost age or country, the genre of decay is an example of the use of the past to learn, to entertain, and also to reflect: Consider Forum Romanum (WHL 91ter, 1980, 1990, 2015), Chichén-Itza (WHL 483, 1988), Angkor (WHL 668, 1992), Hvalsey Church on Greenland, Rapa Nui/Easter Island's "moai" (WHL 715, 1995)! Consider the UK! Consider the USSR! Consider the US! Consider what happened to the others! Consider and learn, so that we or you do not need to follow the same path! Or with malicious pleasure, be prepared for disaster! As a narrative, rise and fall can assume all the well-known forms – romance, tragedy, comedy, and satire.

The use of *spolia* in late Antiquity and the Middle Ages shows that there was an awareness about the past. Even so, ruins as fragmented buildings only became visible – and therefore depicted – from the

Italian Renaissance (Fabricius Hansen 1999: 146, 161ff). But the ruins had multiple meanings. On seeing the ruins of Rome in 1341, the poet Petrarch (Francesco Petrarca), the first to conceptualise a dark Middle Ages, thus thought of the greatness of Rome; conversely, on seeing the same sight in 1764, the historian Edward Gibbon, known for his theory of the decline and fall of the Roman Empire, saw evidence of the decadence of Rome (Petrarca 1934: II, 93; Mommsen 1942: 232f; Gibbon 1966: 136 with note 7).

Where high speed and height are expressions of progress, stationary ruins have often been used as an icon of decay, impermanence, and death. Romanticism in the nineteenth century adored the ruins of Antiquity or the Middle Ages, which were reminders of the greatness of the past. Through their very existence, the ruins might encourage glorious deeds or humility (Roth *et al.* 1997; Woodward 2001; Eriksen 2014: 64ff).

The deindustrialisation of the West in recent decades has left a landscape of ruins that is speedily being redefined as heritage and becoming its own field of research – industrial heritage. The ruins of industrial society may be regarded as something unpleasant, disfiguring, and frightening that should simply be demolished, or as premises that provide possibilities of alternative activities – or as a heritage worthy of admiration, protection, and preservation.

The transformation of a factory into heritage and the reuse of premises with new functions such as arts centres, museums, offices, or housing have attracted attention in many studies, with World Heritage sites such as Ironbridge Gorge in England (WHL 371, 1986) and Zollverein in Germany (WHL 975, 2001) as already classic examples (e.g. Storm 2008; Willim 2008; also Alzén 1996). This is a narrative of the successful transition from the industrial to the post-industrial society – a narrative of success, in which defeat is transformed into victory.

Alternatively, abandoned and dilapidated concrete structures, factories, rusty machinery and cars, and statues are presented in numerous picture books, on websites, and in projects that are characterised by melancholy aesthetics, existential reflection, or criticism of the present time; urban decay places us at the edge of the abyss (e.g. Burström 2004; Edensor 2005; Burström *et al.* 2011; Jörnmark & Hausswolff 2011; Olsen & Pétrusdóttir 2014). One clear and early example here is Detroit in Michigan, an epicentre of the American dream, whose development from rise and expansion to decay and ruin has followed the cycles of car production (e.g. www.camilojosevergara.com).

Here the concrete remains of Benjamin's "storm" and Schumpeter's "creative destruction" are used as moral reminders of the failures of progress, of the impermanence of modernity and ideologies, and of the consequences of capitalism and neoliberalism. This field with its doom-laden book titles demonstrates a neo-Romantic fascination with decay which is quite as intense as the romantic notions about ruins that were rife in the nineteenth century. And at the heart of the field there is an ambiguous nostalgic exoticism, a fascination with a lost epoch and a "foreign country", even though neither the nostalgia nor the exoticism is acknowledged.

Benjamin saw wreckage in the wake of the storm of progress. But all change can create ruins as a consequence of the creative destruction inherent in development. Ruins arose not only in the Reformation, the French Revolution, the industrial revolution, or the Chinese cultural revolution, but every time something has been replaced by something new. Existing expressions of ideas and technology change or are rejected, left behind, or destroyed when something new and – one hopes – better turns up. So progress and decay are inextricably linked, like two different narratives about the same shift.

Ruins are remains of the past which may be icons for both progress and decay. Ruins may be employed in the service of the true, the beautiful, and the good – of knowledge, narratives, and morality. They can be admired, feared, or despised. And paradoxically, ruins represent both dimensions of time: both change and permanence. Ruins are a consequence of constant change; but they are, at the same time, an expression of permanence; that is, something that has survived the renewal.

Abu Simbel is one such expression of the paradoxical duality of time. As temple ruins from the Egypt of the pharaohs, Abu Simbel was first made redundant by developments and forgotten in the sand dunes when dynasties fell and religious faiths changed. Later, though, it was rediscovered and drawn into a Western discourse about the Orient. Then, when the temples of Abu Simbel stood in the way of progress, their permanence was ensured through a radical change, a modernisation of heritage.

The faces of modernity

Words such as modern, modernisation, modernism, and modernity occur everywhere in narratives of human development. They deal with the triumph of progress, enlightenment, rationality, and science, the triumph of individualism, capitalism, urbanisation, industrialisation, and globalisation. But these narratives have been criticised for as long as they have been put forward, and their critics have stressed the dark and destructive reverse side of modernity – alienation, disenchantment, colonialism, genocide, environmental pollution, and climate change. And they are accounts that have been declared dead by postmodernists since the 1970s.

Essentially, modernity may be described as a grand narrative of origins and development, a narrative that is, like other narratives, intended to create meaning and identity in the present. Modernity is the narrative about what is seen as characterising the West, unlike other parts of the world, and the narrative about an epoch in the same way as the Middle Ages. Modernity thus creates a space in time that is thought to be marked by renewal. But open questions remain about what is central to modernity; how it should be defined as a period or in terms of geography; whether modernity is something favourable or unfavourable; and whether modernity ever existed in the first place.

Modernity has many faces. For on closer examination the grand narrative of modernity can be broken up into a number of smaller sub-narratives, each of which gives an account of the growth, impact, and consequences of modernity in a particular field. Depending on the perspective applied, different meanings – and hence varying durations – may be ascribed to modernity. Historians of ideas may stress the importance of science, school education, and religion; historians of technology will speak about the steam engine, railways, and electricity; physicists about the theories of relativity; sociologists about rationality, bureaucracy, and social acceleration; economists about the market economy; historians of architecture, art, literature, or music about experiments with form; human ecologists about the relationship between humans and nature; historians about historical thinking; and archaeologists about the use of tools and images.

In the Western history of ideas, modernity or the modern age is generally defined as beginning in the decades around 1800; that is, the period of the French Revolution and the subsequent Napoleonic Wars. In the work of the influential historian of ideas and philosopher Michel Foucault, we thus find a division between the classical and the modern epoch around 1800, but no explanations for the transition. In *Les mots et les choses* (English: *The Order of Things*), Foucault described a shift in which each epoch or episteme imposed limits on what could be thought and how. This shift meant that God was replaced by history as the interpretative framework, and the

Church and the clergy were succeeded as the shepherding power by the State's new control institutions, the police and the sciences (Foucault 1966 (French); 1971 (English)).

Modernity is also divided up into phases in order to bring out its origins and gradual development since the Renaissance. For instance, the literary historian Marshall Berman has divided modernity into three phases: from the beginning of the sixteenth century to around 1790; from around 1790 to around 1900; and the period after around 1900 (Berman 1982: 16f; cf. also Toulmin 1990).

The changing perspectives make modernity bewilderingly ambiguous both as a phenomenon and as an epoch. For some, modernity is thus something that made its appearance thousands of years ago; for others, it emerged some centuries ago. All epochs can have been modern, modernity can be a finished period in history, or modernity never existed.

Thus modernity has been used since the 1980s to define the emergence of *Homo sapiens* in the Palaeolithic Age; that is, to distinguish modern humans from previous species. Concepts such as "biological modernity" and "behavioural modernity" are used in this context (e.g. Klein 1989; Nowell 2010). Then the debate is about criteria, times, and places pertaining to the emergence of modern humans, but not about whether "modern" is a relevant designation.

Several commentators have undermined the idea of modernity as an epoch of its own. For example, the poet Charles Baudelaire wrote that there has been a modernity for painters of every period (Baudelaire 1863 (French); 1964 (English): 13). And Walter Benjamin described in *Das Passagen-Werk* (*The Arcades Project*) how every period has seen itself as being characterised by unique change and therefore believed that it was modern in its own way (Benjamin 1983 (German): II, 677; 1999 (English): 545). Here modernity is not a period, but a feeling and self-perception of living in a constant crisis caused by change.

When the philosopher Jean-François Lyotard launched the expression "the postmodern condition" in the eponymous book, it had a great impact on the debate in the 1980s and 1990s (Lyotard 1979 (French); 1984 (English); cf. Anderson 1998). Belief in progress and the modern project had expired. Postmodernity or postmodernism was thought to entail the demise of the grand narratives and therefore also the death of the narrative of modernity. Postmodern architecture, art, literature, and history evolved – as did postmodern archaeology, the latter under the name of post-processual archaeology.

One indication that modernity was dead – or was felt to be better dead, or was at least considered to be enfeebled – is that it began to turn up in museum-related and archaeological contexts as a phenomenon and period for critical study (e.g. Prior 2002; Thomas 2004; Ersgård 2007; Lihammer & Nordin 2010). Yet, at the same time, there is little talk about postmodernism or postmodernity these days. The terms have long since lost their news value, become unfashionable, and been filed away among all the other historical "isms". Instead, modernity has experienced a renaissance in the debate.

A curiosity worth mentioning is that, in an often-quoted book about tourism, the landscape architect Dean MacCannell has surprisingly defined modernity as something that arises when industrialisation declines. MacCannell regards post-industrial society as modern – and musealised (MacCannell 1976: 36, 57f, 182). Here the term modernity is being used about what most scholars would call postmodernity.

Finally, the sociologist of science Bruno Latour claims in a book of the same name that *Nous n'avons jamais été modernes* (English: *We Have Never Been Modern*). For modernity is said never to have succeeded in achieving that which was supposed to be characteristic of it, namely the ability to distinguish between nature and culture, science and society, the non-human and the human, and things and signs (Latour 1991 (French); 1993 (English)).

Modernity's narrative of the West has thus been challenged both from the inside and from the outside – from the inside as unwanted and from the outside by other competing narratives.

All that is solid melts

The word "modern" is not itself modern. The first occurrence of *modernus* in the sense of "new" or "newer" is in late Antiquity, in the writings of the prefect and author Flavius Cassiodorus in the sixth century CE, in a period that reused material *spolia* from Antiquity in new buildings (Le Goff 1988 (French): 68f; 1992 (English): 27; Fabricius Hansen 2003: 228f). The word "modern" is used rhetorically to stress the new at the expense of the old. The modern distinguishes past from present and introduces a movement forward, a progress. And the concept "modernity" in the sense of "the present" occurs in the early Enlightenment in seventeenth-century England (*OED*: IX, 947ff; Calinescu 1987: 41ff).

With the idea of progress in the nineteenth century, "modernity" is transformed into a term for the new society that emerges, either as a reality already in existence or as a future utopia, desirable or (often) undesirable. In the essay "Le Peintre de la vie moderne" ("The Painter of Modern Life"), Charles Baudelaire thus characterised modernity as the fleeting and the transient, something that is continually transforming itself, the opposite of the eternal and immovable (Baudelaire 1863 (French); 1964 (English); cf. Calinescu 1987: 41ff; Boym 2001: 19ff). For Baudelaire, modernity was that which was typical of the time and which changes – the opposite of that which endures.

Diagnoses of the present often appear in the debate. New terms are used not only to describe the present, but also to set an agenda and thereby to influence both the present and the future. Since the 1980s, sociologists, and also anthropologists and historians, in Germany, the UK, and France have launched new concepts in order to designate and analyse the state of the world. Modernity is again central; but something new has been added to mark what is typical of the period.

Ulrich Beck described his present as a "risk society" that was entering a "second modernity". New dangers and risks required reflection, and Beck therefore formulated the concept of "reflexive modernity" (Beck 1986 (German); 1992 (English)). Anthony Giddens stresses similar themes such as security, danger, trust, and risk; but he describes the period as "radicalised" or "late modernity" (Giddens 1990). Zygmunt Bauman took the view that the present was insecure, did not permit consolidation, and therefore required flexibility. Bauman used the term "liquid modernity" (Bauman 2000; 2007).

Marc Augé has used the term "surmodernité" (English: "supermodernity") in an examination of what he sees as non-places. These non-places are said to be characterised by movement or travel, examples being airports, bus terminals, hotels, and motorways (Augé 1992 (French); 1995 (English)). Gilles Lipovetsky uses the terms "hypermodern" and "ultra-modern" instead. His view is that the present is characterised by a focus on the now, on movement, changeability, flexibility, greater acceleration, and uncertainty. The past is mobilised as a reaction, with its museums, traditions, heritage, and religious and ethnic identities (Lipovetsky 2004 (French); 2005 (English)).

Speed and acceleration are also central to the work of Hartmut Rosa, who claims that the modernity of the present is characterised by a social and technological acceleration that creates devastation and alienation. This acceleration is described as pathological and totalitarian. Rosa perceives a rising tempo over time from pre-modernity and early modernity via classical modernity to the present late modernity (Rosa 2005 (German); 2012 (German); 2013 (English)).

A specific theme runs through the debate on modernity: it is the importance and consequences of speed. This theme is common to both those who confirm modernity and those who reject it. The theme runs from the nineteenth-century critics of modernity via the twentieth-century Futurists to present-day diagnoses. Where Baudelaire writes about the fleeting and the transient as well as about constant transformation, Beck, Giddens, Bauman, Augé, Lipovetsky, and Rosa have all regarded the present as being characterised by speed and flexibility, two phenomena that transform people and society, nature and culture. For them, then, there is more modernity around these days than ever before.

Speed and its consequences have attracted attention as a social problem and become a separate field of research (e.g. Virilio 1977 (French); 1986 (English); cf. Sokal & Bricmont 1998: 159ff; Tomlinson 2007). And a whole genre of literature has sprung up to describe and reflect on the acceleration of time (e.g. Gleick 1999; Hylland Eriksen 2001). This genre may encourage opposition to the tyranny of time, advise individuals about strategies for economising their time, or present slowness and the unchanging as a virtue. Global anthropogenic changes are now so extensive that they have named a new geological period after humanity – the Anthropocene – a concept that dissolves the boundary between nature and culture (e.g. Hylland Eriksen 2016; Sörlin 2017).

All the sociologists, anthropologists, and historians who describe and analyse the state of the present in the decades around 2000 are critical of modernity. They generally stress the unfavourable consequences of modernity; here the current debate is part of a long tradition of criticism of the present. Transience, acceleration, and the Anthropocene may be a reality; but there is an unmistakably nostalgic tone in the descriptions of modernity ever since the mid-nineteenth century. In earlier times, the present must have been slower, less mobile, fixed. Benjamin's words about the way in which different periods regard themselves as standing at the abyss come back to mind.

It is necessary to have the right diagnosis of the present; but this is not sufficient to understand, explain, and possibly also influence developments. That also requires a theoretical model for the ways in which different phenomena may be interconnected.

Irrespective of how we choose to describe the present, it is apparently characterised by movement and greater speed. The present is modern, and more modern than ever before. The Manifesto of Futurism with its worship of speed, a controversial utopia a century ago, has now become a reality to confirm or regret. Greater speed is a fact that is easy to prove empirically, especially with the aid of information technology. But why transience and acceleration? Several attempts to understand and explain transience and acceleration point to the market economy, which drives developments in the direction of constantly higher speed, efficiency, and profit maximisation.

A few years before Baudelaire's romantic description of the transience of the present, the philosophers Karl Marx and Friedrich Engels wrote about the consequences of modern industrial production in *Manifest der kommunistichen Partei* (English: *The Communist Manifesto*): "Alles Ständische und Stehende verdampft, alles Heilige wird entweiht" (1848: 5; English: "All that is solid melts into air, all that is holy is profaned", 1964: 63). This quotation was used as the title of Marshall Berman's examination of the literature of modernity, *All That is Solid Melts into Air* (1982).

Modernity and the market economy, as well as a phenomenon such as World Heritage with its international convention, are easy to associate with globalisation – that is, how countries are interconnected in economic, cultural, and political terms. But globalisation itself is not a modern phenomenon (e.g. Frank & Gills 1993; Andrén 2011).

Concepts such as progress, modernity, the West, and capitalism are linked up in world-systems theory. The idea of a global system was developed by Immanuel Wallerstein in the trilogy *The Modern World-System* (1974–1989). Wallerstein described an economic development in which centres, with capital accumulation and production, were surrounded by a dependent semi-periphery and periphery both of which supplied raw materials. He regarded historical development as being characterised by cyclical periods in which centres have succeeded one another according to a set deterministic pattern. As a result of competition and rising costs, production – and therefore capital accumulation – moves to new rising centres while the old ones decline or collapse. Capital is decentralised and production moved, so there is a deindustrialisation of the previously dominant centres. In his view, the historical process of changing world-systems can be observed in successive empires and hegemonies since the sixteenth century: Spain, the Netherlands, the UK, and the US.

Inspired by and in opposition to Wallerstein, the social anthropologist Jonathan Friedman has developed a more general model of world-systems, a model that includes the dichotomy modernity versus tradition. This model has been extended backwards in time in order to explain developments since the Bronze Age or even earlier. Friedman's global model is presented in detail in the anthology *Cultural Identity and Global Process* (Friedman 1994).

According to Friedman, modernity can be linked to the rise and culmination of the centres, whereas postmodernity and tradition are seen as characterising their decline. As the Western, that is to say American, hegemony over the world economy decreased from the mid-1970s onwards, belief in progress and modernity ceased. When the hegemony decayed, modernity – which was the central identity of the hegemony – "imploded". A West in economic and political decline instead saw the spread of disorder, postmodern relativism and fragmentation, ethnification, and traditionalism. Dehegemonisation meant dehomogenisation. And traditionalism signified a nostalgic yearning for roots. To quote Friedman, "Modernity moves East, leaving postmodernity in its wake" (Friedman 1994: 15ff, 37ff, 190 quote; 1995; 2005; 2007).

But Friedman's world-systems and view of cycles in the relationship between rise and decline, modernity and tradition, cannot be taken on board without scepticism. For it is remarkable that the nineteenth-century belief in progress and industrial expansion coincided with historicised architecture, the establishment of museums, and a reappearance of traditions. The relationship between modernity and tradition is not a simple dichotomy.

Between modernity and tradition

"You can be a museum, or you can be modern, but you can't be both" (Mellow 1968). The author and art collector Gertrude Stein succinctly formulated a contrast between the modern and the museum. The original context is uncertain; but the words were said either as a critical comment on MoMA, the Museum of Modern Art, in Manhattan in New York, which wanted to take over her collection, or as a justification for why Pablo Picasso's portrait of her went to the nearby Met, the Metropolitan Museum of Art, instead. But are modernity and the museum really mutually exclusive?

Perhaps Stein was inspired by the sociologist Lewis Mumford, who formulated a similar contrast between the modern and the monument: "The notion of a modern monument is veritable [*sic*] a contradiction in terms: if it is a monument, it is not modern, and if it is modern, it cannot be a monument" (Mumford 1938: 438).

On the one side stands modernity with its connotations of future, speed, and acceleration; on the other side stand the museum and the monument with their associations to the past, slowness, and stasis. These opposites also occur in criticism of modern society: on the one side, we find the alienation resulting from capitalism, the rational society with great cities characterised by speed, a lack of rules, root-lessness, and disenchantment, whereas the other side shows us the lost intimacy, community, and enchantment of feudalism, and small towns characterised by slowness, rules, and roots. The contrasts go back to the division of time into change and permanence; but here they are subsumed in nostalgic narratives about how things were better in the old days. The renewals of modernity are critically contrasted with the traditions of the old society. Changes in time are contrasted with the permanence of time.

Crisis theories also contain a patent opposition between modernity and various expressions of the non-modern. Either they interpret the museum, the monument, preservation, in fact the whole heritage sector, including archaeology, as a compensatory and therapeutic reaction to modernity; or they interpret the museum, the monument, preservation, and the heritage sector, including archaeology, as a compensatory and therapeutic reaction to the decline of modernity. In both instances, a dichotomy between modernity and non-modernity is a core premise for the interpretation of developments.

Like the Ritter School, the first, canonical, culture of heritage works towards a compromise, pursuing a balance between renewal and preservation. The second, critical, culture of heritage lines up, in its more extreme forms, with revolutionaries, Futurists, and entrepreneurs in giving the renewal of modernity priority ahead of preservation. Indeed, heritage is an obstacle that has to be confronted and, if possible, overcome. But both cultures presuppose an opposition between modernity and tradition, just as they both presuppose that modernity always means change and tradition always means permanence.

Critics of modernity have usually stressed that modernity is (or was) illogical, inconsistent, and contradictory (e.g. Compagnon 1990 (French); 1994 (English); Latour 1991 (French): 84ff; 1993 (English): 55ff; Thomas 2004: 42ff). Modernity claims one thing, but does the opposite. Modernity is guided by historicism; the idea of progress is followed by a reappearance of the past. The utopia of modernity is built like a medieval cathedral (cf. Källström 2000).

Several scholars have found it odd that modernity, of all things, has been so focused on the past. For instance, the ethnologist Agneta Lilja views modernity's remarkable interest in tradition as a "paradox of modernity" (Lilja 1996: 37). And the archaeologist Cornelius Holtorf finds it ironic that modernism is so obsessed with preserving the past unchanged (Holtorf 2006: 102).

But there does not need to be an opposition between modernity on the one hand and history, memory, and heritage, museums, monuments or traditions on the other. These spheres, with their concepts, are entangled in one another. Modernity can include the apparently non-modern or even anti-modern. It depends on how concepts and phenomena are defined – or not defined, being kept ambiguously open.

When modernity and the museum, modernisation and musealisation, are often set up as mutually contradictory, this is due to our images of modernity as an expression of speed and change – and the museum as an expression of, or the very emblem of, slowness and immutability. On the one hand, urban bustle, density, and clamour; on the other, the peace, space, and quiet of the museum. But it can also be the other way round, depending on the point in time, the place, and – not least – what exhibition is being visited. When posters announce blockbusters such as Monet, Van Gogh, or Picasso – or Tutankhamun – the museum and its exhibition are indisputably part of hectic urban modernity.

On the face of it, the concept of the museum, from the Greek word *museion* meaning "temple", does not contain anything that conflicts with modernity. Museums are built using the architecture current in their time. Walter Benjamin thus described the museum as the dream architecture of his time (Benjamin 1983 (German), 1: 511ff; 1999 (English): 407ff). Nor does the museum as an institution, with its different definitions and practices as a place for collections and exhibitions, exclude the modern. The museum is filled with objects that are not only relics from a lost world but also represent a modern present. Modern art came into museums when modernism was alive, even during Stein's lifetime. Museums were founded early on specifically to collect and show the new – an example being MoMA, which opened in 1929 (www.moma.org), and Moderna Museet in Stockholm from 1958 (www.modernamuseet.se). And now that modernism has long been a canonised part of the history of art, the modern has also become a central part of the collections and exhibitions of most art museums.

Museologists and archaeologists have maintained that modernity is a necessary precondition for the museum as an institution and for archaeology as a discipline – indeed for the whole of rational science. Inspired by Michel Foucault, they describe the museum as an institution that disciplines knowledge, just as prisons, hospitals, factories, and schools are said to discipline people (e.g. Hooper-Greenhill 1992; Olsen & Svestad 1994; Bennett 1995: 95f; Svestad 1995; Prior 2002; Thomas 2004: 52ff). Donald Horne also linked the museum to modern society, but without comparing it to a prison. To him, a tourist visit to a museum – with its timetable, planned route, and focus on the material – reflected the values of industrial society (Horne 1984: 115f).

In line with Foucault's thought, the archaeologists Bjørnar Olsen and Asgeir Svestad interpreted the foundation of the Old Nordic Museum in Copenhagen, and the establishment of archaeology as a practice and a discipline in the course of the nineteenth century, as an opportunity that opened with the breakdown of the classical episteme. They regard the breakdown of the classical episteme in around 1800, with its Genesis narrative and biblical chronology, as meaning that the past was transformed into a fog or darkness which the museum and archaeology, with their ancient objects, could fill with new knowledge. The "modern episteme" with its focus on origins and change thus enabled the growth of museums and archaeology (Olsen & Svestad 1994; Svestad 1995).

Modernity and archaeology are entangled in each other. However, archaeology as excavation and studies of the past existed long before the modern era. But the background of the development of archaeology as an academic discipline is the opening of prehistory; that is, a period before the history of texts. Archaeology uses modern technologies in its methods. Field archaeology is in itself a form of engineering to ensure the expansion of modern society (cf. Rosén 2007). And now, in the twenty-first century, modernity has become a field of research for archaeologists to explore (e.g. Ersgård 2007; Lihammer & Nordin 2010; Anthony 2016).

In principle, this argument may be repeated for monuments, as there is not necessarily any conflict between modernity and monuments. Monuments have all once been "modern" in the sense of "new"; they may be designed in a modern style, and they may serve as reminders not only of something in the past, but also of phenomena in the present or even the future. Temporary monuments may celebrate modern speed, as at the Goodwood Festival of Speed, held in the UK since 1993 (www.goodwood.com).

And monuments can be (re)created using modern light, as has happened at the World Trade Center in Manhattan, New York, and with the Buddha statues in Bamiyan in Afghanistan, which were both destroyed in 2001 (cf. Melotti 2011: 121ff, 134ff). "Tribute in Light" using searchlights pointing up into the sky is thus intended as an annual commemoration of the terror attack on the Twin Towers on 11 September 2001 (www.mas.org/programs/tributeinlight); and the lost Buddha statues were recreated for a short time in a 3D light projection in 2015 (www.youtube.com/watch?v=JDEk9rjM39c).

Modernity and tradition are often presented as a contrast. Modernity may afford associations to capitalism, industrialism, urbanisation, movement, and change, while tradition may carry connotations of feudalism, crafts, rural areas, and stasis. Tradition refers to what survives from one generation to the next, to inheritance, security, repetition, and continuity; to that which endures. In crisis theories, tradition is a reaction to modernity. Conversely, too much tradition can also have a restrictive effect and bring about a need for renewal, for modernity. But modernity and tradition are not mutually contradictory or complementary in the sense of both necessary and incompatible. Innumerable threads run between modernity and tradition, linking them. The concepts are therefore inextricably entangled. Paradoxically, too, tradition can be a modern construction.

The idea that tradition is part of modernity was the influential thesis advocated by the historian Eric Hobsbawm. In his introduction to the collected volume *The Invention of Tradition*, Hobsbawm argued that new symbolic rituals intended to show continuity with the past are particularly apt to be established when rapid change in society weakens or destroys social patterns. Traditions are presented as being extremely old; but they are modern, and they may even be part of modernisation itself (Hobsbawm & Ranger 1983: 1ff; Prickett 2009).

One often cited, albeit contested, example from Hobsbawm's anthology is the kilt, an icon for the Scottish and Highland clans. The kilt is said to be an innovation from around 1730 by an English manufacturer (Trevor-Roper 1983). Another example is ceremonies in the British Royal Family that are intended as evidence of consensus, stability, and community even though – or just because – society is undergoing powerful change; many of these ceremonies were in fact invented in the period between the 1870s and the First World War (Cannadine 1983).

Since the publication of *The Invention of Tradition*, the view that not only traditions but also museums and heritage are part of modernity has had a great impact in the cultural and social sciences. Modernity is said to have created traditions, museums, and heritage in a way that had never existed before. Similarly, urbanisation is said to have led to a new perception of rural areas, industrialisation to a new image of pre-industrial society, and literacy to an interest in oral culture. At the same time, complex society is said to have created a primitive counter-image and civilisation to have defined its own boundaries in relation to barbarity (e.g. Kuper 1988; Malina & Vasícek 1990: 218; Bausinger 1991; Eriksen 1993; Giddens 1999). So the central point is not the opposition, but the connections between modernity and a number of other phenomena.

However, modernity is not only many-faced and transient; it also has weight like a black hole. For modernity swallows other grand narratives or phenomena such as capitalism, industrialism, urbanisation, and secularisation – just as it swallows criticism and compensation. Paradoxically, then, reactions to modernity may themselves also be modern – museums, monuments, archaeology, traditions, and heritage. The core premise of crisis theories, the notion of a dichotomy between modernity and a number of nostalgic or therapeutic reactions, turns out to be false. Both Stein and Mumford were wrong when they contrasted the museum and the monument with the modern. Without a contrast, the paradox of modernity dissolves. The characterisation of modernity as ironic is mistaken as well.

Returning to the debate about heritage, it is possible to uncover a political and history-of-ideas context for the two cultures of heritage and to systematise different individuals and their positions. There are those who confirm modernity, those who want to see modernity, those who accept it because they must, and those who reject it. These positions may, if one so wishes, be discussed in relation to a political scale.

We meet eager modernists verging on Futurism in the shape of Pierre Boulez, who was all for destroying the past in order to move forward (Boulez 1976: 33), and of Cornelius Holtorf, who uses varying arguments and examples to advance the thesis that remains from the past do not need to be preserved and may instead be consumed, renewed, or replaced (e.g. Holtorf 2005: 130ff; 2006; 2018).

Several scholars have given vent to a feeling that modernity has been lost and that this is a thing to be regretted. In doing so, they have indicated where their sympathies lie. Agnes Heller, for instance, argued that Europe has abandoned its true identity, which she saw as progress and modernity (Heller 1988: 155). Robert Hewison wanted to see real industry doing real work (Hewison 1987). Patrick Wright wanted developments to be orientated towards the future (Wright 1985), and Frank Füredi claimed that the crises of modernity had resulted in stagnation, pessimism, and emptiness (Füredi 1992).

The Ritter School, with Joachim Ritter, Herman Lübbe, and Odo Marquard, noted the unfavourable consequences of progress and modernity, but accepted this development as a fact or a necessary evil (cf. Ritter 1961; Lübbe 1982; 1983; 1996; Marquard 1986; 2000). They perceived a task for the humanities, history, memory, and heritage in warding off the worst consequences of progress and modernity and trying to save what could be saved for the future.

Many have seen the unfavourable aspects of modernity and turned away from it, some by adopting postmodernity when it appeared. Norman W. Brown thought that his own present was in a state of sickness on account of civilisation, money, urbanisation, and capitalism (Brown 1959: 234ff). Claude Lévi-Strauss took the view that modern society creates social classes and human exploitation (Lévi-Strauss 1966: 121f). Fred Davis described modern society as characterised by discontinuity and problems (Davis 1979: 97ff). Donald Horne took the view that modernity had caused a crisis (Horne 1984: 21ff). Andreas Huyssen criticised the media and described his present as chaotic, fragmentary, and free-floating (Huyssen 1995: 25ff). And considering Françoise Choay's vigorous condemnation of the electronic technology of our time, she can be classified as an anti-modernist and a neo-Luddite (cf. Choay 1992 (French): 187ff; 2001 (English): 164ff).

Once more, David Lowenthal makes up a category of his own. Lowenthal concluded that modernity was succeeded by postmodernity and regarded both with irony and criticism. If Lowenthal's view of the "isms" is unclear, he was all the clearer in his assessment of the present, which he described as being characterised by traumatic losses and changes and by fear of the future (Lowenthal 1985: 8ff, 394ff; 1997: 1, 5ff; 2015: 31ff, 413ff).

However, Laurent Olivier is, if possible, even more dystopic. Olivier sees the wreck of the Age of Enlightenment since the twentieth century in a series of disasters – the two world wars, the Holocaust, Hamburg, Hiroshima, Chernobyl, the World Trade Center. With references to Benjamin, Heidegger, and Adorno, he looks on the industrialisation of war, the mass production of goods by machines, and the crisis for European civilisation; and he concludes: "There is no Future" (Olivier 2008 (French): 119ff, quotation 120; 2011 (English): 75ff, quotation 76).

To sum up, the canonical tradition of heritage may be positioned close to the Ritter School's conservatism or liberal pragmatism, whereas the critical tradition of heritage spreads to both sides – to the right and, especially, to the left on a traditional political scale.

But modernity is so controversial as a concept and phenomenon that a debate easily runs aground. On the one extreme wing are modernists, revolutionaries, and Futurists, who need the past with its museums, monuments, ancient monuments, traditions, and heritage as a rhetorical counter-image. On the other extreme wing are the opponents of modernity, anti-modernists, reactionaries, and nostalgists, who have a rhetorical urge to defame progress, the present, and utopias. On the one side is the first culture of heritage, where modernity is seen as a threat that must be averted or balanced. On the other side of the gap is the second culture of heritage, in which remains of the past and antiquarian institutions are perceived as a threat.

The disputed position of modernity leads to scepticism when phenomena such as museums, monuments, ancient remains, traditions, and heritage apparently change sides, when they become part of the modern. Despite its many opponents, modernity continues to have a positive ring to it. Does the change of sides represent a new insight about the greater range of modernity? Or is it rather an attempt to win sympathy for something that risks being left behind as ruins after the storm of progress? To make sure that the whole field of history, memory, and heritage is not left behind as something that belongs in a museum, but is also part of the narrative of progress and the future? To make a virtue of necessity? The past must become modern to have a chance. So the past has always been modern.

If, however, modernity is not in conflict with history, memory, and heritage – in conflict with museums, monuments, archaeology, traditions, and nostalgia – then the relationship between modernity and World Heritage may be more complicated than first assumed. Modernity, with the Aswan High Dam and the need for electricity, was initially seen as a threat to the ancient temples of Abu Simbel. Clearly, then, things are not necessarily that simple.

The opponents of modernity

The film *Modern Times* by Charlie Chaplin, who was both director and actor, depicts the US of the 1930s (Chaplin 1936 film). It associates the modern with industrial society, with that society's increasing speed at factory assembly lines, and with unemployment and social unrest. The film communicated a criticism of modernity that was typical of its time, but it did so in a humorous way.

For as long as modernity has been around, it has been fashionable to be critical of it; anti-modern people have always been modern. That massive criticism has been levelled against modernity itself as well as against a number of phenomena interwoven with it – progress, enlightenment, technology, industrialisation, capitalism, urbanisation, and secularisation. This criticism can be defiantly offensive or melancholically resigned. At best, it may contribute additional perspectives on what modernity has been, is, or ought to be. At worst, though, it may contribute to creating pessimistic myths about modernity, myths that liquidate human hope (cf. Tallis 1997).

Consequently, Romanticism and historicism in the nineteenth century may be interpreted as a reaction against the Enlightenment and the radical new elements of belief, science, art, and politics that culminated in the American Revolution, the French Revolution, and the subsequent Napoleonic Wars. In Europe, what was modern at that time was opposed both by the melancholy contemplation of ruins, along with backward-looking architecture, and by a political reaction that reasserted the Church and the authority of the monarchy.

When Charles Baudelaire insightfully characterised modernity as the fleeting and the transient, something that is continually transforming itself, as the change of time, this was a view formulated precisely by a melancholy and nostalgic Romantic (Baudelaire 1863 (French); 1964 (English)). And despite differences, Baudelaire was completely in line with other social critics in his time in this respect.

Modernity, with its changing significance, has been criticised for leading to loss of meaning and alienation, to social and spiritual poverty, and to the disintegration of communities. We meet this criticism first in the UK, Germany, France, and the US, and then in Scandinavia – that is, in countries where industrialisation roared forward in the nineteenth and twentieth centuries. The critics are philosophers such as Karl Marx, Walter Benjamin, Max Horkheimer, Theodor W. Adorno, Martin Heidegger, and Georg Henrik von Wright, sociologists such as Ferdinand Tönnies, Émile Durkheim, Georg Simmel, Max Weber, Zygmunt Bauman, and Hartmut Rosa, and the human ecologist Alf Hornborg. This array is then joined by the philosophers Joachim Ritter, Odo Marquard, and Hermann

Lübbe, the historian and geographer David Lowenthal, the historian Françoise Choay, and the literary historian Andreas Huyssen. These names represent widely different personalities, perspectives, and positions, everything from left to right on the political scale, and everything from analysis to agitation; still, these critics are united in a deep distrust of modernity in their own present.

In philosophy and sociology, several now classic concepts and perspectives are reused – and some new ones minted – in order to characterise the unfortunate consequences of modernity or phenomena linked to modernity: the concept of alienation (German *Entfremdung*) was used by Karl Marx in his "Economic and Philosophic Manuscripts" of 1844 to describe the consequences of capitalism for workers in relation to their work, other people, and nature (Marx 1968 (German); 1975 (English)). Ferdinand Tönnies described the development from the pre-modern community (German *Gemeinschaft*) characterised by the family to the modern, rational society (German *Gesellschaft*) (Tönnies 1887 (German); 2001 (English)). Émile Durkheim used the concept "anomie", the absence of norms, that could arise in both economic growth and decline. Great social changes and imbalances cause a crisis in society, leading to more suicides (Durkheim 1897 (French); 1951 (English)). Later, Georg Simmel described how people in the modern metropolis were affected by the division of labour and the money economy. While life in small towns was slow and characterised by personal contacts, the metropolis was characterised by continuous rapid transformations and impersonal contacts. Rootlessness threatened in the metropolis (Simmel 1903 (German); 1950 (English)). Max Weber employed the concept *Entzauberung* ("disenchantment") in his lecture "Wissenschaft als Beruf" ("Science as Vocation"), delivered to German students in Munich in 1917. The science of the West, with its intellectualisation and rationalisation, meant a disenchantment and secularisation of the world that weakened the magic, mystic, and religious (Weber 1922 (German): 554; 1991 (English): 155). And in the 1940s, Max Horkheimer and Theodor W. Adorno formulated the concept of the culture industry (German *Kulturindustrie*) as part of their criticism of modern mass society and its entertainment industry (Horkheimer & Adorno 1947 (German): 144ff; 2002 (English): 94ff; Adorno 1967 (German); 1979 (English)).

Walter Benjamin's image of progress as a storm was meant in a derogatory sense. The angel of history, Angelus Novus, saw a disastrous storm that created ruins on its way from Paradise (Benjamin

1970 (English): 259f; 1980 (German): 687f). And Benjamin associated modernity with standing at an abyss and with a chronic crisis (Benjamin 1983 (German): II, 677; 1999 (English): 545), which is not remarkable, given his own vulnerable situation as a refugee.

Zygmunt Bauman formulated a weighty but controversial critique of modernity in *Modernity and the Holocaust* (1989). Here, Bauman related modernity to the European trauma, the Holocaust genocide that culminated in the Auschwitz-Birkenau complex (WHL 31, 1979). According to Bauman, the technology and rationality of modernity, its science and bureaucracy, were prerequisites for implementing a genocide on an industrial scale (also Horkheimer & Adorno 1947 (German): 235ff; 2002 (English): 165ff). In his view, then, the Holocaust represented yet another face of modernity.

However, Bauman failed to recognise the irrationality of Nazism and how, for the most part, the Holocaust was *not* in fact implemented rationally or industrially, even at Auschwitz, but constituted a mass murder by traditional means in a society marked by political and administrative anarchy (cf. Snyder 2015; Cannon 2016).

An environmentalist line of thought that is critical of technology can be mapped from the late eighteenth century up to present-day notions about sustainable development. This is a line whose advocates have wanted to see progress and growth, but insisted they should not have unfortunate consequences.

Actual attacks on the new technology manifested themselves in early industrialism in England, where new textile machines were seen as a threat to the old crafts. In the 1810s, Luddites – named after their fictional leader Ned Ludd – thus sabotaged textile machines and factories in violent actions, threatening the lives of the owners if they offered resistance (Jones 2006).

A more abstract critique of technology was advanced by Martin Heidegger. In his essay "Die Frage nach der Technik" ("The Question Concerning Technology"), Heidegger asserts – once again in obscure words – that technology and its essence might be a threat to human beings' pursuit of truth (Heidegger 1954 (German); 1977 (English)).

In recent decades, progress and modernity, with the utopia of boundless growth, have been criticised from many directions as being responsible for destruction of the environment and as a cause of global climate change. Georg Henrik von Wright became a leading figure of the environmentally critical movement against progress and economic growth with his *Myten om framsteget* "The Myth of Progress". He described progress as a myth that would not survive the crisis of modernity in his present. Von Wright was critical of human beings' unrestrained search for knowledge, critical of the ability of natural science and technology to solve the problems they themselves create, critical of growing quantification, and critical of the distortion of traditional patterns of life by industrialisation and what he called quasi-democracy. Instead, von Wright praised the classic modernity of the eighteenth century, the Age of Enlightenment, and the pre-industrial age, when, in his view, technology was useful and sensible (Wright 1993).

Most recently, Alf Hornborg has criticised the central element of progress, modernity, and industrialisation, namely the machine, which he regards as a fetish. According to Hornborg, the idea that machines save time is a myth. What machines actually do is redistribute resources, human time and labour, from the periphery to the centre of the economic world system. Hornborg also claims that industrialisation as we know it in the West is coming to an end. For industrialisation builds on oil and other fossil fuels, and the supply of oil is supposed to have peaked already. And in his view, a transition to other, more sustainable, forms of energy is not realistic (e.g. Hornborg 2001; 2010).

Clearly, then, an enormous importance has been ascribed to modernity as a global force that has reshaped human beings, nature, culture, and society. For there appears to be no end to all the things that modernity is thought to have caused. Masses of phenomena and "isms" have been viewed either as a consequence of or as a reaction to modernity: unemployment, social unrest, alienation, anxiety, stress, secularisation, disenchantment, fascism, Nazism, Islamism, the Holocaust, totalitarianism, fundamentalism, terrorism, environmental pollution, and climate change. It looks as if everything bad or wicked in the world is projected onto modernity. Moreover, Romanticism, nostalgia, modernism, and postmodernism are believed to form a reaction to modernity, as are history, memory, and heritage. Modernity with its many faces must apparently bear the responsibility for both the bad and the good in a development in which each time and place has its own needs, traumas, and crises. Modernity is made a scapegoat for whatever breeds discontent in life.

Indirectly, the criticism recapitulated above outlines a picture of human beings, nature, culture, and society before modernity. Pre-modernity was apparently a golden age characterised by usefulness, reason, employment, order, closeness, community, security, balance, sufficient time, belief, and mystery. There was no fascism or Nazism, no Holocaust and no totalitarianism, fundamentalism, terrorism, environmental pollution, or climate change. Judging by the criticism, the arrival of modernity must therefore have meant an epoch-making break with the past – or, more poetically, a brutal expulsion from Paradise. Things were better in the old days!

Pre-modernity is constructed as a lost paradise or a lost "foreign country". The criticism is clearly a nostalgic reaction which may be counted among modernity's numerous other consequences and counter-reactions. But the question now is whether the criticism of modernity, with its consequences and counter-reactions, has not itself been absorbed by modernity and come to be part of it?

In *Modern Times*, Chaplin made use of a modern mass medium, film, to ridicule modern society. Chaplin made use of the very cultural industry centred on Hollywood that Max Horkheimer and Theodor W. Adorno rejected, even though they lived in Pacific Palisades, just a half-hour trip by car from the Hollywood they criticised. But paradoxically, Chaplin's *Modern Times* was unmodern in that it was Hollywood's last great silent film, speech only appearing in carefully selected sections. Modern and unmodern technology were thus freely united in *Modern Times* and its entertaining criticism of modernity.

Enlightened modernity

Modernity has many faces. Modernity is something that began thousands of years ago, or a couple of centuries ago; or it is something that has not yet happened. Modernity is something that is over and done with, something that is still ongoing, or something waiting to happen in the future. Modernity can mean one thing and then another, depending on the perspective applied. To deepen the confusion, the concepts modern, modernisation, modernism, and modernity are often used randomly without clear distinctions. Moreover, modernity is linked with emphatic opinions as being either a good thing that should be promoted or something bad that we ought to reject. Modernity is thus both an ambiguous and a contested concept.

In linguistic terms the concept of modernity has to do with renewal, with modernising, and it is not restricted to a given field or a certain period or part of the world. Modernity is closely related to progress, which is generally to do with improvement through change, by doing something new. Only human ingenuity and the resources available set limits for what can be renewed and improved.

The metaphorical openness of modernity in terms of both its characteristics and its consequences is hence something we must accept. Modernity is characterised by transience; and it is itself a transient concept which escapes definition.

The goal of renewal or modernisation is modernity. But as a goal in constant movement, modernity remains a utopia, because there is always something that can be modernised, either for the first time or once again. The goal is constantly being moved forward. It is possible to strive for new goals, new utopias. In this sense, to be modern is to be constantly on the way to a new time and a new place.

Modernity has been put to use and given a central role in the narrative of the West and progress. This is a basic narrative about the origins and development of human beings and of society, a story whose details may vary as required. Each field can contribute its own small part of the grand narrative. The pluralism of perspectives creates a common, but somewhat blurred, picture of modernity. Agreement may be reached both on this and that being expressions of modernity, even though, strictly speaking, the views in question are internally opposed. Modernity as a diffuse concept that is, on closer examination, often found to be full of contradictions helps enable different groups to nevertheless agree on a common way forward.

As in many other situations, the purpose of the narrative is to contribute to social cohesion. With its knowledge, form, and reflection, the narrative creates identity. The narrative is about who we are, where we come from, and where we are going. The narrative of modernity creates meaning and identity in an always chaotic present. It can be used to impose a meaning-creating structure both on the past and on the present and the future. But the "we" of identity presupposes the existence of "the others". Hence the narrative of modernity is both inclusive and exclusive.

Modernity is part of the grand narrative of the development of the West, "the West" being another ambiguous concept. Originating in the Latin word for sunset, *occidens*, as opposed to sunrise, *oriens*, "the West" has, in practice, come to mean Europe and North America with their allies, countries seen as having market economies, representative democracy, and civil rights and freedoms. Despite all the differences – and there are many – it is felt that there are some common features that differentiate the West today from earlier periods, or differentiate the West from other areas. So modernity excludes both what happened in earlier times and those "others" who are held to not yet have attained modernity. But modernity as a narrative can, in principle, be all-inclusive, even though it is generally only about a selected part of humanity: the West.

In principle, modernity stands for an apparently innocent endeavour to improve the world. But the occasionally favourable but mostly unfavourable upshot is that modernity has landed in an infected debate about the unfortunate aspects of progress, the Enlightenment, technology, industrialisation, capitalism, urbanisation, and secularisation. In the West's criticism of itself – and in others' criticism of the West – the narrative of modernity has become a tragedy. Here the criticism forgets that modernity has many faces that complement one another.

Just like the Enlightenment, modernity has both a "hard" and a "soft" side (cf. Liedman 1997: 26ff) – or it displays two cultures, in line with C. P. Snow. Modernity is thus both a question of the humanities, and among them especially philosophy and the history of ideas, and natural science, technology, and economics. Modernity can be linked to ideas, concepts, and values – and to experiments, machines, and capital. Moreover, these perspectives are inextricably entangled with one another.

The Age of Enlightenment brought new ideas about the categories of the triad – the true, the beautiful, and the good – all of which are imbued with a universal ambition. Modernity is thus characterised by a new faith in the true, where knowledge is attained by reason and rational scientific methods. Here modernity is often related to the emergence of a new natural science, characterised by experiments since the seventeenth century, and to technological inventions; but modernity may equally be linked to new knowledge in the interpretative humanities. The central point is that the new knowledge lays the foundations for developments (e.g. Toulmin 1990; Liedman 1997).

Modernism is a collection of experimental movements in architecture, art, literature, and music since the end of the nineteenth century, a set of movements that questioned tradition and constantly sought the new. Modernism is normally regarded as a past phenomenon, but the duration of the period depends on what expression is being studied, and a febrile search for new forms of expression has continued. Moreover, according to the literary critic Matei Calinescu, modernity includes not only modernism, but also avant-garde, decadence, kitsch, and postmodernism (*OED*: IX 948f; Calinescu 1987).

Finally, new values have gradually been established from the seventeenth century onwards. They include universal ideas about political and religious freedom and legal, social, and gender equality as well as democracy – the idea that people should be able to elect their leaders (Liedman 1997; Bring 2011). The idea of human rights is a concrete example of conceptual innovation that has been given official status with the UN Universal Declaration of Human Rights (1948). Another concrete example that might be adduced is the global reporting of the degree of personal, civil, and economic freedom, which is measured in the annual Human Freedom Index (www.cato.org/human-freedom-index).

The Age of Enlightenment also brought developments in natural science, medicine, technology, and economics, where there are many statistical possibilities of measuring results or consequences: statistics pertaining to infant mortality, life expectancy, urbanisation, energy consumption, gross domestic product (GDP), the Human Development Index, capital accumulation, the distribution of patents, and the spread of mobile phones or the Internet.

For both the hard and the soft side of modern global development, facts will show a generally favourable trend which contradicts the chronic pessimism of crisis theories (cf. Pinker 2018; Rosling *et al.* 2018). In my view, the hard and the soft side of modernity meet in both concrete and metaphorical terms as light is shed on them.

Light as a guide can overcome the gap between different material and intangible perspectives on modernity. Light is associated with speed and transience, with Enlightenment and illumination. In physics, light is connected with time and matter and represents the highest attainable speed, the speed of light. On the one hand, light can be linked to the ideals of the Age of Enlightenment and is a prerequisite for reading; on the other hand, light can be followed in the culture of everyday life. Light is thus both a concept to think with and something transient that can be measured.

Light can be viewed as an idea-intensive concrete technology, with the development of light sources, windows, window glass, braziers, lamps, paraffin lamps, gas lamps, electricity, light bulbs (now low-energy bulbs), fittings, cables, fuses, transformers, generators in power stations, and solar cells (e.g. Brox 2010; Garnert 2016).

It has been shown that global economic production broadly corresponds to night-sky brightness as seen from a satellite. The contrast shows up clearly between, for instance, dark North Korea and shining South Korea. It is also thought that night-sky brightness may provide a more correct picture of economic activity than the traditional measuring of GDP. This is both because calculations of GDP may be uncertain and because there may be political reasons for over- or understating its size. It is, quite simply, hard to obtain credible global figures for economic activity. Night-sky brightness also permits analyses of regions across or within states (Henderson *et al.* 2009; cf. Croft 1978). The study of night-sky brightness recently advanced to the stage where it is possible to gauge the brightness of individual countries around the globe (Falchi *et al.* 2016).

The light in cities has been seen as a metaphorical expression of modernity, whereas darkness was taken as an expression of the past, the unmodern (Schlör 1991 (German); 1998 (English)). Indeed, several scholars have chosen global night-sky brightness as a concrete expression of modernity, since the quantity of light depends on energy conversion; that is, on the economy or the "technomass", the quantity of machines (e.g. Hornborg 2010; Wienberg 2010).

My immediate reaction is that the picture of night-time brightness is beautiful, like an earthly firmament. But night brightness can also be viewed either as light pollution, an environmental problem (Bogard 2013; www.lightpollution.it/dmsp/index.html), or as a concrete expression of the uneven exchange of goods between the centre and the periphery and therefore as an expression of the skewed distribution of capital (Hornborg 2010: 1, 39, 150, 173f). In the conflicting perceptions of night-time brightness, we therefore again find the debate about developments as either progress or decline in the wake of modernity.

Many have expected that the dissemination of Western market economy and technology would mean that "soft" Western values would also spread globally. The clearest example is the political philosopher Francis Fukuyama, who optimistically wrote the essay "The End of History?" (1989) in the year that saw the fall of the Berlin Wall. Fukuyama concluded that Western market economy and democracy had won and that history had ended; but he also felt nostalgic, since the ideological and conflict-filled post-war period had now been replaced by a boring post-historical future.

A few years later, the political scientist Samuel P. Huntington was berated for the prediction made in his essay "The Clash of Civilisations?" (1993) regarding conflicts along cultural boundaries. According to Huntington, several non-Western countries have had a strategy "to modernize but not to Westernize" (Huntington 1993: 41, quotation 49); that is, to choose the technological and economic part of modernity without including the values of the

West. But Fukuyama was mistaken – and Huntington turned out to be right.

History continued indefatigably and unpredictably. China's growth shows that the market economy and technology are one thing, but that politics and values are something else: state-directed capitalism also works. A rising centre in the world-system is striving after modernity when it comes to technology and the economy, but without necessarily accepting Western values into the bargain. Other examples are Al-Qaeda, which used aircraft in its terror attack on the US in 2001 (Gray 2001), and IS, which has employed the Internet in its propaganda. The Islamic movements are happy to utilise the West's modern technology, but are opposed to the world-system of the US and to modern Western values in general. The West's own critics of modernity have normally associated modernity with technology and the economy as well as with unfortunate consequences; in doing so, they have forgotten other aspects.

The market and modernity are able to exist in symbiosis. Capitalism is able to use modernity as an ideology and a legitimation of an economic system. Economic development is assumed to help enable everyone to be better off, contributing to progress and growth. But modernity is not identical to or completely dependent on capitalism. For renewal can be justified and take place in different types of societies, that is, in widely different cultural, religious, political, and economic circumstances. So a society can accept technological and economic renewal, but oppose religious or political change. This means that the renewal of modernity does not need to be a goal in all areas. Modernity may also have existed before capitalism, and it may continue to exist even if capitalism disappears.

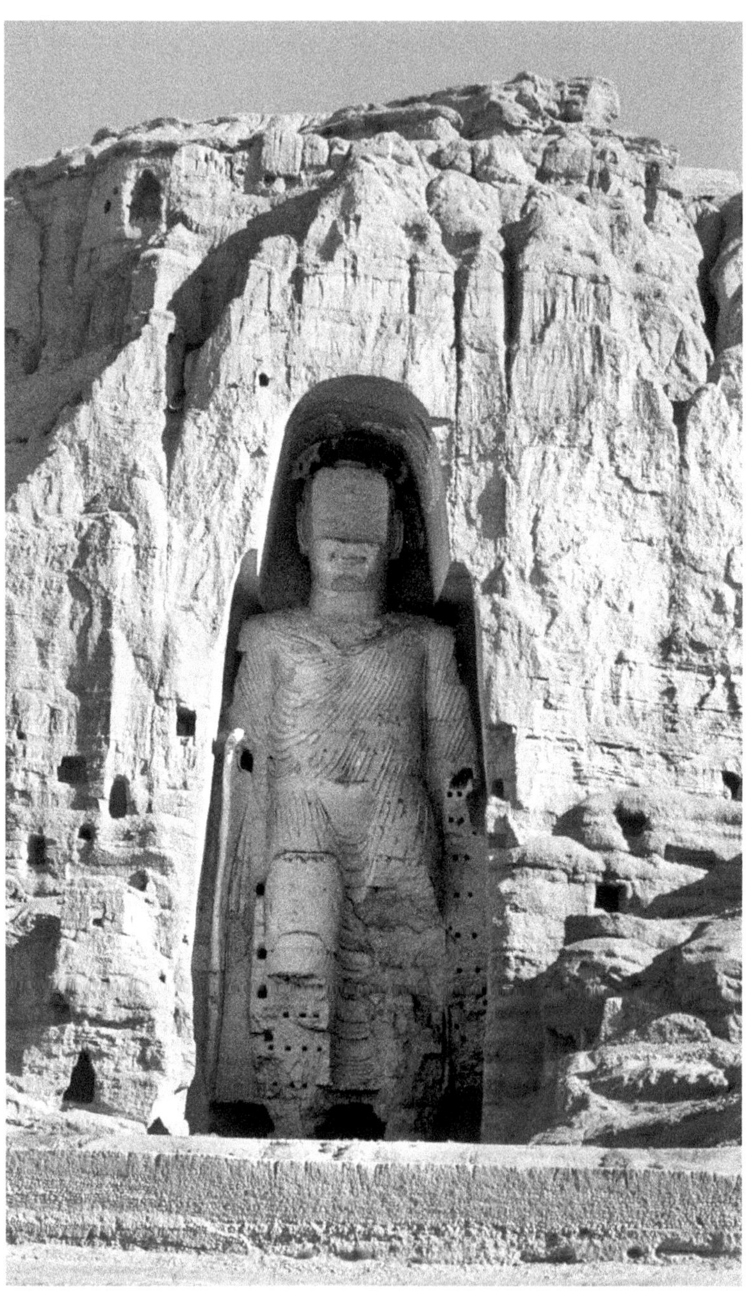

Figure 5 Buddha-statue in Bamiyan before its destruction in 2001.
Photo © Jens Vellev, 1969.

5
Heritage in the present

Heritage is everywhere

David Lowenthal's classic *The Past is a Foreign Country* opens with the sentence "The past is everywhere", and he used exactly the same words three decades later when he revisited that country (Lowenthal 1985: xv; 2015: 1). *The Heritage Crusade and the Spoils of History* begins in much the same way, but here the past has been limited to heritage: "ALL AT ONCE HERITAGE IS EVERYWHERE – in the news, in the movies, in the marketplace – in everything from galaxies to genes" (Lowenthal 1997: ix). The phrase "Heritage everywhere" is later used as the title of the introductory chapter of Rodney Harrison's *Heritage: Critical Approaches* (Harrison 2013: 1).

Lowenthal was not alone in concluding that the past, with its history, memory, and heritage, was intruding on the present. That same observation turns up on a broad front in the West in the 1980s and 1990s. The sense that there was an inflation of the past triggered a wave of critical reflections on this development: Agnes Heller found an increased focus on museums in Europe after the First World War (Heller 1988); Hermann Lübbe noted an increase in musealisation in Switzerland and Germany over the twentieth century (Lübbe 1982); Robert Hewison observed an increase in the number of museums, theme parks, and visitor centres in England since the 1960s and launched the concept "Heritage Industry" (Hewison 1987: 83ff); Françoise Choay perceived an inflation in heritage since the 1960s, reacting particularly strongly against the establishment of industrial monuments and increased heritage tourism (Choay 1992 (French): 158ff; 2001 (English): 138ff); and Andreas Huyssen observed a "relentless museummania" in the 1980s (Huyssen 1995: 14, 20, 25ff). In Sweden, Svante Beckman noted rapid growth in aesthetic and entertainment use of history and heritage, with an ever-larger number of museums and antique markets (Beckman 1993a: 28f).

Referring to the rising number of countries that had ratified the World Heritage Convention and the increasing number of World Heritage sites, Thordis Arrhenius concluded that "[t]he inflation of heritage is today a fact" (Arrhenius 2003: 162). And Rodney Harrison discusses a "heritage boom" and "crisis of accumulation" in late modernity (Harrison 2013: 68ff, 166).

In *The Past is a Foreign Country* (1985; 2015), Lowenthal mainly gathered, presented, and commented on examples in a collage, but he was all the more explicit in his criticism of heritage in *The Heritage Crusade and the Spoils of History* (1997). Other debaters in the 1980s and 1990s were also particularly critical. The background of the development and establishment of "critical heritage" as a separate field of research and education can be sought precisely in the experience that the past, and especially heritage, were occupying more than their fair share of space in the present. This inflation had to be examined and, if necessary, also opposed. But with the gradual maturing of the field, the harsh initial criticism has been toned down and is being replaced by more balanced analysis and reflection (e.g. Harrison 2013: 204ff; Aronsson & Elgenius 2015).

At this time, however, there are many questions to consider. Is heritage actually everywhere? Which cultures are involved in the handling of heritage? When, how, and why does heritage arise and develop as a concept? What characterises heritage? What role do threats and vandalism play for heritage? What is the relationship between heritage and modernity? And what role does, or can, heritage have in the present?

To begin with the first question, is heritage everywhere? On an anecdotal plane, at any rate, it may be noted that David Lowenthal and the old or new edition of his book *The Past is a Foreign Country* turn up everywhere in the debate about the past, history, memory, and heritage. And over three decades, his book has increased in size from 489 to 660 pages.

It can also be noted that the concepts of cultural and natural heritage are well established in present-day legislation, management, and debate. The globalisation of heritage is seen in the establishment of UNESCO's Convention Concerning the Protection of the World Cultural and Natural Heritage (1972). Between 1978 and 2019, the number of World Heritage sites increased from 12 in seven countries to 1121 in 167 countries (*The World's Heritage* 2018; WHL, July 2019). And at the national level, heritage is included in the names of a number of institutions, one example being English Heritage (www.english-heritage.org.uk).

Since the 1980s, "critical heritage" has also gradually become established as a field in its own right. Its establishment is demonstrated by the many universities that conduct some form of education and research concerning heritage, manifested in the appearance of special networks, centres or departments, conferences, journals, textbooks, and theses. Examples are the *International Journal of Heritage Studies* (since 1994) and the Association of Critical Heritage Studies (since 2010; www.criticalheritagestudies.org).

One manifestation of the popularity of the heritage concept is its continual division into sub-categories according to type, period, or geography: cultural heritage and natural heritage, critical heritage, experimental heritage, applied heritage, digital heritage, biological heritage, heritage of war, architectural heritage, maritime heritage, intangible heritage, difficult heritage, classical heritage, heritage of modernity, heritage of the future, English heritage, African heritage, and many more.

Another expression of the popularity of heritage is seen in the way that the concept is constantly becoming relevant to new areas or seeping into closely related fields: heritage is combined with such words as archaeology, art, canon, church, colonialism, commercialism, conservation, criminality, democracy, development, development-assistance policy, economics, education, environment, ethics, forests, future, globalisation, politics of memory, history, human rights, identity, identity policy, landscape, legislation, management, memory, modernity(!), museums, nationalism, peace-building, politics, quality of life, religion, religious services, school, science, settlement, society, sustainable development, tourism, use, use of history, values, and world.

And as has happened with "history", "historicise", and "historisation", as well as with "museum", "musealise", and "musealisation", new words have been formed from "heritage" – words that mark a process and suggest a new disciplinary designation: "heritagisation" and "heritology" (e.g. Walsh 1992: 135ff; Sola 2005).

The thesis according to which there has been an inflation in heritage largely rests on an impressionistic experience that calls for concretisation and confirmation by evidence. Harrison thus substantiates a boom with statistics from the UK – National Trust membership (1895–2007 for England, Wales, and Northern Ireland) and annual visitor figures for Stonehenge (1925–2008) as well as for the British Museum (1760–2010); from the US – Colonial National Historical Park (1932–2010), Chao Culture National Historical Park (1925–2010), Yosemite National Park (1906–2010), and the

Smithsonian Museum (1970–2010); and globally from a number of World Heritage Sites in Danger (1978–2011) (Harrison 2013: 68ff with Figs 4: 1–8).

Harrison claims to identify a boom from around 1970, but his graphs do not show any uniform trend, apart from a gradual increase over a long period of time with breaks for the First and Second World Wars and some temporary deviations. The increase can be demonstrated from the nineteenth century (British Museum) and from the 1920s (Stonehenge, Yosemite), the 1940s (Colonial), and the 1950s (Chao). World Heritage Sites in Danger demonstrates growth since the 1970s, when the list came into being. Only National Trust membership displays a clear steep rise from 1970 onwards, but this growth followed a period of reorganisation and reorientation away from the previous focus on the country houses of the elite (www.nationaltrust.org.uk/lists/our-history-1945–2000).

Harrison's statistics may be supplemented by overviews from other areas: the establishment of national museums in Europe, which is bound up with nationalism and the establishment of nation states, the consequence being that the phenomenon culminates in the nineteenth century (Elgenius 2015); and the establishment of state and state-recognised museums in Denmark (1770–1997), which shows a relative increase over the nineteenth and twentieth centuries (Floris & Vasström 1999: 387ff). In contrast, both the establishment of reconstructions and sites with reconstructions in Scandinavia and the creation of archaeological open-air museums in Europe show a marked increase since the 1960s (Petersson 2003: 399ff; Paardekooper 2011: 79 Fig. 5).

In addition, the relationship between different concepts in the public debate can be illustrated from a long-term perspective with the aid of media archaeology, or "digging" in an archive. The occurrence of the words "history" (Swedish *historia*) and "[cultural] heritage" (Swedish *kulturarv*) can thus be followed in the Swedish newspaper *Svenska Dagbladet* with the aid of a digital archive from the founding of the paper in 1884 until the present (January 2020); *Svenska Dagbladet* is a morning paper, orientated towards the capital, with a conservative profile.

The word "history" appears in all these years with a steadily increasing number of pages; the highest, 4764 pages, occurs in 1994 (Appendix 3). By contrast, the expression "cultural heritage" appears for the first time in 1903; it then reappears regularly, but to a relatively limited extent, before increasing from the end of the 1970s onwards, the biggest number – 261 pages – being recorded for the year 2000. The expression "natural heritage" (Swedish *naturarv*) appears for the first time in 1923 and then makes highly sporadic appearances until the 1990s, when the concept occurs slightly more frequently, peaking in 1999 with seven newspaper pages.

It is notable that the word "history" dominates completely in every single year. The ratio between the expressions "history" and "cultural heritage" presents a clear pattern, the ratio of cultural heritage to history increasing gradually but steadily from 0.1 % in 1903 to its peak of 6.1 % in 2016. In the 1980s and 1990s, decades said to have witnessed an inflation or a boom, "cultural heritage" never rises above a ratio of 3.5 %.

The relative importance of the concepts "history", "memory", and "heritage" is also revealed by a Google search for the words as a quantitative hierarchy, with "history" at the top and "heritage" at the bottom: "history" 12,990 million, "memory" 2,360 million, and "heritage" 1,740 million; "archaeology" with 308 million comes in far below "heritage" (www.google.com; observed on 1 January 2020).

A fresh look at the statistical examples results in a new picture. The past and heritage were not suddenly everywhere. Instead, we observe a gradual increase in museums, museum visits, and heritage tourism that follows on from a general trend in the West with the establishment of nation states, population growth, and more leisure and motorised travel. There has not been a boom, in the sense of something unexpected or sudden; nor has there been any inflation, in the sense of something having ballooned. There has been a general and gradual numerical increase over a very long period, which cannot come as a surprise; and history has maintained its leading position.

The sense that there has been a boom and an inflation with regard to heritage since the 1980s is due to two factors: first, new themes and periods claimed space as the industrial heritage of modernity; second, there was a shift to new forms of mediation, such as reconstructions and re-enactment. The texts of history had to make room for more material expressions such as images, environments, and acts; and more room was demanded for heritage, with its monuments, buildings, sites, and landscapes.

It is the critics of heritage who sound warnings about a boom and an inflation, even though the shift appears to be relatively modest. The critics would prefer to see an orientation towards traditional text-orientated history, traditional exhibitions, and pre-modern themes. The same internal opposition has been encountered by antiquarian practice and disciplines such as history and archaeology when their focus has gradually shifted from exclusive concentration on Antiquity and the Middle Ages so that there is also coverage of the Early Modern and Modern periods, not to mention the present and the future.

But the reaction is exaggerated and partly misleading, since traditional text-based history still dominates completely, as does the museum with its exhibitions. However, once a boom has been described, it becomes a fact that is repeated in an unthinking manner. Both opponents and adherents may have an interest in claiming that heritage has expanded.

There is also a rhetorical rivalry that can be seen from the perspectives chosen: everything is history, everything is memory, or everything is heritage. Each of them wants its particular discourse and concepts to cover the whole field of interest in the past. That the concept of heritage also wants to assert its place is apparently regarded as a provocation.

So what is heritage? When, how, and why does heritage arise and develop, both as a practice and as a concept? Does heritage have its own essence or is it an expression of a transient process? An approach to these questions encounters two traditions, two groups of narratives or discourses, each of which sets out its own version of an answer, supplying two answers that may complement each other – the canonical and the critical.

Canonical heritage

Canon comes from the Greek word *kano'n* meaning "reed" or "guiding principle"; it may also mean "ruler", "measuring stick", "rule", or "model". Canonical scriptures are the genuine or authentic texts in the Bible. Canon law is Roman Catholic legislation that has special status. And saints are canonised, that is, recognised by the Church.

The literary critic Harold Bloom attracted attention and generated debate when, in his book *The Western Canon* (1994), he identified a number of authors and their works as canonical masterpieces, centring on William Shakespeare. Universal or national canonical lists assumed fresh relevance as a reaction against the relativism of postmodernism and a postcolonial criticism of Western values, after having been undeclared and part of general education in earlier times. One example of a formalised hierarchy may be seen in the Danish "Culture Canon" (Danish *Kulturkanon*, 2006), which arose from a political initiative but was compiled by experts. This canon, which was later followed by several others, selected 96 phenomena in seven areas – architecture, visual arts, design and crafts, film, literature, music, and performing arts – of which all Danes ought to be aware.

Canonical lists are not a new phenomenon. For example, the Seven Wonders of the World from Antiquity constitutes a list of outstanding buildings of that period (Klynne 2019). But there is a constant selection of what is considered worth telling about, remembering, or preserving for the future, while other things are consigned to silence, oblivion, or destruction (Assmann 1992 (German): 87ff, 167ff; 2011 (English): 70ff, 147ff). The temples of Abu Simbel represent a monumental canon that communicates an arranged image of Pharaoh Ramses II and the Battle of Kadesh.

Canonical lists are written down in a deliberate attempt to create and maintain hierarchies of values, in which something is considered more valuable than something else. They are written down when there is a need to do so; that is, when something is being threatened by silence, oblivion, or destruction – or is being threatened by alternative priorities. Bloom's canon was produced because he explicitly considered that the Western literary canon was under threat (Bloom 1994: 8). Irrespective of their justifications and motives, then, canons and canonisation are ultimately about power over the discourse.

Heritage represents one such canon. Heritage is used as a concept denoting that part of our inheritance that needs to be protected and preserved for the future. Something is selected as being heritage and given priority, whereas other things are allowed to disappear.

Canonical heritage may stand for an endeavour to protect and preserve selected remains from the past. Canonical heritage is characterised by the notion that the relevant heritage is threatened, but worth protecting and preserving for the future. Canonical heritage is therefore engaged in justifying protection and preservation, in setting criteria for the selection of heritage, and in developing new methods. Canonical heritage brings together individuals, groups, associations, management units, and institutions. Both legislation and a bureaucratic management culture have evolved around work on heritage.

There is extensive literature on the evolution of protection and preservation of remains from the past. This literature is a set of narratives that describe the gradual evolution of protection and preservation, from sporadic initiatives to the present national or international law and conventions. These narratives supply a forward-looking outline of the fight against the threats of various periods. They comprise accounts of the first examples of preservation; of heroic pioneers and their contributions; of government initiatives that were gradually extended to embrace additional categories, periods of time, and countries; and of the establishment of laws and management associated with them. The narratives take us from Antiquity up to the present, often culminating in UNESCO's World Heritage Convention (1972) and the subsequent first national examples of World Heritage sites, which are proudly presented. If the narratives take us any further ahead in time, they will also mention intangible heritage (e.g. Chamberlin 1979; Nielsen 1987; Cowell 2008).

The narratives about the emergence of the protection and preservation of cultural and natural heritage form their own historical genre. They deal with the successful dissemination of heritage preservation as an idea and a practice, even though the concept of heritage makes its appearance relatively late in this developmnt. This is a typical piece of legitimising Whig history-writing (e.g. Southgate 1996: 110f), in which the management practices, laws, and conventions of today are the self-evident aims of an essentially progressive development.

A few scenes from the narratives of the history of preservation are presented here, as examples representing the main lines of that history's development. Taken together, they yield a pattern showing a close connection between destruction – or threats of destruction – and preservation: one causes the other. Alternatively, though, the same actors may both destroy and preserve.

In Memphis, Pharaoh Ramses II's son the priest Khaemwaset saved a statue of Prince Kawab (Schnapp 1993 (French): 328; 1996 (English): 328). Early paradoxical examples of preservation can also be documented in the Roman Empire. For instance, attempts were made in the fourth and fifth centuries to regulate the use of monuments as quarries for *spolia*; this serves as evidence that extensive destruction occurred. The Ostrogoth king Theodoric regretted the destruction in Rome, but he himself imported *spolia* for his construction projects in Ravenna in around the year 500 (Schnapp 1993 (French): 83f; 1996 (English): 83; Fabricius Hansen 2003: 108ff, 157, 238f).

In 1162, the Roman Senate laid down the death penalty and loss of property for anyone who damaged Emperor Trajan's column: "Nous voulons qu'elle demeure intacte, sans corruption, tant que le monde durera" (Schnapp 1993 (French): 94; 1996 (English): 94,

"We wish it to remain intact, without decay, as long as the world shall last"). Pope Pius II prohibited the use of Roman ruins as a quarry in 1462, but the same pope caused Octavian's colonnade in Rome to be destroyed (Schnapp 1993 (French): 338f; 1996 (English): 339f). The Danish King Hans provides an early Scandinavian example of building conservation: in 1508, he proposed renovating the Romanesque crypt at Lund Cathedral (Nielsen 1987: 30f). In the sixteenth and seventeenth centuries, states such as Denmark, Sweden, and England took numerous initiatives to make inventories of, document, and protect monuments that could shed lustre on the history of their realms. In 1666, Sweden was the first to take two initiatives: first, a law called "Signs and decrees on old monuments and antiquities" ("Placat och Påbudh Om Gamble Monumenter och Antiquiteter") and, second, nationwide "Inventories for antiquities" ("Rannsakningar efter antikviteter") (Jensen 2002: 325ff).

The French Revolution, the subsequent Napoleonic Wars, and the Romantic movement brought a new focus on the past, with worship of both Antiquity and the Middle Ages. It is in this period that the museum emerges as an institution, that disciplines such as archaeology, history of art, and history are established, and that the first legislation on protection is enacted. In the midst of the turbulence of the revolution in 1790, the concept "historic monument" was used for the first time by the antiquary Aubin-Louis Millin de Grandmaison as a designation for palaces, churches, and abbeys which could show the history of the country and which therefore needed to be protected from destruction (Choay 1992 (French): 76ff; 2001 (English): 63ff).

It was also during the French Revolution that two new rhetorical concepts, "vandalism" and "heritage", were established as two sides of the same events. In 1794 the Bishop of Blois, Henri Grégoire, employed the term "vandalism" as a piece of invective to describe the destruction of libraries and religious art. At the same time, he used the words "un héritage commun", a common heritage, about what needed to be protected (Choay 1992 (French): 76ff; 2001 (English): 63ff; Gamboni 1997: 17ff; Schildgen 2008: 121ff).

As the art historian Derek Gillman has pointed out, Grégoire must have been inspired by the politician and philosopher Edmund Burke, who had written the following in *Reflections on the Revolution in France* (1790: 47):

You will observe, that from Magna Charta to the Declaration of Right [*sic*], it has been the uniform policy of our constitution to claim and assert our liberties, as an 'entailed inheritance' derived to us from our forefathers, and to be transmitted to our posterity; as an estate specially belonging to the people of this kingdom without any reference whatever to any other more general or prior right.

The book was translated into French, and then "inheritance" became "heritage" (Gillman 2010: 82ff).

These preservation endeavours were intensified with industrialism and nationalism, especially from around 1870 to the First World War, also known as the period of "The Invention of Tradition". To name some examples, Japan's first legislation on preservation came in the 1870s, when the country started a vigorous process of modernisation. Germany began the documentation of monuments at the same time as the country was undergoing a rapid industrialisation. The US was, by contrast, first to have nature conservation, with the national park in Yellowstone in 1872, the Niagara Falls in 1885, and the Grand Canyon in 1919. And the first systematic criteria for the protection of memorials were developed by Alois Riegl in Austria-Hungary after 1900 (Riegl 1903 (German); 1929 (German); 1982 (English)).

Critical heritage

The word "criticism" comes from the Greek word *kritike*, which refers to the art of making judgements. It is related to the word "crisis", which is also of Greek origin, *kri'sis* meaning "decision" or "judgement". In everyday language, the "criticism" is attended by unfavourable connotations since it is, in practice, often a matter of finding faults and defects; but its application does not rule out a neutral or even favourable appraisal. Since the Age of Enlightenment, criticism has also been the name of a distinct genre of reviews whose purpose is to communicate, describe, interpret, and assess fictional and non-fictional texts, art, music, theatre, and film. Ideally, the aim is to enhance the understanding and experience of the works; but reviews may become stuck in the derogatory and dismissive aspect of criticism.

The development of critical heritage as a separate field may, in my view, be divided into three chronological phases: the 1980s, the 1990s, and the twenty-first century. In each phase, Lowenthal has a patent impact through his publications. But first, an account will be provided of the history-of-ideas-related, historical, and political conditions that obtain in this field.

The background in the history of ideas of the emergence of critical heritage is formed by various influences that are not necessarily compatible. Chief among them are the Frankfurt School and critical theory, with names such as Max Horkheimer, Theodor W. Adorno, and later Jürgen Habermas. Here, bourgeois society and its institutions and values are criticised from the left of the political spectrum. It is a criticism that regards traditions, museums, and heritage as conservative phenomena geared to preserving the existing society. According to this line of thought, society should not merely be described; it should be changed as well. Post-structuralism's power-and-discourse criticism follows, with Michel Foucault as the central name. Finally, mention should be made of postcolonialism's reckoning with a Western perspective on the world; one important work here is Edward Said's book *Orientalism* (1978).

Critical theory, poststructuralism, and postcolonialism come together in the critical study of the uses of the past and "the others" that emerged in the 1970s and 1980s. Scholars who belong to this orientation ask what past is examined and mediated, how, where, and when this happens, who does it, and for whom – and ultimately why the past is being examined and mediated at all. Besides the essay "Imperialism and Archaeology" (Bandaranayake 1974) and the book *The Rape of the Nile* (Fagan 1975), many were inspired by the anthology *The Invention of Tradition* (Hobsbawm & Ranger 1983), which showed how history was not only used but also invented. Moreover, inspiration for the critical study of memory, monuments, and memorials came from Pierre Nora's project *Les Lieux de mémoire* (1984 (French); 1989 (English), *Realms of Memory*).

The social, economic, and political developments of the 1970s and 1980s formed a direct precondition for the emergence of critical heritage. Those were turbulent decades during which countries in the West were affected by a lack of belief in progress as well as by oil crises, deindustrialisation, and neoliberalism. There was also a shift in the use of the past from knowledge to experience and reflection – and a shift to new forms of mediation.

Lowenthal had already formulated the basis for critical heritage in the anthology *Our Past Before Us* (Lowenthal & Binney 1981), which summarised a symposium held in London in 1979. In the introduction, Lowenthal noted that "[s]aving historic sites and objects has become a widely popular cause. Although pollution, neglect, and the bulldozer still take a heavy toll, more and more is now being rescued. The growth of the preservation movement is one of the major social phenomena of our time" (1981: 9). And Lowenthal specifically wanted to see a critical analysis: "As a self-conscious movement, preservation is still too new to have attracted much critical analysis" (1981: 10). He also includes an early variant of later statements about the past and heritage being everywhere: "Remnants of our past lie all around us, some whole, some decayed, some in shreds and tatters, some to be discerned only in traces" (1981: 10).

Critical heritage had a breakthrough in the mid-1980s with the publication of three now "canonical" books that generated attention and debate (cf. Sørensen & Carman 2009: 17ff; Harrison 2013: 98ff): David Lowenthal's *The Past is a Foreign Country* (1985), Patrick Wright's *On Living in an Old Country* (1985), and Robert Hewison's *The Heritage Industry* (1987). Two of the key works supplied Lowenthal's own extensive reply to the wonderment expressed in his introduction, where nostalgia came in for especially harsh criticism; Wright's criticism of the use of history as a diversionary political manoeuvre in the present; and Hewison's devastating criticism of the heritage industry as a new sector of the economy.

It should be pointed out that these three books all represented Western self-criticism originating in personal experience from the UK and the US. The next point to note is that this first phase of criticism was itself nostalgic, polemic, and very critical in a negative sense.

The 1990s then saw a broadening of the field, widely dissimilar disciplines being inspired by Lowenthal's book in particular. Now there was a gradual "academicisation", in which heritage emerged as a research field in its own right. The periodical *International Journal of Heritage Studies* (1994ff) was founded in this period. In Sweden, a research project was completed and published in the anthology *Modernisering och Kulturarv* ("Modernisation and Heritage", Anshelm 1993). And Lowenthal himself published *The Heritage Crusade and the Spoils of History* (1997), which was hypercritical of the whole phenomenon of heritage.

The final establishment of critical heritage as an academic field in its own right has come in the twenty-first century. This is when teaching and research are established at centres and departments whose scholars focus on heritage. The first real textbooks have been published during this period, for instance *The Heritage Reader* (Fairclough *et al.* 2009) and *Heritage Studies* (Sørensen & Carman 2009). Cooperation between academics at universities in Australia, Sweden, and the UK has led to the formation of the Association of

Critical Heritage Studies (since 2010; www.criticalheritagestudies. org). Mention may also be made of the textbook *Heritage: Critical Approaches* (Harrison 2013). There was a reprint of Wright's *On Living in an Old Country* in 2009, and Lowenthal has revised his standard work in *The Past is a Foreign Country – Revisited* (2015). But there has not been a new impression of Hewison's *The Heritage Industry*.

As with criticism more generally, it should be possible to regard critical heritage as an endeavour to mediate, describe, interpret, and assess the protection, preservation, and use of heritage. Ideally, the purpose would be to increase the understanding of heritage in the context of impending change. Critical heritage may therefore be concerned with what heritage is protected, preserved, and used; how, where, and when this happens; and who it is done by and for whom – and also why heritage is protected, preserved, and used in the first place.

My description or definition of critical heritage as typical genre criticism is fairly open. The reason is that in practice, critical heritage displays great breadth, not least in terms of perspectives and attitudes.

The first and most radical form of criticism is aimed against heritage itself as an idea. It rejects the view that the past with its history, memory, and heritage is in any way a good or necessary thing. Strikingly often, though, rhetoric and invective take the place of arguments, heritage being linked to threats, disease, and religion – or interest in heritage being viewed unfavourably as a "heritage industry". This is how critical heritage is introduced by David Lowenthal, Patrick Wright, and Robert Hewison; but similar attitudes are voiced by many others, among them Norman O. Brown, Pierre Boulez, Donald Horne, Agnes Heller, Françoise Choay, Andreas Huyssen, Frank Füredi, and Svante Beckman. However, this radical criticism appears to belong chiefly to the 1980s and 1990s as an initial reaction against a perceived expansion of heritage.

The second form of criticism focuses on the use, in the sense of consumption, of heritage, taking the view that protection and preservation should not prevent continued use or new modes of use, even if heritage is affected in the process. In the choice between preservation and destruction, the argument is that destruction is acceptable or even preferable. For instance, archaeologist Cornelius Holtorf maintains that heritage may be allowed to be consumed, or worn out, since new heritage is always at hand; he views heritage as an enduring resource (Holtorf 2005: 130ff). Even though heritage is not rejected in principle, this attitude is, in practice, reminiscent of the first radical criticism in that it consistently argues that a specific piece of heritage may be allowed to disappear for some reason.

The third, and now most widespread, criticism is concerned with the choice of heritage – the point being that the existing heritage has been too narrowly defined. The established heritage administered by institutions such as UNESCO and ICOMOS is regarded as being too traditional, as bearing the imprint of Western thinking, and as being dominated by material culture and monuments linked precisely to the West. This criticism wants to see an extension of heritage in both theoretical and practical terms. The material therefore needs to be supplemented by the intangible, so that more people around the world can have their heritage – and therefore their identity – recognised. To be specific, more representation of heritage is needed in relation to neglected subjects, periods, geographical areas and, especially, groups in society with respect to class, gender, and ethnicity. The selection of heritage should not be directed from above, but should be carried out locally (e.g. Smith 2006; Meskell 2018).

One unambiguous example of the third form of criticism is a manifesto formulated for the Association of Critical Heritage Studies at a conference in Gothenburg in Sweden in 2012 and signed by the archaeologist Laurajane Smith: it is a postcolonial programme for change, in which "ruthless criticism of everything existing" is considered necessary in order to rebuild heritage studies from scratch. Smith's onslaught on the existing is indeed ruthless: "The old way of looking at heritage – the Authorised Heritage Discourse – privileges old, grand, prestigious, expert approved sites, buildings, and artefacts that sustain Western narratives of nation, class and science" (www.criticalheritagestudies.org/history).

As a consequence of the third form of criticism, a large number of attempts are under way both to update and to democratise heritage in the present. Such endeavours may involve activating the heritage in relation to issues of sustainable development and human rights, as well as creating a dialogue with the public and local engagement for heritage (e.g. Alzén & Aronsson 2006; Harrison 2013: 140ff, 204ff; Högberg 2013).

The name "critical heritage" embodies a hint that there is an established alternative, namely something that might be referred to as "uncritical heritage". That this is actually held to be the case is stated clearly in the 2012 manifesto. It was formulated in explicit opposition to the established, which is described as the "Authorized

Heritage Discourse", abbreviated as AHD (Smith 2006: 85ff). The manifesto's desire to be "ruthless" and to build something new from scratch is revolutionary and iconoclastic. Paradoxically, though, it is Western academic experts on heritage who are formulating the criticism.

Even so, the rhetoric cannot conceal the fact that critical heritage has been in the making for three decades. Critical heritage is established and has networks, centres, departments, teaching programmes, academic staff, conferences, journals, textbooks – and a manifesto. Representatives of critical heritage act as established experts and "gatekeepers". Consequently, an ACHD – the "Authorized Critical Heritage Discourse" – now also exists.

At the same time, the disparagingly named "Authorized Heritage Discourse", and UNESCO especially, have been extremely alert to issues involving representation, topicality, and dialogue. Hence, the distinction between old and new, between established and revolutionary, is not as great as the rhetoric wants to claim.

Even if the differences between canonical and critical heritage become blurred over time, there is still a distinct difference when it comes to defining cultural and natural heritage, as well as in relation to such themes as decay and vandalism, and modernity.

Heritage and authenticities

The origin of the word *heritage* is the Old French word *heritage* or *eritage* with the verb *heriter*, "to inherit", which comes from the Latin *heriditare*; so the word "heritage" may be a linguistic legacy from both the Norman invasion and the Roman Empire. "Heritage" is explained as "[p]roperty that is or may be inherited". "Heritage" is also used as an antiquarian term about "[v]alued objects and qualities such as historic buildings and cultural traditions that have been passed down from previous generations" (*OED*: VII, 167). Consequently, the meaning of "heritage" is closely associated with the concept of "tradition", which is used about that which is passed on.

As a wide-ranging and ambiguous concept, "heritage" may form part of numerous contexts, for instance The Heritage Foundation, a conservative think tank in the US. "Heritage" may also be the name of a film, a novel, or a political party, and it may even be used as a surname.

The antiquarian concept of "heritage" may be specified as either cultural heritage or natural heritage. In the Nordic languages, however, "heritage" is often translated as *kulturarv*, corresponding lexically to "cultural heritage", which does not cover the entire field. And despite the French origin of the word "heritage", the term *patrimoine*, "paternal inheritance", is used in France instead.

In antiquarian contexts, as well as in everyday speech, heritage serves as a name for valuable remains of the past. Heritage is then used both as an explanation why something is actually being protected and preserved for the future – well, it is heritage – and as a slogan, raising a call to action: this is heritage, so it needs protection and preservation. Employing the concept is likely to be a good choice in that it creates favourable connotations around the past in a present where the public debate is dominated by economic priorities. And if there is a tendency towards specialisation and fragmentation in research, management, and mediation, "heritage" is able to gather different phenomena under a single umbrella. For like history and memory, heritage covers an extensive field of remains from the past.

In order to be able to explain and understand the emergence of the heritage concept, we can follow the development of what is designated by the concept; that is, both thinking and practice concerning the need to protect and preserve remains from the past for the future. The history of preservation from Antiquity to the present is very clearly set out in narratives intended to legitimise current antiquarian legislation and institutions.

Over time, changing concepts have been used to designate what is to be protected and preserved: antiquities, historic monuments, and heritage. In *From Antiquities to Heritage* (2014), the cultural historian Anne Eriksen has linked the varying concepts to different "regimes of historicity", drawing inspiration from the historian François Hartog, who is, in turn, inspired by several other scholars, including Michel Foucault with his concept of the episteme (Hartog 2003 (French); 2015 (English)).

Both Hartog and Eriksen want to connect the heritage concept with "presentism", or the current preoccupation of the present. Heritage is used as a concept referring to everything from the past that someone will inherit and therefore assume responsibility for as an exclusive resource. The concept is also linked to the development of individualism and liberalism (Hartog 2003 (French): 113ff, 163ff; 2015 (English): 97ff, 149ff; Eriksen 2014: 132ff, 149ff). Heritage is hence directly bound up with questions of identity and identity policy. But once again, as in crisis theories, one may suspect that heritage as a contested concept and practice is entangled with topical political phenomena in the present about which the authors are sceptical.

The formal and actual breakthrough of heritage as a central antiquarian, but also popular, concept came with the adoption of UNESCO's Convention Concerning the Protection of the World Cultural and Natural Heritage (1972). But even then, the concept had been around for quite a long time. For instance, "cultural heritage" has a prominent place in the Hague Convention for the Protection of Cultural Property in the Event of Armed Conflict (1954, Chapter 1, Article 1).

Consequently, it is not wholly convincing when Patrick Wright claims – with reference to Hannah Arendt and others – that the heritage concept was regarded in an unfavourable light before the 1980s (cf. Wright 2009: xff). Even so, heritage may have conveyed unfortunate associations with the German word *Ahnenerbe* ("ancestral heritage"), which was the name of a research institute within the SS, the Schutzstaffel, 1933–1945 (Pringle 2006). And generally speaking, the heritage concept may have been viewed as non-progressive by those who were striving for modernisation.

In Sweden, the breakthrough for the use of the heritage concept has been dated as having occurred in the late 1980s and interpreted as part of a realignment of cultural policy (Pettersson 2003: 9, 56ff, 93, 157). Sweden ratified the World Heritage Convention in 1985 (Annex 1; whc.unesco.org/en/statesparties/se). In 1887, however, the concept *kulturarf* ("heritage", in the old Swedish spelling) appears for the first time in Sweden in a lecture by the author Viktor Rydberg on the Middle Ages and what the "Romano-Gauls" had taken over from Antiquity (Rydberg 1905: 582). After that, the heritage concept was often referred to in public debate, the media, and book titles throughout the twentieth century. So even if the 1980s and 1990s brought a political and economic realignment, the question is whether heritage might not once more be identified by critics as a scapegoat for a development they did not wish to see.

With the establishment of heritage as a central concept, numerous definitions appear, that is, attempts to specify just what heritage is. To begin with, heritage actually describes something limited, a situation where something is worth protecting and preserving, worth canonising, while something else can be omitted from the list of priorities. But heritage was given a relatively broad definition early on, and since that time it has been expanded even further.

A strikingly broad definition of cultural heritage as an overarching concept is found in the Hague Convention, even though "cultural property" is the main concept here:

> movable or immovable property of great importance to the cultural
> heritage of every people, such as monuments of architecture, art or
> history, whether religious or secular; archaeological sites; groups of
> buildings which, as a whole, are of historical or artistic interest;
> works of art; manuscripts, books, and other objects of artistic, historical
> or archaeological interest; as well as scientific collections, and important
> collections of books or archives or of reproductions of the property
> defined above. (Hague Convention, 1954, Chapter 1, Article 1a)

A long-term tendency may be observed regarding what may or should be heritage, that is, what is heritable. It tends to gradually move closer in time, cover more categories, and be globally disseminated: from Antiquity via the Middle Ages to the Early Modern and Modern period, all the way to the present; from single monuments and buildings to whole environments or landscapes; and from individual countries to the whole world.

The widening of heritage has entailed the inclusion of a number of expressions that refer specifically to the modern period and modernity. The physical movements of modernity by way of trains, cars, planes, rockets, and laser beams; railways, roads, airports, launchpads, and power stations – all become of interest as heritage to explore, protect, and preserve for the future. One monumental example is controversial nuclear power stations such as Barsebäck in Sweden and Ignalina in Lithuania (Storm 2010; 2014: 69ff, 94ff). Human exploration of space offers another example of cutting-edge heritage conceptions (O'Leary & Capelotti 2014).

An expansion also took place when material or tangible heritage was supplemented by immaterial or intangible heritage, the dual intention being to represent the diversity of heritage more adequately and to make sustainable development possible. The relevant principles were laid down in the Convention for the Safeguarding of the Intangible Cultural Heritage (2003; cf. Smith & Akagawa 2009). Antiquarian management transforms the intangible cultural heritage so that it actually becomes tangible (cf. Baxter 2012).

One example of a broad definition was supplied by English Heritage in 2008: "All inherited resources which people value for reasons beyond mere utility" (Conservation Principles, English Heritage, 2008; the definition no longer appears on the English Heritage website, but it is quoted on the Historic England website under Heritage Definitions, https://historicengland.org.uk/advice/hpg/hpr-definitions). The definition is so general that what is regarded as heritage under it cannot be differentiated from, or will include, the religious sphere with its notions of what is sacred.

An extension of the concept is also visible in official texts from the Swedish National Heritage Board. In 2017, the Board defined heritage as, in principle, everything created or influenced by human beings: "Heritage refers to all material and intangible expressions of human influence – for instance traces, remains, objects, constructions, environments, systems, structures, activities, traditions, naming customs, knowledge, etc." (www.raa.se/kulturarv/definition-av-kulturarv-och-kulturmiljo; cf. *Räkna med kulturarvet* ("Count on heritage"), 2017: 7). Here, heritage has been transformed from a broad yet defined concept to something boundless, indeed potentially to everything in the present. As Harrison puts it, "almost anything can be perceived to be 'heritage'" (Harrison 2013: 3).

The tendency to extend definitions of heritage has been criticised. For instance, the lawyer Jeanette Greenfield points out in *The Return of Cultural Treasures* that the term cultural heritage is used in such arbitrary, inexact, broad, and general ways that it is, in point of fact, useless and ineffective. In addition, she criticises UNESCO for producing rhetoric without practical significance (Greenfield 1996: 254f, 258).

When "almost anything can be perceived to be 'heritage'", the canonical model, in which the very best and finest is selected, must be replaced by a more representative model (Harrison 2013: 3 quotation, 18). And in line with this extension, a new view of heritage has developed. On the one hand, there is a traditional essential perspective that is concerned with the existence of a tangible and intangible heritage which has survived from the past until today. This heritage needs to be identified and assessed in relation to set criteria, so that it may then be protected and preserved for the future. On the other hand, there is a constructivist perspective in which heritage is a category created in the present in negotiations between different actors and interests; to quote from Laurajane Smith, "There is, really, no such thing as heritage" (Smith 2006: 11). Here, heritage is something that is defined in what is called a heritage process.

With the widening of heritage and a constructivist perspective, heritage is now, in the twenty-first century, emphasised as something dynamic that is changed and recreated along with the world we live in, and as a process in itself (e.g. Convention for the Safeguarding, 2003: Article 2; Aronsson & Hillström 2005; Harrison 2013: 10; Högberg 2013; Schofield 2015).

Heritage as a concept is on the move, just like the world around us. Heritage is modernised. Heritage has become part of an adaptable modernity, constantly restless and heading towards new goals. Or, to put it differently: heritage and modernity, permanence and change, have become so entangled with one another that they have in effect coalesced into one.

The crucial value of heritage is often claimed to be its authenticity, from the adjective authentic, which comes from the Latin word *authenticus* and the Greek word *authen'tia* for principal or genuine (*OED* I, 1989: 795ff). The authentic can be seen as the original, that which was there at the beginning, and then it approaches the meaning of the *arche* concept. "Authenticity" is a set heading immediately after the criteria in the presentation of individual World Heritage sites in the UNESCO list (whc.unesco.org/en/list).

Heritage is expected by definition to be a genuine or true trace of the past, irrespective of whether heritage is defined narrowly or broadly, tangibly or intangibly. But authenticity is a contested quality. There is thus no single way of understanding authenticity; there are many ways. The concept should therefore be presented in the plural as authenticities.

It is supposedly the authenticity of heritage, its closeness to the true past, the past in itself, that creates the foundation for heritage tourism (MacCannell 1976: 2f, 91ff, 145ff; Horne 1984: 16f). A need for authenticity has also been said to account for an upturn for heritage and museums; this need is regarded as a reaction against the electronic, the technological, and the artificial in the present (Choay 1992 (French): 158ff, 187ff; 2001 (English): 138ff, 164ff). And more generally, the wish for authenticity has been interpreted as an expression of a modern loss of belief and meaning, that is, as yet another example of a reaction to modernity (e.g. Lindholm 2008; Jones 2010: 186ff).

Many scholars have pointed to analogies between heritage and religion. Remains from the past may be compared with church relics, museums with temples, antiquarians with priests, and tourism with pilgrimage (e.g. MacCannell 1976; 1999; Horne 1984; Wangefelt Ström 2006). Heritage is selected in a process that is reminiscent of canonisation; and it may be described as a phenomenon that satisfies a craving for enchantment where secularisation is gaining ground.

The fundamental common feature here may be the special quality called "sacred" in the religious sphere and "authentic" in the antiquarian sphere. The sacredness of religion and the values of heritage are one of several expressions of the much-discussed division into sacred and profane. With regard to that debate, I want to align myself with the interpretation offered by the historian of religion Mircea Eliade in *Das Heilige und das Profane* (*The Sacred and the Profane*): "daß das *Heilige* und das *Profane* zwei Weisen des In-der-Welt-Seins bilden, zwei existentielle Situationen, die der Mensch im Lauf seiner Geschichte ausgebildet hat" (Eliade 1957 (German): 10, "that *sacred* and *profane* are two modes of being in the world, two existential situations assumed by man in the course of his history"; 1987 (English): 14). These are, however, two perspectives that are not necessarily mutually exclusive, and the boundary between them may shift and slide.

Even so, "sacred" and "profane" are intangible qualities whose status can only be maintained by distancing. Both sacredness and authenticity are dependent on authoritative contexts, the existence of religious or antiquarian experts who provide confirmation. And on close inspection both sacredness and authenticity melt into air, as does every tangible or intangible thing – heritage included – that encounters the force of modernity.

The Western view of authenticity has been supplemented by an "Asian" view. What has happened is that an essential interpretation of authenticity as permanence on the part of the material has been supplemented by a more constructivist approach. That approach emphasises continuity in ideas, forms, and craft traditions – more intangible qualities, in other words.

According to the Nara Conference in Japan in 1994, authenticity should not be interpreted according to set criteria: "heritage properties must be considered and judged within the cultural contexts to which they belong". The intention is to show respect for the global diversity of cultures and heritages, which may be both tangible and intangible (*The Nara Document on Authenticity*, 1994: 11). The well-known examples here are stupas, Buddhist buildings for relics, and Japanese temples that have been renewed time and again but are still perceived as old and well preserved, since the underlying ideas are unchanged (Byrne 1995; Larsen 1995). From 2005 onwards, the view of the Conference that authenticity depends on the cultural context also came to cover World Heritage sites (e.g. *Operational*, 2019: §79ff).

The critics rightly want to remind us that the authenticity of heritage is not always decisive; that it can often be difficult to determine what is old or new; and that heritage may consist of parts from different periods, or be completely replaced by copies or reconstructions. In the words of Cornelius Holtorf, "pastness" is a characteristic that can be constructed (Holtorf 2005: 113f; 2013a).

Authenticity as a quality therefore depends not only on which type of heritage – cultural or natural – is in focus, or on whether the heritage is tangible or intangible, but also on the choice of perspective. The meaning of authenticity depends on the purpose of the protection, preservation, and use – whether it is knowledge of truth, a narrative of beauty, or the ethics of goodness. If the purpose is to experience the past, the truth of authenticity may therefore be subordinate to the narrative's own inner "truth".

"Pastness" constructed with a view to reducing the wear-and-tear on the authentic past may be exemplified by the copy of the cave at Lascaux in France (WHL 85, 1979). And "pastness" created for mediation can be exemplified by the copies of Abu Simbel and by the exhibition with Tutankhamun's tomb that is touring the world. But in the case of investments in art, fakes are destroyed when revealed. So just as authenticity may vary, the stance adopted in relation to authenticity – or its absence – may shift, depending on perspective and context.

At Abu Simbel, it is possible to discuss what is authentic and whether it is a crucial value: seen from a distance, the location and architecture can be described as authentic, but at close range they cannot. For the temples stand beside the Nile, but not in their original location, even though their orientation in relation to the sun is unchanged; they have, after all, been moved. And from a distance, the rock and architecture seem authentic; but at close hand and in comparison with older pictures, it is revealed that they have been cut up, moved, and resited in a modern structure. Nor can the monuments as tourist attractions be described as "authentic" in the sense of "original" with their present lighting to enhance the experience, with walkways and ventilation as protection and for the comfort of visitors. Abu Simbel thus has both authentic and non-authentic parts, representing both tradition and modernity, and the visitor is not always made aware of where the boundaries are. And for anyone who is unable to make the trip to Abu Simbel, copies or representations in words, images, and film may be a perfectly satisfactory way of learning, experiencing, and assessing.

Ambivalent vandalism

Pierre Boulez praised vigorous, expanding civilisations without memory or monuments and continued, "our Western civilization would need Red Guards to get rid of a good number of statues or even decapitate them. The French Revolution decapitated statues in churches; one may regret this now, but it was proof of a civilisation on the march" (Boulez 1976: 33; originally to *Der Spiegel*, 25 September 1967). Boulez thus wanted assistance from Mao Zedong's Red Guards, who were active in the Chinese Cultural Revolution in 1966–1976. His statement was made in the second year of the Cultural Revolution and printed in the year when the Revolution ended.

Boulez's wish had been fulfilled a couple of years earlier, in 1965, but at that point the West was able to cope without Red Guards. As part of an international campaign under the leadership of UNESCO, Pharaoh Ramses II's faces were sawn off and removed, just like the rest of his colossal statues and temples of Abu Simbel. But it hardly happened the way Boulez had imagined. For in 1968, the reconstructed temples with the statues of Ramses II could be reopened at new sites, where the rising waters of the Nile no longer threatened them.

Still, Boulez's wish has been granted on many other occasions. Through the ages, history is attended by the deliberate destruction of monuments, buildings, sites, and landscapes, both tangible and intangible heritage; this is especially so in the last century with its world wars, civil wars, and terror. Since 2000 alone, episodes of destruction in Bamiyan (WHL 208rev, 2003), Timbuktu (WHL 119rev, 1988), Aleppo (WHL 21, 1986), and Palmyra (WHL 23bis, 1980) have shocked the world.

Understandably, these instances of destruction have generated extensive debate and literature across the two cultures of heritage, both about specific localities and what can, must, or ought to happen to them, and, more generally, about destruction through the ages (e.g. Lambourne 2001; Kramer 2007; Boldrick *et al.* 2013; Noyes 2013; Kolrud & Prusac 2014; Bevan 2016).

The events that have taken place after the turn of the new millennium raise both specific questions and issues of principle concerning motives and values; protection, preservation, and continued use; and possible restoration or reconstruction. The events leave no doubt that the remains of the past do, in fact, play a central role in the present, for otherwise there would be no reason to deliberately destroy these remains or to subsequently endeavour to recreate them. But interest in these events may also border on an ambivalent fascination with violence, destruction, and death.

The events may be described in neutral terms as a deliberate change; but they are more apt to be designated in derogatory terms such as damage, destruction, iconoclasm, or vandalism. Alternatively, the actors themselves and their adherents want to be able to describe the events as a cleansing or clean-up, in which the world is liberated from something unseemly and unwanted.

"Iconoclasm" means "the breaking or destruction of images". "Iconoclasm" comes from the Greek word *eikonokla'stes*, *eiko'n* for "a likeness or image" and *kla'o* for "breaking" (*OED*: VII, 609). The iconoclasm concept is used to describe the deliberate destruction of images that function as collective symbols. This process may involve religious images and monuments which are attacked as part of a reformation or revolution. During the invasion of Iraq, for instance, the taking down and humiliation of a statue of President Saddam Hussein in Paradise Square in Baghdad in 2003 was seen as a symbolic demonstration of the capture of the capital and the shift of political power (e.g. Bevan 2016: 120ff).

"Vandalism" is another term that is used more generally about aggressive and reprehensible destruction. The term refers to the sacking of Rome by the Vandals in 455 and was used by Henri Grégoire in 1794 – at the same time as the establishment of the heritage concept (*OED*: XIX, 425; Choay 1992 (French): 76ff; 2001 (English): 63ff; Gamboni 1997: 17ff; Schildgen 2008: 121ff).

In the rhetoric surrounding the destruction and removal of ancient monuments and antiquities from their original archaeological sites, those acts are occasionally referred to as rape; that is, they are metaphorically equated with a violent sexual assault (e.g. Fagan 1975; Amery & Cruickshank 1975; Romer & Romer 1993). Rape is germane to war situations as the social order is being dissolved.

Both canonical and critical heritage focus on the destruction of heritage, but there is a distinct difference of attitude between the cultures. While canonical heritage wants to argue for preserving, protecting, and defending heritage, critical heritage – at any rate as encountered in its more extreme variants – argues along various lines for not preserving, protecting, or defending. The difference in attitudes is so marked that it can be claimed to define the two cultures.

Threats and destruction play a crucial part in canonical heritage when it comes to legitimising the need for protection and preservation. The fact that threats and destruction have and have had an important role, both rhetorically and in reality, is clear from the field's own narratives about the ways in which preservation, antiquarian institutions, legislation, conventions, and management have evolved. The story told by these narratives keeps emphasising threats against remains from the past which it was necessary to avert.

Here mention may be made of the returning fascination with the salvage of iconic World Heritage sites that are under very visible threat – Abu Simbel threatened by the Aswan High Dam (WHL 88, 1979), the Tower of Pisa threatened by gravity (WHL 395bis, 1987, 2007), and Venice threatened by both rising waters and tourists (WHL 394, 1987). In the specific case of World Heritage sites there is a special List of World Heritage in Danger, which is updated annually (Convention 1972: Article 11.4; also *Operational* 2019: §§177–191).

Critical heritage has also been fascinated by threats and destruction; but for several reasons, it has been sceptical about defending, protecting, and preserving heritage. The argument may be that it is not that important to preserve an example of heritage that is being considered at a particular time; something else is or will be more relevant or representative. The argument may also be that vandalism is part of the history of heritage, so there is no point in trying to prevent it; graffiti may become part of the monument's biography. Moreover, the argument may be that heritage destroyed can be of greater importance or value than heritage preserved; more people are engaged in the memory of a lost monument than in one that is still in place. In addition, the responsibility is sometimes assigned not to the agents but to the antiquarian authorities; the claim made in such contexts is that the vandalism would never have happened if the site had not had heritage or even World Heritage status. By elevating a site to World Heritage, UNESCO is seen as creating a "soft target"; World Heritage sites attract threats, risk destruction, and can contribute to ongoing conflicts (e.g. Gamboni 2001; Flood 2002; Meskell 2018: 172ff). The argument has points in common with the blaming of a rape victim on the grounds of "provocative" behaviour or clothing.

In this context, Cornelius Holtorf has reused the concept of creative destruction in order to stress that the destruction of heritage is not necessarily a bad thing. As an example, he mentions the Berlin Wall, fragments of which were spread all over the world as relics (Holtorf 2005: 144f).

But nowhere have the canonical and critical arguments been as clear as in respect of the blasting of the two sixth-century Buddha statues in Bamiyan Valley in Afghanistan in 2001. Defenders regard the statues as valuable, viewing the event as an example of cultural terrorism and an infringement of international law, holding the Taliban responsible (Francioni & Lenzerini 2003). Critics, by contrast, put the blame on the West. The Buddha statues are not considered to have been valuable. Their empty niches have become part of history, and more people than before are taking an active interest in Bamiyan. Therefore, the statues should not be reconstructed (e.g. Gamboni 2001; Flood 2002; Holtorf 2006).

To this I would like to reply that the Buddha statues had value for the knowledge that they alone could provide and the narratives they could communicate; that the empty niches are allowing the violence of the Taliban to win; and that the statues may be recreated using digital methods.

But most of all I want to recall the connection between the destruction of remains of the past and the expulsion, rape, and murder of human beings. Vandalism and mass murder are companions in conflicts (Kramer 2007; Bevan 2016). The French Revolution, eulogised by Boulez, is an early and illuminating example. In the course of it, quite a number of both humans and statues were decapitated. And the past century supplies notorious examples of bombings or massacres such as Guernica in 1937; Coventry in 1940; Oradour-sur-Glane and Warsaw in 1944; Dresden in 1945; Mostar in 1993; Bamiyan in 2001; Timbuktu and Aleppo in 2012, and Palmyra in 2015, in all of which material destruction and massacre took place side by side. In Palmyra, the Roman amphitheatre was thus used in order to stage public executions. The aim in defiling and harming heritage is to defile and harm individuals, groups, peoples, and nations for whom this heritage is important. But it is never the victim who should bear the responsibility.

Remains of the past that are designated as heritage and World Heritage are given greater attention and normally attract more tourists. That makes for tourism that threatens to bring greater wear and degradation. At well-known tourist destinations and World Heritage sites such as the Pyramids (WHL 86, 1979), the Taj Mahal (WHL 252, 1983), Venice (WHL 394, 1987), and Angkor Wat (WHL 668, 1992), tourism is considered a problem. At the Palaeolithic caves at Lascaux (WHL 85, 1979), the problem has been solved by directing tourists to a replica. And at Stonehenge, visitors are kept at a good distance (WHL 373bis, 1986, 2008).

In the choice between preserving and destroying, it is possible to go for both options. Preservation of something may require something else to disappear, or the choice can be made to preserve in one context and destroy in another. Pope Pius II protected ancient ruins in Rome; but the same pope caused other ancient constructions to be dismantled (Schnapp 1993 (French): 338f; 1996 (English): 339f). On its home ground in Sweden, the engineering firm VBB built dams for hydropower plants that entailed the destruction of nature and ancient monuments; but in Egypt it contributed to moving Abu Simbel. Generally speaking, modernity may both rescue and threaten, both create and vandalise.

Something is elevated to heritage – perhaps even to World Heritage – while other things, and more things, are changed and disappear. Most of what has happened is never recorded in history; it is forgotten, and none of it remains. Critics may discern a conspiratorial strategy here. "Cultural reservations" are created and can serve as an alibi to legitimise destruction. But the same strategy can also simply be described as a necessary prioritisation, because everything cannot always stay the same. Preservation must necessarily involve a choice. Priorities are set, selected parts being expected to represent the whole, just as with the metonymic copying and use of *spolia* in the Middle Ages (cf. Krautheimer 1942; 1969).

In critical heritage, a third way between preserving and destroying is also proposed: it consists in letting decay take its course, a post-preservation model – mainly with modern examples. This approach amounts to accepting that everything changes and vanishes, and curating without conserving or controlling (DeSilvey 2017). But a hospice model, watching and perhaps alleviating without actively intervening, is also a choice. It means giving priority to the narrative about and reflection on impermanence, rather than to the possibility of gaining new knowledge or to the physical preservation of evidence. The choice of strategy therefore depends on what one wants with and for the remains of the past.

Abu Simbel was salvaged, but had to be changed as part of the salvage campaign. The temples could also have been documented and then removed. Or it would have been possible to look on, in a contemplative mode, watching the rising Nile and the drowning temples.

However, which solution was and is the right one remains an open question; that is, whether it was and is right to defend, protect, and preserve the temples of Abu Simbel, thereby assisting Pharaoh Ramses II in his ambition to attain monumental immortality. With reference to Kant's categorical and hypothetical imperatives: is the preservation of Abu Simbel a good end in itself? Or is its preservation a means of achieving the good? There is no definitive answer.

Consequently, we cannot avoid the existential challenge of choosing among options all of which may have both good and bad consequences. But if we do not choose ourselves, others will choose for us. We cannot avoid heritage policy.

Heritage and modernity

Heritage and modernity have been described as opposing concepts. However, they are merely examples from a larger field in which expressions are set up as mutually contradictory – like black and white pieces facing one another on a chessboard. On one side of the field stand history, memory, heritage, tradition, monuments, memorials, museums, conservation, and nostalgia, and on the opposite side stand change, progress, modernity, modernisation, modernism, industrialisation, urbanisation, and secularisation.

But as a metaphor, the game of chess soon turns out to be insufficient for describing the relationship between heritage and modernity. For while a move by one side is indeed followed by a countermove by the other, there is no single set of rules of the game, and the pieces seem to be able to change their roles as the game proceeds; in fact, they even seem to be able to change colour and thereby side in the game. The relationship between heritage and modernity is hence characterised by profound ambivalence.

Heritage and modernity may threaten each other. Heritage may prevent further modernisation – and modernisation may threaten the continued existence of heritage. In that case, extensive heritage might mean less modernity – and more modernity might mean less heritage, assuming a zero-sum game with ideas ranged against ideas and materiality ranged against materiality.

At the same time, though, modernity constantly makes more advanced forms of protection and preservation possible, and is therefore also a resource. And heritage may contribute, as a resource, to modernisation. What is a threat and what is a resource thus depends entirely on the perspective adopted.

Outside a zero-sum game of ideas and materiality, the importance of heritage may increase the more it is threatened. This would mean that the importance of the phenomenon of heritage would increase when modernity increases (e.g. Lübbe 1982; 1983; 1996; Marquard 1986; 2000; Choay 1992 (French); 2001 (English); Huyssen 1995). But the importance of heritage might also increase when modernity decreases (e.g. Wright 1985; Hewison 1987; Heller 1988; Füredi 1992; Beckman 1993a; 1993b; Friedman 1994; Lowenthal 2011 YouTube).

There are two tendencies here. First, heritage that is threatened or decreases becomes rarer, and therefore increases in value. Second, changes in modernity, both upturns and downturns, create social uncertainty, for which compensation is sought. And the compensation may appear during periods of social, technological, or economic modernisation with or without confidence in modernity as an idea.

Turning the argument around, I think that the importance of modernity may also increase when heritage increases or decreases.

A modernity that is threatened or decreases becomes more valuable. And changes in heritage may cause an experience of crisis. For here it is possible to observe how the experience of an increase creates unease and irritation among critics of heritage, who want more modernity instead (e.g. Boulez 1976; Hewison 1987; Heller 1988; Füredi 1992). Conversely, a person who is favourably disposed towards heritage, as in canonical heritage, will interpret an increase as a social expansion and democratisation, which gives more people the possibility of acquiring a fair share of heritage (e.g. Kristiansen 1981).

Heritage and modernity as a dichotomy is thus, at a first glance, plausible and rhetorically powerful; but it is a misleading simplification that fails to convince on closer inspection. For the concepts are contested, ambiguous, and entangled with each other.

Heritage and modernity are both contested concepts. They generate either positive or negative associations and rarely leave anyone unaffected. Canonical heritage regards heritage as something positive, a resource that needs to be protected and preserved for the future. Here an increase in heritage may represent a success. In critical heritage, by contrast – as formulated most clearly by Robert Hewison – heritage represents "bogus history" (Hewison 1987: 144). A relative increase in heritage may therefore in itself be interpreted as a sign of crisis. For some, modernity represents progress to strive for; for others, it constitutes an unwanted development.

Heritage has multiple meanings. Heritage can be associated with the unchanging, stasis, and the past; but present-day heritage includes modern examples representing change, speed, and the future. On the one hand, heritage is a modern concept that gradually established itself in the course of the twentieth century. On the other hand, heritage may consist of both tangible and intangible phenomena that may belong to widely different eras, including the modern era.

Modernity has multiple meanings, too. Modernity is associated with speed, transience, and renewal both in the world of ideas and in the material world. Modernity is thus bound up with the universal ideas of the Enlightenment as well as with the market economy and its creative destruction.

The entanglement of heritage and modernity can be demonstrated in several areas – in the modern context of the heritage concept, in the inclusion of modern phenomena in heritage, in the use of heritage in a modernisation of society, and finally in a modernisation of the concept itself.

The concept of heritage belongs, in itself, to the modern epoch. The concept appears in 1794 during the French Revolution, occurs throughout the nineteenth and twentieth centuries, and has its breakthrough in the 1970s as a collective term for whatever should be protected and preserved among the things that previous generations have passed on to posterity.

Heritage may be associated with the unchanging, stasis, and the past; but the boundary for what should be preserved and protected is constantly being moved forward in time, into the modern epoch and closer to the present. For example, in 2014 Sweden specified a limit at 1850 for antiquities (Swedish *fornfynd*) and ancient monuments (Swedish *fornlämningar*) in the Historic Environment Act (1988: 950).

The establishment of industrial heritage as worth protecting and preserving is evidence that heritage now also includes an archetypal expression of modernity. An interest in the remains of early industrialisation emerged in the UK in the decades after the Second World War. But interest in closed-down industries as heritage increased especially after the deindustrialisation of the West in the 1970s (Alzén 1996; Edensor 2005; Storm 2008, 2014; Willim 2008).

Heritage has also come to be used in strategies for improving or modernising society. Here heritage is used as a tool in something that can rightly be called heritage policy, a will to bring about change and improvement using heritage as one of several instruments. Consequently, heritage is regarded as a resource for fostering identity, tourism, and economic development; for generating sustainable development; and for work on diversity and solving other current tasks in the present. This happens without the agents involved themselves necessarily wanting to refer to the strategy as modernisation; on the contrary, modernisation as a controversial concept and phenomenon may be something they consciously reject.

When heritage is redefined from something enduring to something undergoing change, from a stable phenomenon to a process in the present, that redefinition constitutes conclusive evidence of the modernisation of the concept. Heritage as a concept and practice then itself becomes part of modernity where, as is well known, "All That Is Solid Melts into Air" (cf. Berman 1982).

Heritage in the present

The past is everywhere, and heritage is everywhere. Often these words are used a bit haphazardly as synonyms. There is also a tendency for more and more of the past to be regarded as heritage worth protecting and preserving, so the words are gradually coming to denote the same field. But the past and heritage are not identical.

When Lowenthal writes that "The past is everywhere" (Lowenthal 1985: xv; 2015: 1), what he must really mean is that he sees remains of the past everywhere, and that these remains are being given too much attention. And when Lowenthal writes that "heritage is everywhere" (Lowenthal 1997: ix), this is a variant of the same observation, his point being that one type of remains of the past, namely heritage, is spreading at the expense of history and memory.

The past in itself is both gone forever and ever-present. The events of the past are gone forever; but tangible and intangible remains of the past are ever-present as texts, images, memories, objects, and buildings. With their permanence, they reach across to us in our present. Everything in the present is made up of these accumulated remains of the past (Olivier 1999). Even that which we experience as the present moment is a memory, constructed by the brain from previously registered impressions (Eagleman 2016: 39ff). In this way the past may, in an initial response, be said to be everywhere, to quote Lowenthal again. But a more correct statement would be that the remains of the past are everywhere, and remains of the past are everything that exists.

The present is therefore a mosaic of remains of the past, a mosaic whose component parts are of different ages. The development from a past reality to the present-day mosaic is termed a "formation process" in archaeology; this describes the formation of the source material of the present. It is a sequence of events in which the original world is reduced over time, both through natural processes and by means of active human interventions that may be either preservative or destructive. The formation process has attracted methodological interest owing to its potential when it comes to determining, with a fair degree of precision, the extent to which current remains, sources, and durations are representative of a past reality (e.g. Kristiansen 1985; Lucas 2012).

When the present is made up of accumulated remains of the past, the whole of the present can be termed an "inheritance", or something we take over from generations who came before us. And we inherit the remains of the past, whether or not we want to do so. In consequence, every single thing in the present could be termed either cultural heritage or natural heritage; and the formation process could instead be referred to as a heritage process.

But as long as not all remains of the past are regarded as heritage, the heritage process will have to be kept separate from the formation process. First, there is a sequence of events in the course of which the remains of the past are formed – the formation process; then comes a selection of what will be heritage – the heritage process. But after that, the selection of heritage will obviously affect what will survive in the future from the past; that is, what will be given permanence.

The sequence of events in the course of which something comes to be selected as heritage – as worth defending, protecting, preserving, and possibly also continuing to use – is termed the "heritage process" (e.g. Grundberg 2000: 17ff, 47ff). The heritage process is a canonisation process in which parts of the past are assigned special values. It is a sequence of events in which a minor part is selected from the large quantity of remains of the past in a deliberate action that prioritises certain individual component parts of the mosaic for the future.

The heritage process is regulated and made visible both through conventions, legislation, justifications, and criteria, and through established professional practice and antiquarian authorities and institutions. And the heritage process can be examined, discussed, and criticised in relation to issues of representativeness and different interests.

What is given permanence and survives up to the present depends entirely on what remains are involved, when they are from, and in what context they are found. The same applies to what is selected as heritage. Here, however, everyone can assert their own, individual, heritage. But what is crucial for permanence is whether the remains are given collective attention and recognition by those who actually have the possibility and the power to determine that something is not only called heritage, but is also treated accordingly in practice.

In the formation process, the stone temples of Abu Simbel carved out of the cliffs stand a better chance of achieving permanence than the Nubian buildings of clay, just as the narratives of Ramses II have better prospects of surviving than those about the slaves who toiled in their construction. But irrespective of category, irrespective of whether history, memory, or heritage is involved, the great bulk disappears over time. So even if the remains of the past are all that exists, the past has been so much more.

In the heritage process, what can and should be selected for the future is, in principle, an open question. Even though Abu Simbel has lasted until today, more or less unchanged, it did not necessarily also have to be recognised as a heritage worth defending, protecting, preserving, and also continuing to use in the future. Irrespective of the fact that Abu Simbel is part of a World Heritage site, this is a priority set among many potential tangible and intangible cultural heritages, and that priority may be changed in the years ahead.

With the global spread of modernity, with accelerating modernisation, the set of potential cultural heritages is also increasing, while the set of natural heritages is perhaps decreasing to a corresponding degree. Ever more from the modern epoch may therefore come into consideration for protection and preservation, which may force the setting of priorities between pre-modern and modern remains.

What, then, have people through the ages prioritised for protection and preservation? What is it in the inheritance from the past that has been thought to be so valuable that it needs to attain permanence? With a metaphorical analogy to natural selection in evolution, heritage can be identified as the usable part of the past at any moment. What some interested party considered useful has been accorded permanence, provided that that person, group, authority, state, or world community, whoever or whatever they may be, has also had the necessary means to actually ensure permanence. Conversely, it is the non-usable, the useless, that was not prioritised and was allowed to disappear.

What is usable or useful varies over time and space and between different epochs, countries, cultures, groups, and individuals. Priorities are always set between different justifications, motives, and values, and there is always a choice between acting and remaining passive. The heritage process – the selection of what is to be protected, preserved, and possibly also used – is therefore a question of both values and will, of both ethics and politics, of heritage ethics and heritage politics.

Heritage is a term for a way of regarding and relating to a tangible and intangible present. Heritage thus represents both a perspective and a practice. Employing the heritage concept, we bestow values on parts of the present and may choose to act as a consequence of that. We identify parts of the present as usable and useful for the reason that they constitute an important legacy from the past, whereas other parts are allowed to remain unrecorded or be forgotten or destroyed. This means that heritage is here and now. And it connects with everything that engages people in the present – politics, economics, religion, culture, identity, climate, or health. Hence it can come as no surprise that heritage can be – indeed, generally is – controversial.

Questions about heritage are always fundamentally ethical and political because they are about a choice of values and a will to point out a direction in the present. When it is sometimes claimed in a debate that heritage is now being "politicised", this is unreflecting rhetoric. The cry of politicisation means that someone is trying to assert values and an aim that diverge from the established view or the respondent's own standpoint, which is seen as self-evident. The paradigm of normality is being challenged.

Justifications, motives, and values can be categorised, that is, grouped and systematically structured so as to provide an overview. Friedrich Nietzsche identified the use of history as either monumental, antiquarian, or critical (Nietzsche 1874 (German); 2005 (English)), which, when translated into the language of politics, becomes a reactionary, conservative, or revolutionary usage. For my part, I have argued for a different categorisation based on the triad of the true, the beautiful, and the good in the search for knowledge, narratives, or justice. But there are no limits to the justifications, motives, and values that can be formulated. For we constantly find new ways of interpreting the remains of the past so that they remain relevant and useful.

Instead of asking about justifications, motives, and values, we might examine practice, or what happens to heritage. With this change of focus, a practice can be discerned on the basis of the two parts in which the concept of time is divided, change and permanence – a practice that runs along a scale from prioritising and accepting change to prioritising and accepting preservation.

Heritage may be deliberately removed because it is seen as an impediment to change; heritage may be an impediment to modernity – in the construction of a new motorway, for instance. Heritage can be deliberately destroyed, vandalised, as a reaction against what it stands for, as in the case of the Buddha statues in Bamiyan. Heritage may also be deliberately consumed, an act justified by the claim that new and different heritage will always come along and be able to replace the old. And heritage can be allowed to decay and disappear as an instructive example of impermanence, an act of contemplation ahead of the end. The choice of change is the point on the scale where we find the most extreme modernists.

Another option consists in the balancing of change and permanence. Some of the remains of the past are selected as heritage to be protected and preserved, while other traces are allowed to disappear. This is a compromise in which representative or usable parts of a whole are selected. The challenge here is to be able to argue, in each individual case, for how change and permanence are to be balanced. This is the place on the scale where we find canonical heritage with its management, priorities, and criteria.

Finally, the remains of the past may, seen as a whole, be regarded as heritage that should be protected and preserved. Everything can be heritage, as English Heritage and the Swedish National Heritage Board have claimed. For everything may be important to someone, now or in the future. This is where we find the more extreme antiquarian attitude that reacts every time a change is on the way.

The different options along the scale may be concretised in the face of the temples of Abu Simbel: prioritising the modernisation of the Aswan High Dam and letting the temples drown in the Nile;. effecting a compromise in which the temples are relocated, modernised, and remain usable; or prioritising the temples and moving or abandoning the plan for a power plant by the Nile. As we know, the actual outcome was a compromise in the form of UNESCO's salvage action in the 1960s. But in the shadow cast by the famous temples, innumerable other remains were either merely documented or not given any priority at all.

The two cultures of heritage – the canonical and the critical – were both represented in an anthology edited by Lowenthal and the historian of architecture Marcus Binney, *Our Past before Us: Why do we save it?* (1981). Lowenthal appeared in it with his engagement in issues of preservation and heritage, while Binney was already engaged in SAVE Britain's Heritage. Lowenthal concluded with four theses:

> *What to save.* We should save more than we might like to, remembering the pace of destruction and the needs of posterity.
>
> *How to use what we save.* Not everything old belongs in museums or historic precincts; most of what is saved should be a vital part of the present.
>
> *Coping with the contrived.* The past is what we make of it, not only what it was; the process of preservation changes the look and feel, if not the form and substance, of protected sites and artefacts. We must accept many such transformations as inevitable.
>
> *The past as inspiration.* We do not preserve too much but do too little besides; we could treat our heritage more creatively. Past and present should often be commingled, not separated. (Lowenthal in Lowenthal & Binney 1981: 235f)

If, having reached this point, anyone is looking for clear positions, advice, or guidelines about how heritage can, should, or must be handled, I would like to highlight what the relatively "young" David Lowenthal wrote before his criticism of heritage became radicalised.

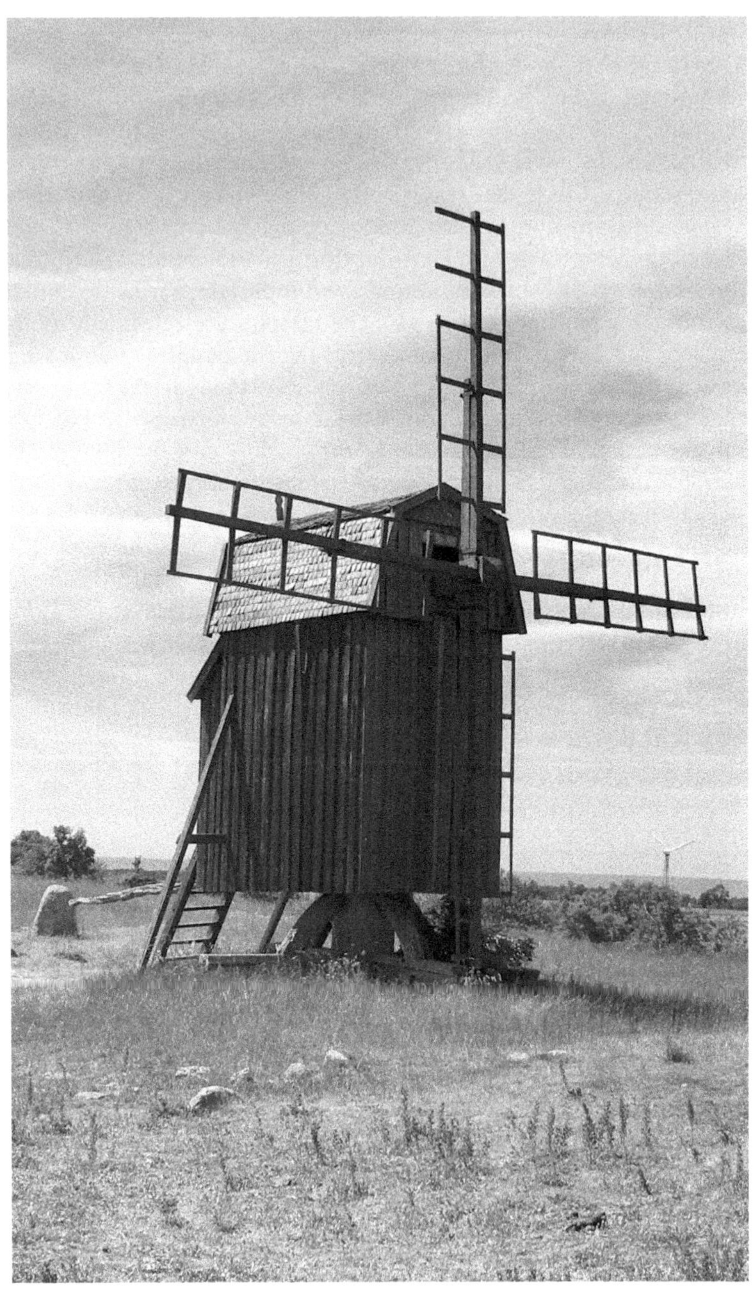

Figure 6 Agricultural landscape of Southern Öland. Photo © Bodil Petersson, 2019.

6

Destination World Heritage

World Heritage Convention

The focus of the inquiry will now shift to World Heritage and to the temples of Abu Simbel and other sites. Focusing on World Heritage means that the inquiry's questions about the past and its history, memory, and heritage will now be given precise coordinates: why, then, identify, examine, document, protect, preserve, mediate, and also develop World Heritage? Is it not a Sisyphean – an absurd or meaningless – task to try to protect and preserve World Heritage for the unlimited future? So, why even bother to define a special category of World Heritage sites?

World Heritage sites are defined as monuments, buildings, and places of outstanding universal value which require protection and preservation for future generations. World Heritage may be cultural heritage, natural heritage, or a combination of both. World Heritage therefore represents both an idea and something concrete that can be visited.

In a world full of diversity and conflicts, where people are separated by gender, language, culture, history, religion, politics, and economics, the World Heritage List is an attempt at a common global perspective and a common global responsibility. In their encounter with World Heritage, human beings are expected to be part of humanity. As both an idea and a practice, World Heritage is therefore connected to the universalism of the Age of Enlightenment.

World Heritage sites have been chosen as Archimedean points to represent heritage globally, or, to use another metaphor, chosen as a main thread throughout this inquiry. There are several reasons for this choice. World Heritage sites form a well-defined category of cultural and natural heritage linked to clearly formulated justifications, criteria, and provisions for their proper use. World Heritage sites are found all over the globe, and they cover all periods and numerous types of monuments, buildings, locations, and landscapes. There is extensive but relatively accessible information at local, national, and international levels about the individual sites, providing facts, descriptions, criteria, protection details, and action plans. The information is available on the Internet and in numerous documents, reports, articles, and books. This makes it possible to compare sites, countries, and regions, to switch focus between individual sites and a broad global overview, and to move between the world of ideas and the material sphere. There is also extensive literature about World Heritage as a phenomenon – about its emergence and establishment and about the upholding of the Convention with its lists. Moreover, World Heritage as both an idea and a practice is surrounded by a debate in which dissimilar perspectives are represented. Once again, World Heritage sites are "good to think with" – and they are good to visit, too.

The roads to the adoption of UNESCO's Convention Concerning the Protection of the World Cultural and Natural Heritage (1972), also known as the World Heritage Convention, are described in many contexts. However, the content of these histories varies with the purposes and perspectives concerned. A point on which they diverge especially markedly is the question how far back in time the origins of the Convention are sought – back to 1965, 1959, 1945, 1919, the 1870s, 1789, or the seventeenth century.

The shortest history was presented by persons involved in the creation of the Convention: two assistant directors-general of UNESCO, the engineer Michel Batisse and the lawyer Gérard Bolla. In *L'invention du "patrimoine mondial"* (2003) (English: *The Invention of "World Heritage"*, 2005), they describe a heroic process in which international agents with different interests presented rival proposals that could finally be reconciled with the Convention as a compromise, a process in which they themselves played a crucial role. The synthesis, which placed protection of nature and of culture within the framework of one and the same convention, is highlighted as a diplomatic achievement; Batisse represented nature conservation and Bolla cultural preservation. They describe the proposal, put forward at a conference at the White House in Washington DC in 1965, for a "World Heritage Trust" to protect "natural and scenic areas and historic sites"; the International Union for Conservation of Nature and Natural Resources (IUCN), which proposed a similar trust in 1968; and UNESCO's own plans for cultural heritage. The solution, which was proposed at a UN conference on the human environment in Stockholm in 1972, was a convention with the name World Heritage, covering both culture and nature and including a fund. The World Heritage Convention was subsequently adopted in Paris on 16 November 1972.

The dominant account of the background to the World Heritage Convention places UNESCO in the centre and starts out from Abu Simbel. It appears in official contexts at UNESCO and its World Heritage Centre and in the literature about World Heritage and the Nubian campaign (e.g. Säve-Söderbergh 1987: 220f; Batisse 1992; 1996: 217f; Batisse & Bolla 2003 (French): 97; 2005 (English): 92; *World Heritage Information Kit*, 2008: 7f; whc.unesco.org/en/convention). The starting point is located at UNESCO's international campaign from 1959 to 1960 to salvage the temples and other threatened ancient monuments along the Nile. Even at this early date, a convention for the protection of cultural heritage is said to have been in preparation. Mention is also made of a step-by-step development with the UNESCO "Recommendation on the Safeguarding of the Beauty and Character of Landscapes and Sites" in 1962, the White House conference in 1965, the campaign spearheaded by UNESCO to save Venice after the floods in 1966, and the IUCN proposal of a World Heritage Trust in 1968. After a first draft presented at the UN Conference in Stockholm in 1972, experts from UNESCO, ICOMOS, and IUCN prepared the final convention proposal, which could be adopted in Paris that same year.

The background to the World Heritage Convention may also be followed back to the Second World War (e.g. Labadi 2013: 26ff). After the war's massive destruction and breakdown of the political order, developments restarted with new organisations. The UN and UNESCO were founded in 1945. And the Hague Convention for the Protection of Cultural Property in the Event of Armed Conflict (1954) laid down provisions for protection that stressed the cultural heritage and its protection as an international responsibility, as is evident in the following quotations: "the cultural heritage of all mankind" and "the preservation of the cultural heritage is of great importance for all peoples of the world and … it is important that this heritage should receive international protection" (Hague Convention, 1954: 8).

The origins of the World Heritage Convention may be traced back to the experience of the First World War, in which many monuments were destroyed. There are accounts of a development that started with the League of Nations, which was founded in 1919; the formation of the International Museums Office; and a conference in Athens in 1931, which resulted in a first international resolution on the protection of historic monuments, the Athens Charter for

Restoration of Historic Monuments (Titchen 1995: 12ff; Labadi 2007: 26ff; Cameron & Rössler 2013: 1ff).

However, there were initiatives for protection and preservation across nations as early as the decades after 1870, a period characterised by colonial great powers of which the British Empire was the greatest. Alongside a gradual professionalisation and the building up of protection and preservation at national level, there were also international contacts, especially in the Church, the universities, and the world of diplomacy (Hall 2011).

The emergence of antiquarian protection and preservation can also be traced back to the Enlightenment ideas of a public sphere and to reactions against the French Revolution in 1789. Here, too, there were international contacts and ambitions, as well as both cooperation and rivalry between the great powers of France, Britain, and Germany (Harrison 2013: 42ff; Swenson 2013).

It is, of course, possible to follow the idea of a canonised cultural heritage even further back in time. Initiatives involving ideas of protection during the wars of the seventeenth century form one example (e.g. Titchen 1995: 13f). So do earlier, more sporadic protection and preservation endeavours, such as preservation through reuse as *spolia* and the wonders of Antiquity that, in the eyes of that age, represented precisely the outstanding and universal.

The World Heritage Convention from 1972 has now itself become history, memory, and an intangible heritage. But what is it that is to be told, remembered, and preserved? Ideas about the Convention's origins vary with the individual commentator's purpose and choice of perspective. Narratives of its background provide an understanding and explanation of the establishment of the Convention, but they do more than that. For history-writing is not solely informative.

The various accounts of the Convention's gradual development, which was attended by difficulties that had to be overcome by means of diplomatic ingenuity and successful campaigns geared to averting threats against it, confer legitimacy both on the Convention in its present form and on UNESCO and the World Heritage Centre as managers of the Convention. This is, once again, a typical Whig writing of history, in which the Convention and, indirectly, its institutions are the self-evident goal of the developmental efforts.

The Convention as innovation

The World Heritage Convention belongs to the modern epoch with its optimism about progress and its universal ambitions in the wake of the Enlightenment. More specifically, ideas about a special category for global protection and preservation emerged gradually in the twentieth century, the salvage campaign for Abu Simbel forming an important milestone. They were realised with UNESCO's Convention Concerning the Protection of the World Cultural and Natural Heritage in 1972 (WHC 1972).

The practical management of the Convention is characterised by modernity, with a thorough bureaucratisation at the World Heritage Centre in Paris and (in principle) rational processes, criteria, and regulations. For instance, the Centre organises annual sessions as well as seminars and workshops, advises countries about nominations, organises financial and other support for World Heritage sites, updates the World Heritage List with the associated database, and develops educational materials. And the Centre itself is based in UNESCO's headquarters at Place de Fontenoy in Paris – a complex of buildings in glass and concrete from 1958, shaped like a three-pointed star, which radiates modern architecture of its period (cf. whc.unesco.org/en/world-heritage-centre).

World Heritage is a new concept, stemming from the idea of a particularly outstanding category of heritage that requires its own status, protection, preservation, and management. And World Heritage is an idea that has been transformed into a practical reality; that is, an innovation.

According to Michel Batisse, the World Heritage Convention has three central components that are perceived as innovative, both jointly and separately. The first is that places of "outstanding universal value" should be seen as a "common heritage". The second is the drawing up of the World Heritage List. And the third is that cultural and natural heritage are given equal standing. Then comes a fourth in the form of the concept of World Heritage itself (Batisse & Bolla 2003 (French): 14ff; 2005 (English): 14ff).

However, national lists of monuments to be protected and preserved can be followed back to the legislation and inventories of the seventeenth century (cf. Jensen 2002: 325ff). The concepts of "common heritage", "universal value", and "universal protection" appear in the appeal made by UNESCO's Director-General Vittorino Veronese on behalf of the Nubian campaign in 1960 (Veronese 1960: 7). The word "outstanding" is not found in the appeal, but it contains a related phrase: "[w]ondrous structures, ranking among the most magnificent on earth". The concept of a "World Heritage Fund" was formulated by the lawyer Russell E. Train in Washington in 1965; but for linguistic reasons (there is no equivalent of "trust

fund" in French) it had to be changed to World Heritage (Batisse &
Bolla 2003 (French): 17ff, 48, 98f; 2005 (English): 16f, 44, 94). The
coordination of cultural and natural heritage was the final element
to be put in place.

The concept of innovation comes from the Latin word *innovare*,
which means "to renew" and originates from the word *novus* for
"new". Innovations are new ideas, products, or methods that have
also come into use. The words "innovation" and "modernisation"
are partial synonyms. Innovations are thus something central, but
not unique, to modernity.

Innovation is an extensive field of research in its own right where
researchers have, for instance, worked on models for the chronological and geographical dissemination of new technologies. Particular
inspiration is provided by the classic work *Diffusion of Innovations*
(2003) by the sociologist Everett M. Rogers. On the basis of a great
deal of empirical material, Rogers tried to systematise and generalise
the course of the innovation process, examining when, where, and
how innovations spread in social networks. According to Rogers,
this development follows a bell-shaped curve when frequency
is measured over time and an S-shaped curve when it is regarded as
a cumulative process. He divided the agents involved in the process
of innovation into five phases – innovators (2.5 %), early adopters (13.5 %), early majority (34 %), late majority (34 %), and
laggards (16 %) (Rogers 2003).

Instead of analysing technical innovations such as tiles, clocks,
phones, or tractors, the present discussion focuses on an international convention in which traces of the past are canonised. Inspired
by Rogers, I wonder when, where, and how the World Heritage
Convention was and is being disseminated as an idea and as a
practice. Does it adhere to the same curve as other innovations?
Who were the social agents involved in the process? Moreover, how
was World Heritage as an innovation affected by criticism and by
potential competition? And is World Heritage as an idea threatened
by creative destruction, like other innovations?

On the basis of facts collected directly from UNESCO and the
World Heritage Centre, World Heritage can be analysed as an innovation (Appendix 2). It is possible to follow how ever more countries ratify the Convention over time, and to identify the points in
time when signatory countries are given their first World Heritage.
In preparing and interpreting the statistics, account must be taken
of the fact that the potential "market" grows over time with the
formation of new states. There has thus been a striking increase in

the number of UN member states that can accede to the Convention since 1972, when it was 132 countries, to the present number of 193 (whc.unesco.org/en/statesparties; September 2020).

The World Heritage Convention came into being in 1972; and the first country to ratify it, in 1973, was the US, which had also played a central role in the whole process (cf. Batisse & Bolla 2003 (French): 32, 89; 2005 (English): 29, 85) – as one of the world's two superpowers at that time, serving as a model for others. In 1974, a further nine countries followed – Egypt (7 February), Iraq (5 March), Bulgaria (7 March), Sudan (6 June), Algeria (24 June), Australia (22 August), Democratic Republic of the Congo (23 September), Nigeria (23 October), and Niger (23 December). By the end of 1974, 10 (7.2 %) of the UN's then 138 member states had ratified the Convention. The Convention was formally able to enter into force when ratified by 20 countries, and this number was reached with the accession of Switzerland in 1975. The first 20 countries hence created the necessary critical mass for the continued existence of the Convention.

It may be noted here that out of the first 10 ratifying countries, 6 were involved in UNESCO's salvage campaign in Nubia, either as hosts or as donors (cf. Säve-Söderbergh 1987: 232). Moreover, with these first 20 countries, all 5 inhabited continents were represented; that is, both the "old" and the "new" world.

If we follow Rogers, the innovators would be the first 2.5 %, a figure achieved with the accession of Bulgaria in March 1974. This would mean that four countries were the innovators – the US, Egypt, Iraq, and Bulgaria. But that would amount to interpreting the material in an overly formalistic way. In view of the differences in respect of administrative and political systems between these countries, it would be a mistake to attribute too much importance to a few months or a year here or there in the date of ratification.

In the course of the subsequent years, the number of countries ratifying the Convention remained relatively constant between 0 (2008, 2013, 2015) and, at most, 10 (1975) new countries per year. Phase 1 (innovators, 2.5 %) was thus reached in 1974, phase 2 (early adopters, cumulative figure 16 %) in 1976, phase 3 (early majority, 50 %) in 1984, and phase 4 (late majority, 84 %) in 2000, while phase 5 (laggards, up to 100 %) closed in 2020. More than 90 % of UN member states had ratified the Convention by 2002 – and those ratifying thereafter are mostly small or new states like Swaziland (2005), Cook Islands (2009), South Sudan (2016) and then, most recently, Somalia (2020). The dissemination of the innovation over time may be described as relatively rapid, as 50 % was attained a mere 12 years after the Convention came into being.

It is worth observing that France, as the seat of UNESCO and the World Heritage Centre, joined in 1975 in phase 2 while the Nordic countries, for instance, belong to phase 3 (Norway 1977, Denmark 1979) or phase 4 (Sweden 1985, Finland 1987, Iceland 1995).

At first sight, the innovation process would appear to be complete, since 193 states have ratified the World Heritage Convention and the UN has 193 member states. But these figures conceal a statistical complication. Three UN member states have still not ratified the Convention; they are Liechtenstein (1990, not a member of UNESCO), Nauru (1999), and Tuvalu (2000). By contrast, four other states that are not UN member states, but have observer status or are members of UNESCO, have ratified it; they are Niue (ratified in 2001), Cook Islands (2009), Holy See/Vatican (2011, not a member of UNESCO), and Palestine (2011). All UNESCO's 195 member states have ratified the Convention. The last was Somalia, a country long ravaged by civil war, which ratified the convention in July 2020. Countries belonging to the group of "laggards" were not ignored; on the contrary, they have been the subject of special action to persuade all of them to join. Here it can be noted that Taiwan represented China up until 1971, but has not been a member of the UN or UNESCO since that time – and has therefore not been able to ratify the Convention either. But irrespective of how the counting is done, there is, in principle, global consensus about World Heritage. And no country has chosen to leave the Convention after signing it.

Statistical accounts of World Heritage sites generally present their growing number and much discussed geographical distribution across the world. Italy and China have the largest number with 55 each, followed by Spain with 48, Germany with 46, and France with 45. The regional distribution is Africa 96 (8.6 %), the Arab countries 86 (7.7 %), Asia and the Pacific 268 (23.9 %), Europe and North America 529 (47.2 %), Latin America and the Caribbean 142 (12.7 %). Of the 193 states that have ratified the Convention, 26 (13.5 %) do not have a World Heritage (yet) – nor does Taiwan.

Social agents and networks have been and continue to be important, both formally and informally. Agents with their positions and contacts were crucial at the establishment of the World Heritage Convention, and they may continue to be so in future work on determining which heritages will be entered in the list. On the one hand, there is a formal process in which nations nominate a proposal for a coming World Heritage from tentative lists. This proposal is then assessed by the International Centre for the Study of the Preservation and Restoration of Cultural Property (ICCROM), ICOMOS, and IUCN, while UNESCO's World Heritage Committee makes decisions at its annual meeting of selected delegates. On the other hand, there is the work behind the scenes where individuals with their knowledge, personality, contacts, and lobbying may be of crucial importance for the success of a nomination, as may chance circumstances (e.g. Turtinen 2006).

The archaeologist Lynn Meskell has presented a chilling picture of how work in UNESCO with its World Heritage Committee is characterised by geopolitical intrigue, power-wielding states, alliances, rivalry, self-interest, and inconsistencies, in which small states and minorities are ignored, as are recommendations from UNESCO's own expert bodies. World Heritage is reduced to a cultural commodity in the international game (Meskell 2018).

As early as the salvage campaign for the temples of Abu Simbel, the importance of single individuals was in the foreground. Initiatives by named individuals – a minister of culture, an assistant director-general, an Egyptologist, and several others – are presented as heroes in the narrative of a sequence of events characterised by pressure of time and obstacles that had to be overcome (cf. Säve-Söderbergh 1987: 64ff; 1996: 59ff).

However, what catches the eye in the literature about the salvage campaign and the establishment and administration of the Convention is how the texts are given legitimacy by a succession of forewords by individuals higher up in the hierarchy (e.g. Desroches-Noblecourt & Gerster 1968: 7, 9), and how those involved either describe themselves as central agents or are so described by others. This is sometimes followed up by photographs showing those involved in single portraits, at gatherings, in meetings, or in front of monuments (e.g. Batisse & Bolla 2003 (French): 47ff; 2005 (English): 43ff; Cameron & Rössler 2013). In sumptuous publications, the forewords may also be accompanied by conspicuous portrait photographs (e.g. Anker & Snitt 1997: 5, 8f). And in the media, politicians and high officials appear at the inauguration of a new World Heritage site, at the same time as the number of sites in the country concerned is apt to be noted with pride.

World Heritage sites are thus not only places to protect and preserve for the future, but also a capital that may yield a cultural, social, and political dividend for the countries, institutions, and individuals involved. There is prestige in being responsible for a World Heritage site. Publications about World Heritage sites are thus part of a social game about positions and memory, in which the agents try to associate themselves with valuable World Heritage. These agents cause themselves to be depicted in an endeavour to obtain a share of the outstanding and eternal – at least as its heroic defenders.

And no one is allowed to share this honour undeservedly. The evening before the reinauguration of Abu Simbel in 1968, UNESCO's Secretary-General discovered a memorial praising the efforts of the then President Abdul Nasser without mentioning UNESCO or its member states. In the face of the threat that the Secretary-General would not attend the ceremony, the memorial was speedily excised (Säve-Söderbergh 1996: 99; not mentioned in the English edition of 1987).

The interplay between the international, national, and local levels in the process of having a World Heritage site established may be followed in several studies. For instance, the establishment of the Hanseatic Town of Visby (WHL 731, 1995) and the Agricultural Landscape of Southern Öland (WHL 968, 2000), both in Sweden, is discussed in several articles and books, favourably by agents involved (Jonsson 2015) and more critically by researchers from the outside (e.g. Saltzman 2001: 205ff; Turtinen 2006: 140ff; Ronström 2007: 120ff). Another study of this kind of interplay concerns Angra do Heroismo on the Azores in Portugal (WHL 206; 1983; Johansson 2015). A third is a critical account of how Çatalhöyük in Turkey became a World Heritage site (WHL 1405, 2012; Meskell 2018: 134ff).

It is normal for new products to be met by criticism from consumers, and for producers to then try to improve their product so as not to lose market shares. World Heritage has not been reinvented, but it has been adjusted as an idea and a practice in relation to critical views. The management of the World Heritage Convention from 1972 has thus been changed over the nearly five decades that have passed: thematically new categories are constantly being added, culture and nature meet in mixed sites, new countries are included, national borders are crossed, more sites from a modern epoch have gradually been inscribed in the list, and attempts are made to redress any geographical or thematic imbalances (cf. *WHL Filling*, 2004).

In 1992, the World Heritage Convention was complemented by a scheme called the Memory of the World Programme, whose purpose was to protect and highlight particularly valuable documents or collections in archives and libraries. Since 1997 its Register includes, for example, Memory of the Suez Canal (1997), Declaration of the Rights of Man and of the Citizen (2003), Ingmar Bergman Archives (2007), Diaries of Anne Frank (2009), documents about Timor-Leste, On the Birth of a Nation: Turning points (2013), and The Scientific and Mathematical Papers of Sir Isaac Newton (2015). The Register now consists of 427 memories in 118 countries (www. unesco.org/new/en/communication-and-information/memory-of-the-world/homepage; *Memory of the World*, 2012; overview July 2019).

The traditional World Heritage is tangible, material, and frequently monumental. To complement this, UNESCO has defined a new category of intangible cultural heritage that is also to be protected for the future – "oral traditions and expressions", "performing arts", "social practices, rituals, and festive events", "knowledge and practices concerning nature and the universe", and "traditional craftsmanship". In 2003, the Convention for the Safeguarding of the Intangible Cultural Heritage (2003) was therefore put in place. So far, it has been ratified by 178 (91.3 %) of UNESCO's 195 member states (ich.unesco.org/en/convention; December 2019). The list includes, for instance, Vanuatu sand drawings (2008), Chinese calligraphy (2009), falconry (2010), the gastronomy of the French (2010), traditional carpet-weaving skills in Kashan in Iran (2010), and Fado singing in Portugal (2011). At the outset, in 2008, the list covered 90 instances of cultural heritage in 70 countries. The intangible cultural heritage items on the list have been divided into three categories: cultural heritage in urgent need of protection, the representative list, and good examples/good safeguarding practices. Now there are a total of 549 intangible cultural heritage elements in 127 (65.1 %) of member states (ich.unesco. org/en/lists; December 2019).

Can World Heritage as an idea and a practice be subjected to creative destruction just like other innovations, in other words be replaced by new and better solutions? This raises the question of what needs World Heritage is expected to meet.

The purpose of the World Heritage Convention is to select sites of particular value that are to be protected and preserved for future generations. But the idea of preservation is a phenomenon that arose in specific historical conditions. Protection and preservation became more important in the modern epoch from the end of the eighteenth century, and the concept of World Heritage belongs to the late twentieth century. It may be imagined that in the future, humanity will have other priorities, and that the protection and preservation of nature and culture will have to give way to other considerations; if nothing else, history demonstrates the importance of the unforeseen. World Heritage status may then become irrelevant.

So far, only two World Heritage sites have been removed from the list on account of other priorities. The first is the Arabian Oryx Sanctuary in Oman, which was delisted in 2007 when the protected area was reduced by 90 % (WHL 654, 1994; delisted 2007). The second example is Dresden, where the construction of a new motorway bridge was thought to be more important than Dresden Elbe Valley as a World Heritage site (WHL 1156, 2004; delisted 2009). Here World Heritage had to give way to the latest manifestation of modernity.

The conditions for World Heritage may also become different if the present world community built up around the UN and its subsidiary organisations such as UNESCO is dissolved or replaced by something else. The UN is a historical construction both created and characterised by the victorious great powers after the Second World War. It is an organisation where states can meet, and it is neither better nor worse than its members – not necessarily democratic or effective when that might be desired. Its future is not self-evident. The known world community is changing. For example, both the US and Israel have withdrawn from UNESCO as of 31 December 2018.

The purpose of listing as a World Heritage site is protection and preservation for the future; but the outcome may be the opposite. Listing can give the site a status, attention, and an association to modernity which, contrary to its purpose, attracts destruction. Greater tourism may entail undesirable wear and tear, which antiquarian authorities try to regulate with plans for management. Furthermore, World Heritage status may also increase the risk of vandalism, as has already been seen in Mali and Syria, for example. Listing as a World Heritage site creates a well-defined target for attacks. But it is doubtful whether this means that agents will or should refrain from making nominations.

Since 1978, the World Heritage Centre has supplemented the World Heritage List with its own list which shows World Heritage sites that are in the danger zone for various reasons – World Heritage in Danger. Of the 1121 World Heritage sites, 53 (4.7 %) are in danger: they consist of 36 cultural and 17 natural World Heritage sites in 33 (19.8 %) of the 167 countries with World Heritage (whc.unesco.org/en/158; overview July 2019); and current war zones such as Congo, Iraq, Libya, Mali, Syria, and Yemen are abundantly represented.

Rogers has demonstrated an innovation paradox – that those who have least need of an innovation are the first to adopt it, whereas those who would have the greatest need show the greatest resistance and are among the last (Rogers 2003: 295f). But in the present context it is noteworthy that the war zones of our time, by contrast, acceded to the Convention at a relatively early date – Congo (1987), Iraq (1974), Libya (1978), Mali (1977), Syria (1975), and Yemen (1980).

If a regional or national ambition for World Heritage is to increase tourism and economic development, disappointed expectations may lead to reconsidered priorities. In the work to achieve World Heritage status, unrealistically high aims may easily be set. For instance, two decades after listing, it must be concluded that the Agricultural Landscape of Southern Öland (WHL 968; 2000) is perhaps unable to meet the great expectations for a peripheral rural district. Moreover, current plans for new windmills appear to collide with the status of the area – even though Öland does, in fact, have a long tradition of windmills.

If the purpose of the Convention, and of listing, is to protect, preserve, and make accessible, solutions other than physical preservation and restoration may also be considered in the years ahead. Digitalisation is rapidly gaining ground, so the future may bring schemes of "preservation" in the form of digital documentation that includes an experience using all the senses. Since 2003, for instance, World Heritage sites are documented in 3D as part of their preservation for the future (www.cyark.org).

Digital documentation may be a break with a traditional Western view of preservation and authenticity, but protection and preservation through transformation into documentation is nothing new; it is, for example, done all the time in archaeological excavations. And the Western view of authenticity as concrete material continuity is not the sole possibility given the "Asian" model, which stresses continuity in ideas and crafts, not the material dimension (cf. Larsen 1995; Labadi 2013: 113ff; *Operational* 2019: §§78ff).

But if the purpose of World Heritage is to define an exclusive heritage category in a reaction against the inflation in heritage, the constant increase in World Heritage sites must be a problem. The brand loses value if too many products are in circulation. The project of the seven new wonders of the world, New7Wonders, may be regarded as an attempt to re-establish an overarching category of excellence; but it has not succeeded in replacing World Heritage.

New7Wonders was founded by the filmmaker and museum curator Bernard Weber. The organisation wanted to contribute to creating a global and democratic memory with precisely seven wonders which everyone can remember, and which should be protected and preserved for the future. Global votes were used to select New 7 Wonders of the World (2000–2007), New 7 Wonders of the World Nature (2007–2011), and New 7 Wonders Cities (2011–2014) (www.new7 wonders.com).

The New 7 Wonders of the World were chosen on the basis of a list of 177 potential monuments. 77 of the 177 were nominated in a voting procedure. A panel of experts, headed by a former director-general of UNESCO, then selected 21 finalists that went on to a vote in which around 100 million people took part. Most votes went to the Great Wall of China (WHL 438, 1987), Taj Mahal in India (WHL 252, 1983), Machu Picchu in Peru (WHL 274, 1983), Chichén-Itzà in Mexico (WHL 483, 1988), the statue of Jesus Christ at Rio de Janeiro in Brazil (WHL 1100rev, 2012), the Colosseum in Rome in Italy (WHL 91ter, 1980, 1990, 2015), and Petra in Jordan (WHL 326, 1985). After Egyptian protests, the pyramids in Giza (WHL 86, 1979) were given their own place of honour as the sole preserved site among the seven original wonders of Antiquity (www.new7wonders.com).

Not unexpectedly, voters chose much-visited tourist destinations and national monuments in populous countries which, with one exception, already had World Heritage status: the statue of Jesus Christ received it in 2012 (WHL 1100, 2012). Consequently, no great difference can be observed between what is accepted in UNESCO by national representatives and experts and what people think more generally. High culture and popular culture coincide, but the reason for that may be that the selection involved both experts and the general public. And both cases involve a democratic process – in the case of World Heritage representative democracy and in the case of New7Wonders direct democracy, at any rate in choosing between the finalists.

If inflation in heritage and World Heritage is a problem, UNESCO can put a ceiling on how many can be inscribed on the list. UNESCO can simply put a stop to more World Heritage sites – or not list any new ones unless old ones are removed – in brief, by prioritising. But at the moment there is no formal limit to the total number of World Heritage items that may be listed (cf. *Operational* 2019: §58).

The 42 years in the period 1978–2019 saw the listing of 1121 sites of World Heritage, which amounts to an average of 26.7 new sites per year. UNESCO could, for instance, set a ceiling at a maximum of 1200 World Heritage sites, a figure that would, at the present rate, be reached in 2022, on the 50th anniversary of the Convention. But that kind of self-imposed restriction is probably impossible to apply in view of cultural-policy considerations, being attractive neither to individual UNESCO member states nor to the World Heritage Centre as an organisation.

Outstanding, universal, and representative

The World Heritage Convention has been ratified by virtually all countries, and after nearly five decades there are World Heritage sites everywhere on earth. World Heritage sites are spread across all continents with the exception of Antarctica and across variations in language, culture, history, religion, politics, and economics. The great popularity of World Heritage may be a cause of wonder – wonder that a world deeply divided in many contexts is able to come together in the protection and preservation of an increasing number of monuments, buildings, places, and landscapes. What is it, then, that so many can agree on?

The core of the Convention, and the common denominator of all listed instances of World Heritage, is the requirement of "outstanding universal value" (e.g. Labadi 2013). This involves two different values that have to be fulfilled at the same time: a World Heritage site has to be assessed as being both outstanding and universal. By way of specification, the *Operational Guidelines* document (2019: §49, §77) sets out ten criteria, at least one of which has to be met for listing as a World Heritage site. The guidelines also point out that "Nominations of immovable heritage which are likely to become movable will not be considered" (*Operational* 2019: §48). However, the prior relocation was apparently not an impediment to nominating and listing the temples of Abu Simbel as part of a World Heritage site.

This shows us that the Convention and its World Heritage concept are dependent on a difficult balance; for the terms "outstanding" and "universal" may coincide, but they may also contradict each other. On the one hand, there is the assessment of the outstanding, pre-eminent, the superbly ingenious, or the excellent, and on the other, the assessment of the universal or general. The complication arises when the outstanding is not universal and the universal is not outstanding. The outstanding may be reserved for a few and the universal may be something that just does not stand out. A specification in ten criteria does not solve the problem; it merely moves the assessment to a different level. This does not address the fundamental difficulty, which is coming to an agreement about what is both outstanding and universal; that is, attaining a common human consensus about what is valuable in nature and culture.

My truth, beauty, and goodness need not be yours, too. My proposal for World Heritage does not need to be yours as well. What I see as outstanding and universal, you may reject as indifferent, provincial, or perhaps typically Western. When this is combined with questions of nationalism, identity, tourism, growth, and geopolitics, a chasm of potential conflicts opens up. If my or our World Heritage proposal is not accepted, then it is I, my people or country, my nature or culture, my nation, identity, development, and economy that is being ignored or insulted. Respect!

The established or so-called "authorized heritage", including World Heritage, has been criticised for not being universal or sufficiently representative. The Convention is also seen as having elevated a typical Western view of cultural and natural heritage to a general norm. In addition, it is regarded as having, in practice, favoured elite monuments and buildings in the West. History, memory, and heritage belonging to hitherto neglected nations, groups, and genders are thought to require more attention (e.g. Smith 2006: 85ff).

Lynn Meskell wants to see a more general prioritisation of living people before the stones of the past; of archaeological investigations before the preservation of monuments, and of visions of peace before technological assistance. The early, global UNESCO under the leadership of the biologist Julian Huxley was intended to be peopled by intellectuals and academics; but the organisation then developed into an intergovernmental technocracy characterised by consultants, bureaucrats, and politicians. Meskell nevertheless takes the view that UNESCO would have to be reinvented if it did not exist (Meskell 2018: 1ff, 59ff, 76, 226).

However, UNESCO, with its World Heritage General Assembly, Committee, and Secretariat, has tried to respond to the criticism. For instance, there has, in principle, been criticism of the selection of sites ever since the Convention came into practice with the listing of the first World Heritage sites in 1978. The uneven geographical distribution came in for particular criticism.

First, ICOMOS established a Global Study Working Group from 1989 onwards, and then, in 1994, a Global Strategy was adopted for greater representativeness, balance, and credibility. Analyses were carried out to demonstrate what was represented or under-represented in relation to categories, chronology, regions, and themes. There was, for example, said to be an over-representation of cultural heritage in Europe, of historic towns, religious monuments, Christianity, historical periods, and "elitist" architecture. ICOMOS concluded that imbalances could be attributed to countries not having overviews of their heritage and systems for protection and preservation, as a result of which the necessary tentative lists were either flawed or not provided at all. UNESCO's strategy has therefore been to encourage, assist, and include, with a view to inscribing new alternative sites to supplement the existing ones. It therefore encouraged the establishing of new World Heritage sites within the framework of cultural landscapes, cultural routes, agricultural settlement, secular architecture, industrial heritage, and the modern period (whc.unesco.org/en/globalstrategy; *WHL Filling*, 2004; *Operational* 2019: §§54–61). Finally, the establishment of a convention for Intangible Cultural Heritage (ich.unesco.org/en/convention) in 2003 can be interpreted as an attempt to complement the World Heritage Convention, which was characterised by a Western material view of cultural heritage, with a new convention focusing on the intangible.

World Heritage must not only be outstanding and universal; it has to be representative too. But the equation with three variables is not unique to the World Heritage Convention. The same problems are to be found in the debate on human rights.

Intimations of human rights can be found far back in time, actually as far back as pharaonic Egypt. However, the Age of Enlightenment has been assigned a special role in the narrative of human rights, with the American Declaration of Independence in 1776 and the French Revolution's Declaration of the Rights of Man and of the Citizen in 1789 as milestones. The UN's Universal Declaration of Human Rights (1948) is usually regarded as a reaction against the atrocities of the 1930s and 1940s. The Declaration was adopted by 48 UN member countries, while 8 abstained (Bring 2011: 11ff).

But human rights are disputed. What is at issue here is the interpretation of the Declaration's background in the history of ideas, the importance of individual agents, and, more specifically, different political and religious views about how human rights can, should, or must be formulated. From the very beginning, the rights were criticised for being too limited and for being too extensive. The UN Declaration has been criticised for imposing a Western norm on the countries of the world as universal. Another critical view holds that the rights may be in conflict with cultural or religious requirements. For example, the Organisation of the Islamic Conference adopted an alternative Cairo Declaration on Human Rights in Islam (1990), in which the rights are delimited in relation to Sharia (hrlibrary. umn.edu/instree/cairodeclaration.html).

Several commentators have asked whether heritage is a human right. In one instance, the answer is unclear (Kristiansen 2001: 150f), and in another, it is negative (Barthel-Bouchier 2013: 27ff). Referring to human rights may be a rhetorical strategy geared to gaining further support for heritage since, despite all the conflicts, these rights do have a relatively high international legitimacy. Even so, there is no mention of heritage at all in the Universal Declaration of Human Rights (1948). Nor is there any such mention in the Cairo Declaration on Human Rights in Islam (1990) or, for instance, in the International Covenant on Economic, Social and Cultural Rights (1966/1976).

Is World Heritage a human right? Anyone who wishes to assert that it is must also consider what that would entail. Is it the right of all groups, peoples, or nations precisely to "their" cultural and natural heritage as World Heritage? Or is it World Heritage that is a right for everyone as a collective, that is, for the whole of humanity? And in both instances, what would that mean more specifically? For instance, it may be noted that while World Heritage is laid down in a binding treaty, the Declarations may be more prestigious, but they are not binding.

There is, however, an ongoing debate precisely about the relationship between World Heritage and human rights. The debate may, for instance, deal with the fact that a World Heritage site can as such become a symbol of rights, an example being Robben Island in South Africa (WHL 916, 1999). It may also address the fact that the absence of the establishment of a World Heritage may be regarded as a violation of rights. In addition, it may be about whether the management of World Heritage sites should take account of the rights of, for example, indigenous peoples. And it may be about the fact that different principles can collide – universalism, diversity, and relativism. The debate may also arise on account of vandalisation of World Heritage sites (e.g. Silverman & Fairchild Ruggles 2007; Langfield *et al.* 2010; Logan 2012; Harrison 2013: 140ff; Ekern *et al.* 2015; Bille Larsen 2018; Meskell 2018: 218ff).

The relationship between the outstanding and the universal in the case of World Heritage is part of a larger debate about the particular and the general. On one side is the universalism of the Age of Enlightenment, with humanity as an imagined collective, and on the other is the particularism of Romanticism, with its emphasis on the distinctive character of specific nations, peoples, and individuals with their culture and history. We meet the latter in the preoccupation of the present with identities – who you "are", not who or what you may become.

How can the paradoxical oppositions built into the very design of the World Heritage Convention be resolved? Tentative World Heritage sites are nominated nationally, conferring national legitimacy on a proposal. Here the particular perspective is taken into account. Decisions on nomination and listing are subsequently made by international representatives in consultation with expert bodies. This amounts to considering the global perspective. Consequently, a negotiation is evolved in which the particular and the universal, the local and the global, the national and the international, try to meet. Combining several levels, World Heritage becomes "glocal", with double legitimacy (cf. Robertson 1995; also Turtinen 2006: 62). The global "product" is to a certain extent adapted to local conditions. It is a matter of the art of the possible, of diplomacy and politics, where there is give and take. A diplomatic negotiation ensues – if you accept my World Heritage, I will accept yours.

When the World Heritage Convention has been a success enveloped in practically global consensus, this is due partly to its particularly ingenious design, which unites opposites, and partly to responsive management, which has taken account of the priorities of different decades. The Convention has gained permanence through adjustments and supplements that served to modernise it – just like World Heritage itself.

What is particularly ingenious is that the Convention succeeds in embracing a number of apparent opposites: culture and nature, the particular and the universal, the local or national and the global, the popular and the elitist. For each country nominates what that country considers important. World Heritage occurs globally, but it is managed locally. And despite being steered by experts, it also appeals to local and popular engagement. World Heritage is of use when it comes to asserting antiquarian protection and preservation as well as national pride and identity, and it is often included in a strategy for increased tourism and growth.

Even so, the strength of the design of World Heritage, with national nominations and an international decision, is, at the same time, its weakness. States cannot have their cultural or natural heritage accepted as World Heritage against the will of the international community – and the international community cannot impose World Heritage on a country.

Just as the Universal Declaration of Human Rights (1948) may come into conflict with religious views, the World Heritage Convention (1972), as practised, may collide with the sacred in religion. This is likely to be the reason why the Kaaba in Mecca is not a World Heritage site as a building. It undoubtedly meets one or more criteria; but it has such a central role as a shrine in the Muslim world, and for Saudi Arabia, that there is no question of placing it on a tentative list. By contrast, other holy monuments, buildings, and sites are instances of World Heritage – for example St Peter's Basilica in Vatican City (WHL 286, 1984) and Durham Cathedral in England (WHL 370bis, 1986, 2008). Cultural heritage and the sacred can live in symbiosis, but not without complications, not without compromises, and not in all contexts (e.g. Clausén 2016: 95ff, 117ff). If the "sacred" in an antiquarian context competes with the sacred in a religious context, and coexistence is not possible, a choice must be made. For instance, the currents of tourists pouring into cathedrals can be seen as a problem for their use precisely as churches.

The weakness of the design also becomes visible in relation to contested heritage. Why should Poland take responsibility for Auschwitz-Birkenau (WHL 31, 1979) as a World Heritage site when it is a Nazi German facility? How can, must, or should Jerusalem be managed as a World Heritage site (WHL 148rev, 1981) when three world religions and several nations make claims on the site? And can Hebron/al-Khalil on the West Bank in Palestine be managed as a new World Heritage site (WHL 1565, 2017) in the face of Israeli protests? Conflicts in the present also become conflicts about the past.

If a map is a model of reality, a map can also reshape this reality. Similarly, reality can be shaped through written words in declarations and conventions. The World Heritage Convention shapes our view of the listed monuments, buildings, sites, and landscapes, and hence has an impact on their actual future. The Convention talks about something outstanding, universal, and representative for which everyone is responsible. An idea is fused with materiality, and something new is created.

Exclusive World Heritage

UNESCO's organisation of World Heritage is reminiscent of the structure of the UN, with member states that meet in a general assembly, a security council, expert bodies, and a secretariat; but there are no permanent member states that hold a veto. The member states of the Convention meet every other year for over-arching discussions in a General Assembly. Decisions on inscription in the World Heritage List – and on the List of World Heritage in Danger – are made annually in the World Heritage Committee. The Committee consists of elected representatives of 21 member states, who serve on the Committee for a period of at most six years (WHC 1972: Article 8; *Operational* 2019: §§17–26). A secretariat is required to assist the World Heritage Committee, and in conjunction with the 20th anniversary of the Convention in 1992 it was set up in a World Heritage Centre in Paris (WHC 1972: Article 14; *Operational* 2019: §§ 27–29; whc.unesco.org/en/world-heritage-centre). Its work is to take place in consultation with experts from the Rome Centre (now also called ICCROM), ICOMOS, and IUCN (*Operational* 2019: §§30–37).

UNESCO's intentions with World Heritage are explicitly stated in the Convention from 1972, and they amount to "ensuring the identification, protection, conservation, presentation, and transmission to future generations of the cultural and natural heritage" (WHC 1972: Article 4).

To achieve this aim, each of the participating countries is under express obligations pertaining to five areas:

1. to adopt a general policy which aims to give the cultural and natural heritage a function in the life of the community and to integrate the protection of that heritage into comprehensive planning programmes;
2. to set up within its territories, where such services do not exist, one or more services for the protection, conservation, and presentation of the cultural and natural heritage with an appropriate staff and possessing the means to discharge their functions;
3. to develop scientific and technical studies and research and to work out such operating methods as will make the State capable of counteracting the dangers that threaten its cultural or natural heritage;

4. to take the appropriate legal, scientific, technical, administrative, and financial measures necessary for the identification, protection, conservation, presentation, and rehabilitation of this heritage; and

5. to foster the establishment or development of national or regional centres for training in the protection, conservation, and presentation of the cultural and natural heritage and to encourage scientific research in this field. (WHC 1972: Article 5)

On the basis of the World Heritage sites proposed by individual countries, the Committee established a World Heritage List, as well as a List of World Heritage in Danger, in respect of which active measures may be required (Article 11). In addition, a World Heritage Fund, based on both compulsory and voluntary contributions, was established to support the work of individual countries (Article 15).

The process by which something is elevated to a World Heritage site, and is entered in the list, is lengthy and involves laypeople, experts, and politicians at several levels over a good many years. The process generally starts with local lobbying work in which sites compete with one another for inclusion on a national tentative list. Each country then presents proposals drawn from this list – and the international lobbying can start or continue. As of 2018, each country will only be able to nominate one World Heritage site, and at most 35 nominations will be assessed. The decisions are made by UNESCO's World Heritage Committee once a year after receiving advice from the experts in ICOMOS and IUCN, in a process that is reminiscent of a peer-review process for the publication of academic articles and books (cf. WHC 1972; *Operational* 2019: §§34–37, §§45–95, §§143–151).

Since 2010, nomination work has included an "Upstream Process" that provides advice, consultation, and analysis (whc.unesco.org/en/upstreamprocess). The tentative lists are public (whc.unesco.org/en/tentativelists), and UNESCO offers guidance on how to go about the nomination itself (whc.unesco.org/en/nominations).

A fundamental point about World Heritage sites is that they have to possess outstanding universal value: monuments and buildings must have "outstanding universal value from the point of view of history, art or science", and sites must have "outstanding universal value from the historical, aesthetic, ethnological or anthropological point of view" (WHC 1972: 1; *Operational* 2019: §§45–53).

Outstanding value is characterised by ten criteria, and a World Heritage has to meet one or more of them. From the first instructions in 1977 until 2004, there were two lists of criteria – one for culture with six criteria (i–vi) and one for nature with four (i–iv). Since 2005, a common list is applicable:

(i) represent a masterpiece of human creative genius; (ii) exhibit an important interchange of human values, over a span of time or within a cultural area of the world, on developments in architecture or technology, monumental arts, town-planning or landscape design; (iii) bear a unique or at least exceptional testimony to a cultural tradition or to a civilization which is living or which has disappeared; (iv) be an outstanding example of a type of building, architectural or technological ensemble or landscape which illustrates (a) significant stage(s) in human history; (v) be an outstanding example of a traditional human settlement, land-use, or sea-use which is representative of a culture (or cultures), or human interaction with the environment especially when it has become vulnerable under the impact of irreversible change; (vi) be directly or tangibly associated with events or living traditions, with ideas, or with beliefs, with artistic and literary works of outstanding universal significance. (The Committee considers that this criterion should preferably be used in conjunction with other criteria); (vii) contain superlative natural phenomena or areas of exceptional natural beauty and aesthetic importance; (viii) be outstanding examples representing major stages of earth's history, including the record of life, significant on-going geological processes in the development of landforms, or significant geomorphic or physiographic features; (ix) be outstanding examples representing significant on-going ecological and biological processes in the evolution and development of terrestrial, fresh water, coastal, and marine ecosystems and communities of plants and animals; (x) contain the most important and significant natural habitats for in-situ conservation of biological diversity, including those containing threatened species of Outstanding Universal Value from the point of view of science or conservation. (*Operational* 2019: §§77–78)

Moreover, a monument, building, or location has to have integrity and/or authenticity, adequate protection, and a management system to ensure its safeguarding.

The document *Operational Guidelines for the Implementation of the World Heritage Convention* (2019) supplies a detailed presentation, description, and definition of everything conceivable with a connection to World Heritage – the Convention, the participating countries, the General Assembly and Committee, the Secretariat, advisory bodies, the definition of World Heritage, representativity, balance and credibility, tentative lists, assessment criteria, integrity and authenticity, protection and management, the process of preparations for nomination containing format and content, requirements, registration, evaluation, withdrawal and decisions, modifications to the boundaries of World Heritage properties or of the criteria used, the timetable, reactive monitoring, the List of World Heritage in Danger with guidance, criteria, and evaluation, reporting on the implementation of the Convention, encouraging support for the Convention in the form of awareness-raising, education, and research, information about the fund and international assistance, the World Heritage emblem, sources of information, forms, and a bibliography.

The emblem and plaques may be mentioned as an example of the degree of detail in the *Operational Guidelines*. A thorough account is given of the World Heritage emblem, setting out its meaning and proper use in a large number of sections (*Operational* 2019: §§258–279). One recommendation is that a plaque should be set up at every new World Heritage, and there is a description of where it should in that case be placed and how it should be designed, including a suggestion regarding the wording on it (*Operational* 2019: §§269–272). Clearly, nothing is left to spontaneous initiatives or to chance.

The purpose of this extremely carefully established process, all the instructions and documents, must be twofold: first, to generate rational uniformity and predictability in assessment and management; second, to bestow international legitimacy on the Convention and the World Heritage Centre and hence also on the World Heritage List.

The number of new World Heritage sites listed each year has varied all the time. In the first year, 1978, 12 World Heritage sites were listed in 7 countries. The fewest, a mere 7, were listed in the politically turbulent year 1989, whereas the largest number, 61, was listed in the year 2000. Of the 1121 World Heritage sites that have been listed in 167 countries, 869 are cultural, 213 natural, and 39 mixed (WHL; overview July 2019; Appendix 1).

A World Heritage site can be justified by several criteria. For example, the Nubian monuments from Abu Simbel to Philae were justified by three criteria – i, iii, and vi (WHL 88; 1979). By making searches in the World Heritage List, it is possible to obtain statistics about the use of criteria. The distribution is as follows: criterion i is found in 254 (22.7 %) of all 1121 World Heritage sites, ii in 449 (40.1%), iii in 466 (41.6 %), iv in 597 (53.3 %), v in 157 (14.0 %), vi in 246 (22.9 %), vii in 146 (13.0 %), viii in 93 (8.3 %), ix in 128 (11.4 %), and x in 156 (13.9 %). In other words, the cultural criterion iv occurs most often and natural criterion viii least often (WHL; statistics July 2019).

In a broad sense, World Heritage sites may be said to be representative of heritage and the past. World Heritage covers all periods of human history; and as is the case with cultural heritage, there is a gradual shift so that modern monuments, buildings, sites, and landscapes are also being included in the List to a greater extent. Geographically, World Heritage sites have spread to most of the earth, even though (so far) not all countries that have acceded to the Convention have their own World Heritage sites. And thematically, World Heritage represents a wide range of nature and culture (*Operational* 2019: §§54–61). The wording of the criteria also shows that World Heritage sites have to be representative (i) and to act as "examples" of something greater (iv, v, viii, ix) (*Operational* 2019: §77). Different regions and cultures in the world have to be represented on the World Heritage Committee (WHC 1972: §8:2).

Paradoxically, however, while all World Heritage sites are part of cultural or natural heritage, they differ from it on several key points – in their definition, process, growth, and need for protection. Cultural heritage and natural heritage are therefore both more and less than World Heritage.

Unlike cultural heritage, which is an open and expansive concept that can cover all tangible and intangible expressions of human influence, World Heritage is a well-defined concept reserved for monuments, buildings, and sites that meet one or more set criteria. But World Heritage may, at the same time, be something different from cultural heritage, since it also covers outstanding and universal natural heritage.

While everyone is perfectly free to claim that something is heritage, the requirements for becoming a World Heritage are formalised in a particular way. The organisation and process surrounding World Heritage has been laid down to the very last political, economic, legal, and bureaucratic detail. There are an international World Heritage Convention, a World Heritage Committee, a Secretariat at the World Heritage Centre, *Operational Guidelines* that have been adjusted numerous times, a large number of directions and reports, meetings, conferences, and a website containing masses of additional information, statistics, and references.

And while the concept of heritage can grow freely, while more and more is constantly being seen as heritage, the increase in the number of World Heritage sites is strictly regulated. Each year, an announcement is made as to how many new World Heritage sites have been inscribed.

At first sight, the importance of threats and destruction in justifying protection would seem to be something that heritage and World Heritage have in common. The very first lines of the Convention formulate the need for its existence by referring specifically to threats: "*Noting* that the cultural heritage and the natural heritage are increasingly threatened with destruction not only by the traditional causes of decay, but also by changing social and economic conditions which aggravate the situation with even more formidable phenomena of damage or destruction ..." (WHC 1972: 2, italics in the original; also *Operational* 2019: §4).

Further on, the Convention specifies possible examples of threats in connection with the establishment of a separate List of World Heritage in Danger:

> the threat of disappearance caused by accelerated deterioration, large-scale public or private projects or rapid urban or tourist development projects; destruction caused by changes in the use or ownership of the land; major alterations due to unknown causes; abandonment for any reason whatsoever; the outbreak or the threat of an armed conflict; calamities and cataclysms; serious fires, earthquakes, landslides; volcanic eruptions; changes in water level, floods, and tidal waves. (WHC 1972: Article 11.4; also *Operational* 2019: §§177–191)

The temples of Abu Simbel were threatened in the 1950s by the modernisation of Egypt, by the Aswan High Dam and by the higher water level in the Nile; but when Nubian monuments from Abu Simbel to Philae became a World Heritage site in 1979 (WHL 88, 1979), they were no longer threatened. And this is typical of the great majority of monuments, buildings, places, and landscapes listed as World Heritage sites. For even though threats are stressed as a justification for the Convention, the tentative World Heritage sites are rarely if ever threatened. They generally belong to the heritage category that has long come in for national, and often also international, attention. Inscription is more of a final confirmation of a pre-existing canonisation as something outstanding and universal. But why categorise something as World Heritage to be protected for the future if it is already protected? What is the need for a convention for the protection of World Heritage sites with reference to threats, if these threats have no real existence?

To understand and explain World Heritage as a phenomenon, I want to focus on the points where World Heritage differs from heritage. The paradoxical relationship between heritage and World Heritage is the very place to look for an answer, because while heritage is open, informal, and expansive, World Heritage is bounded, formalised, and regulated. While everyone is entitled to assert a heritage, experts determine what will be World Heritage. Everything can be heritage, whereas World Heritage is something outstanding and exclusive. And if heritage should, just like World Heritage, be protected, it can be noted that World Heritage is protected already.

If we look at what the Convention does not explicitly express but what it actually does, it distinguishes an extremely exclusive group of cultural heritage and natural heritage sites as something exceptional. While Sweden, for example, has thousands of cemeteries filled with memorials, only one of them, the Woodland Cemetery (*Skogskyrkogården*) in Stockholm, has been made a World Heritage site (WHL 558rev, 1994). The Woodland Cemetery is outstanding.

The canonical exclusiveness of World Heritage is also clear to see in a report produced by the Swedish National Heritage Board: Sweden has 15 World Heritage sites, 43 cultural reserves, 264 listed government buildings, 1647 museums, 1650 national interests for cultural environment protection, 2266 listed non-government buildings, 3422 protected churches, 30,011 buildings marked in municipal plans for their heritage value (but this statistic is based on information from only 11 of 21 counties/regions), 283,669 ancient monuments, 595,872 other cultural heritage remains, and a total of 7,608,094 buildings (*Räkna med kulturarvet*, 2017: 7). Summarised as a simple and instructive statistic, there are thus 507,206 buildings for every World Heritage site in Sweden.

The Convention creates a category separated from the mass of heritage. When a gradual democratisation of heritage has created inflation in the concept, a new category, managed by an elite, is introduced. When everything can, in principle, be designated as heritage, a carefully selected part is given certified status as World Heritage. The devaluation of the heritage concept leads to the establishment of a new currency. The establishment of World Heritage can therefore be interpreted as a compensatory response to the inflation in heritage.

The Convention establishes a hierarchy of values that not only has consequences for the handling of the remains of the past, but also confers social status on the countries, institutions, and individuals involved. The Convention has created what may be called a "distinction", to use a concept borrowed from the sociologist Pierre

Bourdieu (1979 (French); 1984 (English)). Consequently, World Heritage is not (only) about protection and preservation; it is (also) about distancing.

In order to be able to manage the World Heritage sites and maintain hierarchical distance, no depreciation of their value can be permitted. This makes it essential to have sharp definitions, specific criteria, a difficult process, and a regulation of their growth. Here UNESCO's World Heritage Centre, with its Committee, functionaries, Convention, and Guidelines, functions as a gatekeeper. Rejections of applications are essential to maintain the standard, and any potential threats must be given careful consideration: the outstanding must not become too general (e.g. Batisse 1992: 30). Still, it is difficult to maintain a distance. Innumerable monuments, buildings, places, and landscapes are competing to become World Heritage sites. And sites that do become World Heritage rise in popularity, so that the frequently desired tourism becomes a new menace.

However, it is inconsistent when the journalist Peter Hanneberg regrets the tourism and the inflation in the number of World Heritage sites – cultural ones in particular – while writing frequently in the media about trips to World Heritage sites and publishing coffee-table books lavishly illustrated with photographs geared to augmenting interest in them (Hanneberg 1998; cf. 2012). And it is inconsistent, or at any rate problematic, when the local level has hopes of increased tourism while increased tourism may become a threat.

This brings to mind the Nobel Prize for Literature, an exclusive distinction for something and someone already honoured; there, however, the distinction is accompanied by a cash reward. And for 50 years, secrecy shrouds who was nominated and exactly how the discussion went, unless somebody breaks their obligation to remain silent...

Modern World Heritage

You can be a World Heritage site; but if you are, you must be modern too. World Heritage as both a concept and a reality can be surprisingly modern. And if World Heritage is not modern to begin with, it can be brought into modernity through modernisation, management, and representations. On the face of it, World Heritage is expected to be remains of the past to be protected and preserved for the future – monuments such as the temples of Abu

Simbel. But World Heritage as a concept and as a collection of actual sites does not by any means represent the past only. The very categorisation as World Heritage, with its Convention and management, is a modern phenomenon. And in the course of the process of being accepted as World Heritage – or, subsequently, as a consequence of that acceptance – a World Heritage is irretrievably thrown into a modernity characterised by change, renewal, and movement.

Most cultural World Heritage sites are of an impressive age, measured in centuries or millennia. The natural World Heritage sites may even be of an age that can be measured in millions of years, for instance the Grand Canyon in the US (WHL 75, 1979) and the Dolomites in Italy (WHL 1237rev, 2009), at the same time as nature with its plants and animals is constantly being recreated in the present. But modernity is also abundantly represented, with more than 50 World Heritage sites from the eighteenth, nineteenth, and twentieth centuries. They include sites that mark crucial historical events, the architecture of modernism, and the infrastructure of industrialism with its bridges, tunnels, canals, railways, and factories.

The first modern World Heritage site on the list is also perhaps the most controversial one, namely Auschwitz-Birkenau (WHL 31, 1979) of 1940–1945, which became a World Heritage site in 1979, the second year of listing. The problematic character of the site is indirectly shown by the fact that the UNESCO list officially gives it a supplementary designation as a "German Nazi Concentration and Extermination Camp" – not a Polish camp, even though it is geographically located in Poland, and not just "German" either. The question of where the camp belongs is a disputed issue. On good grounds, neither Poland nor democratic Germany wants to recognise the site as "its" heritage. Otherwise, Germany is known and recognised for its *Vergangenheitsbewältigung*, that is, its exertions to deal with a problematic past (e.g. Dudek 1992). In 2018, Poland adopted a law that imposes a sentence of imprisonment for up to three years for calling Auschwitz-Birkenau a "Polish death camp". As a World Heritage site, Auschwitz-Birkenau can represent a modern epoch, a site of crimes against humanity that must not be forgotten – and according to Zygmunt Bauman a modern rational (death) industry (Bauman 1989).

The next modern example is less controversial and represents the emergence of revolutionary ideas. It is Independence Hall, or Pennsylvania State House (WHL 78, 1979), which also became a

World Heritage site in 1979. The building is not primarily being preserved for its style, which is Georgian. The reason for the building's status is that it is where the Declaration of Independence and the US Constitution were signed, in 1776 and 1787 respectively.

The first example of modern uncontroversial industrial heritage as World Heritage is the Ironbridge Gorge (WHL 371, 1986) in England, with its bridge erected in 1779. The subsequent decades saw the addition of a large number of modern World Heritage sites – the capital city of Brasilia (WHL 445, 1987), Bauhaus in Weimar, Dessau, and Bernau (WHL 729bis, 1996, 2017), the Hiroshima Peace Memorial (WHL 775, 1996), Zollverein Coal Mine Industry (WHL 975, 2001), Mountain Railways of India (WHL 994ter, 1999, 2005, 2008), White City of Tel Aviv (WHL 1096, 2003), Grimeton Radio Station (WHL 1134, 2004), Central University City Campus at UNAM in Mexico (WHL 1250, 2007), 17 buildings by the architect Charles-Édouard Jeanneret, known as Le Corbusier (WHL 1321rev, 2016), Bikini Atoll Nuclear Test Site on the Marshall Islands (WHL 1339, 2010), Japan's Meiji Industrial Revolution (WHL 1484, 2015), Asmara: a Modernist City of Africa (WHL 1550, 2017), eight buildings by the architect Frank Lloyd Wright (WHL 1496rec, 2019) – and many more.

The youngest World Heritage so far is the architect Jørn Utzon's Sydney Opera House (WHL 166rev, 2007), erected in the period 1957–1973. The Sydney Opera House represents modernism, is an icon of Australia's largest city, and became a World Heritage site in 2007.

But it is probably only a matter of time before a monumental construction work in the present – such as the Millennium Wheel from 1999, also called the London Eye – achieves World Heritage status. Another candidate might be the "Bird's Nest", as Beijing's National Stadium at the 2008 Olympic Games is known; the artist Ai Weiwei was involved in its design, but his political activism may prove an obstacle. As yet, none of these examples appears on a tentative World Heritage list.

In fact, most of the World Heritage sites – or, at any rate, most of the cultural ones – may be connected to the concept of modernity, since they were once modern in the sense of constituting something new in their own present. For example, one of the very first World Heritage sites on the list is Chartres Cathedral (WHL 81bis, 1979, 2009) in France, where the Gothic building style of the twelfth century was an expression of bold new ideas about light, form, and technology. Another example that was modern in the sense of being a technical innovation is the Ottoman Stari Most (Old Bridge) in Mostar (WHL 946rev, 2005) in Bosnia-Herzegovina. When Stari Most was opened in 1566, its free span across the Neretva River was supposedly the broadest ever. In Walter Benjamin's words, every epoch has been able to feel modern (Benjamin 1983 (German): 2, 677; 1999 (English): 545).

If a World Heritage site is not already modern, it can be modernised so as to remain relevant and useful. For example, a good many sites have been renewed or substantially restored in order to even come under consideration as World Heritage. Others have been modernised or given modern additions as a result of their listing. Notably, many World Heritage sites have had to build parking places, paths, and visitor centres, and many have been illuminated so as to be able to attract or regulate an expected or actual increase in tourist numbers.

Like other examples of heritage, World Heritage sites are managed by antiquarian and environmental authorities in a process called heritage management. In the canonical tradition of heritage, there is a continual production of manuals, journals, articles, reports, courses, and conferences about how heritage can, should be, or is managed in relation to threats, protection, preservation, and accessibility, with general recommendations, instructions, and examples adapted to the legislation of different countries or to international conventions (e.g. Leask & Fyall 2006).

The World Heritage Centre has, for instance, published a series of manuals for the management of World Heritage sites, covering what are termed "Disaster Risks" and referring to both natural and cultural World Heritage (whc.unesco.org/en/managing-cultural-world-heritage). And the World Heritage List contains a careful presentation, under the heading "Protection and management requirements", of what antiquarian regulations apply in each individual case and what action is going to be taken (WHL). The concept of management refers to principles for leading operations or organisations that are, as such, typical expressions of rational modern society.

Wooden buildings in Asia may be perceived as old and authentic, even though they have been renewed a number of times. Here authenticity is linked not to the materiality in itself, because wooden structures are often replaced, but to the preservation of the craft tradition and architecture, which amounts to applying a view of authenticity that differs from what is traditional in the West (Byrne 1995; Larsen 1995). One example is found in the World Heritage site in the previous capital Kyoto in Japan. This site comprises wooden buildings and gardens from the tenth century up to and including the sixteenth; but both buildings and gardens have been fully or partly renewed since they were first constructed (WHL 688, 1994).

However, constant change and renewal are not unique to an "Asian" way of thinking. Continuous management also occurs as a strategy in the West in the form of repeated restorations, full or partial reconstructions, and other interventions. At the World Heritage site of Stonehenge (WHL 373bis, 1986, 2008), stones were raised again and secured throughout the twentieth century; a nearby road with heavy traffic has been closed; footpaths and car-parking spaces have been created; and 2013 saw the opening of the new Stonehenge Visitor Centre, placed further away from the monument than its predecessor (Chippindale 2012; www.english-heritage.org.uk/visit/places/stonehenge).

At the Acropolis in Athens (WHL 404, 1987; Beard 2010; Sandis 2014: 57ff), the Classical period has been given priority with the temple of the Parthenon, which is intended to legitimise the Greek State. In 1834, only a few years after the country's new-won independence, the Parthenon was opened as an ancient monument and as a symbol of the young nation. During the subsequent decades, the Acropolis was "liberated" from buildings or ruins that were not from Antiquity – traces of the Parthenon as a Byzantine or French cathedral or as an Ottoman mosque, Roman and Florentine remains, and Turkish settlements. A restoration of the ancient Acropolis has been under way since 1975, and its justification as a World Heritage site puts special emphasis on the Classical period. A new Acropolis Museum was opened in 2009, to provide more room for the many tourists visiting the site and to act as a setting for a long-sought-for return of the Parthenon frieze (also known as the Elgin Marbles) from the British Museum (e.g. Melotti 2011: 191ff).

Another example is Jelling (WHL 697, 1994, 2018; Hvass 2000; 2011) in Denmark, where the buildings in the railway-station community around grave mounds, rune-stones, and the church have been bought up and removed since the 1910s, so as to be able to uncover the monuments – not without conflicts with local people who wanted to protect business and trade. A nearby visitor centre called Kongernes Jelling was built in 2000 and has since been renewed. Shortly after the act of graffiti vandalism in 2011, in the course of which "GELWANE" was painted on the largest stone, both rune-stones were placed in outdoor display cases. The excavated remains of a large ship-setting, a palisade, and halls were marked clearly in concrete in 2013. The whole area now looks like a gigantic outdoor installation from the 2000s.

In a few cases, the character of modern restorations and reconstructions has itself been sufficient to justify the status of a site as a World Heritage site. This applies, for instance, to Warsaw, where more than 85 % of the historic centre of the capital city was destroyed during the rising in 1944, but where the city centre was practically reconstructed in full during the period 1945–1984 (WHL 30bis, 1980, 2014; Appelbom Karsten 1987: 72ff). Another example is the Fortified City of Carcassonne (WHL 345rev, 1997) in France, which was threatened with demolition but where the architect Eugène Viollet-le-Duc succeeded in carrying out an extensive restoration in 1853–1879, which was continued after his death. Viollet-le-Duc's modern restoration is an important reason why Carcassonne was made a World Heritage site.

In addition, there are World Heritage sites that have not yet been completed but where the construction process is under way. For instance, seven works by the architect Antoni Gaudí (WHL 320bis, 1984, 2005) became World Heritage sites in Spain in 1984. However, the church of La Sagrada Familia in Barcelona, which was started in 1882 and where Gaudí had time to contribute to the crypt and the facade before his death in 1926, is not expected to be (largely) completed until 2026.

A renewal in the form of a reconstruction or a radical restoration may also be taken into consideration when a World Heritage site has been destroyed in war or through acts of terrorism. For example, the Stari Most bridge in Mostar (WHL 946rev, 2005; Nikolic 2012: 53ff) in Bosnia-Herzegovina was fired on and destroyed by Croatian artillery in 1993; but it was reconstructed and reopened in 2004 as a symbol of reconciliation, cooperation, and coexistence. Mausoleums in the World Heritage in Timbuktu (WHL 119rev, 1988) in Mali, which were destroyed in 2012, are being reconstructed as well. By contrast, the reconstruction of the Buddha statues in Bamiyan in Afghanistan, which were both destroyed in 2001, has been abandoned (WHL 208rev, 2003).

However, the lack of any great measure of consistency in dealing with the reconstruction, restoration, and modernisation of World Heritage sites is clear from the different positions that are taken from site to site. For instance, the Dresden Elbe Valley (WHL 1156, 2004, delisted 2009) in Germany became a World Heritage site in 2004. Dresden, with its baroque architecture, was largely destroyed in bomb raids in 1945. After the reunification of Germany, the Frauenkirche (Church of Our Lady) was reconstructed in the period 1994–2005, as were parts of the surrounding buildings from the eighteenth century. The World Heritage site also includes modern industrial heritage with bridges, a cableway, and a railway; one example is the Loschwitzer Bridge, also called the "Blaues Wunder" ("Blue Wonder"), a steel bridge from 1891–1893. But when a new motorway bridge of steel and concrete, the Waldschlösschen Bridge, was planned in order to reduce city traffic, it was a bridge too far. The World Heritage Centre warned that Dresden risked being removed from the World Heritage List and proposed building a tunnel instead. A referendum was held, as were court hearings, but work on the bridge continued. Dresden Elbe Valley was placed on the List of World Heritage in Danger in 2006 and was removed from the World Heritage List in 2009. Or, to be correct, it still appears on the list; but now it is firmly crossed out as a reminder that it has been discredited. The new bridge was opened in 2013.

The temples of Abu Simbel are excellent examples when it comes to illustrating a modern World Heritage site. With their style and size, the temples constituted something new in the Nubian frontier region in their pharaonic present. They were rediscovered and investigated in what has been classed as the modern epoch, in which the past as well as territories were colonised by European great powers. Nature was to be tamed so as to modernise postcolonial Egypt as well. The Aswan High Dam and the power stations would compel the waters of the Nile to produce electricity, and the annual floods would be regulated. But the dam project created a lake that threatened the temples of Abu Simbel and other remains of the past. Modernity threatened heritage. The solution was a gigantic salvage campaign, a feat of engineering that lifted the temples above the rising water mirror of the Nile (*The Salvage of the Abu Simbel Temples* 1976: 200). The temples were brought into modernity as reconstructions at nearby new sites. They were "reborn" into a modern time and a modern society.

The temples of Abu Simbel were cut up, moved, and reassembled using modern science and technology under arched domes of concrete and hidden in artificial hills. The temples were illuminated both internally and externally, and their interior was given modern ventilation. Modern buildings, hotels, roads, and an airport were constructed nearby (*The Salvage of the Abu Simbel Temples* 1976; Säve-Söderbergh 1987; 1996). The salvage action was regarded as an international success, which paved the way for the phenomenon of World Heritage – and for Nubian monuments from Abu Simbel to Philae to become a World Heritage site as early as 1979, the second year of listing (WHL 88, 1979). The temples were thus adapted to Egyptian tourism, in which visitors could be driven, sailed, or flown to the site. It was a development in which the first European adventurers and the select few who had travelled along the Nile in earlier times paved the way for latter-day mass tourism encouraged by travel guides, (crime) novels, film, and advertising.

There was a modernisation of Abu Simbel in the world of representations too. There is a technological development from the first drawings and watercolours to the photographs of the 1850s, the film of the 1900s, and the 3D scans of the twenty-first century. Pictures of the temples were mass-produced and widely disseminated. In 1959, before the cutting and relocation, the temples were also documented by photogrammetry (Desroches-Noblecourt & Gerster 1968; *The Salvage of the Abu Simbel Temples* 1976: 33, 72 with Fig. 13.1:1). The temples can be visited virtually, sitting in front of a computer screen. In the virtual world, too, the temples can be reconstructed digitally and coloured to give viewers an experience of their original appearance (e.g. Siliotti 1997). Today, the drawing pad, the easel, and the relatively slow technology of the photographic apparatus have been replaced by a smartphone, in which tourists at the site are able to instantly share images and films from their visit with other people all over the world. Obviously, representation is also subject to the acceleration of modernity.

The reconstruction of Abu Simbel included careful planning of how the temples would be illuminated both internally and externally. First and foremost, the great temple was orientated so that the sun could continue to penetrate to the statues in its interior twice a year, as before. Then artificial lighting was created, lighting that would on the one hand permit studies and on the other hand imbue the temples with a "mysterious and sacred atmosphere" (*The Salvage of the Abu Simbel Temples* 1976: 191f with Fig. 20: 1). The light was thus intended to permit both the clarity of knowledge and the enchantment of beauty.

In this respect, Abu Simbel is only one of numerous World Heritage sites whose dark interiors have been made accessible to the scrutiny of human eyes by means of artificial lighting, and whose exteriors are illuminated at night in order to create an experience, and perhaps also as a preventive measure for protection. Abu Simbel, Auschwitz-Birkenau, Independence Hall, the Ironbridge Gorge, the Sydney Opera House, Chartres, the Bridge in Mostar,

Timbuktu, the Acropolis, Jelling's rune-stones, Warsaw, Carcassonne, and La Sagrada Familia – all are floodlit at night, whereas this is not normally the case at Stonehenge or Bamiyan. Light moves World Heritage into modernity.

Destination World Heritage

The Past is a Foreign Country! We often employ metaphors in order to describe our relationship to the past. We travel – or escape – to or from another time or another country. In nostalgia, a home country or a lost time is being missed. People also travel more tangibly to monuments, buildings, and places that represent the past. But why do we travel to seek out the past?

The temples of Abu Simbel were destinations from the very moment of their construction; they must have required a great inflow of labour. Greek graffiti from 592 BCE on the legs of the statues of Ramses II, the name of the adventurer Belzoni from 1817, and other inscriptions are memories of numerous visits (MacQuitty 1965: 76, 84, 91, 98f, 134; Desroches-Noblecourt & Gerster 1968: 30f). After their rediscovery, the temples became destinations on cruises along the Nile. Travel books, novels, and films established Abu Simbel as Egyptian icons along with destinations including the Museum of Egyptian Antiquities, the pyramids of Giza, the Valley of the Kings, Karnak, and Luxor; upper-class travel paved the way for mass tourism. The salvage campaign of the 1960s increased the attraction of the temples by means of a new narrative, and the construction of a town, hotels, roads, an airport, and a port made even more visits possible. Inscription on the World Heritage List along with other Nubian monuments between Abu Simbel and Philae (WHL 88, 1979) only confirms the importance of the temples as tourist destinations.

The World Heritage List contains numerous other sites that have been destinations for centuries. They include places of religious pilgrimage, for instance Jerusalem (WHL 148rev, 1981), St Peter's Basilica in Rome (WHL 286, 1984), and Santiago de Compostela in Spain (WHL 347, 1985). Another is Venice in Italy (WHL 394, 1987), which became a destination at an early date. Most World Heritage sites were established tourist destinations long before being entered on a tentative national list, nominated, and inscribed. Even so, most destinations for pilgrimage or tourism are of course not World Heritage sites.

The linking of tourism and World Heritage is not a matter of chance. Established World Heritage sites are usually already important destinations. And when nominations are made, there is often a local hope that the new World Heritage site will become a destination that attracts more visitors and therefore promotes development and economic growth in the local area. World Heritage sites are "modernised"; that is, they are adapted to the needs of the tourist industry with signage, illumination, visitor centres, paths and trails, and car parks.

However, UNESCO's ambition for World Heritage sites is not limited to development and the economy. According to the anthropologist Michael A. Di Giovine in *The Heritage-scape* (2009), UNESCO's aim is to create a new global system and a new global identity with the aid of World Heritage sites. UNESCO wants (or wanted) to create a borderless and peaceful world (cf. also Meskell 2018).

At the same time, there is constant criticism of tourism to World Heritage sites. That criticism stresses how World Heritage sites themselves are adversely affected by commercialisation and wear and tear from mass tourism. The effects of the many visitors on the local population and the surroundings are a factor too.

At such destinations as the Ironbridge Gorge in the UK (WHL 371, 1986), Visby in Sweden (WHL 731, 1995), and Venice in Italy (WHL 394, 1987), the point is made that the gradual transition to heritage and World Heritage has led to a gentrification, in other words a change of the social mix in the area. Conflicts of interest may also arise between the local population, newcomers, and tourists (e.g. Ronström 2007; White & Devlin 2007). For example, in the summer of 2017, there were demonstrations in Venice against mass tourism and its consequences. The city now has more tourists every day than it has permanent year-round residents. The World Heritage site with its souvenir shops has become a threat to modern city life, with its need for shops for convenience goods. But gentrification of attractive urban environments in recent decades is a widespread phenomenon, not solely the preserve of World Heritage; and it began long before the concept of World Heritage had been devised.

UNESCO has worked actively to regulate tourism at World Heritage sites in the awareness that it can have both benefits and drawbacks. For instance, strategies were formulated at an early stage for "sustainable" tourism that works with, and not against, the local population (World Heritage Sustainable Tourism Programme, 2001; Bourdeau *et al.* 2015; 2017; whc.unesco.org/en/tourism).

If one wishes to claim that the primary purpose of World Heritage is to create tourist destinations, the response will be that the great majority were destinations already. But listing has undoubtedly served to attract more attention. The sites become part of an international branding exercise. But why, then, do people visit the past at all?

In *The Great Museum* (1984), Donald Horne compared heritage tourism in Europe to medieval pilgrimages, museums to churches, exhibited objects to relics, and tourists to pilgrims – and many others have thought along the same lines. The attraction is the perception of authenticity in a period of modernity, industrialism, crisis, and nervousness. But tourism is extensive, and it is growing swiftly, irrespective of whether the present can be characterised as modern or postmodern, as bearing the stamp of industrialism or deindustrialisation. Tourism is growing in Europe; and it is growing in China as well. Everywhere people are given the opportunity to travel – sufficient freedom, leisure, money, and health – they go and visit other places. Tourism is growing because more and more people are being given the opportunity to travel, something that used to be the preserve of a few.

There is no single reason to travel, no single reason to visit World Heritage sites. At this point, I would again like to invoke the triad of truth, beauty, and goodness. Travel to the past can engender new knowledge, contribute to the forming of new experiences, and make reflection possible.

Enchantment and expectations

World Heritage is everywhere. While the list, when started in 1978, consisted of 12 World Heritage sites in seven countries, there are now 1121 World Heritage sites in 167 countries (WHL, July 2019). But why does a special category called World Heritage exist in the first place, and why did the temples of Abu Simbel become World Heritage sites?

UNESCO's World Heritage Convention came into being in 1972 in order to protect and preserve monuments, buildings, and sites that possess "outstanding universal value" for future generations. To justify this need, the Convention refers to increasing and new threats to cultural and natural heritage (WHC 1972: 1). In other contexts, the campaign at Abu Simbel in the 1960s is highlighted as an important background, since threatened monuments were salvaged through international cooperation (e.g. Batisse 1992;

whc.unesco.org/en/convention). Nubian monuments along the Nile from Abu Simbel to Philae were listed as World Heritage site in 1979, with the criteria of being (i) a masterpiece (ii) testimony to a vanished civilisation, and (vi) an open-air museum that represents the unfolding of a long sequence of Egyptian pharaonic history (WHL 88, 1979).

The temples of Abu Simbel are undoubtedly masterpieces and represent a vanished civilisation; but are they not already lost, at least partly? For salvaging the temples from drowning meant that they had to be broken up, relocated, and reconstructed at a new site under concrete arched domes in artificial hills. So the temples became World Heritage despite debatable authenticity. The temples of Abu Simbel appear as they did at the time of Ramses II, but are largely the result of a modernisation in the 1960s.

Several other World Heritage sites mix old and new. The wooden buildings in Kyoto in Japan have been renewed repeatedly (WHL 688, 1994); the Fortified City of Carcassonne in France was substantially renewed in the nineteenth century (WHL 345rev, 1997); and Warsaw in Poland was reconstructed after the Second World War (WHL 30bis, 1980, 2014). Here, too, continued permanence was achieved through radical changes where that which appears, at first sight, to be from Antiquity – or to be pre-modern – may in fact be modern.

The past is indeed everywhere; for the whole of our present, everything in our "now", has been accumulated from parts of various ages. The present consists of innumerable "archaeological" layers in a complicated stratigraphy. The view from my remembered or current office is composed of parts, some of which have existed for centuries while others are modern; and the view is in constant change. But in point of fact, this present, this now, is also already past, since it takes time for my senses to register and coordinate the impressions into an interpretation in my brain (Eagleman 2016: 52f). Consequently, we can state that the past is everywhere and that this is, in itself, not problematic.

The composition of my view depends on where I am and where I direct my gaze. It also depends on how my surroundings are affected over time in the course of interplay between humans, culture, and nature, with an ongoing building up and breaking down. In archaeology, this is called taphonomic or formation processes.

What survives from the past to the present, what gains permanence – the temples of Abu Simbel, for example – depends on which materials were used from the outset, on forces of nature including the climate and weather at the location, and on human interventions such as clearing from sand after rediscovery. The choice made by Pharaoh Ramses II to have the temples carved out in the rock has ensured permanence for thousands of years. And the campaign in the 1960s ensured further permanence into the future when the Aswan High Dam brought the threat of flooding and destruction, but it was a permanence that entailed radical changes.

In an analogy with evolution, what has survived until today may be described as a process of selection in which only the useful survives. The past with its history, memory, and heritage survives until the present if the prerequisites for permanence exist thanks to the choice of durable materials or favourable conditions for preservation. And it is not sufficient to have an environment that counters natural degradation; the past also has to be useful in the present, and that is why it comes in for attention and is told about, remembered, and protected. That which is not "of use" will be ignored, go undocumented, be forgotten, or be allowed to decay. At the same time, every retelling, recalling, or preservation involves a change on the part of that which is to remain. This is why nature is not alone in "developing"; history, memory, and heritage do so too.

With another analogy, the past is a landscape of ruins from which *spolia* are gathered that may be moved to new places and given a new use. History, memory, and heritage are invested with new meanings as the issues and needs of the present shift. The past may thus be used for the true, the beautiful, and the good – and for the false, the ugly, and the evil. With this perspective, nostalgia is not a longing for a lost or "foreign country", but a hunt for narratives that can be reused. Lowenthal's books, with their innumerable examples and contradictory interpretations, are precisely that kind of quarry, where everyone can find something that suits whatever they may be building. That is the reason for their attraction and popularity, despite Lowenthal's critical attitude.

That the past is everywhere is nothing to be surprised about. For heritage to suddenly be everywhere is a completely different matter. If heritage is everywhere – or if everything can be heritage – that means that everything should also be protected and preserved. The ultimate consequence of such a principle is that all change, all renewal, is forced to cease. This is not realistic. So how did the perception that heritage is everywhere arise?

The inflation in the demand for preservation is a consequence of the acceleration of change. The phenomenon has been given many names – modernity, supermodernity, late capitalism, the great acceleration, or a completely new period in which the impact of humans dominates around the globe, the Anthropocene epoch. Since the industrialisation of the nineteenth century, continuing during the twentieth century, since the Second World War, and especially since the 1970s, with more countries sharing in modernity, the speed of change has increased. The quantity of accumulated past – and the rate of turnover of this past – has grown.

Asserting heritage everywhere and for everything is a compensatory and psychological reaction to the great acceleration. Nor is this reaction illogical, since experience shows that remains of the past can be useful now or at some time in the future in contexts that we cannot predict. But since everything cannot be preserved and protected, because then society would ossify, several methodological and overlapping strategies can be discerned.

One established strategy is to prioritise and only preserve selected parts, whereas other remains are allowed to disappear with or without documentation. An archaeological excavation does not document everything, just as not all finds are transported for exhibition or storage in museums. Similarly, priorities are set among narratives, memories, and heritage sites. These priorities are, in principle, assigned on the basis of what the present finds relevant; that is, useful. Speculation about what might become relevant in the future occasionally forms part of this process.

But the preservation of original remains of the past in libraries, archives, and museums for future use is under pressure, since it is costing more all the time. There is, however, a rapid development of (relatively expensive) digital methods for documentation and reconstruction. We can hence envisage ever more remains being documented and preserved digitally, so as to be recreated later as required. With a less "Western" and more "Asian" attitude to authenticity, this would be a strategy that could be combined with a continuation of the rapid developments in this area.

Prioritisation can be combined with creative reuse, in which heritage is modernised so as to remain relevant. Monuments, buildings, sites, and landscapes can be given new functions and meanings. Abu Simbel becomes a tourist destination, while industrial heritage buildings become offices, homes, or hotels. In my view, this extensive "management" amounts to a strategy in which cultural and natural heritage are deliberately adapted to the present – not least tourism.

Still, it is also possible to choose not to tell, not to remember or preserve. Here two different attitudes meet: the futurists, who

want to confirm progress, modernity, and the future, so away with
the remains of the past, and the romantics, who want to leave well
alone and contemplate the beauty of decay or decline, so let the
remains of the past go away naturally. From widely different starting
points, they arrive at attitudes that have the same consequences –
the disappearance of heritage.

The World Heritage Convention is a modernist strategy for prioritisation and management, so that the outstanding and universal
is protected and preserved for the future while being adapted to
the ideological and economic needs of the time. World Heritage is
thus a compensatory reaction both against the great acceleration
and against the subsequent inflation in heritage. The Convention
and its highly organised bureaucracy recreate order, hierarchy, and
distance. But if there is inflation in World Heritage as well, then the
process may start again with the creation of new priority categories.

Should the temples of Abu Simbel go, so that progress is not
impeded, or should they be blown up or drown? No: when the
modernisation of Egypt with the Aswan High Dam formed a threat,
the choice that was made was an international salvage campaign
which also partly modernised the temples, so that they continued
to be of use. Otherwise, both futurists and romantics would have
been able to look on while the faces of Ramses II slipped below the
water's surface day by day – either relieved to be rid of the past or
reflecting pensively on what had disappeared.

Abu Simbel represents cultural heritage; but the same attitudes
can, in principle, be transferred to natural heritage: prioritise, document, modernise, root out, or leave be. If it is part of modernity to
distinguish between nature and culture, the opponents of modernity have some explaining to do if they want to treat (the heritage
of) culture in one way and (the heritage of) nature in a completely
different way. For modernity is, after all, a human creation, and as
such it is also a consequence of a "natural" development.

The World Heritage Convention represents order, hierarchy,
and distance in relation to proliferating heritage. At the same time,
though, listing as a World Heritage adds something invisible. The
special elevated and distanced status of World Heritage as outstanding and universal may be described as a modern "enchantment", or
something sacred in a more or less secularised modern world. This
is why World Heritage as a phenomenon may be compared with the
sacred in the religious sphere. In both spheres, the enchanted represents different perspectives and narratives that may both coexist
and collide.

Not unexpectedly, there is enormous faith in World Heritage; it is expected to be able to work miracles – or it is blamed for erroneous deeds. Either World Heritage is expected to contribute to greater knowledge, growth, diversity, and peace, or World Heritage is held responsible for abuse, mass tourism, gentrification, and destruction. World Heritage becomes a projection plane for the hopes and frustrations of the present. And either it is not possible to have enough of history, memory, heritage, and especially World Heritage – or there is already far too much.

But why focus so much on history, memory, and heritage? Why not focus on modernity instead? The main problem may, for better or worse, be that "modernity is everywhere".

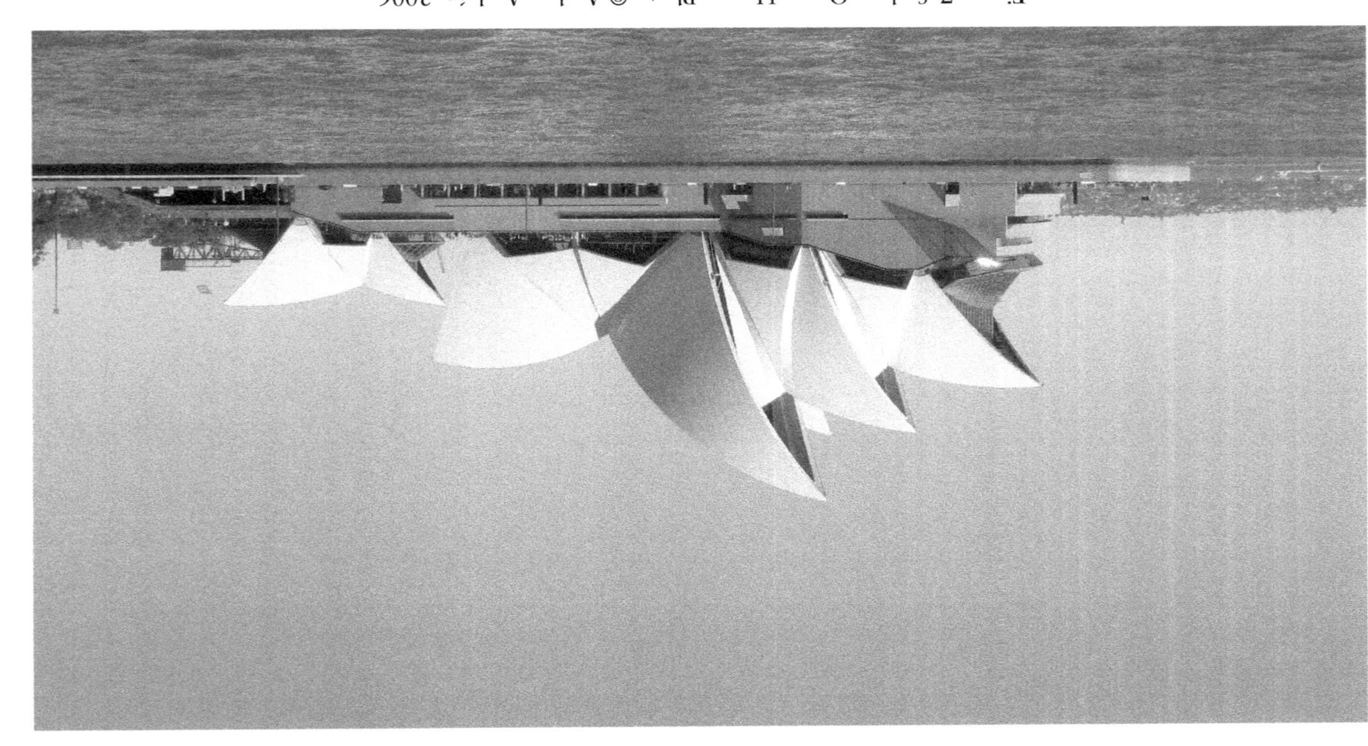

Figure 7 Sydney Opera House. Photo © Anders Andrén, 2006.

7
World Heritage and modernity

Heritopia

UNESCO's salvage campaign in Nubia, with the temples of Abu Simbel as its main attraction, was described as a great success both at the time and afterwards. The Aswan High Dam's threats to the ancient monuments could be averted. The temples of Pharaoh Ramses II were saved from the rising water level of the Nile by being cut up, moved, and reassembled in a new and safer place. Heritage had been threatened by Egypt's modernisation, but it was salvaged in an international campaign that employed the rational organisation, finances, knowledge, and technology of modernity in order to succeed.

Even so, despite all the words about success, the campaign appears to have been associated with seven paradoxes, which may be reformulated as questions. The contradictions are to do with the impossibility of preserving the past; the relationship between preservation and change; protection and preservation as an exception; the significance of threats; the relationship between heritage and modernity; trends and tendencies in modernity; and heritage as both local and global. The paradoxes and the associated questions will be discussed in this concluding chapter in order to round up my inquiry, but they will be reviewed in the reverse of the order in which they were first presented.

It was noted that World Heritage, with Abu Simbel as an example, does not at first sight fit in with a postmodern interpretation of the present, since World Heritage is a category for protection and preservation geared to creating structure, unity, wholeness, and universalism. World Heritage as a phenomenon is one of many expressions of a globalisation; but it includes national and local places, where diversity is also deliberately pursued. World Heritage can thus be designated as glocal; that is, a phenomenon that combines the global and the local. But glocality as a concept is not an exhaustive answer, since the World Heritage Convention with its list of World Heritage sites crosses borders in several respects: in its intentions; in relation to the categories of nature and culture; in respect of World Heritage themes; and with regard to chronology, geography, and engagement.

The fundamental intention of the World Heritage Convention is to protect and preserve heritage that is viewed as outstanding and universal (WHC 1972: 1). But since the establishment of the Convention, additional objectives to which World Heritage is meant to contribute have also been developed, one example being sustainable development (*Operational*, 2019: §6; cf. Bille Larsen & Logan 2018). However, the overall objective of protection and preservation and the subordinate objective concerning development are not always compatible. Indeed, they may be opposed.

The combination of the categories of nature and culture in the same convention for protection and preservation was presented with pride by the convention's agents (Batisse & Bolla 2003 (French); 2005 (English)). The great achievement consisted in making two established discourses and bureaucratic fields, each with its own agenda and ambitions, work together. The specific combination of nature and culture is symbolically expressed in the World Heritage emblem – a square inscribed in a circle, designed by the artist Michel Olyff. The emblem is intended to symbolise how "the results of human skills and inspiration" represented by the square are accommodated in and bound up with "gifts of nature" represented by the circle, and how the circle also refers to the globe of the earth (whc.unesco. org; *Operational* 2019: §§258–279). Besides, the emblem may serve to recall the ground plan of a passage grave from the Stone Age, and also, in simplified form, the ground plan of the temples of Abu Simbel in their artificial hills.

If the division between nature and culture is something characteristic of modernity, we can observe that the Convention of 1972 presented an attempt to unite the two several years before Jean-François Lyotard proclaimed the arrival of the postmodern condition in 1979 (Lyotard 1979 (French); 1984 (English)). But the symbiosis between nature and culture only came about gradually. Until 2004, there were two separate lists of criteria; and even after they were brought together in a single list, it is still obvious that criteria i–vi apply to culture and criteria vii–x to nature. The provision of advice is also split between different bodies with, by and large, ICOMOS for culture and IUCN for nature. The integration is clearer in the 39 so-called "mixed" World Heritage sites

(WHL, noted in July 2019), examples being the "Holy Mountain" Mount Athos in Greece (WHL 454, 1988) and Machu Picchu in Peru (WHL 274, 1983).

In the same way as the Convention covers both nature and culture, it also accommodates various types of World Heritage that have to be protected and preserved, namely monuments such as buildings and sites, objects that may belong in different institutions and disciplines. The theme of cultural landscapes, which was added in 2002, is a cross-cutting perspective, in which the landscape may contain elements of differing ages (Fowler 2004). There are 112 World Heritage sites that are characterised as cultural landscapes (WHL, noted in July 2019). One example is the Bamiyan Valley in Afghanistan, with the niches of the destroyed Buddha statues as well as other remains (WHL 208rev, 2003).

The chronological range of the Convention is enormous. It extends from nature such as the Grand Canyon in the US, with deposits up to 2 billion years old (WHL 75, 1979), to the Sydney Opera House, which was begun in 1957 and opened in 1973 (WHL 166rev, 2007). Once again, the Convention gathers objects across institutions and disciplines, the Grand Canyon being connected with paleogeology and the Sydney Opera House with modern architectural history.

In conjunction with the World Heritage List, the Convention operates at several geographical levels. It deals with local sites, nominated by the nation for elevation to an international level, where they become not only a national responsibility but also a responsibility for everybody, in practice under the supervision of UNESCO with the World Heritage Centre. More specifically, World Heritage sites may extend across one or more national borders; there are thus 39 "transboundary" World Heritage sites (WHL, July 2019). One example is the Struve Geodetic Arc, a chain of survey triangulations along a meridian through ten countries in Europe from Norway to Ukraine (WHL 1187, 2005); a second example is the Architectural Work of Le Corbusier with buildings in seven countries (WHL 1321rev, 2016); and a third is the Silk Roads through China, Kazakhstan, and Kyrgyzstan (WHL 1442, 2014).

The glocality of World Heritage sites is also reflected by the people involved. Initiatives concerning cultural and natural heritage often begin locally; but they are obliged to persuade a regional and national level, so as to be included in a tentative list and then actually be nominated. Work at local, regional, and national levels may take place in consultation with representatives of the World

Heritage Centre; and the decision to approve inscription is made by the World Heritage Committee with its 21 representatives, following opinions from ICOMOS, IUCN, and ICCROM as expert bodies. The process up to potential inscription as a World Heritage thus involves a large number of agents with widely different roles, at different levels, and in many countries.

The World Heritage Convention with its World Heritage List crosses borders in a number of areas. Features that would, at first sight, come across as obstacles – such as separate categories, types, periods, or levels – are allowed to work together here. In my view, it is the very cross-border character of the Convention, and of World Heritage, that has laid the foundation for its success. Here international cooperation succeeds – and it cannot be stopped by a veto, as in the UN Security Council. A need is met; and problems have been solved in a relatively pragmatic spirit, in a way that is responsive to current needs and trends.

For despite all the criticism of the World Heritage Convention – criticism of the process from initiative to inscription, of the actual selection of World Heritage sites, and of how the World Heritage sites are managed – it is easy to establish that the Convention is a great success. This is seen from accession to the Convention, which proceeded relatively rapidly in the period from 1972 onwards and has since, without defections, reached a level amounting to a global consensus; as of July 2020, even Somalia has ratified the convention. It is also apparent from the tentative lists, in which numerous monuments, buildings, and sites are queuing to become World Heritage sites. Besides, it is clear from the intensive work being done in many places to get a monument, building, site, or landscape on to the tentative list and nominated; some of these efforts are new attempts to win approval after a previous rejection. Places are prepared for nomination, being "modernised" in order to be experienced as relevant.

Two examples of tentative World Heritage sites that I have run into in my work as a historical archaeologist are Viking Monuments and Sites, with cooperation between Denmark, Iceland, Latvia, Norway, and Germany, and The Rise of Systematic Biology, with cooperation between Australia, England, France, the Netherlands, Sweden, and South Africa. The latter example involves botanical gardens and sites from the eighteenth century, places that are linked to the botanist Carl Linnaeus in Sweden (whc.unesco.org). At local, regional, or national levels, there is great keenness to attain World Heritage status for one thing or another. The nomination of a presumptive World Heritage site is associated with great hopes for attention, funding, and development. World Heritage status is attractive.

It may briefly and counterfactually be concluded that if the World Heritage Convention had not existed, it would have been necessary to (re)invent it, for the need and its popularity cannot be doubted.

The genius of the Convention is based on its cross-border ambitions and capabilities. It combines the apparently contradictory. The Convention is a creative construction, since it has generated new thinking and practice both about what can be cultural and natural heritage and about what protection and preservation may mean.

World Heritage sites are cross-border and glocal; but the full complexity of the phenomenon is not captured by the glocal concept. A similarity to franchising in business may be pointed out, too; there, payments are made to obtain a share of a well-known brand. In the case of World Heritage, however, the point is not to trade under a certain brand name but to have a right to protection, preservation, and promotion under the World Heritage emblem. States pay UNESCO as well as making both mandatory and voluntary payments to the World Heritage Fund; they may then apply for a monument, a building, a site, or a landscape to be made part of the World Heritage brand, which confers the right to use the Convention's emblem. But most of the responsibility and the work remains local, regional, and national. If the rules are not adhered to, a site may, after warnings, lose the right to call itself a World Heritage site and use the emblem, as happened to the Arabian Oryx Sanctuary in Oman (WHL 654, 1994, delisted 2007) and the Dresden Elbe Valley (WHL 1156, 2004, delisted 2009).

Sites are modernised in order to become World Heritage – and they are modernised after having achieved this status. But in actual fact, nothing happens on inscription. It is a matter of recognition of a pre-existing status. If a site is inscribed in the World Heritage List, it is because it is in fact already outstanding and universal. This is reminiscent of the canonisation of a person as a saint after several stages of scrutiny. The deceased was already a saint, but is now officially deemed to be worthy of the respect due to such a personage. Nonetheless, recognition as a World Heritage after a long and often difficult process is associated with so much hope and prestige. A World Heritage site is not just a material place; it is also a starting point for utopian expectations.

The World Heritage Convention and the inscription of a site as World Heritage adds something invisible. The special status or increased value as a World Heritage site is best described as a modern "enchantment" that makes everything possible. The World Heritage site is lifted into its own elevated sphere, a sphere characterised by the immoveable, invaluable, and eternal; here heritage is united with the no-place of utopia, and the sphere may hence be designated as *Heritopia*.

In Heritopia, paradoxes are no obstacles; if anything, they enhance the enchantment. The analogy with the sacred and religious is thus entirely justified and does not necessarily convey unfavourable connotations. That World Heritage sites by no means remain untouched, but are visited by large numbers of tourists; that they are valued in terms of money, generally in the form of paying visitors and hotel nights; and that they do not remain unchanged, but are actually modernised – all this is part of the narrative of the border-crossing paradoxes inherent in World Heritage.

The new concept Heritopia, made by uniting Heritage and Utopia, signifies the land of the future, which is being pursued with the aid of a modernised heritage and World Heritage. Here, remains of the past are used to create the future in a manner completely opposed to Zygmunt Bauman's depressing concept "Retrotopia". The future is not being sought nostalgically in the past, but looked for as a utopia with the aid of the past. While my inquiry opened with a sense of wonderment about the temples of Abu Simbel and the Nubian campaign, Heritopia may serve to summarise the optimistic final outcome of this inquiry. In more ways than one, Heritopia is a place and a situation to long for.

Regardless of trends

Both more and less modernity creates heritage. On the one hand, the ambition of modernising Egypt through the Aswan High Dam launched an international campaign in the course of which the cliff temples of Abu Simbel were salvaged and later inscribed in the World Heritage List together with other temples along the Nile. On the other hand, the decline of modernity, the emergence of postmodernity, and deindustrialisation entailed a transition to a "heritage industry". Here income from industrial production is replaced by income from heritage tourism, and at the same time the remains of industry may themselves be reclassified as heritage worth protecting, preserving, and visiting. In Egypt, however, tourism was an important "industry" long before the construction of the Aswan High Dam, indeed before all talk of postmodernism, deindustrialisation, and World Heritage. Ramses II's temples at Abu Simbel have been important destinations ever since their (re)discovery in 1813.

In crisis theories, both more and less modernity can be made to bear the responsibility for varying periods' obsession with the past. Consequently, the more – or less – modernity, the more history, memory, and heritage. The paradox can be explained in several ways, however. First, the view taken of the concept of modernity varies in different crisis interpretations. Second, examples are chosen that may strengthen a particular thesis concerning the past and modernity, while others are overlooked or deliberately excluded. Third, all change can create relics in need of protection and preservation, irrespective of whether a rise or decline of modernity is involved.

An emerging modernity means new ideas, new monuments, buildings, places, and landscapes; but it also means that earlier ideas lose their relevance and that the older infrastructure is transformed, abandoned, or destroyed. Modernity leaves relics that may live on as history, memory, and heritage. But modernity in decline creates relics too. When industry moves to new places or countries with cheaper labour or lower taxes, ideas, technologies, factories, and housing that were modern once become redundant. The creative destruction of ideas as well as materiality is common to both rise and decline.

In view of how heritage may be combined with both modernity and post-modernity, both industrialisation and deindustrialisation, it can be no surprise that the same tendencies appear regarding World Heritage. Here, however, the picture is even clearer. Thus, there are no simple correlations between the establishment of World Heritage and trends in the history of ideas and the economy.

The World Heritage Convention came into being in 1972, right at the end of a unique period of economic growth and confidence in modernity in the West. The Convention was developed in the 1960s during a modern boom, which coincided with the establishing of new states after decolonisation. As an idea, the Convention thus belongs to modernity with its ambition to protect and preserve remains of the past that modernisation is threatening directly, or risks abandoning as useless relics. Shortly after the adoption of the Convention came the turning point of the Oil Crisis of 1973–1974, which marked the end of the economic boom, and of optimism, in the West.

Consequently, the situation had changed when the Convention was to be implemented in practice with the inscription of the first World Heritage sites in 1978. The UK, the former colonial great power, was in an economic and political crisis in the 1970s because of deindustrialisation and unemployment. The concept of postmodernism was established to characterise the new tendencies in the history of ideas.

The Convention is managed pragmatically in relation to the new needs of the time, as is seen in varying editions of the *Operational Guidelines* (most recent from 2019). The Convention was justified by threats and needs for protection and preservation; but its management at the World Heritage Centre came to be about identity, tourism, multiplicity, sustainable development, representativeness, balance, and credibility. More than ever, the Convention is becoming a political project in which choices must be made between different objectives, interests, and values.

One concrete expression of how the Convention is managed as an idea in a period with new conditions and needs is seen in the inscription of industrial heritage as World Heritage. This is a question both of a general interest in the early history of industrialisation with its material remains and of facilities that economic cycles have made redundant. One example of early industrialisation is the Ironbridge Gorge (WHL 371, 1986) in the UK; and an example of a topical closure is the Zollverein Coal Mine Industry in Germany (WHL 975, 2001), where industrial activities ended in 1986.

Another concrete expression of the relevance of the Convention in a new period is the nomination and designation of monuments, buildings, places, and landscapes that have national iconic status. States have proposed and received acceptance for World Heritage sites that are central to the narrative of their country's history and identity, often doing so at a relatively early stage in the Convention's history. Examples include the Giza pyramids in Egypt (WHL 86, 1979), the Persepolis in Iran (WHL 114, 1979), the Taj Mahal in India (WHL 252, 1983), Machu Picchu in Peru (WHL 274, 1983), the Statue of Liberty in New York (WHL 307, 1984), Petra in Jordan (WHL 326, 1985), Great Zimbabwe in Zimbabwe (WHL 364, 1986), the Acropolis in Athens, Greece (WHL 404, 1987), the Great Wall in China (WHL 438, 1987), Uluru (Ayers Rock-Mount Olga) in Australia (WHL 447rev, 1987, 1994), and Jelling in Denmark (WHL 697, 1994, 2018).

A third concrete expression is the modernisation carried out before and/or after sites have been inscribed as World Heritage. This is modernisation both of the sites themselves by providing signs, paths, lighting, and ventilation, and of their surroundings by means of the provision of visitor centres, car parks, and access roads – all to make the World Heritage sites attractive as destinations in an expansive tourist industry. One example here is the temples of Abu Simbel (WHL 88, 1979); Stonehenge in England (WHL 373bis, 1986, 2008) is another, and a third is Jelling in Denmark (WHL 697, 1994, 2018).

If the World Heritage Convention and its practical management are seen not only as an antiquarian project for protection and preservation of the outstanding and universal, but also as a political project shaped by states in both rivalry and cooperation, other patterns emerge. First and foremost, note must be taken of the remarkable consensus about the Convention, with ratifications by 193 states (noted in September 2020). The types of World Heritage vary between states, but they appear across economic, political, and religious classifications of the world. Thus, around the same number of World Heritage sites exists in the US (24; 1973; noted in July 2019), Iran (24; 1975), Russia (29; 1988), and Japan (23; 1992).

Iran ratified the Convention as early as 1975 and obtained its first World Heritage in 1979, the same year as the revolution. But no new World Heritage sites were added in the period 1980–2002. China, which deliberately destroyed remains of the past during the Cultural Revolution in 1966–1976, ratified the Convention in 1985, obtained its first World Heritage in 1987, and now has no fewer than 55 World Heritage sites (WHL, July 2019). We may also note the contrast on the Korean Peninsula, where night-time lights also show a clear difference. Capitalist South Korea ratified the Convention in 1998 and has 14 World Heritage sites, the first being inscribed in 1995. Communist North Korea ratified the Convention in 1998 and only has two World Heritage sites, the first dating from 2004.

The World Heritage Convention is thus interpreted and managed with political pragmatism and remains meaningful regardless of trends. As is the case with World Heritage sites themselves, varying meanings may be ascribed to the Convention so that it remains relevant and therefore "useful".

World Heritage and modernity

What is the relationship between World Heritage and modernity? This question has been a pivotal point throughout my inquiry. It is the pivotal point for understanding and explaining how the past is apparently seen everywhere, and how history, memory, and heritage are expanding. The novel *La lenteur* (English *Slowness*) by Milan Kundera formulates an elegant existential mathematics: "le degré de la lenteur est directement proportionnel à l'intensité de la mémoire; le degré de la vitesse est directement proportionnel à l'intensité de l'oubli" (Kundera 1995 (French): 45; 1995 (English): 39, "the degree of slowness is directly proportional to the intensity of memory; the degree of speed is directly proportional to the intensity of forgetting").

Similarly, the relationship between modernity and heritage has often been expressed in a formula, but the concepts that are used in it may vary. For modernity and World Heritage are examples of concepts from a broad field of dichotomies, in which expressions of the future and of the past are set up as opposites. Concepts that may be entered on one side of the dividing line are change, progress, modernity, modernisation, modernism, industrialisation, urbanisation, and secularisation, and concepts that may be written on the other side are history, memory, heritage, tradition, monuments, memorials, museums, conservation, and nostalgia. When modernity increases, so should nostalgia. But paradoxically, when modernity decreases, nostalgia also increases. The formulas synthesise statements or chains of arguments that are seldom if ever accompanied by concrete qualitative reasoning or by the adducing of quantitative evidence.

The point of an "existential mathematics" is undoubtedly to bring persuasive precision and clarity to bear on a problem area in the humanities. At first sight, the formulas look plausible; but the paradoxes that gradually become visible reveal that the assumptions regarding the mathematics are dubious. The paradoxes arise because the concepts that are used are complex, ambiguous, and entangled with one another.

Modernity thus has several faces. It is associated with speed, volatility, and renewal, both in the world of ideas and in the material world. Modernity is therefore connected with the universal ideas of the Enlightenment and with the market economy and its creative destruction.

World Heritage has several faces too. As part of heritage, World Heritage can be associated with the unchanging, with stasis and the past; but the examples of World Heritage include modern ones representing change, speed, and the future. On the one hand, World Heritage as such is a modern concept, linked to the international system organised around the UN that evolved after the Second World War. The World Heritage Convention is managed by a Centre, where the process from tentative lists via nomination to inscription and monitoring is rationally regulated down to the very last bureaucratic detail. On the other hand, World Heritage sites are concrete material monuments, buildings, places, and landscapes that may belong to widely different periods, including the modern era.

We perceive the complex, ambiguous, and entangled not only in the ideal world of concepts, but also in encounters with concrete World Heritage sites. Ramses II's cliff temples at Abu Simbel with their sculptures and images have more or less survived for thousands of years. Consequently, the ancient temples may stand out as a contrast to the modern Aswan High Dam with its turbines and production of electricity. The dam threatened the very existence of the temples, but they survived thanks to a modern international salvage campaign. The temples were sawn into pieces, moved, and recreated in a concrete structure, which an attempt has been made to conceal. The cliff temples thus mix the old and the new. Abu Simbel also acts as one of several important destinations in the Egyptian tourist industry, a place that tourists visit for a few hours.

To deepen the confusion, the canonical tradition of heritage considers that modernity often threatens heritage and World Heritage. But at Abu Simbel, modernity was both a threat (the dam) and a solution to the problem (the salvage campaign). The temples were salvaged by engineers and archaeologists using the most modern knowledge and technology of their time, which may itself become a recognised part of World Heritage in the future: an outstanding and universal "monument to the engineering skill" of the 1960s (cf. Berg 1978: 49). In the critical tradition of heritage, both modernity and heritage may, by contrast, constitute a threat. What is a threat and what is threatened is hence a relative matter.

In my humanities-based mathematics I would instead, despite the conceptual complications, like to call attention to the emergence of a compensatory chain reaction: hypermodernity or the Anthropocene, where humans radically influence nature and society and there is an initial compensatory counter-reaction, with more and more being held up as being natural and cultural heritage worth protecting and preserving for several reasons. As a second compensatory reaction against this inflation of natural and cultural heritage, World Heritage is then constructed as a clearly defined and separate category of its own. And whereas the increase in the changes of modernity and the compensatory expansion in natural and cultural heritage are exponential, the increase in World Heritage is, in principle, linear, with an extremely limited number of new sites each year.

Threats, realities, and rhetoric

Threats of change, decay, or destruction are central to the first, and canonical, culture of heritage. For threats of destruction or change are crucial in establishing remains of the past as heritage. Actual or imagined threats may activate an opinion and generate action and legislation. The mission of the canonical culture is to avert threats to heritage, to protect and preserve it.

Threats of change, decay, or destruction are also central to the second, and critical, culture of heritage. Here, that which is threatened is itself transformed into a threat. For heritage can be an actual or imagined obstacle to development. Criticism of heritage is sometimes transmuted into a particular fascination with change, decay, and destruction. And since heritage is regarded as a constructed category, and therefore as an infinite resource, not only may sustainable use be acceptable but consumption may be so as well.

Threats thus create heritage, and heritage creates threats. Modernity may be one such threat to parts of heritage, at the same time as aspects of modernity may themselves become heritage. So the relationship between threat, heritage, and modernity is, at first sight, confusing and riddled with contradictions. But the paradoxes are due to the simple fact that what is being threatened and what is doing the threatening depends entirely on the perspective applied.

The importance of a threat in activating opinion, generating action, and transforming monuments into World Heritage is graphically illustrated at Abu Simbel (WHL 88, 1979). The construction of the Aswan High Dam threatened the cliff temples with flooding and thereby with destruction. The threat was obvious and could be followed almost day by day in the steadily rising level of the Nile. The patent contrast between present and past, between modernisation and the monuments, between the dam and the cliff temples, created the drama, narrative, and focus necessary for enabling UNESCO to justify, set up, and implement an international salvage action.

The threats to the monuments in Nubia form part of the background to the establishment of the World Heritage Convention. But the background contains other instances of destruction as well, caused by both people and nature. This is the experience of the massive devastation of heritage during the First and Second World Wars. And alongside Abu Simbel, emphasis was placed on UNESCO's action after a natural disaster when wind, high water levels, and violent rain caused flooding in Venice and Florence, Trento and Siena in 1966; subsequently, Venice and its lagoons (WHL 394, 1987), Florence (WHL 174bis, 1982, 2015), and Siena (WHL 717, 1995) all became World Heritage sites.

The World Heritage Convention begins by mentioning the need to protect the outstanding and universal; protection presupposes that something is a threat. And here the Convention explicitly asserts that the heritage is "increasingly threatened". Later, the Convention goes on to specify different threats in detail (WHC 1972: 1 quotation, Article 11: 4).

The importance of threats in the management of the Convention is also shown by the special list of World Heritage in Danger. Here, it is a formal decision that determines – after an investigation, and according to set criteria – whether a World Heritage site should be entered on the list of World Heritage in Danger. The decision is made at the annual meeting of the World Heritage Committee (WHC 1972: Article 11: 4; *Operational* 2019: §§177ff). At present (2019), there are 53 World Heritage sites on the list: 36 cultural and 17 natural in a total of 33 countries, including Jerusalem (whc. unesco.org/en/158; July 2019).

But whether a World Heritage site is threatened or itself constitutes a threat depends on the choice of perspective. At the Dresden Elbe Valley, the plans to build a new motorway bridge of steel and concrete meant that the area was first placed on the list of World Heritage in Danger in 2006 and was then deprived of its status as a World Heritage site in 2009. The matter was presented in an obviously menacing tone by UNESCO: if the bridge was put in place, Dresden would be removed from the World Heritage List. And to make matters clear, Dresden is still on the list, but it has been crossed out (WHL 1156, 2004, delisted 2009)! Here, World Heritage and modernity are presented as each other's opposites. But they could also have been integrated, if the modern bridge had been accepted as part of the World Heritage site. And viewed from another perspective, it was UNESCO's management of the World Heritage site that became a threat to a solution of present-day traffic problems.

Considering that the Dresden Elbe Valley has bridges from different periods, it is strange that the most recent bridge was not interpreted as part of the World Heritage site, as a new annual ring in a historical development. First, modernity is not necessarily an obstacle to status as World Heritage; there are many modern World Heritage sites, including some that are built in concrete. Second, there are World Heritage sites where modern restoration and reconstruction have contributed to the sites becoming World Heritage. Examples are Warsaw city centre, which was reconstructed in the period 1945–1984 (WHL 30bis, 1980, 2014), and Carcassonne (WHL 345rev, 1997) in France, which was restored in 1853–1879. In the same way, the definition of the World Heritage Nubian Monuments from Abu Simbel to Philae (WHL 88, 1979) could be expanded to include the international salvage campaign, with its modern relocation and reconstruction of the Abu Simbel temples beneath arched domes made of concrete.

It is relatively easy to demonstrate inconsistencies in relation to changes in monuments, buildings, places, and landscapes. Old modernities are acceptable, but new ones are not. Graffiti on the leg of Ramses II in front of the great temple, containing the Greek name Potasimto – the military commander of an expedition to Nubia in 592 BCE – is part of World Heritage, as is the name Belzoni from 1817 inside the temple along with other older inscriptions (MacQuitty 1965: 76, 84, 91, 98f, 134; Desroches-Noblecourt & Gerster 1968: 30f; Grove & Thomas 2014: front cover). But when a local teenager sprayed "GELWANE" on the great rune-stone of the Jelling monument in 2011, the green paint was carefully removed, and not many months passed before the rune-stones were protected in outdoor display cases (Hvass 2011: 14ff, 66ff). In Abu Simbel, the graffiti is history to admire – in Jelling, it is heritage crime, which triggered a court order for psychiatric treatment and the payment of compensation for cleaning the stone. The context determines the choice.

At Abu Simbel, the volume of tourists has been regarded as a problem. To reduce damage, Nile cruises were not to be allowed to moor directly at the temples (Hassan 2007: 91). But that was before the Arab Spring.

Venice came into focus again in the summer of 2017. Now, however, the issue was not rising water-levels threatening destruction but tourists. One reason is the rise in tourism, to which listing as a World Heritage site has contributed, although tourism to Venice has a long history. There were even demonstrations against mass tourism and its consequences. Other tourist destinations such as Oxford, Barcelona, San Sebastian, and Palma in Majorca also saw protests, demonstrations, and actions that same summer.

That the defence of a World Heritage site may threaten a modern development became apparent in Dresden, just as it obviously threatens everyday life in Venice; but can the World Heritage Convention itself come under threat as an international convention despite the present consensus? Yes: if "Pax Americana", the global world order after the Second World War with organisations such as the UN and UNESCO, falls, the convention will fall as well. Michel Batisse wrote, "[l]ike many international agreements, the World Heritage Convention remains a fragile instrument, and the list could be seen as a sophisticated house of cards that could tumble down in a storm" (Batisse 1992: 32). In this context, it may be noted that on 31 December 2018, both the US and Israel withdrew from UNESCO. The inscription of Hebron/Al-Khalil Old Town on the West Bank as a World Heritage site (WHL 1565, 2017), and as World Heritage in Danger (whc.unesco.org/en/158) at the same time, is said to have been a contributing factor.

Threats are rhetorical expressions denoting an undesirable change. When a change is desirable, it is described as progress; when it is considered undesirable, it is described as a backward step and, at worst, as a threat. If the aim is to establish sites as heritage and World Heritage, they are represented as threatened and in need of protection; and to critical observers, the sites themselves may constitute a threat. And in the same way, modernity may be both threatening and threatened.

Conspicuous protection

Nubian Monuments from Abu Simbel to Philae were salvaged in UNESCO's international campaign and then inscribed in the World Heritage List (WHL 88, 1979). The outstanding and universal was salvaged. Monuments, buildings, and places that were not as spectacular disappeared into Lake Nasser, after having been examined and documented. Other remains could never be examined, however, and had to be denied priority.

World Heritage, the outstanding and universal, is protected and preserved for future generations; but what happens to everything else? That the outstanding must be an exception cannot come as a surprise. But is World Heritage merely an alibi, so that the outside world can be changed, modernised, or destroyed more or less freely? A temporal reservation for relics of the past? And, more generally, are history, memory, and heritage only islands in a sea dominated by silence, oblivion, and vandalism?

That a World Heritage site may indeed be an exception is seen from the example of Auschwitz-Birkenau (WHL 31, 1979). The

Nazi death camp is a profoundly unsettling metonymic icon of the Holocaust; it is concrete, material testimony to something much more extensive that can be difficult to comprehend. Despite the size of the camp, it was only the centre of a complex with shorter and longer-term satellites, the great majority of which disappeared long ago. Moreover, Auschwitz-Birkenau was one of several death camps, and there were concentration camps and sites where people also died or were murdered across most of Europe (Snyder 2015: 207ff). These matters are not consigned to silence, oblivion, and destruction, although Auschwitz-Birkenau has been given most attention and also World Heritage status. Even so, there are repeated attempts to ignore, minimise, or deny the Holocaust; and here the protection and preservation of actual sites may be of importance as concrete testimony.

The Bridge in Mostar in Bosnia-Herzegovina (WHL 946rev, 2005), the Buddha statues in Bamiyan Valley in Afghanistan (WHL 208rev, 2003), and Palmyra in Syria (WHL 23bis, 1980, 2017) are iconic World Heritage sites that have been vandalised. The sites and their destruction have come in for a great deal of attention; but they are only the tip of an iceberg. Many more and other material and intangible remains of the past, and also of the present, have been vandalised or plundered in wars in these countries without receiving the same attention.

When the Hanseatic Town of Visby on the island of Gotland in Sweden (WHL 731, 1995) became a World Heritage site, this did not mean that change and destruction could be given free rein outside the town wall. In modern, well-organised Sweden, there are rules for development and changes that cover all environments. Consequently, Visby as a World Heritage site is no alibi for changing Gotland's rural districts, even though the degree of protection and preservation may vary from place to place.

When more and more is changed and when, as a psychological reaction, more and more is regarded as heritage worth protecting and preserving, then World Heritage constitutes a special prioritisation of the outstanding and universal. As a reaction against the inflation in the concept of heritage, which has become boundless, a category of conspicuous World Heritage is established with clear distinguishing criteria that have to be met for inscription to be granted. World Heritage becomes something conspicuous, exclusive, and "enchanting" in the mass of gradually "disenchanting" heritage.

The heritage inflation affects both traditions of heritage. When everything can be heritage, the canonical tradition chooses to take the initiative for a new currency with a higher value, namely World Heritage. For something to be designated as an outstanding and universal World Heritage site, set criteria have to be met, and the path goes through a long and strictly regulated process. By contrast, the critical tradition is indignant about the omnipresence of the past and at the increase in heritage, which is held to be threatening. It prefers either "real" history or, at the very least, a different selection of heritage.

But both heritage traditions fail to see that the whole field of history, memory, and heritage is growing because change in society in general is accelerating. And while the focus is on protection and preservation as something either positive or negative, all the more is changed or disappears. While the number of World Heritage sites rises each year under strictly regulated forms, all the more monuments, buildings, places, and landscapes change or disappear. If something needs to be discussed or managed, it is thus not heritage or World Heritage but the underlying causes – the global acceleration of change in both nature and culture.

Permanence through change

The endeavours to protect and preserve heritage lead to heritage changing. However, what is central about heritage is neither preservation, as held by most members of the canonical tradition of heritage, nor change, as is argued by some members of the critical tradition of heritage, but the relationship between preservation and change. Similarly, authenticity – the central capital of heritage – is affected by efforts to protect and preserve.

The preservation of the cliff temples at Abu Simbel took place at the expense of extensive change to the temples themselves and their surroundings. The temples had to be sawn into pieces, lifted away, and reconstructed under concrete arched domes in a new and safe site, using modern technology and materials. The nearby landscape was also changed radically. The cliffs into which the temples were originally carved were replaced by artificial hills. Ramses II had been reflected in the Nile for thousands of years, but now a large lake is spread out in front of the temples. And a new settlement grew up alongside the destinations.

More examples of protection and preservation initiatives leading to changes may be adduced. The Lascaux Cave in France (WHL 85, 1979) had to close as early as 1963 because the many visitors altered the climate inside the cave, affecting the Palaeolithic images;

thereafter, access was relatively restrictive. But since 1983, tourists are able to visit a modern replica of the World Heritage site instead. At Stonehenge in England, visitors are not allowed to approach the monument itself either, except on certain occasions. And here the surrounding landscape was altered for the sake of tourism, with the construction or removal of paths, roads, parking places, and a visitor centre (WHL 373bis, 1986, 2008).

The establishment of the Jelling monuments in Denmark (WHL 697, 1994, 2018) as heritage and World Heritage has taken place at the expense of great changes both to the monuments themselves and to their surroundings. Many surrounding buildings were demolished to clear the site, traffic was reorganised, the church was restored several times, the rune-stones were placed in display cases made of glass, a new visitor centre was constructed, and the archaeological finds of a stone ship, a palisade, and halls were marked clearly in the terrain. The modern alterations to the Jelling monuments may, with time, become part of the narrative about the history of the site and therefore part of the World Heritage. The GELWANE inscription might also have formed part of the World Heritage, as has happened with graffiti at other sites.

The protection and preservation of tentative, nominated, or actual World Heritage sites may be dependent on, or lead to, antiquarian or environmental interventions such as conservation, restoration, reconstruction, and nature conservation. Archaeological investigations can also be carried out so as to obtain more knowledge about a monument, a building, a place, or a landscape.

That protection and preservation for the future is best achieved through continued use, not through functioning as a "museum", has long been a widely held antiquarian attitude. The use involved is often aimed at tourism; but buildings can also be arranged so that they can continue to serve practical purposes, in fortunate cases supporting themselves financially, for instance as housing or as exhibition spaces, assembly rooms, or conference premises. Tourism and continued use may then require alterations to the property itself and to its surroundings with signage, lighting, ventilation, disability adaptation, lifts, sprinkler systems, emergency exits, toilets, a restaurant, and the construction of paths, roads, a car park, and a visitor centre.

World Heritage is modernised in order to remain relevant in the present. The purpose of this modernisation is that by being renewed or made topical, the World Heritage site will remain useful in the face of current requirements – and will therefore also stand a realistic chance to live on for the benefit of future generations. Present-day needs may be to do with knowledge, on-site experiencing, or ethics. They may involve national identity or experience tourism. The modernisation of a World Heritage site brings it into the present. The same process also applies to large parts of heritage in general, which are being adapted to the role of tourist destination.

The changes are bound to lead to a debate in which different values, views, and objectives may collide since they are not immediately compatible, as Alois Riegl observed many years ago (Riegl 1903 (German); 1929 (German); 1982 (English)). The canonical tradition of heritage might be particularly critical of interventions that affect authenticity. But the canonical and the critical tradition will often be able to agree to reject a modernisation that serves commercial objectives, and to view mass tourism as a threat; profit and popularity are controversial across the heritage divide.

When it comes to the concept of authenticity, things are not that simple. The original feature may relate to the material, to the work process, or to the context. Here I would like to see greater freedom in the use of "creative anachronism", in which old and new are combined in new ways (e.g. Petersson 2017). One example is *spolia*, where ancient building components were reused in medieval contexts and given new meanings there. Another example in which new and old, fact and fiction, are combined is the film *Marie Antoinette* by the author and director Sofia Coppola. This film shows the story of the French Queen at Versailles. The narrative and the environment are more or less historically correct; but the colours are exaggerated and the attitudes and music modern, all in order to create proximity and understanding in the present (Coppola 2006 film).

For its time, UNESCO's international salvage campaign was ambitious and bold. But Abu Simbel represents a more discreet example of creative anachronism. Old and new were combined to protect, preserve, and reuse for the future. Both the monuments themselves and their surroundings were renewed, but apart from artificial lighting and ventilation, the modern interventions were concealed from visitors. The cliff temples are intended to appear to be authentic in the material sense – as if nothing had happened since the time of Ramses II.

Here it is tempting to quote from the novel *Il Gattopardo* (English *The Leopard*) by Giuseppe Tomasi di Lampedusa: "Se vogliamo che tutto rimanga come è, bisogna che tutto cambi" (Lampedusa 1958 (Italian): 42; 2007 (English): 19; "If we want things to stay as they are, things will have to change"). But the quotation does not describe what has happened at Abu Simbel and other World Heritage sites. Things do not stay just as they have been, and everything does not need to change. Some things are modernised; others are not. Permanence for the future is created through change, in which the two dimensions of the concept of time balance each other: greater permanence in some parts may mean more change in others.

Sisyphus and Abu Simbel's stone

Is it possible and meaningful to try to protect and preserve Abu Simbel's temples and other World Heritage sites for the future? Is this not impossible and therefore meaningless? For no preservation campaign or move, no elevation to heritage or World Heritage, can prevent change, degradation, and impermanence in the long run.

In the first and canonical heritage tradition, heritage is frequently described as a resource; in the second and critical tradition, heritage is described as a liability. Even an Annales historian may characterise the past as something that needs to be handled so as not to be a burden. Lucien Febvre thus writes about "L'Histoire, qui est un moyen d'organiser le passé pour l'empêcher de trop peser sur les épaules des hommes" (Febvre 1949 (French): 245; 1973 (English): 41; "History is a way of organising the past so that it does not weigh too heavily on the shoulders of men"). Inspired by this, I would argue that World Heritage is a way of setting priorities among natural and cultural heritage phenomena, so that they do not weigh too heavily on human shoulders. But is World Heritage also a burden to be borne into the future?

This brings Sisyphus, King of Corinth, to mind once more – Sisyphus who pushes a great stone up a mountain, from whose top the stone rolls down to the plain again. Sisyphus toils uselessly forever in the land of the dead as punishment for having put Death in chains; that is, for trying to prevent impermanence. The philosopher and author Albert Camus used this myth in order to discuss the hopeless situation of human beings (Camus 1942 (French): 163ff; 2005 (English): 107ff). A few years later, however, Camus changed his standpoint and called for an idealist revolt against the absurdity of life, a revolt against merely accepting one's fate, a revolt against "amor fati" (Camus 1951 (French); 1991 (English)).

Sisyphus is a mythical person who does not need to have existed. Myths are not expected to reflect an ancient reality, but they can communicate existential experiences. The story of Sisyphus is known from ancient images and from Homer's epics *The Iliad* and *The Odyssey* (Homer, *The Iliad*: VI 153f; *The Odyssey*: XI 593), epics dated to the eighth century BCE, although the existence of Homer is open to discussion. Sisyphus has since been commented on and illustrated countless times. Camus thus reuses parts of a both material and intangible heritage in order to reflect on topical (and eternal) issues.

Above the ancient city of Corinth on the plains of Greece, there rises a steep hill bearing the ruins of Acrocorinth, which may have inspired the myth's tale of the great stone rolling down the hillside. I would like to interpret Sisyphus's stone not as a boulder that happened to be lying around but as an ancient worked stone that can be reused time and again. Both Sisyphus and his stone are *spolia* from the past.

The stones of Abu Simbel were not rolled; they were raised up and laid down in a new place. They ought to sit there securely for many generations to come. One of Ramses II's heads fell off during his reign, and it has been left lying on the ground after the reconstruction. But Abu Simbel is no longer two pharaonic temples; that was long ago. They have been transmuted into destinations in Egypt's international tourist industry. The stones of the temple have therefore been given a new meaning.

So, yes, it is possible to protect and preserve Abu Simbel's temples and other World Heritage sites for the future. With modernity, the technological possibilities of protecting and preserving remains of the past have increased dramatically, providing that a more open interpretation of the concepts of preservation and authenticity is accepted. As at Abu Simbel, preservation may involve change, a relocation, and modernisation. And authenticity does not necessarily have to be defined in terms of the material remaining intact.

Preserving remains of the past by transforming them into documentation is no novel idea. This is done every day in archaeological investigations. What is relatively new is that digitalisation using 3D technology makes detailed documentation and reconstruction possible. DNA technology might be of use in recreating threatened or extinct animal species. In addition, in a more traditional and practical vein, monuments, buildings, places – and why not also landscapes – can be moved to new locations where they are no longer threatened, as happened at Abu Simbel.

And, yes, it is also meaningful to protect and preserve Abu Simbel's temples and other World Heritages for the future. For like *spolia*, the monuments, buildings, places, and landscapes of the past can be reused in new and unforeseen contexts. Consequently, protecting and preserving the past for the future is no Sisyphean labour – doing so is both feasible and meaningful.

Remains of the past, such as the temples of Abu Simbel and the myth of Sisyphus of Corinth, are not only good to think with or to visit, but also good as a starting point for action. In the encounter with the past, it is possible to formulate new knowledge, narratives, and ethical reflections that may be put to use in facing the challenges of the present and the future. And there are enough challenges to address.

Appendix 1
World Heritage inscriptions, 1978–2019

World Heritage List – number of properties inscribed each year and the total number accumulated. Source: World Heritage List Statistics, whc.unesco.org/en/list/stat.

1978   12 (12)
1979   45 (57)
1980   27 (84)
1981   26 (110)
1982   24 (134)
1983   29 (163)
1984   22 (185)
1985   30 (215)
1986   29 (244)
1987   41 (285)
1988   27 (312)
1989   7 (319)
1990   16 (335)
1991   22 (357)
1992   20 (377)
1993   33 (410)
1994   29 (439)
1995   29 (468)
1996   37 (505)
1997   46 (551)
1998   30 (581)
1999   48 (629)
2000   61 (690)
2001   31 (721)
2002   9 (730)
2003   24 (754)
2004   34 (788)

2005   24 (812)
2006   18 (830)
2007   22 (851, delisted 1)
2008   27 (878)
2009   13 (890, delisted 1)
2010   21 (911)
2011   25 (936)
2012   26 (962)
2013   19 (981)
2014   26 (1007)
2015   24 (1031)
2016   21 (1052)
2017   21 (1073)
2018   19 (1092)
2019   29 (1121)

Appendix 2

Ratification of the World Heritage Convention, 1973–2020

World Heritage Convention – ratification by states with numbers for each year and also accumulation of numbers and percentages; data from whc.unesco.org/en/statesparties; www.un.org/en/sections/member-states/growth-united-nations-membership-1945-present/index.html.

INNOVATORS 2.5 % ——————————————————————————

1973: 1 (0.7 %) of 135 members
United States of America

EARLY ADOPTERS 2.5 % ——————————————————————

1974: 9, total 10 (7.2 %) of 138 members
6 Algeria (24/6), 7 Australia (22/8), 4 Bulgaria (7/3), 8 Democratic Republic of Congo (23/9), 2 Egypt (7/2), 3 Iraq (5/3), 10 Niger (23/12), 9 Nigeria (23/10), 5 Sudan (6/6)

1975: 10, total 20 (13.9 %) of 144 members
Cyprus, Ecuador, France, Ghana, Iran (Islamic Republic of), Jordan, Morocco, Switzerland, Syrian Arab Republic, Tunisia

EARLY MAJORITY 16 % ——————————————————————

1976: 6, total 26 (17.7 %) of 147 members
Bolivia (Plurinational State of), Canada, Germany, Pakistan, Poland, Senegal

1977: 8, total 34 (22.8 %) of 149 members
Brazil, Costa Rica, Ethiopia, Guyana, India, Mali, Norway, United Republic of Tanzania

1978: 8, total 42 (27.8 %) of 151 members
Argentina, Italy, Libya, Malta, Monaco, Nepal, Panama, Saudi Arabia

1979: 6, total 48 (31.6 %) of 152 members
Afghanistan, Denmark, Guatemala, Guinea, Honduras,
Nicaragua

1980: 7, total 55 (35.7 %) of 154 members
Central African Republic, Chile, Haiti, Portugal, Seychelles, Sri
Lanka, Yemen

1981: 5, total 60 (38.2 %) of 157 members
Côte d'Ivoire, Cuba, Greece, Mauritania, Oman

1982: 9, total 69 (43.9 %) of 157 members
Benin, Burundi, Cameroon, Holy See, Malawi, Mozambique, Peru,
Spain, Zimbabwe

1983: 8, total 77 (48.7 %) of 158 members
Antigua and Barbuda, Bangladesh, Colombia, Jamaica, Lebanon,
Luxembourg, Madagascar, Turkey

LATE MAJORITY 50 % ───

1984: 5, total 82 (51.6 %) of 159 members
Mexico, New Zealand, Qatar, United Kingdom of Great Britain
and Northern Ireland, Zambia

1985: 5, total 87 (54.7 %) of 159 members
China, Dominican Republic, Hungary, Philippines, Sweden

1986: 3, total 90 (56.6 %) of 159 members
Gabon, Maldives, Saint Kitts and Nevis

1987: 8, total 98 (61.6 %) of 159 members
Burkina Faso, Congo, Finland, Gambia, Lao People's Democratic
Republic, Thailand, Uganda, Vietnam

1988: 7, total 105 (66 %) of 159 members
Belarus, Cabo Verde, Malaysia, Paraguay, Republic of Korea,
Russian Federation, Ukraine (+ DDR/German Democratic Republic,
integrated 1990)

1989: 3, total 108 (67.9 %) of 159 members
Albania, Indonesia, Uruguay

1990: 5, total 113 (71.1 %) of 159 members
Belize, Fiji, Mongolia, Romania, Venezuela (Bolivarian Republic of)

1991: 8, total 121 (72.9 %) of 166 members
Angola, Bahrain, Cambodia, El Salvador, Ireland, Kenya, Saint Lucia, San Marino

1992: 9, total 130 (72.6 %) of 179 members
Austria, Croatia, Georgia, Japan, Lithuania, Netherlands, Slovenia, Solomon Islands, Tajikistan

1993: 6, total 136 (73.9 %) of 184 members
Armenia, Azerbaijan, Bosnia and Herzegovina, Czech Republic, Slovakia, Uzbekistan

1994: 3, total 139 (75.1 %) of 185 members
Kazakhstan, Myanmar, Turkmenistan

1995: 6, total 145 (78.4 %) of 185 members
Dominica, Estonia, Iceland, Kyrgyzstan, Latvia, Mauritius

1996: 1, total 146 (78.9 %) of 185 members
Belgium

1997: 5, total 151 (81.6 %) of 185 members
Andorra, Papua New Guinea, South Africa, Suriname, The former Yugoslav Republic of Macedonia

1998: 4, total 155 (83.8 %) of 185 members
Botswana, Democratic People's Republic of Korea, Grenada, Togo

1999: 2, total 157 (83.5 %) of 188 members
Chad, Israel

LAGGARDS 84 % ————————————————————————————

2000: 4, total 161 (85.2 %) of 189 members
Comoros, Kiribati, Namibia, Rwanda

2001: 6, total 167 (88.4 %) of 189 members
Bhutan, Eritrea, Niue, Samoa, Serbia, United Arab Emirates

2002: 8, total 175 (91.6 %) of 191 members
Barbados, Kuwait, Liberia, Marshall Islands, Micronesia (Federated States of), Palau, Republic of Moldova, Vanuatu

2003: 2, total 177 (92.7 %) of 191 members
Lesotho, Saint Vincent and the Grenadines

2004: 1, total 178 (93.2 %) of 191 members
Tonga

2005: 3, total 181 (94.8 %) of 191 members
Sierra Leone, Swaziland, Trinidad and Tobago

2006: 3, total 184 (95.8 %) of 192 members
Guinea-Bissau, Montenegro, São Tomé and Príncipe

2007: 1, total 185 (96.4 %) of 192 members
Djibouti

2008: 0, 185 (96.4 %) of 192 members

2009: 1, total 186 (96.9 %) of 192 members
Cook Islands

2010: 1, total 187 (97.4 %) of 192 members
Equatorial Guinea

2011: 2, total 189 (97.9 %) of 193 members
Brunei Darussalam, Palestine

2012: 1, total 190 (98.4 %) of 193 members
Singapore

2013: 0, total 190 (98.4 %) of 193 members

2014: 1, total 191 (99 %) of 193 members
Bahamas

2015: 0, total 191 (99 %) of 193 members

2016: 1, total 192 (99.5 %) of 193 members
South Sudan

2020: 1, total 193 (100.0 %) of 193 members
Somalia

Holy See Non-member observer status 1964

Palestine Non-member observer status 2012

Appendix 3
Cultural Heritage and Natural Heritage in *Svenska Dagbladet*, 1884–2019

Frequency of words "Historia" ("History"), "Kulturarv"/ "Kulturarf" ("Cultural heritage"), and "Naturarv" ("Natural heritage") in the Swedish broadsheet *Svenska Dagbladet*, 18 December 1884 to 31 December 2019. Source: www.svd.se/arkiv.

Year	History	Cultural Heritage	Natural Heritage
1884	26		
1885	571		
1886	565		
1887	537		
1888	529		
1889	535		
1890	512		
1891	570		
1892	522		
1893	537		
1894	600		
1895	577		
1896	579		
1897	803		
1898	869		
1899	817		
1900	1039		
1901	1092		
1902	1114		
1903	1187	1	
1904	1226	1	
1905	1499	1	
1906	1558	1	
1907	1700	3	
1908	1799	4	
1909	1636	5	

Year	History	Cultural Heritage	Natural Heritage
1910	1628		
1911	1547	3	
1912	1524	1	
1913	1515	2	
1914	1382	1	
1915	1422	2	
1916	1477	2	
1917	1503	3	
1918	1608	5	
1919	1442	11	
1920	1524	16	
1921	1700	3	
1922	1759	3	
1923	2212	3	1
1924	2473	10	
1925	2260	7	
1926	2467	11	
1927	2541	17	
1928	2684	9	
1929	2477	14	
1930	2578	16	
1931	2447	14	
1932	2456	11	1
1933	2317	14	
1934	2448	13	
1935	2660	12	
1936	2636	16	
1937	2581	6	
1938	2584	4	
1939	2269	7	
1940	2003	14	
1941	2319	25	1
1942	2233	24	
1943	2329	18	
1944	2484	14	
1945	2483	17	2
1946	2460	21	
1947	2276	14	
1948	2046	12	
1949	2132	9	
1950	2216	11	
1951	2085	9	1
1952	2104	19	
1953	2230	13	

Year	History	Cultural Heritage	Natural Heritage
1954	2263	22	
1955	2308	11	
1956	2137	18	
1957	2408	12	
1958	2315	12	
1959	2456	19	
1960	2529	18	
1961	2352	25	
1962	2433	26	
1963	2174	17	
1964	2506	27	
1965	2483	22	
1966	2486	26	
1967	2260	13	1
1968	2368	22	1
1969	2153	23	1
1970	2299	34	
1971	2019	16	1
1972	2105	18	
1973	2142	24	
1974	2193	25	1
1975	2291	26	
1976	2222	15	
1977	2209	17	
1978	2578	40	
1979	2582	62	2
1980	2781	72	1
1981	2947	66	1
1982	2826	64	
1983	2875	62	1
1984	3311	88	1
1985	2823	45	
1986	2657	46	
1987	3489	110	1
1988	3663	91	
1989	3777	60	2
1990	3759	93	
1991	4276	120	1
1992	4161	93	
1993	4238	106	1
1994	4764	113	
1995	4097	134	
1996	4243	123	1

Year	History	Cultural Heritage	Natural Heritage
1997	4240	135	3
1998	3936	108	
1999	4230	153	7
2000	4182	261	5
2001	4753	133	5
2002	4055	125	1
2003	3957	149	2
2004	4288	133	
2005	4464	156	1
2006	4510	133	
2007	4519	105	
2008	4748	136	2
2009	3346	95	
2010	3387	60	
2011	3401	89	
2012	2759	70	
2013	2844	53	1
2014	2781	42	
2015	2439	64	1
2016	2692	177	
2017	3189	104	2
2018	3173	53	
2019	3442	49	

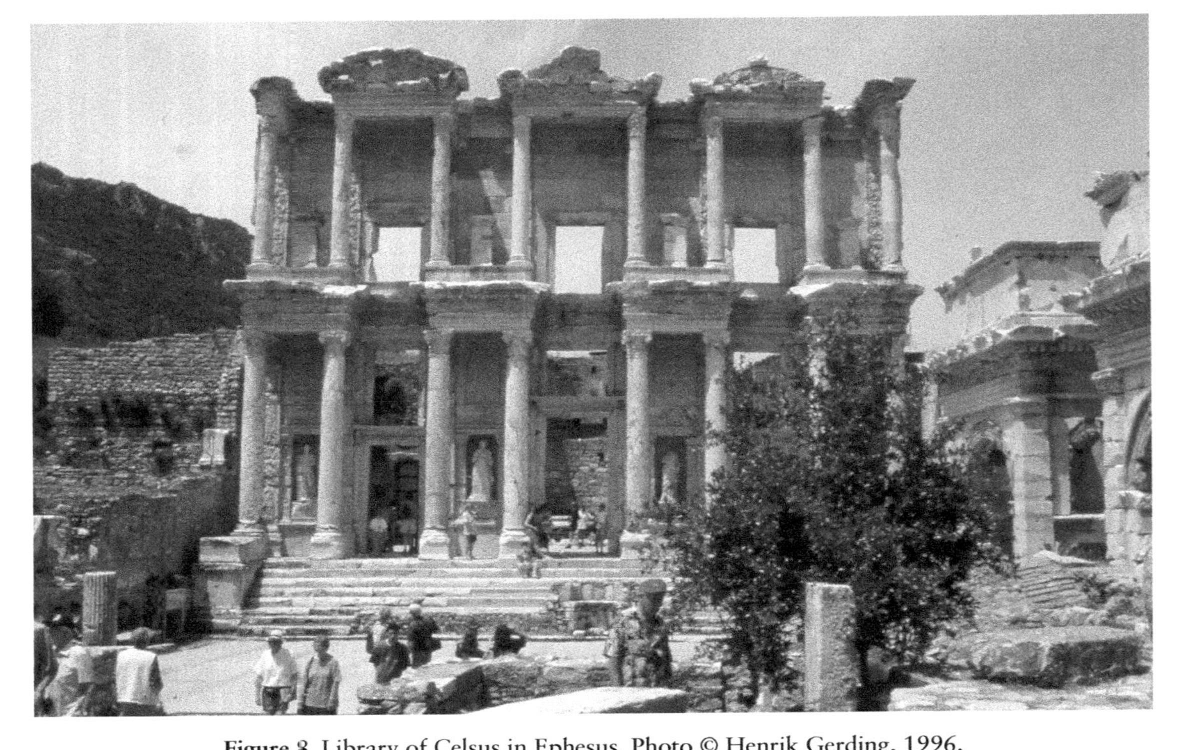

Figure 8 Library of Celsus in Ephesus. Photo © Henrik Gerding, 1996.

Bibliography

Literature

Acemoglu, Daron & Robinson, James A. 2012. *Why Nations Fail: The Origins of Power, Prosperity, and Poverty*. London: Profile Books.

Adler, Alfred 1908. Die Theorie der Organminderwertigkeit und ihre Bedeutung für Philosophie und Psychologie. *Wissenschaftliche Beilage zum 21. Jahresbericht der Philosophischen Gesellschaft an der Universität zu Wien*, pp. 11–26. (English: The Theory of Organ Inferiority and its Philosophical and Psychological Meaning. *The Collected Clinical Works of Alfred Adler*, vol. 2, Journal Articles: 1898–1909. Ed. Henry T. Stein. Bellingham: Classical Adlerian Translation Project, 2002, pp. 78–85.)

Adorno, Theodor W. 1967. Résumé über Kulturindustrie. *Ohne Leitbild. Parva Aesthetica*. Edition Suhrkamp 201. Frankfurt am Main: Suhrkamp Verlag. Pages 60–70. (English: Culture Industry Reconsidered. *The Culture Industry: Selected Essays on Mass Culture*. Routledge Classics. London and New York: Routledge, 1979. Pages 98–106.)

Adriansen, Inge 2010. *Erindringssteder i Danmark: Monumenter, mindesmærker og mødesteder*. Etnologiske Studier 14. Skrifter fra Museum Sønderjylland 4. Copenhagen: Museum Tusculanum.

Allais, Lucia 2013. Integrities: The Salvage of Abu Simbel. *Grey Room 50* (Winter 2013): 6–45.

Allen, Michael J. B. 1975. *Marsilio Ficino: The "Philebus" Commentary*. A Critical Edition and Translation. Center for Medieval and Renaissance Studies 9. Berkeley, Los Angeles, and London: University of California Press.

Almevik, Gunnar & Fridén, Bertil 1996. Vad kostar ett kulturarv? *Kulturmiljövård* 1995.5–6: 92–100.

Alzén, Annika 1996. *Fabriken som kulturarv: Frågan om industrilandskapets bevarande i Norrköping 1950–1985*. Stockholm and Stehag: Brutus Östlings Bokförlag Symposion.

Alzén, Annika & Aronsson, Peter 2006. *Demokratiskt kulturarv? Nationella institutioner, universella värden, lokala praktiker*. Tema Kultur och samhälle, Skriftserie 2006: 1. Norrköping: Linköping University.

Amery, Colin & Cruickshank, Dan 1975. *The Rape of Britain.* London: Elek Books.

Anderson, Benedict 1991. *Imagined Communities: Reflections on the Origin and Spread of Nationalism.* London and New York: Verso. (1st ed. 1983.)

Anderson, Perry 1998. *The Origins of Postmodernity.* London and New York: Verso.

Andersson, Lars M. & Zander, Ulf (eds) 1999. *Tänk om ... Nio kontrafaktiska essäer.* Lund: Historiska Media.

Andrén, Anders (ed.) 2011. *Förmodern globalitet: Essäer om rörelse, möten och fjärran ting under 10 000 år.* Lund: Nordic Academic Press.

Anker, Leif & Snitt, Ingalill 1997. *Our Nordic Heritage: World Heritage Sites in the Nordic Countries.* Ed. Stephan Tschudi-Madsen. Oslo: Kom.

Anshelm, Jonas (ed.) 1993. *Modernisering och Kulturarv: Essäer och uppsatser.* Symposion Bibliotek. Stockholm and Stehag: Brutus Östlings Bokförlag Symposion.

Anthony, Sian 2016. *Materialising Modern Cemeteries: Archaeological Narratives of Assistens Cemetery, Copenhagen.* Lund Studies in Historical Archaeology 18. Lund: Lund University.

Appelbom Karsten, Ingrid 1987. *Minnesmerket – en del av vår identitet: Gjenoppbygging, revaluering og regenerasjon av historiske byer i Polen og Tsjekkoslovakia.* Stockholm: Stockholm University.

Arendt, Hannah 1981. *The Life of the Mind.* San Diego, CA: Harcourt Brace Jovanovich. (1st ed. London: Secker & Warburg, 1978.)

Ariès, Philippe 1974. *Western Attitudes toward Death: From the Middle Ages to the Present.* The Johns Hopkins Symposia in Comparative History. Baltimore, MD: Johns Hopkins University Press.

Arnold, Bettina 1990. The Past as Propaganda: Totalitarian Archaeology in Nazi Germany. *Antiquity* 64.244: 464–478.

Arnold, Bettina 1998. The Power of the Past: Nationalism and Archaeology in 20th Century Germany. *Archaeologia Polona* 35–36: 237–253.

Aronsson, Peter 2004. *Historiebruk – att använda det förflutna.* Lund: Studentlitteratur.

Aronsson, Peter (ed.) 2009. *Platser för en bättre värld: Auschwitz, Ruhr och röda stugor.* Lund: Nordic Academic Press.

Aronsson, Peter 2015. National Museums as Cultural Constitutions. *National Museums and Nation-Building in Europe, 1750–2010: Mobilization and Legitimacy, Continuity and Change.* Eds Peter Aronsson & Gabriella Elgenius. London and New York: Routledge. Pages 167–199.

Aronsson, Peter & Elgenius, Gabriella (eds) 2015. *National Museums and Nation-Building in Europe, 1750–2010: Mobilization and Legitimacy, Continuity and Change.* London and New York: Routledge.

Aronsson, Peter & Hillström, Magdalena (eds) 2005. *Kulturarvens dynamik: Det institutionaliserade kulturarvets förändringar.* Tema Kultur och samhälle, Skriftserie 2005: 2. Linköping: University of Linköping.

Arrhenius, Thordis 2003. *The Fragile Monument: On Conservation and Modernity.* Trita-ARK 2003: 5. Royal Institute of Technology, Stockholm. (Revised: London: Artifice Books, 2012.)

Asplund Ingemark, Camilla (ed.) 2013. *Therapeutic Uses of Storytelling: An Interdisciplinary Approach to Narration as Therapy.* Lund: Nordic Academic Press.

Assmann, Aleida 1999. *Zeit und Tradition: Kulturelle Strategien der Dauer.* Beiträge zur Geschichtskultur 15. Cologne, Weimar, and Vienna: Böhlau.

Assmann, Jan 1992. *Das kulturelle Gedächtnis: Erinnerung und politische Identität in frühen Hochkulturen.* Munich: C. H. Beck. (English: *Cultural Memory and Early Civilization: Writing, Remembrance, and Political Imagination.* Cambridge: Cambridge University Press, 2011.)

Augé, Marc 1992. *Non-Lieux: Introduction à une anthropologie de la surmodernité.* La librairie du XXe siècle. Paris: Le Seuil. (English: *Non-Places: Introduction to an Anthropology of Supermodernity.* London: Verso, 1995.)

Bandaranayake, Senake (pseudonym A. Gidtri) 1974. Imperialism and Archaeology. *Race & Class* XV.4: 431–459.

Bardon, Adrian 2013. *A Brief History of the Philosophy of Time.* Oxford: Oxford University Press.

Barthel-Bouchier, Diana 2013. *Cultural Heritage and the Challenge of Sustainability.* Walnut Creek, CA: Left Coast Press.

Batisse, Michel 1992. The Struggle to Save our World Heritage. *Environment* 34.10: 12–20, 28–32.

Batisse, Michel & Bolla, Gerard 2003. *L'invention du "Patrimoine mondial".* Les Cahiers d'Histoire 2. Paris: Club Histoire, Association des anciens fonctionnaires de l'Unesco. (English: *The Invention of "World Heritage".* History Papers 2. Paris: Association of Former UNESCO Staff Members, 2005.)

Baudelaire, Charles 1863. Le Peintre de la vie moderne. *Le Figaro* 26–29 Nov., 3 Dec. 1863. (English: The Painter of Modern Life. *The Painter of Modern Life and Other Essays.* Ed. Jonathan Mayne. London: Phaidon Press, 1964, pp. 1–41.)

Bauman, Zygmunt 1989. *Modernity and the Holocaust.* Cambridge: Polity Press.

Bauman, Zygmunt 1992. *Mortality, Immortality and Other Life Strategies.* Cambridge: Polity Press.

Bauman, Zygmunt 1993. *Postmodern Ethics.* Oxford: Blackwell.

Bauman, Zygmunt 2000. *Liquid Modernity.* Cambridge: Polity Press.

Bauman, Zygmunt 2007. *Liquid Times: Living in an Age of Uncertainty.* Cambridge and Malden, MA: Polity Press.

Bauman, Zygmunt 2017. *Retrotopia.* Cambridge and Malden, MA: Polity Press.

Bausinger, Herman 1991. Tradition und Moderniserung. *Schweizerisches Archiv für Volkskunde* 87.1–2: 5–14.

Baxter, Ian 2012. *Heritage Transformed*. Oxford and Oakville, CT: Oxbow Books.

Beard, Mary 2010. *The Parthenon. Revised Edition*. Wonders of the World. Cambridge, MA: Harvard University Press (1st ed. London: Profile Books, 2002).

Beck, Ulrich 1986. *Risikogesellschaft: Auf dem Weg in eine andere Moderne*. Edition Suhrkamp N.F. (N.S.) 1365. Frankfurt am Main: Suhrkamp. (English: *Risk Society: Towards a New Modernity*. Theory, Culture & Society. London: Sage, 1992.)

Beckman, Svante 1993a: Oreda i fornsvängen. *Modernisering och Kulturarv: Essäer och uppsatser*. Ed. Jonas Anshelm. Symposion Bibliotek. Stockholm and Stehag: Brutus Östlings Bokförlag Symposion. Pages 25–40. (Also printed in: *Kulturarvet i antikvarisk teori och praktik: Möte på Aronsborg den 4–5 April 1990*. Ed. Gunnel Friberg. Stockholm: Riksantikvarieämbetet (The Swedish National Heritage Board), 1993. Pages 30–44.)

Beckman, Svante 1993b: Om kulturarvets väsen och värde. *Modernisering och Kulturarv: Essäer och uppsatser*. Ed. Jonas Anshelm. Symposion Bibliotek. Stockholm and Stehag: Brutus Östlings Bokförlag Symposion. Pages 61–124.

Beckman, Svante 1997. Fyre N! Varför gör vi vad vi gör? *Tvärsnitt* 1997.4: 3–11.

Beckman, Svante 1998. Vad vill staten med kulturarvet? *Kulturarvets natur*. Ed. Annika Alzén & Johan Hedrén. Stockholm and Stehag: Brutus Östlings Bokförlag Symposion. Pages 13–49.

Beckman, Svante 2005. Utvecklingstendenser i nutida kulturarv. *Kulturarvets dynamik: Det institutionaliserade kulturarvets förändringar*. Eds Peter Aronsson & Magdalena Hillström. Tema Kultur och samhälle, skriftserie 2005: 2. Linköping: Linköping University. Pages 328–340.

Benjamin, Walter 1980. Über den Begriff der Geschichte. *Gesammelte Schriften* I 2. Eds Rolf Tiedemann & Hermann Schweppenhäuser. Frankfurt am Main: Suhrkamp. (1st ed. 1974.) (English: Theses on the Philosophy of History. *Illuminations*. Ed. Hannah Arendt. London: Jonathan Cape, 1970. Pages 255–266.)

Benjamin, Walter 1983. *Das Passagen-Werk*, 1–2. Edition Suhrkamp 1200, N.F. 200. Frankfurt am Main: Suhrkamp. (English: *The Arcades Project*. Eds Howard Eiland, Kevin McLaughlin & Rolf Tiedemann. Cambridge, MA and London: Belknap Press, 1999.)

Bennett, Tony 1995. *The Birth of the Museum: History, Theory, Politics*. Culture: Policies and Politics. London and New York: Routledge.

Berdahl, Daphne 1999. (N)Ostalgie for the present: Memory, Longing, and East German Things. *Ethnos* 64.2: 192–211.

Berg, Ingrid 2019. Abu Simbel – ett kulturarv från det kalla kriget. *Medusa: Svensk tidskrift för antiken* 40.1: 24–31.

Berg, Lennart 1978. The Salvage of the Abu Simbel Temples. *Monumentum: The International Journal of Architectural Conservation* 17: 25–56.

Bergson, Henri 1889. *Essai sur les données immédiates de la conscience.* Paris: Felix Alcan. (English: *Time and Free Will: An Essay on the Immediate Data of Consciousness.* Mineola, NY: Dover Publications, 2001.)

Berman, Marshall 1982. *All That Is Solid Melts into Air: The Experience of Modernity.* New York: Simon and Schuster.

Bevan, Robert 2016. *The Destruction of Memory: Architecture at War.* London: Reaktion Books (1st ed. 2006).

Bille Larsen, Peter (ed.) 2018. *World Heritage and Human Rights: Lessons from the Asia-Pacific and Global Arena.* London and New York: Routledge.

Bille Larsen, Peter & Logan, William (eds) 2018. *World Heritage and Sustainable Development: New Directions in World Heritage Management.* Key Issues in Cultural Heritage. London and New York: Routledge.

Bloch, Marc 1949. *Apologie pour l'histoire ou Métier d'historien.* Cahiers des Annales 3. Paris: Librairie Armand Colin. (English: *The Historian's Craft.* Manchester and New York: Manchester University Press, 1992.)

Bloom, Harold 1994. *The Western Canon: The Books and School of the Ages.* New York: Harcourt Brace.

Bogard, Paul 2013. *The End of Night: Searching for Natural Darkness in an Age of Artificial Light.* London: Fourth Estate.

Boldrick, Stacey, Brubaker, Leslie & Clay, Richard (eds) 2013. *Striking Images, Iconoclasms Past and Present.* Farnham and Burlington, VT: Ashgate.

Boulez, Pierre 1976. *Pierre Boulez – Conversations with Célestin Deliège.* London: Eulenburg Books. (1st ed. Paris: Les Editions du Seuil, 1975.)

Bourdeau, Laurent, Gravari-Barbas, Maria & Robinson, Mike (eds) 2015. *World Heritage, Tourism and Identity: Inscription and Co-Production.* Burlington, VT: Ashgate.

Bourdeau, Laurent, Gravari-Barbas, Maria & Robinson, Mike (eds) 2017. *World Heritage Sites and Tourism: Global and Local Relations.* Heritage, Culture and Identity. Abingdon and New York: Routledge.

Bourdieu, Pierre 1979. *La distinction: Critique sociale du jugement.* Le sens commun. Paris: Les Éditions de Minuit. (English: *Distinction: A Social Critique of the Judgement of Taste.* London: Routledge & Kegan Paul, 1984.)

Boyd, Brian 2009. *On the Origin of Stories: Evolution, Cognition, and Fiction.* Cambridge, MA: Harvard University Press.

Boym, Svetlana 2001. *The Future of Nostalgia.* New York: Basic Books.

Bradley, Richard 1993. *Altering the Earth: Origins of Monuments in Britain and Continental Europe.* The Rhind Lectures 1991–92. Society of Antiquaries of Scotland Monograph series 8. Edinburgh: Society of Antiquaries of Scotland.

Bring, Ove 2011. *De mänskliga rättigheternas väg – genom historien och litteraturen.* Stockholm: Atlantis.

Bring, Ove 2015. *Parthenonsyndromet: Kampen om kulturskatterna.* Stockholm: Atlantis.

Brown, Norman O. 1959. *Life against Death: The Psychoanalytical Meaning of History.* London: Routledge & Kegan Paul.

Brox, Jane 2010. *Brilliant: The Evolution of Artificial Light.* New York: Houghton Mifflin Harcourt.

Burke, Edmund 1790. *Reflections on the Revolution in France, and on the Proceedings in Certain Societies in London Relative to that Event.* London: J. Dodsley.

Burström, Mats 2004. Archaeology and Existential Reflection. *The Interplay of Past and Present: Papers from a session held at the 9th annual EAA meeting in St. Petersburg 2003.* Ed. Hans Bolin. Södertörn Archaeological Studies 1. Södertörn: Södertörn University College. Pages 21–28.

Burström, Mats, Gustafsson, Anders & Karlsson, Håkan 2011. *World Crisis in Ruin: The Archaeology of the Former Soviet Nuclear Missile Sites in Cuba.* Lindome: Bricoleur Press.

Burström, Mats, Winberg, Björn & Zachrisson, Torun 1997. *Fornlämningar och folkminnen.* Stockholm: Riksantikvarieämbetet (The National Swedish Heritage Board).

Byrne, D. 1995. Buddhist *Stupa* and Thai Social Practice. *World Archaeology* 27.2: 266–281.

Calinescu, Matei 1987. *Five Faces of Modernity: Modernism, Avant-Garde, Decadence, Kitsch, Postmodernism.* Durham, NC: Duke University Press.

Cameron, Christina & Rössler, Mechtild 2013. *Many Voices, One Vision: The Early Years of the World Heritage Convention.* Heritage, Culture and Identity. Farnham and Burlington, VT: Ashgate.

Camus, Albert 1942. *Le Mythe de Sisyphe.* Coll. Les Essais xii. Nouvelle Revue francaise. Paris: Gallimard. (English: *The Myth of Sisyphus.* Penguin Modern Classics. Harmondsworth: Penguin Books, 2005.)

Camus, Albert 1951. *L'Homme révolté.* Paris: Gallimard. (English: *The Rebel: An Essay on Man in Revolt.* First Vintage International Edition. New York: Vintage Books, 1991.)

Cannadine, David 1983. The Context, Performance and Meaning of Ritual: The British Monarchy and the "Invention of Tradition", c. 1820–1977. *The Invention of Tradition.* Eds Eric Hobsbawm & Terence Ranger. Past and Present Publications. Cambridge: Cambridge University Press. Pages 101–164.

Cannon, Bob 2016. Towards a Theory of Counter-Modernity: Rethinking Zygmunt Bauman's Holocaust Writing. *Critical Sociology* 42.1: 49–69.

Carlie, Anne & Kretz, Eva 1998. *Sätt att se på fornlämningar: En teoretisk och metodisk grund för värdebedömning inom kulturmiljövården.* Department of Archaeology, Lund, Report Series 60. Lund: Lund University.

Chamberlin, E. R. 1979. *Preserving the Past.* London: J. M. Dent & Sons.

Charbonnier, Georges (ed.) 1961. Horloges et machines à vapeur. *Entretiens avec Claude Lévi-Strauss.* Les lettres nouvelles 10. Paris: Plon

Julliard. Pages 37–46. (English: *Conversations with Claude Lévi-Strauss*. London: Jonathan Cape, 1969.)

Chippindale, Christopher 2012. *Stonehenge Complete*. 4th Edition. London: Thames & Hudson. (1st ed. London: Thames & Hudson, 1983.)

Choay, Françoise 1992. *L'allégorie du patrimoine*. La couleur des idées. Paris: Editions du Seuil. (English: *The Invention of the Historic Monument*. Cambridge: Cambridge University Press, 2001.)

Christie, Agatha 1937. *Death on the Nile*. London: Collins Crime Club.

Claeys, Gregory 2011. *Searching for Utopia: The History of an Idea*. London: Thames & Hudson.

Clark, Kenneth 1928. *The Gothic Revival: An Essay in the History of Taste*. London: Constable. (3rd ed. London: John Murray, 1962.)

Clausén, Marie 2016. *Sacred Architecture in a Secular Age: Anamnesis of Durham Cathedral*. Routledge Research in Architecture. New York and London: Routledge.

Compagnon, Antoine 1990. *Les Cinq Paradoxes de la Modernité*. Paris: Éditions du Seuil. (English: *The Five Paradoxes of Modernity*. New York: Columbia University Press, 1994.)

Connerton, Paul 1989. *How Societies Remember*. Themes in the Social Sciences. Cambridge: Cambridge University Press.

Cowell, Ben 2008. *The Heritage Obsession: The Battle for England's Past*. Stroud: Tempus.

Croft, Thomas A. 1978. Nighttime Images of the Earth from Space. *Scientific America* 239: 68–79.

Däniken, Erich von 1973. *Meine Welt in Bildern: Bildargumente für Theorien, Spekulationen und Erforschtes*. Düsseldorf and Vienna: Econ Verlag. (English: *In Search of Ancient Gods: My Pictorial Evidence for the Impossible*. London: Corgi Books, 1976.)

Davis, Fred 1979. *Yearning for Yesterday: A Sociology of Nostalgia*. New York and London: Free Press and Collier Macmillan.

DeSilvey, Caitlin 2017. *Curated Decay: Heritage beyond Saving*. Minneapolis: University of Minnesota Press.

Desroches Noblecourt, Christiane 2007. *Ramses II: An Illustrated Biography*. Paris: Flammarion.

Desroches-Noblecourt, Christiane & Gerster, Georg 1968. *The World Saves Abu Simbel*. Vienna and Berlin: A. F. Koska.

Diamond, Jared 2005. *Collapse: How Societies Choose to Fail or Succeed*. New York: Viking Press.

Diaz-Andreu, Margarita 2007. *A World History of Nineteenth-Century Archaeology: Nationalism, Colonialism, and the Past*. Oxford Studies in the History of Archaeology. Oxford: Oxford University Press.

Di Giovine, Michael A. 2009. *The Heritage-Scape: UNESCO, World Heritage, and Tourism*. Lanham, MD: Lexington Books.

Dobbs, Betty Jo Teeter 1991. *The Janus Faces of Genius: The Role of Alchemy in Newton's Thought*. Cambridge: Cambridge University Press.

Duby, Georges 1978. *Les trois ordres ou l'imaginaire du féodalisme*. Bibliothèque des Histoires. Paris: Éditions Gallimard. (English: *The Three Orders: Feudal Society Imagined*. Chicago: University of Chicago Press, 1981.)

Dudek, Peter 1992. "Vergangenheitsbewältigung": Zur Problematik eines umstrittenen Begriffs. *Aus Politik und Zeitgeschichte* 42.1–2: 44–53.

Dumézil, Georges 1958. *L'idéologie tripartie des Indo-Européens*. Collection Latomus xxxi. Brussels: Latomus.

Duncan, Carol 1995. *Civilizing Rituals: Inside Public Art Museums*. Re Visions: Critical Studies in the History and Theory of Art. London and New York: Routledge.

Durkheim, Émile 1897. *Le Suicide – étude de sociologie*. Paris: Felix Alcan. (English: *Suicide – a Study in Sociology*. Ed. George Simpson. Glencoe, IL: The Free Press, 1951.)

Eagleman, David 2016. *The Brain: The Story of You*. Edinburgh and London: Canongate Books.

Ebeling, Knut & Altekamp, Stefan (eds) 2004. *Die Aktualität des Archäologischen in Wissenschaft, Medien und Künsten*. Frankfurt am Main: Fischer Taschenbuch.

Eco, Umberto 1980. *Il nome della rosa*. Milan: Bompiani. (English: *The Name of the Rose*. New York: Harcourt, 1983.)

Edensor, Tim 2005. *Industrial Ruins: Space, Aesthetics and Materiality*. Oxford and New York: Berg.

Edwards, Amelia B. 1877. *A Thousand Miles up the Nile*. London: Longmans, Green & Co.

Ekern, Stener, Logan, William, Sauge, Birgitte & Sinding-Larsen, Amund (eds) 2015. *World Heritage Managements and Human Rights*. Abingdon and New York: Routledge.

Elgenius, Gabriella 2015. National Museums as National Symbols: A Survey of Strategic Nation-Building and Identity Politics; Nations as Symbolic Regimes. *National Museums and Nation-Building in Europe, 1750–2010. Mobilization and Legitimacy, Continuity and Change*. Eds Peter Aronsson & Gabriella Elgenius. London and New York: Routledge. Pages 145–166.

Eliade, Mircea 1957. *Das Heilige und das Profane: Vom Wesen des Religiösen*. Rowohlts Deutsche Enzyklopädie. Hamburg: Rowohlt. (English: *The Sacred and the Profane: The Nature of Religion*. A Harvest Book. San Diego, CA and New York: Harcourt Brace, 1987.)

Eriksen, Anne 1993. Den nasjonale kulturarven – en del av det moderne. *Kulturella perspektiv: Svensk etnologisk tidskrift* 1993.1: 16–25.

Eriksen, Anne 2014. *From Antiquities to Heritage: Transformations of Cultural Memory*. Time and the World 1. New York and Oxford: Berghahn.

Ersgård, Lars (ed.) 2007. *Modernitet och arkeologi: Artiklar från VIII Nordic TAG i Lund 2005*. Stockholm: Riksantikvarieämbetet (The National Swedish Heritage Board).

Evans, Richard J. 1997. *In Defence of History.* London: Granta Books.

Evans, Richard J. 2014. *Altered Pasts: Counterfactuals in History.* London: Little, Brown.

Fabricius Hansen, Maria 1999. *Ruinbilleder: Antikfascinationens baggrunde i 1400-tallets italienske maleri.* Copenhagen: Tiderne Skifter.

Fabricius Hansen, Maria 2003. *The Eloquence of Appropriation: Prolegomena to an Understanding of Spolia in Early Christian Rome.* Analecta Romana Instituti Danici, Supplementum XXXIII. Rome: "L'Erma" di Bretschneider.

Fagan, Brian M. 1975. *The Rape of the Nile: Tomb Robbers, Tourists, and Archaeologists in Egypt.* New York: Charles Scribner's Sons.

Fagan, Garrett G. (ed.) 2006. *Archaeological Fantasies: How Pseudoarchaeology Misrepresents the Past and Misleads the Public.* London and New York: Routledge.

Fairclough, Graham, Harrison, Rodney, Jameson, John H. Jr. & Schofield, John (eds) 2009. *The Heritage Reader.* London and New York: Routledge.

Falchi, Fabio, Cinzano, Pierantonio, Duriscoe, Dan, Kyba, Christopher C. M., Elvidge, Christopher D., Baugh, Kimberly, Portnov, Boris A., Rybnikova, Nataliya A. & Furgoni, Riccardo 2016. The New World Atlas of Artificial Night Sky Brightness. *Science Advances* 2.6: 1–25.

Febvre, Lucien 1949. Vers une autre histoire. *Revue de métaphysique et de morale* LVIII.3–4: 225–247. (English: A New Kind of History. *A New Kind of History – from the Writings of Febvre.* Ed. Peter Burke. London: Routledge & Kegan Paul, 1973, pp. 27–43.)

Ferguson, Niall (ed.) 1997. *Virtual History: Alternatives and Counterfactuals.* London: Picador.

Feyerabend, Paul 1978. *Science in a Free Society.* London: New Left Books.

Flood, Finbarr Barry 2002. Between Cult and Culture: Bamiyan, Islamic Iconoclasm, and the Museum. *The Art Bulletin* 84.4: 641–659.

Floris, Lene & Vasström, Annette 1999. *På museum – mellem oplevelse og oplysning.* Humanistisk Historieformidling. Roskilde: Roskilde Universitetsforlag.

Forser, Tomas (ed.) 1978. *Humaniora på undantag? Humanistiska forskningstraditioner i Sverige.* Kontrakurs. Stockholm: Pan and Norstedts.

Foucault, Michel 1966. *Les mots et les choses: Une archéologie des sciences humaines.* Bibliothèque des Sciences Humaines. Paris: Éditions Gallimard. (English: *The Order of Things: An Archaeology of the Human Sciences.* World of Man. New York: Pantheon Books, 1971.)

Foucault, Michel 1969. *L'Archéologie du savoir.* Bibliothèque des Sciences Humaines. Paris: Gallimard. (English: *The Archaeology of Knowledge & The Discourse on Language.* New York: Pantheon Books, 1972.)

Foucault, Michel 1976. *Histoire de la sexualité, 1: La volonté de savoir.* Bibliothèque des Histoires. Paris: Éditions Gallimard. (English: *The History of Sexuality, 1: The Will to Knowledge.* London: Penguin, 1990.)

Fowler, Peter 2004. *Landscapes for the World: Conserving a Global Heritage*. Bollington: Windgather Press.

Francioni, Francesco & Lenzerini, Federico 2003. The Destruction of the Buddhas of Bamiyan and International Law. *European Journal of International Law* 14.4: 619–651.

Frängsmyr, Tore 1980. *Framsteg eller förfall: Framtidsbilder och utopier i västerländsk tanketradition*. Kontenta. Stockholm: LiberFörlag.

Frank, Andre Gunder & Gills, Barry, K. 1993. The 5,000 Year World System: An Interdisciplinary Introduction. *The World System: Five Hundred Years or Five Thousand?* Eds Andre Gunder Frank & Barry K. Gills. London and New York: Routledge. Pages 3–55.

Fredengren, Christina 2012. Kulturarvets värde för en hållbar samhällsutveckling. *I valet och kvalet: Grundläggande frågor kring värdering och urval av kulturarv*. Eds Christina Fredengren, Ola Wolfhechel Jensen & Åsa Wall. Stockholm: Riksantikvarieämbetet (The National Swedish Heritage Board). Pages 189–223.

Freud, Sigm(und) 1930. *Das Unbehagen in der Kultur*. Vienna: Internationaler Psychoanalytischer Verlag. (English: *Civilization and Its Discontents*. Great Ideas 19. London: Penguin Books, 2004.)

Friedman, Jonathan 1994. *Cultural Identity and Global Process*. Theory, Culture & Society. London: Sage.

Friedman, Jonathan 1995. The Implosion of Modernity. *Challenging Boundaries: Global Flows, Territorial Identities*. Eds Michael J. Shapiro & Hayward R. Alker. Borderlines 2. Minneapolis: University of Minnesota Press. Pages 247–256.

Friedman, Jonathan 2005. Plus Ça Change? On Not Learning from History. *Hegemonic Declines: Present and Past*. Eds Jonathan Friedman & Christopher Chase-Dunn. Political Economy of the World-System Annual XXVI–b. Boulder, CO and London: Paradigm Publishers. Pages 89–114.

Friedman, Jonathan 2007. Sustainable Unsustainability: Toward a Comparative Study of Hegemonic Decline in Global Systems. *The World System and the Earth System: Global Socioenvironmental Change and Sustainability since the Neolithic*. Eds Alf Hornborg & Carole Crumley. Walnut Creek, CA: Left Coast Press. Pages 91–108.

Fritzsche, Peter 2004. *Stranded in the Present: Modern Times and the Melancholy of History*. Cambridge, MA: Harvard University Press.

Frykman, Jonas & Ehn, Billy (eds) 2007. *Minnesmärken: Att tolka det förflutna och besvärja framtiden*. Stockholm: Carlssons.

Fuentenebro de Diego, Filiberto & Valiente Ots, Carmen 2014. Nostalgia: A Conceptual History. *History of Psychiatry* 25.4: 404–411.

Fukuyama, Francis 1989. The End of History? *The National Interest* 16 (Summer 1989): 3–18.

Füredi, Frank 1992. *Mythical Past, Elusive Future: History and Society in an Anxious Age*. London and Boulder, CO: Pluto Press.

Gamboni, Dario 1997. *The Destruction of Art: Iconoclasm and Vandalism since the French Revolution*. Picturing History. London: Reaktion Books.

Gamboni, Dario 2001. World Heritage: Shield or Target? *Conservation: The Getty Conservation Institute Newsletter* 16.2: 5–11.

Gärdenfors, Peter 2006. *Den meningssökande människan*. Stockholm: Natur och Kultur.

Gardner, Howard 2011. *Truth, Beauty, and Goodness Reframed: Educating for the Virtues in the Twenty-First Century*. New York: Basic Books.

Garnert, Jan 2016. *Ut ur mörkret: Ljusets och belysningens kulturhistoria*. Lund: Historiska Media.

Gathercole, Peter & Lowenthal, David (eds) 1990. *The Politics of the Past*. One World Archaeology 12. London and New York: Routledge.

Gazin-Schwartz, Amy & Holtorf, Cornelius J. (eds) 1999. *Archaeology and Folklore*. Theoretical Archaeology Group (RAG). London and New York: Routledge.

Gellner, Ernest 1983. *Nations and Nationalism*. New Perspectives on the Past series. Ithaca, NY: Cornell University Press.

Gerding, Henrik & Ingemark, Dominic 1997. Beyond Newtonian Thinking – Towards a Non-Linear Archaeology: Applying Chaos Theory to Archaeology. *Current Swedish Archaeology* 5: 49–64.

Gibbon, Edward 1966. *Memoirs of My Life*. Ed. Georges A. Bonnard. London: Nelson. (1st ed. 1796.)

Giddens, Anthony 1990. *The Consequences of Modernity*. Cambridge: Polity Press.

Giddens, Anthony 1999. *Runaway World: How Globalization is Reshaping Our Lives*. London: Profile Books.

Giere, Ronald N. 2006. *Scientific Perspectivism*. Chicago and London: The University of Chicago Press.

Gillis, John R. (ed.) 1994. *Commemorations: The Politics of National Identity*. Princeton, NJ: Princeton University Press.

Gillman, Derek 2010. *The Idea of Cultural Heritage*. Revised Edition. Cambridge: Cambridge University Press. (1st ed. 2006.)

Gleick, James 1999. *Faster: The Acceleration of Just About Everything*. New York: Pantheon Books.

Golinelli, Gaitano M. (ed.) 2015. *Cultural Heritage and Value Creations: Towards New Pathways*. Heidelberg: Springer.

Gracia, Jorge J. E. 1992. The Transcendentals in the Middle Ages: An Introduction. *Topoi* 11: 113–120.

Graham, Brian, Ashworth, G. J. & Tunbridge, J. E. 2000. *A Geography of Heritage: Power, Culture and Economy*. London: Hodder Arnold.

Gray, John 2001. *Al Qaeda and What It Means to be Modern*. London: Faber and Faber.

Greenfield, Jeanette 1996. *The Return of Cultural Treasures*. Cambridge: Cambridge University Press. (1st ed. 1989.)

Gren, Leif 1994. Petrified Tears: Archaeology and Communication Through Monuments. *Current Swedish Archaeology* 2: 87–110.

Grinder-Hansen, Keld (ed.) 1992. *Rejsen*. Copenhagen: Nationalmuseet (The National Museum).

Grove, Louise & Thomas, Suzie (eds) 2014. *Heritage Crime: Progress, Prospects and Prevention*. Basingstoke and New York: Palgrave Macmillan.

Grundberg, Jonas 2000. *Kulturarvsförvaltningens samhällsuppdrag: En introduktion till kulturarvsförvaltningens teori och praktik*. Gotarc Series C. Arkeologiska skrifter 33. Gothenburg Department of Archaeology, University of Gothenburg.

Grundberg, Jonas 2004. *Historiebruk, globalisering och kulturarvsförvaltning: Utveckling eller konflikt?* Gotarc Series B. Gothenburg Archaeological Thesis No. 28. Gothenburg Department of Archaeology, University of Gothenburg.

Grundsten, Claes & Hanneberg, Peter 2000. *Världsarv: Naturens mästerverk*. Stockholm: Max Ström.

Habermas, Jürgen 1981. *Theorie des kommunikativen Handelns*, 1–2. Frankfurt am Main: Suhrkamp. (English: *The Theory of Communicative Action*, 1–2. London: Heinemann (1); Cambridge: Polity, 1984–1987 (2).)

Habermas, Jürgen 1985. Drei Perspektiven: Linkshegelianer – Rechtshegelianer und Nietzsche. *Der philosophische Diskurs der Moderne: Zwölf Vorlesungen*. Suhrkamp Taschenbuch Wissenschaft 749. Frankfurt am Main: Suhrkamp. Pages 65–94. (English: Three Perspectives: Left Hegelians, Right Hegelians, and Nietzsche. *The Philosophical Discourse of Modernity: Twelve Lectures*. Cambridge: Polity Press, 1990, pp. 51–74.)

Hacke, Jens 2006. *Philosophie der Bürgerlichkeit: Die liberalkonservative Begründung der Bundesrepublik*. Bürgertum Neue Folge. Studien zur Zivilgesellschaft 3. Göttingen: Vandenhoeck & Ruprecht.

Halbwachs, Maurice 1992. *On Collective Memory*. The Heritage of Sociology. Chicago: The University of Chicago Press. (1st ed. in French, 1941 and 1952.)

Hall, Melanie (ed.) 2011. *Towards World Heritage: International Origins of the Preservation Movement 1870–1930*. Heritage, Culture and Identity. Farnham and Burlington, VT: Ashgate.

Halldén, Sören 1983. *Behövs det förflutna? En bok om det gåtfulla vardagslivet*. Stockholm: LiberFörlag.

Hanneberg, Peter 1998. Det har gått inflation i kulturarv. *Dagens Nyheter* 6 Sept. 1998.

Hanneberg, Peter 2012. *Världsarv: Människans mästerverk*. Stockholm: Max Ström.

Hansen, Thorkild 1961. *En kvinde ved en flod*. Copenhagen: Gyldendal.

Hansen, Thorkild 1962. *Det lykkelige Arabien*. Copenhagen: Gyldendal. (English: *Arabia Felix: The Danish Expedition of 1761–1767*. London: Collins, 1964.)

Harrison, Rodney 2013. *Heritage: Critical Approaches*. London and New York: Routledge.

Hartley, Leslie Poles 1953. *The Go-Between*. London: Hamish Hamilton.

Hartog, François 2003. *Régimes d'historicité: Présentisme et expériences du temps*. La librairie du XXIe siècle. Paris: Editions du Seuil. (English: *Regimes of Historicity: Presentism and Experiences of Time*. European Perspectives. New York: Columbia University Press, 2015.)

Hassan, Fekri A. 2007. The Aswan High Dam and the International Rescue Nubia Campaign. *African Archaeological Review* 24: 73–94.

Hassan, Fekri A. 2009. The UNESCO Campaign to Rescue Nubian Archaeology and Monuments. *Managing Egypt's Cultural Heritage: Proceedings of the First Egyptian Cultural Heritage Organisation Conference on: Egyptian Cultural Heritage Management*. Eds L. S. Owens & A. De Trafford. Egyptian Cultural Heritage Organisation Discourses on Heritage Management Series 1. London: Golden House Publications. Pages 59–79.

Hedeager, Lotte & Schousboe, Karen (eds) 1989. *Brugte historier: Ti essays om brug og misbrug af historien*. Copenhagen: Akademisk Forlag.

Heidegger, Martin 1927. *Sein und Zeit*. Jahrbuch für Philosophie und phänomenologische Forschung VIII. Halle: Max Niemeyer. (English: *Being and Time*. SUNY Series in Contemporary Continental Philosophy. New York: State University of New York Press, 1996.)

Heidegger, Martin 1954. Die Frage nach der Technik. *Vorträge und Aufsätze*. Pfullingen: Günther Neske. Pages 13–44. (English: *The Question Concerning Technology and Other Essays*. New York and London: Garland, 1977, pp. 3–35.).

Heller, Agnes 1988. Europe – An Epilogue. *The Postmodern Political Condition*. Eds Agnes Heller & Ferenc Fehér. Cambridge: Polity Press. Pages 146–159.

Henderson, J. Vernon, Storeygard, Adam & Weil, David N. 2009. *Measuring Economic Growth from Outer Space*. NBER Working Paper Series 15199. National Bureau of Economic Research, Cambridge, MA.

Herodotus I–IV, Books I–IX. Ed. A. D. Godley. The Loeb Classical Library 117–120. Cambridge, MA: Harvard University Press, and London: William Heinemann, 1971–1982. (1st ed. 1920–38.)

Hewison, Robert 1987. *The Heritage Industry: Britain in a Climate of Decline*. London: Methuen.

Hobsbawm, Eric 1981. Looking Forward: History and the Future. *New Left Review* 125 (January-February 1981): 3–19. (Also printed in: *On History*. London: Weidenfeld & Nicolson, 1997.)

Hobsbawm, Eric & Ranger, Terence (eds) 1983. *The Invention of Tradition*. Past and Present Publications. Cambridge: Cambridge University Press.

Hofer(us), Johannes 1688 (some title pages erroneously state the year of publication as being 1678): *Dissertatio medica de Nostalgia, Oder*

Heimwehe. Basel: Jacobi Bertschii. (English: "Medical Dissertation on Nostalgia" in *Bulletin of the Institute of the History of Medicine* II.6 (August 1934): 376–391.)

Högberg, Anders 2013. *Mångfaldsfrågor i kulturmiljövården: Tankar, kunskaper och processer 2002–2012.* Lund: Nordic Academic Press.

Holtorf, Cornelius 1997. Towards a Chronology of Megaliths: Understanding Monumental Time and Cultural Memory. *Journal of European Archaeology* 4: 119–152.

Holtorf, Cornelius (with comments by Kathryn Denning & Per Cornell) 2000. Paul Feyerabend: Towards a Democratic Relativism in Archaeology. *Philosophy and Archaeological Practice: Perspectives for the 21st Century.* Eds Cornelius Holtorf & Håkan Karlsson. Gothenburg Bricoleur Press. Pages 241–259.

Holtorf, Cornelius 2005. *From Stonehenge to Las Vegas: Archaeology as Popular Culture.* Walnut Creek, CA: AltaMira Press.

Holtorf, Cornelius 2006. Can Less be More? Heritage in the Age of Terrorism. *Public Archaeology* 5.2: 101–109.

Holtorf, Cornelius 2010. Meta-Stories of Archaeology. *World Archaeology* 43.3: 381–393.

Holtorf, Cornelius 2013a. On Pastness: A Reconsideration of Materiality in Archaeological Object Authenticity. *Anthropological Quarterly* 88.2: 427–443.

Holtorf, Cornelius 2013b. The Past People Want: Heritage for the Majority? *Appropriating the Past: Philosophical Perspectives on the Practice of Archaeology.* Eds Geoffrey Scarre & Robin Coningham. Cambridge: Cambridge University Press. Pages 63–81.

Holtorf, Cornelius 2018. Embracing Change: How Cultural Resilience Is Increased through Cultural Heritage. *World Archaeology* 50.4: 639–650.

Homer: *Iliad*, I–II, books 1–24. Loeb Classical Library. Cambridge, MA: Harvard University Press, 1999–2003.

Homer: *Odyssey*, I–II, books 1–24. Loeb Classical Library. Cambridge, Mass.: Harvard University Press, 1998–2004.

Hooper-Greenhill, Eilean 1992. *Museums and the Shaping of Knowledge.* The Heritage: Cure – Preservation – Management. London and New York: Routledge.

Horkheimer, Max & Adorno, Theodor W. 1947. *Dialektik der Aufklärung: Philosophische Fragmente.* Amsterdam: Querido Verlag (privately printed 1944). (English: *The Dialectic of Enlightenment: Philosophical Fragments.* Cultural Memory in the Present. Stanford, CA: Stanford University Press, 2002.)

Hornborg, Alf 2001. Symbolic Technologies: Machines and the Marxian Notion of Fetishism. *The Power of the Machine: Global Inequalities of Economy, Technology, and Environment.* Globalization and the Environment 1. Walnut Creek, CA: AltaMira Press. Pages 131–153.

Hornborg, Alf 2010. *Myten om maskinen: Essäer om makt, modernitet och miljö*. Gothenburg Daidalos.

Horne, Donald 1984. *The Great Museum: The Re-Presentation of History*. London and Sydney: Pluto Press.

Huntington, Samuel E. 1993. The Clash of Civilizations? *Foreign Affairs* 72.3: 22–49.

Huyssen, Andreas 1995. *Twilight Memories: Marking Time in a Culture of Amnesia*. New York and London: Routledge.

Hvass, Steen 2000. *De kongelige monumenter i Jelling: deres historie, forvaltning og formidling*. Jelling: Kongernes Jelling.

Hvass, Steen 2011. *Jelling-monumenterne: deres historie og bevaring*. Copenhagen: Kulturarvsstyrelsen (The Cultural Heritage Board).

Hygen, Anne-Sophie 1996. *Fornminnevern och forvaltning: En teoretisk og metodisk tilnærming til planlegging og praksis i fornminnevernet*. NIKU Temahefte 1. Oslo: NIKU, Norsk institutt for kulturminneforskning (Norwegian Institute of Cultural Heritage Research).

Hylland Eriksen, Thomas 1996. *Kampen om fortiden: Et essay om myter, identitet og politikk*. Aschehoug Argument. Oslo: H. Aschehoug.

Hylland Eriksen, Thomas 2001. *Tyranny of the Moment: Fast and Slow Time in the Information Age*. London: Pluto Press.

Hylland Eriksen, Thomas 2016. *Overheating: An Anthropology of Accelerated Change*. London: Pluto Press.

International Journal of Heritage Studies 1ff, 1994ff.

Ireland, Tracy & Schofield, John (eds) 2015. *The Ethics of Cultural Heritage*. Ethical Archaeologies: The Politics of Social Justice 4. Heidelberg: Springer and World Archaeological Congress.

Jensen, Ola W. 1998. The Cultural Heritage: Modes of Preservation and the Longing for Eternal Life. *The Kaleidoscopic Past: Proceedings of the 5th Nordic TAG Conference, Gothenburg, 2–5 April 1997*. Eds Anna-Carin Andersson, Åsa Gillberg, Ola W. Jensen, Håkan Karlsson & Magnus V. Rolöf. Gotarc Serie C, Arkeologiska skrifter 16. Gothenburg: Department of Archaeology, University of Gothenburg. Pages 99–118.

Jensen, Ola W. 2002. *Forntid i historien: En arkeologihistorisk studie av synen på forntid och forntida lämningar, från medeltiden till och med förupplysningen*. Gotarc Serie B. Gothenburg Archaeological Theses 19. Gothenburg: Department of Archaeology, University of Gothenburg.

Jensen, Ola W. 2004. Earthly Practice: Towards a History of Excavation in Sweden, in the 17th and 18th Centuries. *Current Swedish Archaeology* 12: 61–82.

Jensen, Ola W. 2010. The Art of Valuating a Heritage: From a Swedish Management Perspective with Past and Present Examples. *Current Swedish Archaeology* 18: 151–176.

Johannisson, Karin 2001. *Nostalgia: En känslas historia*. Bonnier essä. Stockholm: Albert Bonnier.

Johansson, Marit 2015. *Life in a World Heritage City: A Case Study of Discussions and Contested Values in Angra do Heroísmo, the Azores.* Linköping Studies in Arts and Science 646. Linköping: Department of Culture Studies, Linköping University.

Jones, Sîan 2010. Negotiating Authentic Objects and Authentic Selves: Beyond the Deconstruction of Authenticity. *Journal of Material Culture* 15.2: 181–203.

Jones, Steven E. 2006. *Against Technology: From the Luddites to Neo-Luddism.* New York and London: Routledge.

Jonsson, Marita 2015. Hur Visby blev ett världsarv. *Gotländskt arkiv* 87: 25–35.

Jönsson, Lars-Eric & Svensson, Birgitta (eds) 2005. *I industrisamhällets slagskugga: Om problematiska kulturarv.* Stockholm: Carlssons.

Jörnmark, Jan & Hausswolff, Annika von 2011. *Avgrunden.* Gothenburg: Tangent.

Källström, Staffan 2000. *Framtidens katedral: Medeltidsdröm och utopisk modernism.* Stockholm: Carlssons.

Kamil, Jill 1993. *Aswan and Abu Simbel: History and Guide.* Cairo: The American University in Cairo Press.

Kane, Susan (ed.) 2003. *The Politics of Archaeology and Identity in a Global Context.* Archaeological Institute of America, Colloquia and Conference Papers 7. Boston, MA.

Kant, Immanuel 1781. *Critik der reinen Vernuft.* Riga: Johann Friedrich Hartknoch. (English: *Critique of Pure Reason.* Eds Paul Guyer & Allen W. Wood. The Cambridge Edition of the Works of Immanuel Kant. Cambridge: Cambridge University Press, 1998.)

Kant, Immanuel 1784. Beanwortung der Frage: Was ist Aufklärung? *Berlinische Monatsschrift* 1784.12 (December): 481–494. (English: An Answer to the Question: What is Enlightenment? *Practical Philosophy.* Ed. Mary J. Gregor. The Cambridge Edition of the Works of Immanuel Kant. Cambridge: Cambridge University Press, 1996, pp. 11–22.)

Kant, Immanuel 1785. *Grundlegung zur Metaphysik der Sitten.* Riga: Johann Friedrich Hartknoch. (English: *Groundwork of the Metaphysics of Morals.* Ed. Mary Gregor. Cambridge Texts in the History of Philosophy. Cambridge: Cambridge University Press, 1998.)

Kant, Immanuel 1790. *Critik der Urtheilskraft.* Berlin and Libau: Lagarde & Friederich. (English: *Critique of the Power of Judgment.* Ed. Paul Guyer. The Cambridge Edition of the Works of Immanuel Kant. Cambridge: Cambridge University Press, 2000.)

Kant, Immanuel 1798. *Anthropologie in pragmatischer Hinsicht.* Königsberg: Friedrich Nicolovius. (English: *Anthropology from a Pragmatic Point of View.* Eds Robert B. Louden & Manfred Kuehn. Cambridge Texts in the History of Philosophy. Cambridge: Cambridge University Press, 2006.)

Karlsson, Håkan (ed.) 2004. *Swedish Archaeologists on Ethics.* Lindome: Bricoleur Press.

Keating, Rex 1962. *Nubian Twilight.* London: Rupert Hart-Davis.

Keating, Rex 1975. *Nubian Rescue.* London: Robert Hale & Company and New York: Hawthorn Books.

Kennedy, Paul 1987. *The Rise and Fall of the Great Powers: Economic Change and Military Conflict from 1500 to 2000.* New York: Random House.

Khaldûn, Ibn 1958. *The Muqaddimah: An Introduction to History,* 1–3. Transl. Franz Rosenthal. Bollingen series xliii. New York: Pantheon Books.

Kierkegaard, Søren (pseudonym Hilarius Bogbinder) 1845. *Stadier paa Livets Vei: Studier af Forskjellige.* Copenhagen: C. A. Reitzel. (English: *Stages on Life's Way.* Princeton, NJ: Princeton University Press, 1940.)

Kirshenblatt-Gimblett, Barbara 1998. *Destination Culture: Tourism, Museums, and Heritage.* Berkeley, Los Angeles, and London: University of California Press.

Klein, Richard G. 1989. Biological and Behavioural Perspectives on Modern Human Origins in Southern Africa. *The Human Revolution: Behavioural and Biological Perspectives on the Origins of Modern Humans.* Eds Paul Mellars & Chris Stringer. Edinburgh: Edinburgh University Press. Pages 529–546.

Klynne, Allan 2019. *Antikens sju underverk.* Stockholm: Natur och Kultur.

Kolrud, Kristine & Prusac, Marina (eds) 2014. *Iconoclasm from Antiquity to Modernity.* Farnham and Burlington, VT: Ashgate.

Kramer, Alan 2007. *Dynamic of Destruction: Culture and Mass Killing in the First World War.* The Making of the Modern World. Oxford: Oxford University Press.

Krautheimer, Richard 1942. Introduction to an "Iconography of Medieval Architecture". *Journal of the Warburg and Courtauld Institutes* V: 1–33. (Reprint: *Studies in Early Christian, Medieval and Renaissance Art,* London and New York: University of London Press and New York University Press, 1969, pp. 115–150.)

Kristiansen, Kristian 1981. A Social History of Danish Archaeology (1805–1975). *Towards a History of Archaeology.* Ed. Glyn Daniel. London: Thames & Hudson. Pages 20–44.

Kristiansen, Kristian (ed.) 1985. *Archaeological Formation Processes: The Representativity of Archaeological Remains from Danish Prehistory.* Studies in Scandinavian Prehistory and Early History 2. Copenhagen: Nationalmuseet (The National Museum).

Kristiansen, Kristian 1989. "Fortids Kraft og Kæmpestyrke": Om national og politisk brug af fortiden. *Brugte historier: Ti essays om brug og misbrug af historien.* Eds Lotte Hedeager & Karen Schousboe. Copenhagen: Akademisk Forlag. Pages 187–218. (English: "The Strength of the Past and its Great Might": An Essay on the Use of the Past. *Journal of European Archaeology* 1(1993): 3–32.)

Kristiansen, Kristian 1996. Old Boundaries and New Frontiers: Reflections on the Identity of Archaeology. *Current Swedish Archaeology* 4: 103–122.

Kristiansen, Kristian 2001. Resor i tiden. *På resande fot: 23 forskare skriver om turism och upplevelser.* Ed. Margareta Elg. Stockholm: Sellin. Pages 144–153. (Reprinted, with the title "Är kulturarvet en mänsklig rättighet?", *Alba.nu* 2004: 4, www.alba.nu).

Kulturkanon. Copenhagen: Kulturministeriet (Ministry of Culture) and Politikens Forlag, 2006.

Kundera, Milan 1995. *La lenteur.* Paris: Gallimard. (English: *Slowness.* New York: Harper Collins, 1995.)

Kuper, Adam 1988. *The Invention of Primitive Society: Transformations of an Illusion.* London and New York: Routledge.

Kuusamo, Altti 2011. Metaphors of Archaeology in Psychoanalysis. *Times, Things & Places: 36 Essays for Jussi-Pekka Taavitsainen.* Eds Janne Harjula, Maija Helamaa & Janne Haarala. Turku and Helsinki. Pages 80–89.

Labadi, Sophia (ed.) 2007. *World Heritage: Challenges for the Millennium.* Paris: UNESCO World Heritage Centre, 2007.

Labadi, Sophia 2013. *UNESCO, Cultural Heritage, and Outstanding Universal Value: Value-based Analyses of the World Heritage and Intangible Cultural Heritage Conventions.* Archaeology in Society Series. Lanham, MD: AltaMira Press.

Labadi, Sophia & Long, Colin (eds) 2010. *Heritage and Globalisation.* Key Issues in Cultural Heritage. London and New York: Routledge.

Lambourne, Nicola 2001. *War Damage in Western Europe: The Destruction of Historic Monuments During the Second World War.* Societies at War. Edinburgh: Edinburgh University Press.

Lampedusa, Giuseppe Tomasi di 1958. *Il Gattopardo.* Biblioteca di letteratura. Milan: Feltrinelli. (English: *The Leopard.* London: Vintage Books, 2007.)

Langfield, Michele, Logan, William & Craith, Máiréad Nic (eds) 2010. *Cultural Diversity, Heritage and Human Rights: Intersections in Theory and Practice.* Key Issues in Cultural Heritage. London and New York: Routledge.

Laron, Guy 2013. *Origins of the Suez Crisis: Postwar Development Diplomacy and the Struggle Over Third World Industrialization 1945–1956.* Washington DC: Woodrow Wilson Center Press and Baltimore, MD: Johns Hopkins University Press.

Larsen, Knut Einar (ed.) 1995. *Nara Conference on Authenticity in Relation to World Heritage.* Tokyo: Agency for Cultural Affairs.

Latour, Bruno 1991. *Nous n'avons jamais été modernes: Essai d'anthropologie symétrique.* Collection L'Armillaire. Paris: Éditions La Découverte. (English: *We Have Never Been Modern.* Cambridge, MA: Harvard University Press, 1993.)

Latour, Bruno & Woolgar, Steve 1979. *Laboratory Life: The Social Construction of Scientific Facts.* Sage Library of Social Research 80. Los Angeles: Sage. (2nd ed. Princeton, NJ: Princeton University Press, 1986.)

Lauring, Palle 1969. *Hvad skal vi med Historien?* Copenhagen: Carit Andersens Forlag. (2nd ed. 1995.)

Leask, Anna & Fyall, Alan (eds) 2006. *Managing World Heritage Sites.* Oxford and Burlington, VT: Butterworth-Heinemann.

Le Goff, Jacques 1988. *Histoire et mémoire.* Collection folio/histoire. Paris: Gallimard. (English: *History and Memory.* European Perspectives. New York: Columbia University Press, 1992.)

Lévi-Strauss, Claude 1962. *Le totémisme aujourd'hui.* Mythes et religions 42. Paris: Presses Universitaires de France. (English: *Totemism.* Beacon paperback 157. Boston, MA: Beacon Press, 1963.)

Lévi-Strauss, Claude 1966. The Scope of Anthropology. *Current Anthropology* 7.2: 112–123.

Liedman, Sven-Eric 1997. *I skuggan av framtiden: Modernitetens idéhistoria.* Stockholm: Bonnier Alba.

Lightman, Alan 1993. *Einstein's Dreams.* New York: Pantheon Books.

Lihammer, Anna & Nordin, Jonas M. (eds) 2010. *Modernitetens materialitet: Arkeologiska perspektiv på det moderna samhällets framväxt.* The Museum of National Antiquities, Stockholm, Studies 17. Stockholm: Statens Historiska Museum (Museum of National Antiquities).

Liliequist, Inger 2005. Cultural Heritage: A Resource in Urban Development. *Urban Assets: Cultural Heritage as a Tool for Development.* Eds Oscar Hemer & Kristoffer Gansing. Stockholm: SIDA, Urban Development Division. Pages 11–16.

Lilja, Agneta 1996. *Föreställningen om den ideala uppteckningen: En studie av idé och praktik vid traditionssamlande arkiv – ett exempel från Uppsala 1914–1945.* Skrifter utgivna genom Dialekt- och folkminnesarkivet i Uppsala B22. Uppsala: Dialekt- och folkminnesarkivet (Department of Dialectology and Folklore Research).

Lindborg, Rolf 1998. *Anden i naturen: Naturfilosofen Hans Christian Ørsted – experimentalfysiker.* Nora: Nya Doxa.

Lindholm, Charles 2008. *Culture and Authenticity.* Malden, MA: Blackwell.

Linnaeus, Carl 1752. *Quæstio historico naturalis, Cui bono?* Uppsala: Laur. Magn. Höjer. (Swedish: *En fråga, som altid föreställes de Naturkunniga, Då det heter: Hwartill duger det? (Cui bono?).* Stockholm: Lars Salvii, 1753.)

Lipovetsky, Gilles 2004. *Les temps hypermodernes.* Nouveau collège de philosophie. Paris: Éditions Grasset. (English: *Hypermodern Times.* Cambridge and Malden, MA: Polity Press, 2005.).

Little, Barbara J. 2007. *Historical Archaeology: Why the Past Matters.* Walnut Creek, CA: Left Coast Press.

Little, Barbara J. 2009. What Can Archaeology Do for Justice, Peace, Community, and the Earth? *Historical Archaeology* 43.4: 115–119.

Löfgren, Orvar, Andolf, Göran, Lundén, Thomas, Bohm, Peter & Emmelin Lars 1990. *Längtan till landet Annorlunda: Om turism i historia och nutid*. Stockholm: Gidlund.

Logan, William 2012. Cultural Diversity, Cultural Heritage and Human Rights: Towards Heritage Management as Human Rights-Based Cultural Practice. *International Journal of Heritage Studies* 18.3: 231–244.

Logan, William & Reeves, Keir (eds) 2009. *Places of Pain and Shame: Dealing with Difficult Heritage*. Key Issues in Cultural Heritage. London and New York: Routledge.

Lowenthal, David 1985. *The Past is a Foreign Country*. Cambridge: Cambridge University Press. (2nd ed. *The Past is a Foreign Country – Revisited*. Cambridge: Cambridge University Press, 2015.).

Lowenthal, David 1997. *The Heritage Crusade and the Spoils of History*. London: Viking. (US version published as: *Possessed by the Past: The Heritage Crusade and the Spoils of History*. New York: Free Press, 1996.)

Lowenthal, David & Binney, Marcus (eds) 1981. *Our Past before Us: Why Do We Save It?* London: Temple Smith.

Lübbe, Hermann 1982. *Der Fortschritt und das Museum: Über den Grund unseres Vergnügens an historischen Gegenständen*. The 1981 Bithell Memorial Lecture. London: University of London, Institute of Germanic Studies. (Also in: *Die Aufdringlichkeit der Geschichte: Herausforderungen der Moderne vom Historismus bis zum Nationalsozialismus*. Graz: Styria, 1989, Ch. 1.1, pp. 13–29.)

Lübbe, Hermann 1983. *Zeit-Verhältnisse: Zur Kulturphilosophie des Fortschritts*. Herkunft und Zukunft 1. Graz: Styria, pp. 9–32.

Lübbe, Hermann 1996. *Zeit-Erfahrungen: Sieben Begriffe zur Beschreibung moderner Zivilisationsdynamik*. Akademie der Wissenschaften und der Literatur. Abhandlungen der Geistes- und Sozialwissenschaftlichen Klasse, Jahrgang 1996, No. 5. Stuttgart: Franz Steiner.

Lucas, Gavin 2012. *Understanding the Archaeological Record*. Cambridge: Cambridge University Press.

Lutyk, Carol Bittig (ed.) 1987. *Our World's Heritage*. Washington DC: National Geographic Society.

Lyotard, Jean-François 1979. *La condition postmoderne: Rapport sur le savoir*. Collection Critique. Paris: Les Éditions de Minuit. (English: *The Postmodern Condition: A Report on Knowledge*. Theory and History of Literature 10. Minneapolis: University of Minnesota Press, 1984.)

MacCannell, Dean 1976. *The Tourist: A New Theory of the Leisure Class*. New York: Schocken Books. (2nd ed. Berkeley: University of California Press 1999.)

Macdonald, Sharon 2009. *Difficult Heritage: Negotiating the Nazi Past in Nuremberg and Beyond*. London and New York: Routledge.

MacQuitty, William 1965. *Abu Simbel*. London: Macdonald.

Magnusson Staaf, Björn 2013. Att lita på krisen? Om kris som komponent i historieteori. *Kris och kultur: Kulturvetenskapliga perspektiv på kunskap, estetik och historia.* Eds Mats Arvidson, Ursula Geisler & Kristofer Hansson. Lund: Sekel. Pages 29–48.

Malina, Jaroslav & Vasícek, Zdenek 1990. *Archaeology Yesterday and Today: The Development of Archaeology in the Sciences and Humanities.* Cambridge: Cambridge University Press.

Malraux, André 1960. L'homme arrache quelque chose à la mort. *Le UNESCO Courrier* XIII (Mai 1960): 8–11. (English: T.V.A. of Archaeology. *The UNESCO Courier* XIII (May 1960): 8–11.)

Mankell, Henning & Vera, Yvonne 2000. *Homo Narrans – the Storytelling Man: A Conversation.* Stockholm: Millenniekommittén (The Millennium Committee).

Marinetti, Filippo Tommaso 1909. Le Futurisme. *Le Figaro,* 20 février 1909. (English: The Founding and Manifesto of Futurism 1909. *Futurist Manifestos.* Ed. Umbro Apollonio. The World of Art Library, Modern Movements. London: Thames & Hudson, 1973. Pages 19–24.)

Marquard, Odo 1986. *Apologie des Zufälligen: Philosophische Studien.* Universal-Bibliothek 8351. Stuttgart: Philipp Reclam jun.

Marquard, Odo 2000. *Philosophie des Stattdessen: Studien.* Universal-Bibliothek 18049. Stuttgart: Philipp Reclam jun.

Martin, Hans-Peter & Schumann, Harald 1996. *Die Globaliserungsfalle: Der Angriff auf Demokratie und Wohlstand.* Reinbek bei Hamburg: Rowohlt. (English: *The Global Trap: Globalization and the Assault on Prosperity and Democracy.* London: Zed Books, 1997.)

Marx, Karl 1968. Die entfremdete Arbeit. *Karl Marx, Friedrich Engels Werke* 40. Berlin: Dietz–Verlag, pp. 510–522. (English: Estranged Labour. *Karl Marx, Frederick Engels, Collected Works* 3, London: Lawrence & Wishart 1975, pp. 270–282.)

Marx, Karl & Engels, Friedrich 1848. *Manifest der kommunistichen Partei.* London: Bildungs-Gesellschaft für Arbeiter. (English: *The Communist Manifesto.* New York: Pocket Books, 1964.)

May, Rollo 1975. *The Courage to Create.* New York: W. W. Norton.

McAnany, Patricia A. & Yoffee, Norman 2009. *Questioning Collapse: Human Resilience, Ecological Vulnerability, and the Aftermath of Empire.* Cambridge: Cambridge University Press.

McKirahan, Richard 1998. Arche. *Routledge Encyclopedia of Philosophy 1.* Ed. Edward Craig. London and New York: Routledge. Pages 359–361.

Mellow, James R. 1968. The Stein Salon Was the First Museum of Modern Art. *The New York Times* 1 Dec. 1968.

Melotti, Marxiano 2011. *The Plastic Venuses: Archaeological Tourism in Post-Modern Society.* Cambridge: Cambridge Scholars.

Memory of the World: The Treasures that Record our History from 1700 BC to the Present Day. Paris and Glasgow: UNESCO Publishing, HarperCollins, 2012.

Meskell, Lynn (ed.) 1998. *Archaeology under Fire: Nationalism, Politics and Heritage in the Eastern Mediterranean and Middle East.* London and New York: Routledge.

Meskell, Lynn 2002. Negative Heritage and Past Mastering in Archaeology. *Anthropological Quarterly* 75.3: 557–574.

Meskell, Lynn 2018. *A Future in Ruins: UNESCO, World Heritage and the Dream of Peace*. Oxford: Oxford University Press.

Moberg, Carl-Axel 1984. Den nyttiga fornforskningen: En skiss till en åskådnings historia och karakteristik. *Lychnos, Lärdomshistoriska Samfundets Årsbok* 1984. Pages 133–157.

Møller, Lis 1994. Viljen til viden: Freud som "Conquistador" og arkæolog. *Slagmark: Tidsskrift for idéhistorie* 22: 17–37.

Mommsen, Theodore E. 1942. Petrarch's Conception of the "Dark Ages". *Speculum: A Journal of Medieval Studies* 17.2: 226–242.

Moro (More), Thomo (Thomas) 1516. *Libellus vere aureus nec minus salutaris quam festivus de optimo reipublicae statu, deque nova Insula Utopia*. Louvain: Theodorici Martini (Thierry Martens). (English: *Utopia*. Penguin Classics. London: Penguin, 2012.)

Mumford, Lewis 1938. *The Culture of Cities*. New York: Harcourt Brace.

Musil, Robert 1936. Denkmale. *Nachlaß zu Lebzeiten*. Zurich: Humanitas. Pages 87–93. (English: Monuments. *Posthumous Papers of a Living Author*. New York: Archipelago Books, 2006, pp. 64–68.)

Navrud, Ståle & Ready, Richard C. (eds) 2002. *Valuing Cultural Heritage: Applying Environmental Valuation Techniques to Historic Buildings, Monuments and Artifacts*. Cheltenham and Northampton: Edward Elgar.

Nielsen, Ingrid (ed.) 1987. *Bevar din arv: 1937 – Danmarks fortidsminder – 1987*. Copenhagen: G. E. C. Gads forlag & Skov- og Naturstyrelsen (Danish Forest and Nature Agency).

Nielsen, Niels Kayser 2010. *Historiens forvandlinger: Historiebrug fra monumenter til oplevelsesøkonomi*. Aarhus and Copenhagen: Aarhus Universitetsforlag.

Nietzsche, Friedrich 1874. *Vom Nutzen und Nachtheil der Historie für das Leben*. Unzeitgemässe Betrachtungen II. Leipzig: Verlag von E. W. Fritzsch. (English: *On the Use and Abuse of History*. Cosimo Classics. New York: Cosimo, 2005.)

Nikolic, Dragan 2012. *Tre städer, två broar och ett museum: Minne, politik och världsarv i Bosnien och Hercegovina*. Lund: Department of Cultural Sciences, Ethnology.

Niles, John D. 1999. *Homo Narrans: The Poetics and Anthropology of Oral Literature*. Philadelphia: University of Pennsylvania Press.

Nilsson Stutz, Liv 2008. Archaeology, Identity, and the Right to Culture: Anthropological perspectives on repatriation. *Current Swedish Archaeology* 15–16: 157–172.

Nora, Pierre 1984. Entre Mémoire et Histoire: La problématique des lieux. *Les Lieux de mémoire*. 1. *La République*. Ed. Pierre Nora. Bibliothèque illustrée des histoires. Paris: Gallimard. Pages xvii–xlii. (English: Between Memory and History: Les Lieux de Mémoire. *Representations* 26 (Spring 1989): 7–24. Also: General Introduction: Between Memory and

History. *Realms of Memory: Rethinking the French Past*. I. *Conflicts and Divisions*. Eds. Pierre Nora & Lawrence D. Kritzman. New York: Columbia University Press 1996. Pages 1–20.)

Nordin, Svante 1989. *Från tradition till apokalyps: Historieskrivning och civilisationskritik i det moderna Europa*. Symposion Bibliotek. Stockholm, Lund, and Stehag: Symposion.

Nordin, Svante 2008. *Humaniora i Sverige: Framväxt – Guldålder – Kris*. Stockholm: Atlantis.

Nowell, April 2010. Defining Behavioral Modernity in the Context of Neandertal and Anatomically Modern Human Populations. *Annual Review of Anthropology* 39: 437–452.

Noyes, James 2013. *The Politics of Iconoclams: Religion, Violence and the Culture of Image-Breaking in Christianity and Islam*. London and New York: I.B. Tauris.

Nussbaum, Martha 1988. Non-Relative Virtues: An Aristotelian Approach. *Midwest Studies in Philosophy* XIII.1: 32–53. (New version: *The Quality of Life*. Eds Martha Nussbaum & Amartya Sen. Oxford: Clarendon Press, 1993, pp. 242–269.)

Nyerup, Rasmus 1806. Oversyn over Fædernelandets Mindesmærker fra Oldtiden, saaledes som de kan tænkes opstillede i et tilkommende National-Museum: Et Forsøg. *Historisk-statistisk Skildring af Tilstanden i Danmark og Norge i ældre og yngre Tider*, 4. Copenhagen: A & S. Soldin.

Olaus Magnus 1555. *Historia de Gentibus Septentrionalibus*, I–XII. Rome: Olaus Magnus. (Swedish: *Historia om de nordiska folken*. Hedemora: Gidlund, 1982.)

O'Leary, Beth Laura & Capelotti, P. J. (eds) 2014. *Archaeology and Heritage of The Human Movement into Space*. Heidelberg: Springer.

Olivier, Laurent C. 1999. Duration, memory and the nature of the archaeological record. *Glyfer och arkeologiska rum – en vänbok till Jarl Nordbladh*. Eds Anders Gustafsson & Håkan Karlsson. Gotarc Series A 3. Gothenburg: Department of Archaeology, University of Gothenburg. Pages 529–535. (Also printed in: *It's about Time: The Concept of Time in Archaeology*. Ed. Håkan Karlsson. Gothenburg: Bricoleur Press, 2001. Pages 61–70.)

Olivier, Laurent 2008. *Le sombre abîme du temps: Mémoire et archéologie*. La Couleur des idées. Paris: Éditions du Seuil. (English: *The Dark Abyss of Time: Archaeology and Memory*. Archaeology in Society Series. Lanham, MD: AltaMira Press, 2011.)

Olsen, Bjørnar & Pétursdóttir, Thora 2014 (eds): *Ruin Memories: Materialities, Aesthetics and the Archaeology of the Recent Past*. Archaeological Orientations. London and New York: Routledge.

Olsen, Bjørnar & Svestad, Asgeir 1994. Creating Prehistory: Archaeology, Museums and the Discourse of modernism. *Nordisk Museologi* 1994.1: 3–20.

Orwell, George 1949. *Nineteen Eighty-Four.* London: Secker & Warburg.

Ossian, Clair 2007. The Egyptian Court. *Kmt, A Modern Journal of Ancient Egypt* 18.3: 64–73.

The Oxford English Dictionary, Second Edition, I–XX. Eds J. A. Simpson & E. S. C. Weiner. Oxford: Clarendon Press, 1989.

Paardekooper, Roeland 2011. Experimental Activities: A European Perspective. *Experimental Archaeology: Between Enlightenment and Experience.* Eds Bodil Petersson & Lars Erik Narmo. Acta Archaeologica Lundensia, Series in 8, 62. Lund: Lund University, Department of Archaeology and Ancient History. Pages 69–85.

Petersson, Bodil 2003. *Föreställningar om det förflutna: Arkeologi och rekonstruktion.* Lund: Nordic Academic Press.

Petersson, Bodil 2017. Anachronism and Time Travel. *The Archaeology of Time Travel: Experiencing the Past in the 21st century.* Eds Bodil Petersson & Cornelius Holtorf. Oxford: Archaeopress. Pages 281–297.

Petrarca, Francesco: *Le Familiari, Edizione critica,* I–IV. Ed. Vittorio Rossi. Edizione Nazionale delle opere di Francesco Petrarca, X–XIII. Florence: Casa Editrice Le Lettere, 1933–42.

Pettersson, Richard 2003. *Den svenska kulturmiljövårdens värdegrunder: En idéhistorisk bakgrund och analys.* Skrifter från forskningsprogrammet Landskapet som arena 7. Umeå: Umeå University.

Pinker, Steven 2018. *Enlightenment Now: The Case for Reason, Science, Humanism and Progress.* London: Allen Lane.

Plato. *Complete Works.* Ed. John M. Cooper. Indianapolis, IN: Hackett, 1997.

Pollock, Griselda 2006. The Image in Psychoanalysis and the Archaeological Metaphor. *Psychoanalysis and the Image: Transdisciplinary Perspectives.* Ed. Griselda Pollock. New Interventions in Art History. Malden, MA: Blackwell. Pages 1–29.

Popper, Karl 1935. *Logik der Forschung: Zur Erkenntnistheorie der modernen Naturwissenschaft.* Schriften zur wissenschaftlichen Weltauffassung 9. Vienna: Springer. (English: *The Logic of Scientific Discovery.* London: Hutchinson, 1959.)

Popper, Karl 1957. *The Poverty of Historicism.* London: Routledge & Kegan Paul.

Poulot, Dominique 1995. Revolutionary "Vandalism" and the Birth of the Museum: The Effects of a Representation of Modern Cultural Terror. *Art in Museums.* Ed. Susan Pearce. New Research in Museum Studies 5. London: Athlone. Pages 192–214.

Poulot, Dominique 1997. *Musée, nation, patrimoine, 1789–1815.* Bibliothèque des Histoires. Paris: Éditions Gallimard.

Prickett, Stephen 2009. *Modernity and the Reinvention of Tradition: Backing into the Future.* Cambridge: Cambridge University Press.

Pringle, Heather Anne 2006. *The Master Plan: Himmler's Scholars and the Holocaust.* New York: Hyperion.

Prior, Nick 2002. *Museums and Modernity: Art Galleries and the Making of Modern Culture*. Leisure, Consumption and Culture. Oxford and New York: Berg.

Prozesky, Martin 2014. "Homo Ethicus": Understanding the Human Nature that Underlines Human Rights and Human Rights Education. *Journal for the Study of Religion* 27.1: 283–301.

Räkna med kulturarvet: Kulturarvets bidrag till en hållbar samhällsutveckling. Stockholm: Riksantikvarieämbetet (The Swedish National Heritage Board), 2017.

Ranke, Leopold 1824. *Geschichten der romanischen und germanischen Völker von 1494 bis 1514*, I. Leipzig and Berlin: G. Reimer. (English: *History of the Latin and Teutonic Nations, 1494–1514*. London: George Bell & Sons, 1909. – However, Ranke's foreword is missing from this edition.)

Reid, Donald Malcolm 2002. *Whose Pharaohs? Archaeology, Museums, and Egyptian National Identity from Napoleon to World War I*. Berkeley: University of California Press.

Reid, Donald Malcolm 2015. *Contesting Antiquities in Egypt: Archaeology, Museums, & the Struggle for Identities from World War I to Nasser*. Cairo: The American University in Cairo Press.

Reisch, George A. 1991. Chaos, History, and Narrative. *History and Theory* XXX.1: 1–20.

Renfrew, Colin & Bahn, Paul 2016. *Archaeology: Theories, Methods and Practice*. 7th Edition. London: Thames & Hudson. (1st ed. 1991.)

Ricoeur, Paul 1983–1985. *Temps et récit*, 1–3. L'Ordre philosophique. Paris: Éditions du Seuil. (English: *Time and Narrative*, 1–3. Chicago: University of Chicago Press, 1984–88.)

Riegl, Alois 1903. *Der moderne Denkmalkultus, sein Wesen und seine Entstehung*. K. K. Zentral-Kommission für kunst- und historische Denkmale. Vienna and Leipzig: W. Braumüller. (Also in *Gesammelte Aufsätze*. Augsburg and Vienna: Dr. Benno Filser Verlag, 1929. Pages 144–193. English: The Modern Cult of Monuments: Its Character and Its Origin. *Oppositions: A Journal for Ideas and Criticism in Architecture* 25 (1982): 21–51.)

Ritter, Joachim 1961. Die Aufgabe der Geisteswissenschaften in der modernen Gesellschaft. *Jahresschrift 1961 der Gesellschaft zur Förderung der Westfälischen Wilhelms-Universität zu Münster*. Pages 11–39. (Also in the series called Schriften der Gesellschaft zur Förderung der Westfälischen Wilhelms-Universität zu Münster 51, Münster Westf.: Verlag Aschendorff, 1963, pp. 5–33.)

Robertson, Roland 1995. Glocalization: Time-Space and Homogeneity-Heterogeneity. *Global Modernities*. Eds. Mike Featherstone, Scott Lash & Roland Robertson. Theory, Culture & Society. London: Sage, pp. 25–44.

Rogers, Everett M. 2003. *Diffusion of Innovations.* 5th ed. New York: Free Press. (1st ed. 1962.)

Romer, John & Romer, Elizabeth 1993. *The Rape of Tutankhamun.* London: Michael O'Mara Books.

Ronström, Owe 2007. *Kulturarvspolitik. Visby: Från sliten småstad till medeltidsikon.* Stockholm: Carlssons.

Rosa, Hartmut 2005. *Beschleunigung: Die Veränderung der Zeitstrukturen in der Moderne.* Suhrkamp Taschenbuch Wissenschaft 1760. Berlin: Suhrkamp. (English: *Social Acceleration: A New Theory of Modernity.* New York: Columbia University Press, 2013.)

Rosa, Hartmut 2012. *Weltbeziehungen im Zeitalter der Beschleunigung: Umrisse einer neuen Gesellschaftskritik.* Suhrkamp Taschenbuch Wissenschaft 1977. Berlin: Suhrkamp.

Rosén, Christina 2007. Uppdragsarkeologi och modernitet. *Modernitet och arkeologi: Artiklar från VIII Nordic TAG i Lund 2005.* Ed. Lars Ersgård. Stockholm: Riksantikvarieämbetet (The Swedish National Heritage Board). Pages 9–24.

Rosling, Hans, Rosling, Ola & Rosling Rönnlund, Anna 2018. *Factfulness: Ten Reasons We're Wrong about the World – and Why Things Are Better than You Think.* London: Hodder & Stoughton.

Roth, Michael S. with Claire Lyons & Charles Merewether 1997. *Irresistible Decay: Ruins Reclaimed.* Bibliographies & Dossiers: Collections for the Getty Research Institute for the History of Art and the Humanities 2. Los Angeles: Getty Research Institute for the History of Art and the Humanities.

Rovelli, Carlo 2017. *L'Ordine del tempo.* Piccola Biblioteca 705. Milan: Adolphi. (English: *The Order of Time.* London: Penguin, 2019.)

Rowlands, Michael 1999. Remembering to Forget: Sublimation as Sacrifice in War Memorials. *The Art of Forgetting.* Eds Adrian Forty & Susanne Küchler. Oxford and New York: Berg. Pages 129–145.

Rudebeck, Elisabeth 2009. Inledning. *Arkeologisk framtid: Arkeologmötet 2008.* Eds Tore Artelius & Anna Källen. Lund: Svenska Arkeologiska Samfundet (The Swedish Archaeological Society). Pages 11–19.

Rüsen, Jörn 1994. *Historische Orientierung.* Cologne, Weimar, and Vienna: Böhlau.

Rüsen, Jörn 2001. *Zerbrechende Zeit: Über den Sinn der Geschichte.* Cologne, Weimar, and Vienna: Böhlau.

Rydberg, Viktor 1905. *Kulturhistoriska föreläsningar, IV. Föreläsningar öfver den äldre medeltidens kulturhistoria.* Stockholm: Albert Bonnier.

Sabloff, Jeremy A. 2008. *Archaeology Matters: Action Archaeology in the Modern World.* Key Questions in Anthropology. Walnut Creek, CA: Left Coast Press.

Said, Edward W. 1978. *Orientalism.* London: Routledge & Kegan Paul.

Said, Edward 1994. *Representations of the Intellectual: The Reith Lectures.* New York: Pantheon.

Saltzman, Katarina 2001. *Inget landskap är en ö: Dialektik och praktik i öländska landskap*. Lund: Nordic Academic Press.

The Salvage of the Abu Simbel Temples: Concluding Report, December 1971. Ed. Vattenbyggnadsbyrån (VBB; The Swedish Hydraulic Engineering Company). Stockholm: Vattenbyggnadsbyrån (VBB), 1976.

Samuel, Raphael 1994. *Theatres of Memory 1. Past and Present in Contemporary Culture*. London and New York: Verso.

Sandis, Constantine (ed.) 2014. *Cultural Heritage Ethics: Between Theory and Practice*. Cambridge: OpenBooks.

Säve-Söderbergh, Torgny (ed.) 1987. *Temples and Tombs of Ancient Nubia: The International Rescue Campaign at Abu Simbel, Philae and Other Sites*. London: Thames & Hudson, and Paris: UNESCO.

Säve-Söderbergh, Torgny 1996. *Uppdrag Nubien: Hur världen räddade ett lands kulturminnen*. Stockholm: Atlantis.

Schiffer, Michael Brian 2017. *Archaeology's Footprints in the Modern World*. Salt Lake City: The University of Utah Press.

Schildgen, Brenda Deen 2008. *Heritage or Heresy: Preservation and Destruction of Religious Art and Architecture in Europe*. New York and Basingstoke: Palgrave Macmillan.

Schlör, Joachim 1991. *Nachts in der großen Stadt*. Paris, Berlin, London 1840 – 1930. München: Artemis und Winkler. (English: *Nights in the Big City: Paris, Berlin, London 1840–1930*. Topographics. London: Reaktion Books, 1998.)

Schnapp, Alain 1993. *La conquête du passé: Aux origines de l'archéologie*. Paris: Éditions Carré. (English: *The Discovery of the Past: The Origins of Archaeology*. London: British Museum Press, 1996.)

Schofield, John (ed.) 2014. *Who Needs Experts? Counter-Mapping Cultural Heritage*. Heritage, Culture and Identity. London and New York: Routledge.

Schofield, John 2015. Forget About "Heritage": Place, Ethics and the Faro Convention. *The Ethics of Cultural Heritage*. Eds Tracy Ireland & John Schofield. Ethical Archaeologies: The Politics of Social Justice 4. Heidelberg: Springer and World Archaeological Congress. Pages 197–209.

Schumpeter, Joseph A. 1942. *Capitalism, Socialism and Democracy*. New York and London: Harper & Brothers.

Sedikides, Constantine, Wildschut, Tim & Baden, Denise 2004. Nostalgia: Conceptual Issues and Existential Functions. *Handbook of Experimental Existential Psychology*. Eds Jeff Greenberg, Sander L. Koole & Tom Pyszczynski. New York and London: The Guilford Press. Pages 200–214.

Shanks, Michael & Tilley, Christopher 1987. *Re-Constructing Archaeology: Theory and Practice*. New Studies in Archaeology. Cambridge: Cambridge University Press.

Siliotti, Alberto 1997. The Adventure of Abu Simbel. *Virtual Archaeology: Great Discoveries Brought to Life Through Virtual Reality*. Eds Forte, Maurizio & Siliotti, Alberto. London: Thames & Hudson. Pages 66–69.

(Italian: *Archeologia: Percorsi virtuali nelle civiltà scomparse*. Milan: Arnoldo Mondadori, 1996.)

Silverman, Helaine & Fairchild Ruggles, D. (eds) 2007. *Cultural Heritage and Human Rights*. New York: Springer.

Simmel, Georg 1903. Die Großstädte und das Geistesleben. *Die Großstadt: Vorträge und Aufsätze zur Städteausstellung*. Jahrbuch der Gehe-Stiftung Dresden IX. Pages 185–206. (English: The Metropolis and Mental Life. *The Sociology of Georg Simmel*. Ed. Kurt H. Wolff. Glencoe, IL: The Free Press, 1950. Pages 409–424.)

Singer, Peter 2016. *One World Now: The Ethics of Globalization*. New Haven, CT: Yale University Press. (1st ed. *One World*, 2002.)

Small, Helen 2013. *The Value of the Humanities*. Oxford: Oxford University Press.

Smith, Anthony D. 1983. Nationalism and Classical Social Theory. *The British Journal of Sociology* 34.1: 19–38.

Smith, George S., Messenger, Phyllis Mauch & Soderland, Hilary A. (eds) 2010. *Heritage Values in Contemporary Society*. Walnut Creek, CA: Left Coast Press.

Smith, Laurajane 2006. *Uses of Heritage*. London and New York: Routledge.

Smith, Laurajane & Akagawa, Natsuko (eds) 2009. *Intangible Heritage*. Key Issues in Cultural Heritage. London and New York: Routledge.

Snow, C(harles) P(ercy) 1959. *The Two Cultures and the Scientific Revolution*. The Rede Lecture, 1959. Cambridge: Cambridge University Press.

Snyder, Timothy 2015. *Black Earth: The Holocaust as History and Warning*. New York: Tim Duggan Books.

Sokal, Alan & Bricmont, Jean 1998. *Intellectual Impostures: Postmodern Philosophers' Abuse of Science*. London: Profile Books. (1st ed. *Impostures intellectuelles*. Paris: Éditions Odile Jacob, 1997.)

Sola, Tomislav 2005. What Theory? What Heritage? *Nordisk Museologi* 2005.2: 3–16.

Solli, Brit 1996. *Narratives of Veøy: An Investigation into the Poetics and Scientifics of Archaeology*. Universitetets Oldsaksamlings Skrifter, Ny rekke (New Series) 19. Oslo: Universitetets Oldsaksamling (Collection of Antiquities, University of Oslo).

Sørensen, Marie Louise Stig & Carman, John (eds) 2009. *Heritage Studies: Methods and Approaches*. London and New York: Routledge.

Sörlin, Sverker 2017. *Antropocen: En essä om människans tidsålder*. Stockholm: Svante Weyler Bokförlag.

Southgate, Beverley 1996. *History: What & Why? Ancient, Modern and Postmodern Perspectives*. London and New York: Routledge.

Southgate, Beverley 2000. *Why Bother with History? Ancient, Modern and Postmodern Motivations*. Harlow: Pearson Education.

Southgate, Beverley 2005. *What is History For?* London and New York: Routledge.

Storm, Anna 2008. *Hope and Rust: Reinterpreting the Industrial Place in the Late 20th Century.* Stockholm Papers in the History and Philosophy of Technology, Trita–Hot–2057. Stockholm: Royal Institute of Technology.

Storm, Anna 2010. Kärnkraft som minnesplatser. *Nordisk Museologi* 2010.2: 96–102.

Storm, Anna 2014. *Post-Industrial Landscape Scars.* Palgrave Studies in the History of Science and Technology. Basingstoke and New York: Palgrave Macmillan.

Sundin, Bo 1996. Vetenskapens många ansikten. *Forskning och Framsteg* 96.3: 42–49.

Svestad, Asgeir 1995. *Oldsakenes orden: Om tilkomsten av arkeologi.* Oslo: Universitetsforlaget.

Swenson, Astrid 2013. *The Rise of Heritage: Preserving the Past in France, Germany and England, 1789–1914.* New Studies in European History. Cambridge: Cambridge University Press.

Tainter, Joseph A. 1988. *The Collapse of Complex Societies.* New Studies in Archaeology. Cambridge: Cambridge University Press.

Tallis, Raymond 1997. *Enemies of Hope: A Critique of Contemporary Pessimism. Irrationalism, Anti-Humanism and Counter-Enlightenment.* Basingstoke: Macmillan, and New York: St. Martin's Press.

Tegnér, Esaias 1828. *Smärre samlade dikter.* Stockholm: H. A. Nordström.

Tekippe, Rita W. 2004. Copying Power: Emulation, Appropriation, and Borrowing for Royal Political Purposes. *Visual Resources* XX.2–3: 143–159.

Thomas, Julian 2004. *Archaeology and Modernity.* London and New York: Routledge.

Thomson, David 1969. *The Aims of History: Values of the Historical Attitude.* The Central Studies Library. London: Thames & Hudson.

Timothy, Dallen J. 2011. *Cultural Heritage and Tourism: An Introduction.* Aspects of Tourism Texts. Bristol: Channel View Publications.

Titchen, Sarah M. 1995. On the construction of outstanding universal value: UNESCO's World Heritage Convention (Convention concerning the Protection of the World Cultural and Natural Heritage, 1972) and the identification and assessment of cultural places for inclusion in the World Heritage List. Doctoral thesis for the Australian National University, April 1995.

Tomlinson, John 2007. *The Culture of Speed: The Coming of Immediacy.* Los Angeles and London: Sage.

Tönnies, Ferdinand 1887. *Gemeinschaft und Gesellschaft: Abhandlung des Communismus und des Socialismus als empirischer Culturformen.* Leipzig: Fues's Verlag. (English: *Community and Civil Society.* Ed. José Harris. Cambridge Texts in the History of Political Thought. Cambridge: Cambridge University Press, 2001.)

Tosh, John 2008. *Why History Matters.* Basingstoke and New York: Palgrave Macmillan.

Toulmin, Stephen 1990. *Cosmopolis: The Hidden Agenda of Modernity.* New York: Free Press.

Toulmin, Stephen & Goodfield, June 1965. *The Discovery of Time.* Ancestry of Science 3. London: Hutchinson.

Trevor-Roper, Hugh 1983. The Invention of Tradition: The Highland Tradition of Scotland. *The Invention of Tradition.* Eds Eric Hobsbawm & Terence Ranger. Past and Present Publications. Cambridge: Cambridge University Press. Pages 15–41.

Trigger, Bruce G. 1984. Alternative Archaeologies: Nationalist, Colonialist, Imperialist. *Man,* New Series 19.3: 355–370.

Trigger, Bruce G. 1989. *A History of Archaeological Thought.* Cambridge: Cambridge University Press.

Trigger, Bruce G. 1990. Monumental Architecture: A Thermodynamic Explanation of Symbolic Behaviour. *World Archaeology* 22.2: 119–132.

Tunbridge, John E. & Ashworth, G. J. 1996. *Dissonant Heritage: The Management of the Past as a Resource in Conflict.* Chichester: John Wiley & Sons.

Turtinen, Jan 2006. *Världsarvets villkor, intressen, förhandlingar och bruk i internationell politik.* Acta Universitatis Stockholmiensis, Stockholm Studies in Ethnology 1. Stockholm: Stockholm University.

Unnerbäck, Axel 2002. *Kulturhistorisk värdering av bebyggelse.* Stockholm: Riksantikvarieämbetets förlag (The Swedish National Heritage Board).

Urry, John 1990. *The Tourist Gaze: Leisure and Travel in Contemporary Societies.* Theory, Culture & Society. London: Sage.

Veronese, Vittorio 1960. Appeal. *The UNESCO Courier* XIII (May 1960): 6–7.

Virilio, Paul 1977. *Vitesse et Politique: Essai de dromologie.* Paris: Éditions Galilée. (English: *Speed and Politics. An Essay on Dromology.* Semiotext(e) Foreign Agents series. New York: Semiotext(e), 1986.)

Vitelli, Karen D. (ed.) 1996. *Archaeological Ethics.* Walnut Creek, CA: AltaMira Press.

Wallerstein, Immanuel 1974–89: *The Modern World-System,* I-III. Studies in Social Discontinuity. New York, London, and San Diego, CA: Academic Press.

Wallerstein, Immanuel 2003. *The Decline of American Power: The U.S. in a Chaotic World.* New York: The New Press.

Walsh, Kevin 1992. *The Representation of the Past: Museums and Heritage in the Post-Modern World.* The Heritage: Care – Preservation – Management. London and New York: Routledge.

Wangefelt Ström, Helena 2006. Kulturarv – ikon för en sekulariserad tid? *Kulturella perspektiv: Svensk etnologisk tidskrift* 15.3: 67–76.

Ward, Colin 1985. Blue Plaques and Dead Elms. *The Times Educational Supplement* 3615, 11 October 1985, p. 27.

Weber, Max 1922. Wissenschaft als Beruf. *Gesammelte Aufsätze zur Wissenschaftslehre.* Tübingen: J. C. B. Mohr, pp. 524–555. (English:

Science as a Vocation. From *Max Weber: Essays in Sociology*. Eds Hans Heinrich Gerth & C. Wright Mills. Routledge Sociology Classics. Abingdon: Routledge, 1991 (1st ed. 1948), pp. 129–156.)

Weibull, Lauritz 1953: *Lunds domkyrka: Dess ombyggnad 1860–1880*. Malmö: Allhem.

Weissglas, Gösta, Paju, Martin, Westin, Lars & Danell, Torbjörn 2002. *Kulturarvet som resurs för regional utveckling: En kunskapsöversikt.* Report from Riksantikvarieämbetet (The Swedish National Heritage Board) 2002: 1. Stockholm: Riksantikvarieämbetet.

Westman, Anna & Tunón, Håkan 2010. Kulturarv och hållbar utveckling. *Bebyggelsehistorisk tidskrift* 59: 99–106.

White, Hayden 1973. *Metahistory: The Historical Imagination in Nineteenth–Century Europe*. Baltimore, MD: The Johns Hopkins University Press.

White, Roger & Devlin, Harriet 2007. From Basket-Case to Hanging-Baskets: Regeneration, Alienation and Heritage in Ironbridge. *World Heritage: Global Challenges, Local Solutions. Proceedings of a conference at Coalbrookdale, 4–7 May 2006 hosted by the Ironbridge Institute*. Eds Roger White & John Carman. BAR International Series 1698. Oxford: Archaeopress. Pages 47–51.

Wienberg, Jes 1999. The Perishable Past: On the Advantage and Disadvantage of Archaeology for Life. *Current Swedish Archaeology* 7: 183–202.

Wienberg, Jes 2004. Sakral geometri: veje og vildveje til viden. *Ordning mot kaos: Studier av nordisk förkristen kosmologi*. Eds Anders Andrén, Kristina Jennbert & Catharina Raudvere. Vägar till Midgård 4. Lund: Nordic Academic Press. Pages 23–57.

Wienberg, Jes 2007. Kanon og glemsel: Arkæologiens mindesmærker. *Kuml: Årbog for Jysk Arkæologisk Selskab* 2007. Pages 237–282.

Wienberg, Jes 2009. Agenda arkeologi: upplysning, terapi eller moral. *Arkeologi och samhälle*. Eds Bodil Petersson, Kristina Jennbert & Cornelius Holtorf. Acta Archaeologica Lundensia Series in 8°, 58. Lund: Arkeologiböcker. Pages 53–64.

Wienberg, Jes 2010. Ljusets arkeologi: Att bejaka moderniteten. *Modernitetens materialitet: Arkeologiska perspektiv på det moderna samhällets framväxt*. Eds Anna Lihammer & Jonas M. Nordin. The Museum of National Antiquities, Stockholm, Studies 17. Stockholm: Statens historiska museum. Pages 17–25.

Willim, Robert 2008. *Industrial cool: Om postindustriella fabriker.* HEX 2. Lund: Joint Faculties of Humanities and Theology, Lund University.

Wilson, David Sloan 2002. *Darwin's Cathedral: Evolution, Religion and the Nature of Society*. Chicago: The University of Chicago Press.

Wilson, Edward O. 2012. *The Social Conquest of Earth*. New York and London: Liveright and W. W. Norton.

Wimmer, Andreas & Glick Schiller, Nina 2002. Methodological Nationalism and Beyond: Nation-State Building, Migration and the Social Sciences. *Global Network* 2.4: 301–334.

Winter, Tim 2013. Clarifying the Critical in Critical Heritage Studies. *International Journal of Heritage Studies* 19.6: 532–545.

Wood, Denis 1993. *The Power of Maps.* London: Routledge.

Woodward, Christopher 2001. *In Ruins.* London: Vintage.

The World's Heritage: The definitive guide to all 1073 World Heritage sites. 5th ed. Paris: UNESCO Publishing, 2018. (1st ed. Paris: UNESCO Publishing, 2009.)

Wright, Georg Henrik von 1971. *Explanation and Understanding.* International Library of Philosophy and Scientific Method. London: Routledge & Kegan Paul.

Wright, Georg Henrik von 1993. *Myten om framsteget: Tankar 1987–1992 med en intellektuell självbiografi.* Stockholm: Albert Bonnier.

Wright, Patrick 1985. *On Living in an Old Country: The National Past in Contemporary Britain.* London and New York: Verso. (2nd ed. Oxford: Oxford University Press, 2009.)

Wyschogrod, Edith 1998. *An Ethics of Remembering: History, Heterology and the Nameless Others.* Religion and Postmodernism. Chicago: University of Chicago Press.

Council of Europe

European Convention on the Value of Cultural Heritage for Society (Faro Convention, 2005): www.coe.int/en/web/culture-and-heritage/faro-convention.

ICOMOS www.icomos.org

Charter for the Protection and Management of the Archaeological Heritage (1990).

The Nara Document on Authenticity (1994).

The World Heritage List: Filling the Gaps – an Action Plan for the Future. Paris: ICOMOS, 2004. (Abbreviated: *WHL Filling,* 2004).

UNESCO – conventions, manuals, lists, and other information; whc.unesco.org

Convention Concerning the Protection of the World Cultural and Natural Heritage. Paris: UNESCO, 1972. (Abbreviated: World Heritage Convention or WHC 1972).

Convention for the Safeguarding of the Intangible Cultural Heritage (2003).

Hague Convention for the Protection of Cultural Property in the Event of Armed Conflict (1954).

Intangible cultural heritage: ich.unesco.org/en/lists.

Memory of the World: www.unesco.org/new/en/communication-and-information/memory-of-the-world/homepage.

Operational Guidelines for the Implementation of the World Heritage Convention. UNESCO: World Heritage Centre 2019. (1. Ed. 1977) (Pdf: whc.unesco.org/en/guidelines; abbreviated: *Operational*).

World Heritage Information Kit. Paris: UNESCO World Heritage Centre, 2008.

World Heritage List (abbreviated: WHL).

World Heritage Sustainable Tourism Programme. Paris: UNESCO, 2012/2001.

United Nations Human Rights (www.ohchr.org)

International Covenant on Economic, Social and Cultural Rights (1966/1976).

Universal Declaration of Human Rights (1948).

Internet

Association of Critical Heritage Studies (ACHS): criticalheritagestudies.org.

British Museum: www.britishmuseum.org.

Cairo Declaration on Human Rights in Islam: hrlibrary.umn.edu/instree/cairodeclaration.html.

Camilo José Vergara, Tracking Time: www.camilojosevergara.com.

CyArk: www.cyark.org.

English Heritage: www.english-heritage.org.uk.

EUNAMUS, European National Museums: www.ep.liu.se/eunamus.

Gesellschaft Berliner Schloss: www.historisches-stadtschloss.de.

Global Times 25 June 2016, Britain steps backward as EU faces decline: www.globaltimes.cn/content/990440.shtml.

Goodwood: www.goodwood.com.

Google: Google.com.

Historic England: https://historicengland.org.uk/advice/hpg/hpr-definitions.

Human Freedom Index: www.cato.org/human-freedom-index.

Humboldt Forum: www.humboldtforum.com.

Image of Destroyed Bamiyan Buddhist Statue Recovered by Chinese with Lighting Technology: www.youtube.com/watch?v=JDEk9rjM39c.

Gardaland: www.gardaland.it.

Kulturmiljölagen (the Swedish Historic Environment Act): www.riksdagen.se/sv/dokument-lagar/dokument/svensk-forfattningssamling/kulturmil-jolag-1988950_sfs-1988–950.

Lightpollution: www.lightpollution.it/dmsp/index.html.

Louvre: www.louvre.fr.

Lowenthal, David 2011. Personal Reflections on the State of Heritage. Lecture at University of Cambridge, 3 Nov. 2011: www.youtube.com/watch?v=KzJMbMw1L7c.

Moderna Museet, Stockholm: www.modernamuseet.se.

Museum of Modern Art (MoMa): www.moma.org.

National Trust: www.nationaltrust.org.uk.

Natural History Museum: www.nhm.ac.uk.

Riksantikvarieämbetet (Swedish National Heritage Board): www.raa.se.

SCA, Society for Creative Anachronism: www.sca.org.

Stolpersteine: www.stolpersteine.eu.

Tribute in Light: www.mas.org/programs/tributeinlight.

University of Minnesota, Human Rights Library: hrlibrary.umn.edu.

Vasamuseet (The Vasa Museum), Stockholm: www.vasamuseet.se.

Vikingeskibsmuseet (The Viking Ship Museum), Roskilde: www.viking eskibsmuseet.dk.

World Heritage: whc.unesco.org (abbreviated WH).

World Heritages in Sweden: worldheritagesweden.se.

World of New 7 Wonders: www.new7wonders.com.

Films

Bergman, Ingmar 1957. *Det sjunde inseglet* (*The Seventh Seal*). Svensk Filmindustri.

Chaplin, Charlie 1936. *Modern Times*. United Artists.

Coppola, Sofia 2006. *Marie Antoinette*. Columbia Pictures.

Guillermin, John 1978. *Death on the Nile*. EMI Films.

Franck, Herbert M. 1967. *The World Saves Abu Simbel*. UNESCO.

Heimlich, Rüdiger & Weidenbach, Thomas 2005. *Abu Simbel: Ein Tempel bewegt die Welt*. Bayerischer Rundfunk.

Monty Python & The Holy Grail 1975. EMI Films.

Reinl, Harald 1970. *Erinnerungen an die Zukunft*. (English: *Chariots of the Gods*). Terra-Filmkunst.

Roundhay Garden Scene 1888. (https://www.youtube.com/watch?v=nR2r__ZgO5g).

Tarkovsky, Andrei 1983. *Nostalghia*. Opera Film.

Tykwer, Tom 1998. *Lola rennt*. X Filme Creative Pool GmbH.

Index

EU authorised representative for GPSR:
Easy Access System Europe, Mustamäe tee 50,
10621 Tallinn, Estonia
gpsr.requests@easproject.com

www.ingramcontent.com/pod-product-compliance
Ingram Content Group UK Ltd.
Pitfield, Milton Keynes, MK11 3LW, UK
UKHW021812150726
7214IPUK00004B/15